BEST OF
QUICK
cooking

BEST OF QUICK cooking

Editor: Krista Lanphier
Art Director: Rudy Krochalk
Layout Designer: Kathy Crawford
Content Production Supervisor: Julie Wagner
Proofreader: Linne Bruskewitz
Recipe Asset Management System: Coleen Martin (Manager), Sue A. Jurack (Specialist)
Editorial Assistant: Barb Czysz
Indexer: Jean Duerst

Food Director: Diane Werner RD
Test Kitchen Manager: Karen Scales
Recipe Editors: Mary King, Christine Rukavena
Studio Photographers: Rob Hagen (Senior), Dan Roberts, Jim Wieland, Lori Foy
Food Stylists: Sarah Thompson (Manager), Kaitlyn Besasie
Set Stylists: Jenny Bradley Vent (Senior), Stephanie Marchese (Senior), Melissa Haberman, Dee Dee Jacq
Assistant Food Stylists: Alynna Malson, Shannon Roum, Leah Rekau
Photo Studio Coordinator: Kathleen Swaney

Vice President, Executive Editor/Books: Heidi Reuter Lloyd
Senior Editor/Books: Mark Hagen
Creative Director: Ardyth Cope
Creative Director/Creative Marketing: Jim Palmen
Vice President/Book Marketing: Dan Fink
Chief Marketing Officer: Lisa Karpinski
Senior Vice President, Editor in Chief: Catherine Cassidy
President, Food & Entertaining: Suzanne M. Grimes
President and Chief Executive Officer: Mary G. Berner

Cover Photography: Dan Roberts (Photographer),
Jenny Bradley Vent (Senior Set Stylist),
Sarah Thompson (Food Styling Manager),
Jennifer Janz (Food Stylist)

Taste of Home Books
©2009 Reiman Media Group, Inc.
5400 S. 60th Street
Greendale, WI 53129

International Standard Book Number (10): 0-89821-638-9
International Standard Book Number (13): 978-0-89821-638-7
Library of Congress Control Number: 2008933650

Pictured on front cover: Clockwise from upper left, Meatball Sub Casserole (p. 151), Veggie Chowder (p. 103), Light Chicken Cordon Bleu (p. 218) and Makeover Chocolate Truffle Dessert (p. 288).
Pictured on back cover: Clockwise from right, Peach Almond Bars (p. 284), Calzone Pinwheels (p. 34) and Buffalo Chicken Lettuce Wraps (p. 110).

Pictured on title page: Raspberry Truffle Brownies (p. 285).
Pictured on the Table of Contents page: From left to right, Bavarian Meatballs (p. 26), Fantastic Fish Tacos (p. 222) and Ice Cream Pretzel Cake (p. 283).

Table *of* Contents

Cooking *has never been* easier!

Over a decade ago, we listened to thousands of our readers who wrote in and expressed how they wanted quality recipes and home-cooked meals that were fast and easy. Soon after, *Quick Cooking* magazine was born. Although it had a makeover in 2006 with a new name, *Simple & Delicious*, the magazine's mission of bringing fast-to-fix recipes to you has carried on. To celebrate *Quick Cooking's* success, we've compiled the best recipes since it began.

Welcome to *The Best of Quick Cooking*, which captures over 650 of the most popular recipes and tips from its first 10 years. In this attractive full-color cookbook, you'll find hundreds of eye-catching recipes that are as easy as they are delicious!

Here are just a few of the book's special standout features:

grand prize winners

As you may already know, each issue of *Quick Cooking* and *Simple & Delicious* includes the winners of national recipe contests. We've featured those amazing handpicked dishes from the very first issue of *Quick Cooking*, all the way through the 2008 issues of *Simple & Delicious*!

Fabulous Grand Prize recipes include Chicago-Style Pan Pizza on page 206, scrumptious Pumpkin Waffles with Orange Walnut Butter on page 239 and irresistible Macadamia Berry Dessert on page 299. To spot Grand Prize winning dishes quickly, just look for the blue ribbons next to the recipe titles!

favorite fast recipes from readers like you!

"30 Minutes to Mealtime" and "Readers' Favorite Meals" profile busy home cooks who created easy dinner menus for their own families. These two chapters are perfect when you need meals that come together in a jiffy.

And the recipes only get more amazing and easier to make with "10 Minutes to the Table" and "Give Me 5 or Fewer." Our readers demonstrate how innovative they really are by showing how easy it is to make delicious, impressive dishes in only 10 minutes or with only five ingredients or less. For cooks on the go, it's a dream come true!

holiday & seasonal pleasers

From festive holidays to the opening of farmers markets everywhere, there's always a reason to celebrate the arrival of a new season. In this chapter, there are plenty of yummy recipes that use the wonderful produce that becomes available during the spring, summer and fall months.

You'll also discover that fancy recipes for special occasions, like Easter, Halloween, Thanksgiving and Christmas, can still be easy on the cook. No matter what the season, there's a fast and easy recipe for every reason!

helpful kitchen tips & nutrition facts

Throughout the book, you'll discover plenty of helpful hints, fascinating culinary information and kitchen shortcuts for harried home cooks. You may find that many of these ideas help you through an already busy day!

We've also made it easy for you to find recipes that are lower in fat, calories or sodium and that include Nutrition Facts and Diabetic Exchanges. Just look for the apple icon next to the recipe title.

hundreds of mouth-watering recipes

There are so many amazing recipes to choose from in this big collector's edition book that you can make a different recipe from it every day well past a year-and-a-half! From elegant entrees to showstopping desserts, the endless variety of easy-to-make dishes will ensure your family is satisfied any day of the week. And like all of our recipes, rest assured, these have been tested and approved by our Test Kitchen staff.

After viewing the vibrant color photographs in this book, no doubt you'll be tempted to start cooking from it immediately. So don't waste any time getting started, because hundreds of quick, delicious and easy recipes await busy cooks like you. From our home to yours, we wish you many fast, happy and successful cooking adventures!

30minutes to mealtime

Our Test Kitchen home economists paired reader recipes with some of their own quick creations to produce terrific menus for busy home cooks like you. From start to finish, preparing each delicious menu will take you a mere 30 minutes...or less!

When your hectic schedule doesn't allow you to spend even a full hour in the kitchen, rely on these speedy and satisfying meals that come together in no time at all.

Quick Chicken Cordon Bleu &
Almond Rice Pilaf
(recipes on p. 15)

Vicki Smith from Okeechobee, Florida uses traditional Greek ingredients to make this delicious supper. "I like to serve this meal with crusty bread and dipping oil. Just add a tablespoon of Italian seasoning to 1/3 cup of extra-virgin olive oil."

Greek Tossed Salad

Prep/Total Time: 10 min.

5	cups ready-to-serve salad greens
3/4	cup sliced cucumber
1	medium tomato, cut into wedges
2	tablespoons crumbled feta cheese
2	tablespoons sliced ripe olives
2/3	cup Greek vinaigrette *or* salad dressing of your choice

In a salad bowl, combine the greens, cucumber, tomato, cheese and olives. Drizzle with dressing; toss to coat. **Yield:** 4 servings.

Bacon-Feta Stuffed Chicken

Prep: 15 min. | Cook: 25 min.

4	boneless skinless chicken breasts (4 ounces *each*)
1/4	cup crumbled cooked bacon
1/4	cup crumbled feta cheese
1/2	teaspoon salt
1/4	teaspoon pepper
1	tablespoon canola oil
2	cans (14-1/2 ounces *each*) diced tomatoes
1	tablespoon dried basil

Carefully cut a slit in the deepest part of each chicken breast. Fill with bacon and cheese; secure with toothpicks. Sprinkle with salt and pepper. In a large skillet, brown chicken in oil.

Drain one can of tomatoes; add to skillet. Stir in the remaining tomatoes; sprinkle with basil. Cover and simmer for 10 minutes. Simmer, uncovered, for 5 minutes longer or until a meat thermometer inserted in the chicken breasts reads 170° and the tomato mixture is thickened. Discard toothpicks. **Yield:** 4 servings.

Fresh *flavors are the hallmark of meals at Gloria Warczak's dinner table in Cedarburg, Wisconsin, where she and her husband raised their family.*

"I enjoy all phases of cooking, including gardening, canning and freezing vegetables, drying herbs and baking yeast breads," she says. Gloria shares one of her quick menus here. "The original recipe for Microwaved Cod came from my grandmother, who baked it in the oven," she recalls.

Gloria takes advantage of her garden bounty every summer to prepare Sauteed Summer Squash. To round out the meal, she tosses together a refreshing fruit-and-vegetable medley.

Sauteed Summer Squash
Prep/Total Time: 25 min.

2	small zucchini, julienned
2	small yellow summer squash, julienned
1	small sweet red pepper, julienned
1	small onion, julienned
2	tablespoons canola oil
1-1/2	teaspoons seasoned salt
1/2	teaspoon pepper

In a large skillet, saute the zucchini, summer squash, red pepper and onion in oil for 8 minutes or until the vegetables are crisp-tender. Sprinkle with seasoned salt and pepper.
Yield: 6 servings.

Pineapple Cucumber Salad
Prep/Total Time: 10 min.

1	can (8 ounces) pineapple chunks
2	medium cucumbers, halved and thinly sliced
1	cup seedless grapes
2	teaspoons snipped chives
2/3	cup mayonnaise
1/3	cup sugar
1	teaspoon prepared mustard
1/4	teaspoon celery seed
1/4	teaspoon prepared horseradish

Drain pineapple, reserving 1 tablespoon juice (discard remaining juice or save for another use). In a bowl, combine the pineapple, cucumbers, grapes and chives. In another bowl, combine the mayonnaise, sugar, mustard, celery seed, horseradish and reserved pineapple juice. Pour over pineapple mixture; gently stir to coat. Serve with a slotted spoon.
Yield: 6 servings.

Microwaved Cod
Prep/Total Time: 15 min.

1-1/2	pounds cod *or* haddock fillets
1/2	cup white wine *or* chicken broth
2	tablespoons lemon juice
1	tablespoon grated lemon peel
1	tablespoon minced chives
1	tablespoon minced fresh parsley
1/2	teaspoon dried tarragon

Pepper to taste

Place the fillets in an ungreased 11-in. x 7-in. microwave-safe dish. Cover and cook on high for 6 minutes; drain. Add wine or broth, lemon juice, lemon peel, chives, parsley, tarragon and pepper.

Cover and cook 4-5 minutes longer or until the fish flakes easily with a fork. Let stand for 5 minutes before serving.
Yield: 6 servings.

Editor's Note: This recipe was tested in a 1,100-watt microwave.

Our home economists combined the following reader recipes into this must-try menu that uses popular convenience foods and other pantry staples.

When time is tight, Beverly Menser whips up Pasta Meatball Soup in her Madisonville, Kentucky home. The savory Italian soup relies on items most cooks have on hand. Karin Bailey of Golden, Colorado adds a little pizzazz to store-bought bread for the Herbed French Bread recipe. And Jacquie Troutman of Zephyrhills, Florida tops salad greens with a sweet dressing, hard-cooked eggs, tomato and onion.

Creamy Lettuce Salad

Prep/Total Time: 15 min.

  3   hard-cooked eggs
  1   package (16 ounces) ready-to-serve salad greens
  1   medium tomato, diced
1/4   cup diced onion
DRESSING:
3/4   cup mayonnaise
  3   to 4 tablespoons milk
  2   tablespoons sugar
  2   tablespoons cider vinegar

Cut one egg into wedges for garnish; set aside. Chop remaining eggs. In a salad bowl, combine the greens, tomato, onion and eggs.

In a jar with tight-fitting lid, combine the dressing ingredients; shake well. Pour over salad and toss to coat. Garnish with reserved egg wedges. **Yield: 10 servings.**

Herbed French Bread

Prep/Total Time: 10 min.

  1   loaf (1 pound) French bread
1/2   cup butter, softened
1/4   cup minced fresh parsley
1/4   cup minced chives

Cut the bread into 1-in. slices. In a small bowl, combine the butter, parsley and chives; spread over one side of each slice of bread.

Place buttered side up on an ungreased baking sheet. Broil 4 in. from the heat for 1-2 minutes or until golden brown. **Yield: 10 servings.**

Pasta Meatball Soup

Prep/Total Time: 25 min.

      1   cup uncooked spiral *or* shell pasta
     32   frozen Italian meatballs (about 1 pound), thawed
      2   cans (14-1/2 ounces *each*) chicken broth
      1   can (28 ounces) diced tomatoes, undrained
1-1/2   cups frozen sliced carrots, thawed
      1   can (16 ounces) kidney beans, rinsed and drained
      1   jar (14 ounces) meatless spaghetti sauce
      1   jar (4-1/2 ounces) sliced mushrooms, drained
      1   cup frozen peas

Cook the pasta according to package directions. Meanwhile, combine the remaining ingredients in a soup kettle or Dutch oven. Bring to a boil; cover and simmer for 5 minutes. Drain the pasta. Add to the soup; heat through. **Yield: 10 servings (3 quarts).**

You don't need dozens of recipes to serve a satisfying meal to guests. Our Test Kitchen proves that by pairing two reader recipes into a menu for six that's a snap to prepare on the stovetop.

"I'm a busy mother and my husband has unpredictable hours at work, so quick and delicious meals are my mainstay," writes Lara Priest of Gansevoort, New York. "A dear friend shared the recipe for Chicken Milan a few years ago," she recalls. "Since then, I've prepared this memorable main dish for both family meals and get-togethers."

For an easy accompaniment, fix Cajun Vegetables from Chrissy Fessler of Hazleton, Pennsylvania. "This snappy side dish is not only fast and nutritious, but delicious as well," she relates. "Choose whatever frozen vegetables your family prefers."

Cajun Vegetables
Prep/Total Time: 20 min.

1	package (16 ounces) frozen vegetable blend
1	cup frozen cut green beans
1	cup sliced fresh mushrooms
2	tablespoons butter
1	tablespoon olive oil
1	can (15-1/4 ounces) whole kernel corn, drained
2	to 3 teaspoons Cajun seasoning

Cook the vegetable blend and green beans according to package directions. Meanwhile, in a large skillet, saute mushrooms in butter and oil for 1 minute or until crisp-tender. Add corn; saute for 1 minute longer or until heated through. Drain vegetable blend and beans; add to skillet. Stir in Cajun seasoning. **Yield: 6 servings.**

An Easy Dessert Option

If you don't have time to prepare dessert, make cookie dough when you do have some spare time. Most cookie doughs, including chocolate chip and peanut butter, may be refrigerated or frozen and then baked later. With airtight wrapping, unbaked cookie dough can be refrigerated for a week or frozen up to a year.

To freeze cookie dough, drop tablespoonfuls onto baking sheets, freeze, then transfer to freezer bags. To thaw, place the frozen dough on baking sheets and allow to stand 30-45 minutes at room temperature, then bake according to directions!

Chicken Milan
Prep/Total Time: 20 min.

8	ounces uncooked linguine
1	tablespoon minced garlic
3	tablespoons olive oil, *divided*
1/2	teaspoon dried parsley flakes
1/2	teaspoon pepper, *divided*
1/4	cup all-purpose flour
1	teaspoon dried basil
1/2	teaspoon salt
2	eggs
1-1/2	pounds boneless skinless chicken breasts, cut into strips

Cook linguine according to package directions. Meanwhile, in a large skillet, saute garlic in 1 tablespoon oil for 2-3 minutes or until tender; stir in parsley and 1/4 teaspoon pepper. Remove to a small bowl and set aside.

In a shallow bowl, combine the flour, basil, salt and remaining pepper. In another shallow bowl, whisk the eggs. Dredge chicken strips in flour mixture, then dip in eggs.

In the same skillet, cook chicken in remaining oil over medium-high heat for 8-10 minutes or until no longer pink. Drain linguine and place on a serving platter. Pour reserved garlic mixture over linguine and toss to coat; top with chicken. **Yield: 6 servings.**

*Nutrition Facts: 3 ounces cooked chicken with 1/2 cup linguine (prepared with egg substitute) equals 349 calories, 10 g fat (2 g saturated fat), 63 mg cholesterol, 295 mg sodium, 32 g carbohydrate, 2 g fiber, 31 g protein. **Diabetic Exchanges:** 3 lean meat, 2 starch, 1/2 fat.*

Forget about fast-food kiddie meals! Put this casual menu of short-order classics on the table, and even the gloomiest day looks a little brighter. Just watch the pickiest eaters in your household dig right into these diner favorites!

Start with hearty Grilled Ham 'n' Jack Cheese sandwiches from Jayne Ward of Eldon, Missouri, and you have the kind of comfort food that's the stuff of childhood memories. "These sandwiches are fast, filling and nice enough for company," Jayne says.

Complete the meal with toasty Herbed Steak Fries and thick, fudge-rippled Cola Floats from our Test Kitchen. What's not to like?

Herbed Steak Fries

Prep/Total Time: 25 min.

    4   cups frozen steak fries
    1   tablespoon olive oil
1-1/2   teaspoons dried basil
1-1/2   teaspoons dried parsley flakes
  1/4   teaspoon garlic salt
  1/4   teaspoon seasoned salt
  1/4   cup grated Romano cheese

In a large bowl, combine the first six ingredients; toss to coat. Arrange steak fries in a single layer in a greased 15-in. x 10-in. baking pan.

Bake at 450° for 15-20 minutes or until lightly browned. Sprinkle with cheese. **Yield: 4 servings.**

Cola Floats

Prep/Total Time: 5 min.

    4   cups cherry cola, chilled
    1   teaspoon vanilla extract
    8   scoops fudge ripple ice cream
Whipped cream in a can, optional
    4   maraschino cherries

In a pitcher, combine cola and vanilla. Place two scoops of ice cream in each of four chilled glasses. Pour cola over ice cream; top with whipped cream if desired and cherries. **Yield: 4 servings.**

Grilled Ham 'n' Jack Cheese

Prep/Total Time: 15 min.

    4   tablespoons butter, softened
    8   slices Texas toast
    4   slices sharp cheddar cheese
   16   thin slices deli ham
    4   slices red onion, optional
    4   tablespoons prepared ranch salad dressing
    4   slices pepper Jack cheese

Butter one side of each slice of Texas toast. On the unbuttered sides of four slices, layer the cheddar cheese, half of the ham, onion if desired and remaining ham; spread with ranch dressing. Top with pepper Jack cheese and remaining toast, buttered side up.

In a small skillet over medium heat, toast the sandwiches for 3-4 minutes on each side or until the cheese is melted. **Yield: 4 servings.**

Easy does it when it comes to outdoor entertaining. Our Test Kitchen grouped three kitchen-tested recipes that are a natural together. This complete meal tastes delicious.

Start with Orange Roughy with Cucumber Salsa. The moist fillets are topped with a cool and colorful seven-ingredient salsa. Pair the fish with a warm, buttery side dish of Basil Walnut Fettuccine, studded with toasted walnuts and lightly flavored with garlic and basil. The combination of regular spinach fettucine is eye-catching, but you can use any flavor or shape of pasta you have on hand.

Finish the meal off with the fresh-squeezed flavor of Poppy Seed Lemon Pie. Guests will love this tangy and fluffy finale to dinner.

 Orange Roughy with Cucumber Salsa
Prep/Total Time: 20 min.

1	cup chopped cucumber
1/2	cup chopped yellow summer squash
2	plum tomatoes, chopped
1/4	cup chopped red onion
1	tablespoon lime juice
2	teaspoons olive oil
1/4	teaspoon salt
2	teaspoons lemon-pepper seasoning
6	fresh *or* frozen orange roughy fillets (6 ounces *each*)

For the salsa, in a small bowl, combine the first seven ingredients; set aside. Sprinkle the lemon pepper over both sides of fillets.

Place on a broiler pan coated with cooking spray. Broil 4-6 in. from the heat for 3-4 minutes on each side or until the fish flakes easily with a fork. Serve with the cucumber salsa. **Yield:** 6 servings.

*Nutrition Facts: 1 fillet with 1/4 cup salsa equals 143 calories, 3 g fat (trace saturated fat), 34 mg cholesterol, 362 mg sodium, 3 g carbohydrate, 1 g fiber, 26 g protein. **Diabetic Exchange:** 4 very lean meat.*

Basil Walnut Fettuccine
Prep/Total Time: 20 min.

1	package (12 ounces) fettuccine
1	teaspoon minced garlic
6	tablespoons butter, *divided*
1/4	cup finely chopped walnuts, toasted
1	tablespoon minced fresh basil *or* 1 teaspoon dried basil
1/4	teaspoon salt
1/8	teaspoon pepper

Cook fettuccine according to package directions. In a large skillet, saute garlic in 1 tablespoon butter for 1 minute or until crisp-tender. Add the walnuts, basil, salt, pepper and remaining butter; cook and stir for 2 minutes or until heated through. Drain fettuccine; add to skillet and toss to coat. **Yield:** 6 servings.

Poppy Seed Lemon Pie
Prep/Total Time: 10 min.

1	can (14 ounces) sweetened condensed milk
1/3	cup lemonade concentrate
1	carton (8 ounces) frozen whipped topping, thawed, *divided*
1	graham cracker crust (9 inches)
1	tablespoon poppy seeds
10	to 12 drops yellow food coloring, optional

In a large bowl, beat milk and lemonade concentrate until smooth (mixture will begin to thicken). Fold in 2 cups whipped topping. Spread half into the crust.

Add poppy seeds and food coloring if desired to the remaining lemon mixture; stir until blended. Spoon over first layer. Spread with the remaining whipped topping. Refrigerate until serving. **Yield:** 6-8 servings.

Sitting down to a delicious steak dinner doesn't have to mean spending a lot of time preparing it. Begin with the Grilled Peppered Steaks created by Stephanie Moon from Nampa, Idaho and Great Garden Veggies from Chris Schmidt of Clarksville, Tennessee, which make a colorful accompaniment. And the Citrus Shortcake from Eileen Warren of Windsor, Ontario, makes a fabulous finale.

Great Garden Veggies

Prep/Total Time: 15 min.

1	medium zucchini, cut into 1/4-inch slices
1	medium yellow summer squash, cut into 1/4-inch slices
1/4	cup sliced onion
1	tablespoon butter
1	medium tomato, cut into wedges
1/4	teaspoon salt
1/4	teaspoon garlic salt
1/4	teaspoon dried basil
1/4	teaspoon pepper
2	tablespoons grated Parmesan cheese

In a large skillet, saute the zucchini, yellow squash and onion in butter until crisp tender. Add the tomato, salt, garlic salt, basil and pepper. Cook 2-3 minutes longer or until heated through. Sprinkle with Parmesan cheese. **Yield: 4 servings.**

Grilled Peppered Steaks

Prep/Total Time: 25 min.

1-1/2	to 2 teaspoons coarsely ground pepper
1	teaspoon onion salt
1	teaspoon garlic salt
1/4	teaspoon paprika
4	New York strip steaks (about 8 ounces *each*)

In a small bowl, combine the pepper, onion salt, garlic salt and paprika if desired. Rub onto both sides of steaks.

Grill, covered, over medium heat for 8-10 minutes on each side or until meat reaches desired doneness (for medium-rare, a meat thermometer should read 145°; medium, 160°; well-done, 170°). **Yield: 4 servings.**

Citrus Shortcake

Prep/Total Time: 10 min.

1	cup (8 ounces) lemon yogurt
1	cup whipped topping
4	individual round sponge cakes
1/4	cup orange juice
2-2/3	cups sliced fresh strawberries

In a small bowl, combine the yogurt and whipped topping. Place sponge cakes on dessert plates; drizzle with orange juice. Spread with half of the yogurt mixture. Top with strawberries and remaining yogurt mixture. **Yield: 4 servings.**

When time's tight, busy cooks look for delicious recipes that can be prepared in a hurry. These two fuss-free dishes are both easy and impressive.

Classic chicken cordon bleu is remade with a need for speed in this quick-to-fix microwave version from Louise Gilbert of Quesnel, British Columbia. "If your family prefers, you can subsitute cheddar cheese for the Swiss," Louise notes. Serve it with a side of Almond Rice Pilaf from Mary Jo Nikolaus of Mansfield, Ohio. "Whenever I want a side dish other than potatoes or noodles, I prepare this rice dish. It goes well with grilled or broiled meats," she says.

To round out the meal, serve cubes of fresh watermelon or any other favorite fruit for a light and refreshing dessert.

Almond Rice Pilaf

Prep/Total Time: 25 min.

- 3/4 cup chopped onion
- 1/2 cup slivered almonds
- 1 tablespoon butter
- 2 cups chicken broth
- 2 cups uncooked instant rice
- 1/2 cup frozen peas
- 1/2 teaspoon salt
- 1/4 teaspoon pepper

In a large skillet, saute onion and almonds in butter for 5-6 minutes or until onion is tender and almonds are golden brown. Add broth. Bring to a boil. Stir in the rice, peas, salt and pepper. Cover and remove from the heat. Let stand for 6-8 minutes or until liquid is absorbed. **Yield: 4 servings.**

Quick Chicken Cordon Bleu

Prep/Total Time: 25 min.

- 4 boneless skinless chicken breast halves (6 ounces *each*)
- 4 thin slices deli ham
- 2 slices Swiss cheese, halved
- 1/4 cup butter, melted
- 1 envelope seasoned coating mix

Flatten chicken to 1/4-in. thickness. Place ham and cheese down the center of each; roll up and secure with a toothpick. Place butter and coating mix in separate shallow bowls. Dip chicken in butter, then roll in coating mix.

Place in a greased 2-qt. microwave-safe dish. Cover loosely and microwave on high for 5-7 minutes on each side or until no longer pink. Let stand for 5 minutes. Discard toothpicks. **Yield: 4 servings.**

Editor's Note: This recipe was tested in a 1,100-watt microwave.

Fixing a cozy meal can be simple when you follow this fuss-free menu. Since the dessert needs time to chill, start by preparing refreshing Raspberry Yogurt Pie first from Margaret Schneider of Utica, Michigan. Try it with your favorite yogurt flavor and berries or fruit slices.

After placing the pie in the refrigerator, stir up the buttery Seasoned Green Beans from Katherine Firth of Oro Ballay, Arizona. While the beans steam, fix the savory Chicken with Peach Stuffing from Theresa Stewart of New Oxford, Pennsylvania.

Seasoned Green Beans

Prep/Total Time: 15 min.

3-1/2	cups fresh *or* frozen green beans (about 1 pound)
2	tablespoons butter, melted
1/4	to 1/2 teaspoon seasoned salt
1/4	to 1/2 teaspoon chili powder
1/8	teaspoon garlic powder
1/8	teaspoon onion powder

Place beans in a steamer basket; place in a saucepan over 1 in. of water. Bring to a boil; cover and steam for 7-8 minutes or until crisp-tender. In a small bowl, combine the butter and seasonings. Drain beans; add butter mixture and toss to coat. **Yield:** 4 servings.

Chicken with Peach Stuffing

Prep/Total Time: 25 min.

1	can (15-1/4 ounces) sliced peaches
4	boneless skinless chicken breast halves (4 ounces *each*)
2	tablespoons canola oil
2	tablespoons butter
1	tablespoon brown sugar
1	tablespoon cider vinegar
1/8	teaspoon ground allspice
1	package (6 ounces) chicken stuffing mix

Drain peaches, reserving syrup. Set aside eight peach slices for garnish; dice the remaining peaches. Add enough water to the syrup to measure 1 cup. Set peaches and syrup aside.

In a large skillet, cook chicken in oil for 4-5 minutes on each side or until a meat thermometer reads 170°. Add the butter, brown sugar, vinegar, allspice and reserved syrup.

Bring to a boil. Reduce heat; cover and simmer for 5 minutes. Add dry stuffing mix and diced peaches. Remove from the heat; cover and let stand for 5 minutes. Serve with peach slices. **Yield:** 4 servings.

Raspberry Yogurt Pie

Prep/Total Time: 10 min.

2	cartons (8 ounces *each*) raspberry yogurt
1	carton (8 ounces) frozen whipped topping, thawed
1	graham cracker crust (9 inches)

Fresh raspberries, optional

Place yogurt in a bowl; fold in whipped topping. Spoon into crust. Garnish with raspberries if desired. Refrigerate until serving. **Yield:** 8 servings.

Nutrition Facts: 1 piece (prepared with fat-free yogurt, reduced-fat whipped topping and a reduced-fat graham cracker crust) equals 200 calories, 6 g fat (4 g saturated fat), 2 mg cholesterol, 137 mg sodium, 28 g carbohydrate, 0 fiber, 4 g protein. **Diabetic Exchanges:** *1-1/2 starch, 1 fat, 1/2 fat-free milk.*

Graham Cracker Crust

When a recipe calls for a 9-in. graham cracker crust, it's easy to make one from scratch in a pretty pie plate. Finely crush 24 graham cracker squares to yield 1-1/2 cups crumbs. Combine the crumbs, 1/4 cup sugar, and 1/3 cup melted butter. Press the mixture onto the bottom and up sides of an ungreased 9-in. pie plate. Refrigerate for 30 minutes before filling.

Joyce Key of Snellville, Georgia says made-in-minutes menus, like the one she shares here, are especially handy when camping. An envelope of onion soup mix adds the speedy seasoning to Three-Step Stroganoff, a quick version of the traditional entree. "The original called for ground beef, but we prefer it with sliced beef," Joyce states.

While her main dish simmers, Joyce prepares Orange Lettuce Salad. A flavorful dressing sparks fresh greens that are tossed with colorful oranges and green onion. For dessert, Cream-Topped Grapes look lovely when served in sherbet glasses.

 ## Orange Lettuce Salad
Prep/Total Time: 15 min.

- 8 cups torn Bibb lettuce *or* salad greens of your choice
- 3 green onions, sliced
- 1 can (15 ounces) mandarin oranges, drained
- 1/4 cup canola oil
- 2 tablespoons white vinegar
- 2 tablespoons sugar
- 2 tablespoons minced fresh parsley
- 1/2 teaspoon salt, optional

Dash pepper

- 4 drops hot pepper sauce
- 1/4 cup slivered almonds, toasted, optional

In a salad bowl, toss the lettuce, onions and oranges; set aside. In a jar with a tight-fitting lid, combine the oil, vinegar, sugar, parsley, salt if desired, pepper and hot pepper sauce; shake well. Drizzle desired amount over salad; toss to coat. Sprinkle with almonds if desired. Refrigerate any remaining dressing. **Yield: 8 servings.**

Nutrition Facts: 1 serving (prepared with artificial sweetener equivalent to 2 tablespoons sugar and without salt and almonds) equals 104 calories, 7 g fat (0 saturated fat), 0 cholesterol, 7 mg sodium, 11 g carbohydrate, 1 g fiber, 1 g protein. **Diabetic Exchanges:** *1 vegetable, 1 fat, 1/2 fruit.*

Cream-Topped Grapes
Prep/Total Time: 10 min.

- 1 pound seedless grapes
- 1 cup (8 ounces) sour cream
- 1/4 cup packed dark brown sugar

Place grapes in six dessert cups. Combine sour cream and brown sugar until smooth. Refrigerate until ready to serve. Spoon over grapes. **Yield: 6 servings.**

 ## Three-Step Stroganoff
Prep/Total Time: 30 min.

- 1-1/2 pounds boneless beef top round steak, thinly sliced
- 1 tablespoon canola oil
- 1 can (10-3/4 ounces) condensed cream of mushroom soup, undiluted
- 1/2 cup water
- 1 envelope onion soup mix
- 1/2 cup sour cream

Hot cooked noodles
Minced fresh parsley, optional

In a large skillet, cook the sliced beef over medium-hot heat in the oil until the meat is no longer pink; drain. Stir in the soup, water and onion soup mix. Reduce heat; cover and simmer for 20 minutes.

Stir in the sour cream; cook until heated through (do not boil). Serve with the noodles; sprinkle with parsley if desired. **Yield: 6 servings.**

Nutrition Facts: 1 cup (prepared with reduced-fat cream of mushroom soup, reduced-sodium onion soup mix and reduced-fat sour cream; calculated without noodles) equals 250 calories, 9 g fat (0 saturated fat), 81 mg cholesterol, 521 mg sodium, 10 g carbohydrate, 0 fiber, 29 g protein. **Diabetic Exchanges:** *3-1/2 lean meat, 1 starch.*

Green Chili Burritos

Prep/Total Time: 30 min.

    1   can (16 ounces) refried beans
    8   flour tortillas (6 inches), warmed
  1/2   pound ground beef, cooked and drained
    1   cup (4 ounces) shredded sharp cheddar cheese,
        divided
    1   can (4 ounces) chopped green chilies

Spread refried beans over tortillas. Top each with beef and 2 tablespoons of cheese. Fold ends and sides over filling and roll up; place seam side down in a greased 13-in. x 9-in. baking dish. Sprinkle with chilies and remaining cheese.

Bake, uncovered, at 350° for 20 minutes or until heated through. **Yield: 4 servings.**

Mexican Cookies

Prep/Total Time: 20 min.

    4   flour tortillas (6 inches)
  1/2   cup semisweet chocolate chips
  3/4   teaspoon shortening
  1/4   cup confectioners' sugar
  1/4   teaspoon ground cinnamon

Cut each tortilla into eight wedges; place on ungreased baking sheets. Bake at 400° for 10-12 minutes or until lightly browned. Meanwhile, in a microwave, melt chocolate chips and shortening. Stir until smooth; keep warm.

In a large resealable plastic bag, combine confectioners' sugar and cinnamon. Add tortilla wedges a few at a time; shake to coat. Place on waxed paper-lined baking sheets. Drizzle with melted chocolate. Refrigerate until serving. **Yield: 32 cookies.**

Kathy Ybarra and her husband, who is a minister, are busy running their congregation in Rock Springs, Wyoming. So when she has free time, Kathy likes to try new recipes. "After a woman in our congregation shared the recipe for hearty Green Chili Burritos, they became a favorite in our home. When I serve them at church potlucks, they disappear fast." Fresh-tasting Taco Salad is the perfect side dish to the zippy burritos. And the light, crunchy cookies make a sweet and tasty ending.

Taco Salad

Prep/Total Time: 15 min.

      6   cups chopped iceberg lettuce
    1/2   cup finely chopped onion
    3/4   to 1 cup kidney beans, rinsed and drained
  1-1/2   cups (6 ounces) shredded cheddar cheese
      1   medium tomato, chopped
      4   cups taco-flavored tortilla chips
    1/2   cup Thousand Island salad dressing

In a large bowl, layer the first five ingredients in order listed. Just before serving, add chips and salad dressing; toss to coat. **Yield: 4-6 servings.**

Leftover Tortilla Treats

Here are some ways to use up extra flour tortillas:

- *Make a breakfast burrito by spooning scrambled eggs, salsa and shredded cheddar cheese down the center of the tortilla and rolling up.*

- *Spread peanut butter, apple butter or cream cheese on a tortilla and roll it up for a quick snack sandwich. Eat it cold or heated in the microwave.*

- *Let tortillas dry on racks until brittle, then crumble into small pieces to use on soups or salads in place of croutons.*

Our Test Kitchen created the German Bratwurst and Pretzels with Mustard for this wonderful fall meal. The Sauerkraut Mashed Potatoes, from Betsy Esley of Three Mile Bay, New York, make it complete. An added bonus is that you use the bacon from the bratwurst in the mashed potato recipe!

German Bratwurst
Prep/Total Time: 30 min.

     4   bacon strips, diced
     5   uncooked bratwurst links
     1   teaspoon cornstarch
   1/4   cup chicken broth
     2   tablespoons Dijon mustard
     1   tablespoon brown sugar
     1   tablespoon white wine *or* additional chicken broth
     1   tablespoon cider vinegar
   1/8   teaspoon celery seed

In a large skillet, cook bacon over medium heat until crisp. Using a slotted spoon, remove to paper towels (save for another use). Drain, reserving 4 tablespoons drippings. In the drippings, cook bratwurst for 10-15 minutes or until no longer pink. Remove and keep warm. Drain skillet.

In a small bowl, combine cornstarch and broth until smooth; set aside. Add the mustard, brown sugar, wine or additional broth, vinegar and celery seed to skillet; cook and stir over medium heat until mixture is hot and bubbly.

Gradually add cornstarch mixture. Bring to a boil; cook and stir until thickened. Return bratwurst to the pan; cook and stir for 1-2 minutes or until glazed. **Yield: 5 servings.**

Pretzels with Mustard
Prep/Total Time: 5 min.

   1/2   cup Dijon mustard
   1/3   cup honey
     1   tablespoon white wine vinegar
     2   teaspoons sugar
Large soft pretzels, warmed

In a small bowl, whisk the mustard, honey, vinegar and sugar until blended. Serve with soft pretzels. **Yield: 3/4 cup.**

Sauerkraut Mashed Potatoes
Prep/Total Time: 20 min.

   2-2/3   cups water
     2/3   cup milk
     1/4   cup butter, cubed
       1   teaspoon salt
   2-2/3   cups mashed potato flakes
     1/2   cup sauerkraut, rinsed and well drained
     1/3   cup chopped onion
       4   bacon strips, cooked and crumbled

In a large saucepan, combine the water, milk, butter and salt; bring to a boil. Stir in potato flakes. Remove from the heat; cover and let stand for 5 minutes.

Meanwhile, in a small skillet coated with cooking spray, cook onion over medium heat until tender. Stir sauerkraut into potatoes; sprinkle with onion and bacon. **Yield: 5 servings.**

Kicking off the weekend with a delicious breakfast doesn't require waking up at sunrise to prepare it. With these easy eye-openers from our home economists, you'll have no trouble surprising family members with a hearty morning meal.

A batch of Cranberry Bran Muffins conveniently starts with a boxed mix. And the Sweet 'n' Spicy Bacon requires the same temperature as the muffins! The sensational Strawberry Cream Crepes come together easily and are guaranteed to impress.

Cranberry Bran Muffins
Prep/Total Time: 25 min.

1	package (8.1 ounces) apple cinnamon muffin mix
1/2	cup All-Bran, crushed
1/2	cup dried cranberries
1/2	cup milk

In a large bowl, combine the muffin mix, bran and cranberries. Stir in milk just until moistened. Fill greased or paper-lined muffin cups three-fourths full. Bake at 450° for 15-20 minutes or until a toothpick comes out clean. Cool muffins for 5 minutes before removing from pan to a wire rack. Serve warm. **Yield: 6 muffins.**

Sweet 'n' Spicy Bacon
Prep/Total Time: 25 min.

1	teaspoon chili powder
1/8	teaspoon cayenne pepper
1/8	teaspoon curry powder
1/8	teaspoon ground cinnamon
8	bacon strips
3	tablespoons maple syrup

Combine the seasonings; sprinkle over both sides of the bacon strips. Place on a rack in an ungreased 15-in. x 10-in. baking pan. Bake at 450° for 10 minutes. Drizzle with 1 tablespoon maple syrup. Turn the bacon and drizzle with remaining maple syrup.

Bake for 6-10 minutes longer or until browned. Remove to paper towels. Serve warm. **Yield: 4 servings.**

Strawberry Cream Crepes
Prep/Total Time: 30 min.

1/2	cup biscuit/baking mix
1	egg
1/2	cup milk
1/4	teaspoon vanilla extract
2	packages (3 ounces *each*) cream cheese, softened
1/4	cup sour cream
2	tablespoons sugar
1/4	teaspoon ground cinnamon
1	package (10 ounces) frozen sweetened sliced strawberries, thawed and drained
1/2	cup strawberry glaze

In a large bowl, combine the biscuit mix, egg, milk and vanilla. Cover and refrigerate for 1 hour.

Heat a lightly greased 8-in. nonstick skillet over medium heat; pour 2 tablespoons of the batter into the center of the skillet. Lift and tilt the pan to coat the bottom evenly. Cook until the top of the crepe appears dry; turn and cook 15-20 seconds longer. Remove to a wire rack. Repeat with the remaining batter, greasing the skillet as needed. When cool, stack the crepes with waxed paper or paper towels in between.

In a small bowl, beat the softened cream cheese, sour cream, sugar and ground cinnamon until blended. Spoon 2 rounded tablespoonfuls of the cream cheese mixture down the center of each crepe; roll up.

In a microwave-safe bowl, combine the thawed strawberries with the strawberry glaze. Cover and microwave on high for 1-2 minutes or until heated through. Spoon the strawberry sauce over the crepes. **Yield: 4 servings.**

Forget fast-food restaurants when lunchtime rolls around, because our home economists came up with this mouth-watering menu you can assemble in only a half hour.

Heated in the oven, Warm Layered Sandwich gives hungry diners eight different kinds of classic sandwich staples. To continue the no-fuss feast, toss together Pepperoni Floret Salad in no time at all. Dessert's a cinch with yummy, easy-to-make Chocolate-Oat Toffee Bars.

Pepperoni Floret Salad
Prep/Total Time: 5 min.

- 2 cups fresh cauliflowerets
- 2 cups fresh broccoli florets
- 1 can (6 ounces) pitted ripe olives, drained
- 1/2 cup sliced pepperoni
- 1/4 cup pickled pepper rings
- 1/2 cup Italian salad dressing

In a large bowl, combine the cauliflower, broccoli, olives, pepperoni and pepper rings. Drizzle with dressing; toss to coat. Refrigerate leftovers. **Yield: 6 servings.**

Warm Layered Sandwich
Prep/Total Time: 25 min.

- 1 unsliced round loaf (1 pound) Italian bread
- 2 tablespoons honey mustard
- 1/4 pound thinly sliced deli turkey
- 1/4 pound thinly sliced hard salami
- 1/4 pound sliced part-skim mozzarella cheese
- 2 thin slices red onion, separated into rings
- 1/4 pound thinly sliced deli ham
- 1/4 pound sliced Monterey Jack cheese
- 1 medium plum tomato, sliced
- 3 romaine leaves, torn

Cut the bread in half. Carefully hollow out the bottom and top of loaf, leaving a 3/4-in. shell (discard the bread that was removed or save for another use). Spread mustard on cut sides of bread.

On bread bottom, layer the turkey, salami, mozzarella cheese, onion, ham, Monterey Jack cheese and tomato. Replace top.

Wrap in heavy-duty foil; place on a baking sheet. Bake at 450° for 12-15 minutes or until heated through. Place romaine over tomato. Cut into wedges. **Yield: 6 servings.**

Chocolate-Oat Toffee Bars
Prep/Total Time: 30 min.

- 6 tablespoons butter, cubed
- 1 cup all-purpose flour
- 1 cup quick-cooking oats
- 1/3 cup packed brown sugar
- 3 tablespoons corn syrup
- 1 cup (6 ounces) semisweet chocolate chips
- 1/3 cup English toffee bits *or* almond brickle chips
- 1/3 cup chopped pecans

In a microwave-safe bowl, melt butter; stir in flour, oats, sugar and corn syrup. Press into greased 9-in. square baking pan.

Bake at 450° for 8-12 minutes or until golden-brown. Place on a wire rack. Sprinkle with chips. Let stand for 5 minutes; spread chocolate over crust. Sprinkle with toffee bits and pecans. Refrigerate until chocolate is set. **Yield: 15 servings.**

Different Oats

After quick-cooking or old-fashioned oats are processed, they are referred to as groats. Old-fashioned groats are steamed and flattened. Quick-cooking groats have been cut into pieces before being steamed and rolled. Both can be used interchangeably, although old-fashioned oats may give your recipe more texture.

Searching for quick-to-fix fare with old-fashioned appeal? Start with Breaded Dijon Pork Chops shared by Shannon Gerardi from Dayton, Ohio. The golden breading that coats the tender chops is subtly seasoned with Dijon mustard.

Marybeth Thompson of Thurmont, Maryland uses convenient pantry items to make Corn Bread Dressing. And Margaret McNeil of Memphis, Tennessee created the warm side dish with a heavenly aroma of Cinnamon Baked Apples.

Cinnamon Baked Apples

Prep/Total Time: 30 min.

3	large tart apples, peeled and cut into wedges
2	tablespoons lemon juice
2/3	cup apple juice
2/3	cup packed brown sugar
2	tablespoons butter
1/4	teaspoon ground cinnamon
4	cinnamon sticks (3 inches), optional

Whipped topping, optional

Place apples in an ungreased 11-in. x 7-in. baking dish. Drizzle with lemon juice; toss to coat. Set aside.

In a small saucepan, combine the apple juice, brown sugar, butter and cinnamon. Cook and stir over medium heat until sugar is dissolved and butter is melted. Pour over apples. Add cinnamon sticks if desired.

Bake, uncovered, at 375° for 20 minutes or until apples are tender. Discard cinnamon. Serve warm with whipped topping if desired. **Yield: 4 servings.**

Corn Bread Dressing

Prep/Total Time: 30 min.

1	package (8 ounces) corn bread stuffing cubes
1	medium onion, finely chopped
1	celery rib, finely chopped
1	can (8-3/4 ounces) cream-style corn
1	cup water
1	tablespoon butter, melted
1	tablespoon spicy brown mustard

In a large bowl, combine the stuffing, onion, celery, corn and water. Spoon into a greased 8-in. square baking dish. Combine the butter and mustard; drizzle over stuffing. Bake, uncovered, at 375° for 20 minutes or until heated through. **Yield: 4-6 servings.**

Breaded Dijon Pork Chops

Prep/Total Time: 30 min.

3/4	cup crushed saltines (about 20 crackers)
1/2	teaspoon dried thyme
1/4	teaspoon pepper
1/8	to 1/4 teaspoon rubbed sage
3	tablespoons Dijon mustard
4	pork rib chops (1/2 inch thick and 7 ounces *each*)
1/4	cup canola oil

In a small bowl, combine the cracker crumbs, thyme, pepper and sage. Spread mustard on both sides of pork; coat with crumb mixture.

In a large skillet, cook pork in oil over medium-high heat for 4-5 minutes on each side or until golden brown and meat juices run clear. **Yield: 4 servings.**

If you visit the quaint country town of Greenbriar, Pennsylvania, you're likely to find Nicole Harris happily cooking away in her kitchen, fixing meals for her family. She prepares Rosemary Lime Chicken, Zesty Garden Salad and Mandarin Berry Cooler as a quick, easy and flavorful meal.

Rosemary Lime Chicken
Prep/Total Time: 20 min.

4	boneless skinless chicken breast halves (5 ounces *each*)
2	tablespoons canola oil
1/2	cup white wine *or* chicken broth
1/4	cup lime juice
2	tablespoons minced fresh rosemary *or* 2 teaspoons dried rosemary, crushed
1/2	teaspoon salt
1/4	teaspoon pepper

Flatten chicken to 1/2-in. thickness. In a large skillet, brown chicken in oil over medium-high heat. Add the remaining ingredients. Cook, uncovered, for 5-7 minutes or until chicken is no longer pink. **Yield: 4 servings.**

Nutrition Facts: 1 chicken breast equals 244 calories, 9 g fat (1 g saturated fat), 82 mg cholesterol, 389 mg sodium, 2 g carbohydrate, 0.55 g fiber, 33 g protein. **Diabetic Exchanges:** *4 lean meat, 1/2 fat.*

Zesty Garden Salad
Prep/Total Time: 5 min.

4	cups torn romaine
1	can (2-1/4 ounces) sliced ripe olives, drained
1/2	cup chopped tomato
1/2	cup shredded cheddar cheese
1/4	cup pickled pepper rings
1/2	cup Italian salad dressing

In a large salad bowl, toss the romaine, olives, tomato, cheese and pepper rings. Just before serving, drizzle with dressing and toss to coat. **Yield: 4 servings.**

Mandarin Berry Cooler
Prep/Total Time: 5 min.

1	can (11 ounces) mandarin oranges, drained
1	can (8 ounces) crushed pineapple, drained
1	cup sliced fresh strawberries
1	medium ripe banana, cut into chunks
6	ice cubes
3/4	cup milk

In a blender, combine the oranges, pineapple, strawberries and banana; cover and process until blended. Add ice and milk; cover and process until blended. Pour into chilled glasses; serve immediately. **Yield: 4 servings.**

swift snacks
& easy appetizers

Whether you need a fancy hors d'oeuvre for a holiday get-together or just a simple snack to tide hungry ones over until dinnertime, this chapter is the solution! You're a speedy recipe away from making scaled-down recipes for any occasion.

Every appetizer in this chapter takes just minutes to prepare. Your guests will be thrilled when they bite into Bacon-Stuffed Mushrooms, Chunky Blue Cheese Dip or Mini Apricot Cheesecakes. Every delightful morsel comes together in a jiffy to give you tasty munchies in no time flat.

Calzone Pinwheels
(recipe on p. 34)

Bavarian Meatballs

Hot Crab Dip

Prep: 5 min. | Cook: 3 hours

I work full-time and coach soccer and football, so I appreciate recipes like this one that are easy to assemble. This warm and creamy seafood appetizer is perfect for large get-togethers.
—Teri Rasey-Bolf, Cadillac, Michigan

1/2	cup milk
1/3	cup salsa
3	packages (8 ounces *each*) cream cheese, cubed
2	packages (8 ounces *each*) imitation crabmeat, flaked
1	cup thinly sliced green onions
1	can (4 ounces) chopped green chilies

Assorted crackers

In a small bowl, combine milk and salsa. Transfer to a greased 3-qt. slow cooker. Stir in cream cheese, crab, onions and chilies. Cover and cook on low for 3-4 hours, stirring every 30 minutes. Serve with crackers. **Yield: about 5 cups.**

Sausage Egg Rolls

Prep: 25 min. | Cook: 5 min./batch

I use a packaged coleslaw mix for my easy eggrolls, so they're a breeze to put together. Serve them with your favorite brand of sweet 'n' sour sauce to suit your family's taste.
—Janet Hommes, Surprise, Arizona

1/2	pound bulk pork sausage
1/4	cup chopped green pepper
2	tablespoons plus 1-1/2 teaspoons chopped onion
1/2	teaspoon minced garlic
3-3/4	cups coleslaw mix
1/4	teaspoon pepper
1/8	teaspoon salt
16	egg roll wrappers

Oil for frying
Sweet-and-sour sauce

In a large skillet, cook the sausage, green pepper, onion and garlic over medium heat until meat is no longer pink; drain. In a large bowl, combine the coleslaw, pepper and salt; stir in sausage mixture.

Place 1/4 cupful of the filling in the center of each egg roll wrapper. Fold the bottom corner over filling, then fold the sides toward center over filling. Moisten remaining corner with water; roll up tightly to seal.

In an electric skillet or deep-fat fryer, heat 1 in. of oil to 375°. Fry egg rolls, a few at a time, for 2-3 minutes on each side or until golden brown. Drain on paper towels. Serve with sweet-and-sour sauce. **Yield: 16 egg rolls.**

Bavarian Meatballs

Prep: 15 min. | Cook: 3-1/2 hours

These mouth-watering meatballs are a guaranteed crowd-pleaser when I serve them as party appetizers...or a yummy, filling sandwich spooned over crusty rolls and topped with cheese.
—Peggy Rios, Mechanicsville, Virginia

1	package (38 ounces) frozen cooked Italian meatballs
1/2	cup chopped onion
1/4	cup packed brown sugar
1	envelope onion soup mix
1	can (12 ounces) beer *or* nonalcoholic beer
12	hoagie buns, split
3	cups (12 ounces) shredded Swiss cheese

In a 3-qt. slow cooker, combine the meatballs, onion, brown sugar, soup mix and beer. Cover and cook on low for 3-1/2 to 4-1/2 hours or until heated through.

Serve with toothpicks for an appetizer. Or for sandwiches, place six meatballs on each bun bottom. Sprinkle each sandwich with 1/4 cup cheese. Place on baking sheets. Broil 4-6 in. from the heat for 2-3 minutes or until cheese is melted. Replace bun tops. **Yield: 12 servings.**

Frosted Peanut Butter Fingers

Prep: 25 min. | Bake: 15 min. + cooling

I first learned about these quick crowd-pleasers from a next-door neighbor when I sniffed the delightful aroma of a batch baking. Topped with extra peanut butter and chocolate frosting, the chewy bars became a family favorite that day when she brought us a plateful and shared the recipe.

—Leah Gallington, Corona, California

1	cup butter, softened
1-1/2	cups packed brown sugar
1	cup sugar
2-1/2	cups creamy peanut butter, *divided*
1	egg
1-1/2	teaspoons vanilla extract
2-1/2	cups quick-cooking oats
2	cups all-purpose flour
1	teaspoon baking soda
1/2	teaspoon salt

CHOCOLATE FROSTING:

6	tablespoons butter, softened
4	cups confectioners' sugar
1/2	cup baking cocoa
1	teaspoon vanilla extract
6	to 8 tablespoons milk

In a large bowl, cream butter and sugars until light and fluffy. Beat in 1 cup peanut butter, egg and vanilla. Combine oats, flour, baking soda and salt; gradually add to creamed mixture, beating well after each addition.

Spread into a greased 15-in. x 10-in. baking pan. Bake at 350° for 13-17 minutes or until golden brown. Cool slightly on a wire rack, about 12 minutes. Spread with remaining peanut butter. Cool completely.

For the frosting, in a large bowl, beat the butter, confectioners' sugar, cocoa, vanilla and enough milk to achieve spreading consistency. Spread over peanut butter. Cut into bars. **Yield: about 3 dozen.**

Editor's Note: Reduced-fat or generic brands of peanut butter are not recommended for this recipe.

Slow Cooker Mexican Dip

Prep: 15 min. | Cook: 1-1/2 hours

My husband and I love to entertain and this hearty, 7-ingredient dip is always a hit...as well as a request. It couldn't be much easier to put together, and using our slow cooker leaves us free to share some quality time with our guests.

—Heather Courtney, Ames, Iowa

1-1/2	pounds ground beef
1	pound bulk hot Italian sausage
1	cup chopped onion
1	package (8.8 ounces) ready-to-serve Spanish rice
1	can (16 ounces) refried beans
1	can (10 ounces) enchilada sauce
1	pound process cheese (Velveeta), cubed
1	package tortilla chip scoops

In a Dutch oven, cook the beef, sausage and onion over medium heat until meat is no longer pink; drain. Heat rice according to package directions.

In a 3-qt. slow cooker, combine the meat mixture, rice, beans, enchilada sauce and cheese. Cover and cook on low for 1-1/2 to 2 hours or until cheese is melted. Serve with tortilla scoops. **Yield: 8 cups.**

Slow Cooker Mexican Dip

Rosemary Cheese Patties

Prep/Total Time: 25 min.

We're a family that loves snacks and I combined some of our favorite ingredients in this fast, easy and delicious recipe. Great for entertaining, it can be prepared ahead of time and browned just before guests arrive. It's quickly doubled for a crowd and is extra special with marinara sauce.

—Judy Armstrong, Prairieville, Louisiana

1	package (8 ounces) cream cheese, softened
1	cup grated Parmesan cheese
3/4	cup seasoned bread crumbs, *divided*
2	eggs
1-1/2	to 2 teaspoons minced fresh rosemary
1-1/2	teaspoons minced garlic
1/8	to 1/4 teaspoon cayenne pepper
2	tablespoons olive oil

Marinara sauce, warmed, optional

In a large bowl, beat the cream cheese, Parmesan cheese, 1/4 cup bread crumbs, eggs, fresh rosemary, minced garlic and cayenne until blended.

Place the remaining crumbs in a shallow bowl. Shape heaping tablespoonfuls of cheese mixture into 1-1/2-in. balls; flatten to 1/2-in. thickness. Coat with bread crumbs.

In a large skillet, brown patties in oil in batches over medium heat until golden brown. Drain on paper towels. Serve warm with marinara sauce if desired. **Yield: 12 servings.**

Hot Artichoke Spread

Prep/Total Time: 30 min.

Green chilies add a bit of zip to this thick spread that's terrific on crackers and pita bread. I serve it often at parties because it makes a lot, is quick to prepare and looks so pretty with the chopped red tomatoes and green onions on top.

—Victoria Casey, Coeur d'Alene, Idaho

1	can (14 ounces) water-packed artichoke hearts, rinsed, drained and chopped
1	cup mayonnaise
1	cup grated Parmesan cheese
1	can (4 ounces) chopped green chilies, drained
1	garlic clove, minced
1	cup chopped fresh tomatoes
3	green onions, thinly sliced

Crackers *or* pita bread

In a large bowl, combine the artichoke hearts, mayonnaise, cheese, green chilies and garlic. Spread into a 1-qt. baking dish or 9-in. pie plate.

Bake, uncovered, at 350° for 20-25 minutes or until the top is lightly browned. Sprinkle with the chopped fresh tomatoes and sliced green onions. Serve with crackers or pita bread. **Yield: 4-1/2 cups.**

Editor's Note: Reduced-fat or fat-free mayonnaise is not recommended for this recipe.

Rosemary Cheese Patties

Frosty Mocha Drink

Frosty Mocha Drink
Prep/Total Time: 15 min.

I like to make this chilly chocolate-flavored coffee drink when friends stop by for a visit. I always double the recipe, however, because I know they'll come back for seconds. For a richer and creamier version, replace the milk with half-and-half cream.
—Lauren Nance, San Diego, California

1	cup milk
3	tablespoons instant chocolate drink mix
2	tablespoons instant coffee granules
2	tablespoons honey
1	teaspoon vanilla extract
14	to 16 ice cubes

In a blender, combine all the ingredients; cover and process until smooth. Pour into chilled glasses; serve immediately. Yield: 4 servings.

Tomato Guacamole Dip
Prep/Total Time: 15 min.

With just six ingredients, this refreshing dip is a snap to whip up. It's so light and fresh, it's the perfect way to start our dinner.
—Jill Perez, Racine, Wisconsin

2	medium ripe avocados, peeled and chopped
1	tablespoon lime juice
1	small tomato, seeded and chopped
3	tablespoons sour cream
1/2	teaspoon salt
1/2	teaspoon minced garlic

Tortilla chips

In a small bowl, mash the avocados and lime juice with a fork. Stir in the chopped tomato, sour cream, salt and garlic. Cover and refrigerate for 5 minutes. Serve with tortilla chips. Yield: 2-1/3 cups.

Tortellini Appetizers
Prep: 20 min. | Bake: 20 min. + cooling

The festive green and red of this appetizer will make it a welcomed addition to your holiday buffet table. Store-bought pesto keeps the preparation fast. Sometimes I like to heat the garlic in a skillet and use skewers for a different look.
—Cheryl Lama, Royal Oak, Michigan

4	garlic cloves, peeled
2	tablespoons olive oil, *divided*
1	package (10 ounces) refrigerated spinach tortellini
1	cup mayonnaise
1/4	cup grated Parmesan cheese
1/4	cup milk
1/4	cup prepared pesto
1/8	teaspoon pepper
1	pint grape tomatoes
26	frilled toothpicks

Place the garlic cloves on a double thickness of heavy-duty foil; drizzle with 1 tablespoon olive oil. Wrap foil around the garlic. Bake at 425° for 20-25 minutes or until tender. Cool for 10-15 minutes.

Meanwhile, cook tortellini according to package directions; drain and rinse in cold water. Toss with remaining oil; set aside. In a small bowl, combine the mayonnaise, Parmesan cheese, milk, pesto and pepper. Mash garlic into pesto mixture; stir until combined.

Alternately thread tortellini and tomatoes onto toothpicks. Serve with pesto dip. Refrigerate leftovers. **Yield: about 2 dozen (1-1/2 cups dip).**

Tortellini Appetizers

Olive Bruschetta

Olive Bruschetta

Prep/Total Time: 30 min.

This time-saving and colorful party classic can be made several days in advance. In fact, it actually tastes better if prepared ahead so all the fresh flavors can blend together. It's best served at room temperature with a crusty loaf of toasted French bread or your favorite crackers.

—Linda Austin, Lake Hopatcong, New Jersey

2	cups grape tomatoes, quartered
2	celery ribs, chopped
1/2	cup shredded carrot
1/4	cup sliced ripe olives
1/4	cup sliced pimiento-stuffed olives
1/4	cup minced fresh flat-leaf parsley
1/4	cup chopped red onion
1	teaspoon minced garlic
3	tablespoons olive oil
2	tablespoons balsamic vinegar
1/4	teaspoon salt
1/8	teaspoon pepper
1	loaf (1 pound) French bread baguette, sliced and toasted

In a large bowl, combine the first eight ingredients. In a small bowl, combine the oil, vinegar, salt and pepper; pour over vegetables and toss to coat. Serve on toasted baguette slices. **Yield: 2-1/2 dozen.**

Broccoli Bites

Prep: 25 min. | Bake: 15 min.

Seasoned stuffing and Parmesan cheese add a wonderful, savory flavor to the broccoli in these cute appetizers. They're so easy to make and super-convenient because the extra appetizers can be frozen. The recipe yields several dozen, so you can just take however many you need out of the freezer.

—Laurie Todd, Columbus, Mississippi

6	cups frozen chopped broccoli
2	cups crushed seasoned stuffing
1	cup grated Parmesan cheese
6	eggs, lightly beaten
1/2	cup butter, softened
1/2	teaspoon salt
1/4	teaspoon pepper

Cook the chopped broccoli according to the package directions; drain and place in a bowl. Stir in the stuffing, Parmesan cheese, eggs, softened butter, salt and pepper. Shape into 1-in. balls.

Place in a greased 15-in. x 10-in. baking pan. Bake at 350° for 11-12 minutes or until golden brown. Or place in a single layer in a freezer container and freeze for up to 1 month.

To use frozen appetizers: Place in a greased 15-in. x 10-in. baking pan. Bake at 350° for 16-18 minutes or until golden brown. **Yield: about 5 dozen.**

Banana Shakes

Prep/Total Time: 10 min.

I love bananas and these shakes are the best. Though we're stationed overseas, I've fed my two young kids these made-in-moments drinks since they were babies. Pop them into the freezer for a few minutes if you like them thicker. Or try different flavors using chocolate or strawberry ice cream.

—Martha Miller, Tokyo, Japan

  1 cup half-and-half cream
  4 cups vanilla ice cream, softened
  1 medium banana, sliced
  1/4 teaspoon banana extract

In a blender, combine all the ingredients; cover and process until smooth. Pour into chilled glasses; serve immediately. **Yield: 4 servings.**

Raspberry Cheese Spread

Prep: 10 min. + chilling

A party guest brought this attractive appetizer to our home, and we fell in love with it. Now I often make it myself for company.

—Jane Montgomery, Hilliard, Ohio

  4 ounces cream cheese, softened
  1 cup mayonnaise
  2 cups (8 ounces) shredded part-skim mozzarella cheese
  2 cups (8 ounces) shredded cheddar cheese
  3 green onions, finely chopped
  1 cup chopped pecans
  1/4 cup seedless raspberry preserves
Assorted crackers

Raspberry Cheese Spread

Mini Spinach Frittatas

In a small bowl, beat cream cheese and mayonnaise until smooth. Beat in cheeses and onions. Stir in pecans. Spread into a plastic wrap-lined 9-in. round dish. Refrigerate until set, about 1 hour.

Invert onto a serving plate; spread with preserves. Serve with crackers. **Yield: about 3 1/2 cups.**

Mini Spinach Frittatas

Prep/Total Time: 30 min.

These mini frittatas are a cinch to make and just delicious. It doubles easily for a crowd and even freezes well.

—Nancy Statkevicus, Tucson, Arizona

  1 cup ricotta cheese
  3/4 cup grated Parmesan cheese
  2/3 cup chopped fresh mushrooms
  1 package (10 ounces) frozen chopped spinach, thawed and squeezed dry
  1 egg
  1/2 teaspoon dried oregano
  1/4 teaspoon salt
  1/4 teaspoon pepper
  24 slices pepperoni

In a small bowl, combine the first eight ingredients. Place a slice of pepperoni in each of 24 greased miniature muffin cups. Fill muffin cups three-fourths full with cheese mixture.

Bake at 375° for 20-25 minutes or until a toothpick comes out clean. Carefully run a knife around edges of muffin cups to loosen. Serve warm. **Yield: 2 dozen.**

Cheese Fries

Prep/Total Time: 20 min.

I came up with this recipe after my daughter had cheese fries at a restaurant and couldn't stop talking about them. She loves that I can fix them so quickly at home. The frozen fries help to make this an easy recipe.

—Melissa Tatum, Greensboro, North Carolina

- 1   package (28 ounces) frozen steak fries
- 1   can (10-3/4 ounces) condensed cheddar cheese soup, undiluted
- 1/4   cup milk
- 1/2   teaspoon garlic powder
- 1/4   teaspoon onion powder

Paprika

Arrange the steak fries in a single layer in two greased 15-in. x 10-in. baking pans. Bake at 450° for 15-18 minutes or until tender and golden brown.

Meanwhile, in a small saucepan, combine the condensed cheddar cheese soup, milk, garlic powder and onion powder; heat through. Drizzle over the steak fries; sprinkle with paprika. **Yield: 8-10 servings.**

Cheese Fries

French Fries with Pizzazz!

It's super simple to turn Cheese Fries into any number of specialty french fries. Add a little chili to make chili cheese fries. Add a few drops of hot sauce and some chopped green onion to the cheese sauce for a zippier version. For an Italian flair, sprinkle garlic salt over the fries and add Parmesan cheese and chopped tomato to the sauce.

Jalapeno Chicken Wraps

Jalapeno Chicken Wraps

Prep: 15 min. | Grill: 20 min.

These easy appetizers are always a hit at parties! Zesty strips of chicken and bits of onion sit in jalapeno halves that are wrapped in bacon and grilled. Serve them with blue cheese or ranch salad dressing for dipping.   *—Leslie Buenz, Tinley Park, Illinois*

- 1   pound boneless skinless chicken breasts
- 1   tablespoon garlic powder
- 1   tablespoon onion powder
- 1   tablespoon pepper
- 2   teaspoons seasoned salt
- 1   teaspoon paprika
- 1   small onion, cut into strips
- 15   jalapeno peppers, halved and seeded
- 1   pound sliced bacon, halved widthwise

Blue cheese salad dressing

Cut the chicken into 2-in. x 1-1/2-in. strips. In a large resealable plastic bag, combine the garlic powder, onion powder, pepper, seasoned salt and paprika; add the chicken and shake to coat. Place a chicken and onion strip in each jalapeno half. Wrap each with a piece of bacon and secure with toothpicks.

Grill, uncovered, over indirect medium heat for 9-10 minutes on each side or until chicken is no longer pink and bacon is crisp. Serve with blue cheese dressing. **Yield: 2-1/2 dozen.**

Editor's Note: When cutting hot peppers, disposable gloves are recommended. Avoid touching your face.

Baked Chicken Nachos

Prep: 20 min. | Bake: 15 min.

Here's a colorful, party appetizer that's delicious and so simple. Rotisserie (or leftover) chicken keeps it quick, and the seasonings and splash of lime juice lend fantastic flavor. My husband likes this snack so much he often requests it for dinner!

—Gail Cawsey, Fawnskin, California

- 2 medium sweet red peppers, diced
- 1 medium green pepper, diced
- 3 teaspoons canola oil, *divided*
- 1 can (15 ounces) black beans, rinsed and drained
- 1 teaspoon minced garlic
- 1 teaspoon dried oregano
- 1/4 teaspoon ground cumin
- 2-1/4 cups shredded cooked rotisserie chicken (skin removed)
- 4-1/2 teaspoons lime juice
- 1/8 teaspoon salt
- 1/8 teaspoon pepper
- 7-1/2 cups tortilla chips
- 8 ounces pepper Jack cheese, shredded
- 1/4 cup thinly sliced green onions
- 1/2 cup minced fresh cilantro
- 1 cup (8 ounces) sour cream
- 2 to 3 teaspoons diced pickled jalapeno peppers, optional

In a large skillet, saute peppers in 1-1/2 teaspoons oil for 3 minutes or until crisp-tender; transfer to a small bowl. In the same skillet, saute the beans, garlic, oregano and cumin in remaining oil for 3 minutes or until heated through.

PB&J Spirals

Meanwhile, combine the chicken, lime juice, salt and pepper. In a greased 13-in. x 9-in. baking dish, layer half of the tortilla chips, pepper mixture, bean mixture, chicken, cheese, onions and cilantro. Repeat layers.

Bake, uncovered, at 350° for 15-20 minutes or until heated through. Serve with sour cream and pickled jalapenos if desired. **Yield: 16 servings.**

PB&J Spirals

Prep/Total Time: 30 min.

Kids young and old love these peanut butter and jelly treats. Using refrigerated crescent roll dough, they're a fun snack for hungry youngsters to assemble. Parents help with the baking.

—Lisa Renshaw, Kansas City, Missouri

- 1 tube (8 ounces) refrigerated crescent rolls
- 8 teaspoons creamy peanut butter
- 8 teaspoons grape jelly
- 1/4 cup chopped unsalted peanuts
- 2 tablespoons confectioners' sugar

Unroll crescent dough; separate into triangles. Spread 1 teaspoon each of peanut butter and jelly on the wide end of each triangle; sprinkle with peanuts. Roll up from the wide end and place point side down 2 in. apart on an ungreased baking sheet. Curve ends to form a crescent shape.

Bake the crescents at 375° for 11-13 minutes or until lightly browned. Dust with confectioners' sugar. Serve warm. **Yield: 8 servings.**

Baked Chicken Nachos

Calzone Pinwheels

Reuben Spread

Prep: 5 min. | Cook: 2 hours

I received the recipe for this hearty spread from my daughter. It tastes just like a Reuben sandwich. Serve it from a slow cooker set to low so the spread stays warm.

—Rosalie Fuchs, Paynesville, Minnesota

1	jar (16 ounces) sauerkraut, rinsed and drained
1	package (8 ounces) cream cheese, cubed
2	cups (8 ounces) shredded Swiss cheese
1	package (3 ounces) deli corned beef, chopped
3	tablespoons prepared Thousand Island salad dressing

Snack rye bread *or* crackers

In a 1-1/2-qt. slow cooker, combine the first five ingredients. Cover and cook for 2 hours or until the cheeses are melted; stir to blend. Serve warm with snack bread or crackers. **Yield: 3-1/2 cups.**

Calzone Pinwheels

Prep/Total Time: 30 min.

Once you try these mini-sized calzones, you may never go back to the large ones. Not only do these pretty bites take advantage of convenient refrigerator crescent rolls, they can be made ahead and popped in the oven right before company arrives. No one can eat just one and people love the cheesy, fresh taste!

—Lisa Smith, Bryan, Ohio

1/2	cup ricotta cheese
1	teaspoon Italian seasoning
1/4	teaspoon salt
1/2	cup shredded part-skim mozzarella cheese
1/2	cup diced pepperoni
1/4	cup grated Parmesan cheese
1/4	cup chopped fresh mushrooms
1/4	cup finely chopped green pepper
2	tablespoons finely chopped onion
1	package (8 ounces) refrigerated crescent rolls
1	jar (14 ounces) pizza sauce, warmed

In a small bowl, combine the ricotta, Italian seasoning and salt. Stir in the mozzarella, pepperoni, Parmesan, mushrooms, green pepper and onion. Separate crescent dough into four rectangles; seal perforations.

Spread cheese mixture over each rectangle to within 1/4 in. of edges. Roll up jelly-roll style, starting with a short side; pinch seams to seal. Cut each into four slices.

Place cut side down on greased baking sheets. Bake at 375° for 10-15 minutes or until golden brown. Serve warm with pizza sauce. Refrigerate leftovers. **Yield: 16 appetizers.**

Bacon-Stuffed Mushrooms

Prep/Total Time: 20 min.

I first tried these broiled treats at my sister-in-law's house. The juicy mushroom caps and creamy filling were so fabulous that I had to get the recipe. They're super fast and easy.

—Angela Coffman, Stewartsville, Missouri

1	package (8 ounces) cream cheese, softened
1/2	cup real bacon bits
1	tablespoon chopped green onion
1/4	teaspoon garlic powder
1	pound whole fresh mushrooms, stems removed

In a small bowl, beat cream cheese until smooth. Stir in the bacon, onion and garlic powder. Spoon into mushroom caps. Broil 4-6 in. from the heat for 4-6 minutes or until heated through. Serve warm. **Yield: about 2 dozen.**

Bacon-Stuffed Mushrooms

Bread Bowl Seafood Dip

Prep: 15 min. | Bake: 45 min.

Every Christmas Eve, our family has a special hors d'oeuvre supper, and this seafood-stuffed dip is a much-requested staple. I got the recipe from a friend, who made it for my daughter's wedding shower. It's so rich, elegant and creamy—and a huge hit at parties any time of year at all!

— Terry Flewelling, Lacombe, Alberta

1	package (8 ounces) cream cheese, softened
1/2	cup mayonnaise
1-1/2	teaspoons Dijon mustard
1	can (6 ounces) small shrimp, rinsed and drained
1	can (6 ounces) crabmeat, drained, flaked and cartilage removed
2/3	cup shredded Monterey Jack cheese, *divided*
1/2	cup chopped green onions
1	round loaf (1 pound) sourdough bread

Assorted fresh vegetables

In a large bowl, beat the cream cheese, mayonnaise and mustard until smooth. Stir in the shrimp, crab, 1/3 cup Monterey Jack cheese and onions.

Cut the top fourth off the loaf of bread; carefully hollow out bottom, leaving a 1/2-in. shell. Cube the bread that was removed; set aside.

Spoon seafood mixture into bread shell. Sprinkle with remaining cheese. Wrap tightly in heavy-duty foil and place on a baking sheet.

Bake at 350° for 25 minutes. Unwrap; bake 20-25 minutes longer or until the cheese is melted and the dip is heated through. Serve with assorted vegetables and reserved bread cubes. **Yield: 2-1/4 cups.**

Spinach Deviled Eggs

Prep/Total Time: 15 min.

Spinach adds unexpected color and flavor to this tasty variation on deviled eggs. They're easy to make with leftover eggs and an attractive addition to a party spread.

—Dorothy Sander, Evansville, Indiana

12	hard-cooked eggs
1/4	cup mayonnaise
2	tablespoons white vinegar
2	tablespoons butter, softened
1	tablespoon sugar
1/2	teaspoon pepper
1/4	teaspoon salt
4	bacon strips, cooked and crumbled
1/2	cup frozen chopped spinach, thawed and squeezed dry

Cut eggs in half lengthwise. Remove yolks; set whites aside. In a small bowl, mash yolks. Add the mayonnaise, vinegar, butter, sugar, pepper and salt; mix well. Stir in bacon and spinach. Stuff or pipe into egg whites. Refrigerate until serving. **Yield: 2 dozen.**

Italian Snack Mix

Prep/Total Time: 15 min.

This munchable no-bake medley can be put together in minutes, and it stores well in an airtight container. With a hint of garlic and yummy Parmesan cheese, the pretzel-and-cereal combination makes a wonderful after-school treat.

—*Nancy Zimmerman, Cape May Court House, New Jersey*

- 8 cups Crispix
- 4 cups sourdough pretzel nuggets
- 3 tablespoons vegetable oil
- 1/4 cup grated Parmesan cheese
- 1 tablespoon spaghetti sauce mix
- 2 teaspoons garlic powder

In a 2-gal. resealable plastic bag, combine the cereal and pretzels. Drizzle with oil; seal bag and toss to coat. Combine the Parmesan cheese, spaghetti sauce mix and garlic powder; sprinkle over cereal mixture. Seal bag and toss to coat. **Yield: about 3 quarts.**

Chunky Blue Cheese Dip

Prep/Total Time: 10 min.

Every time I make this quick dip, someone asks for the recipe. It only requires a few items, so it's a snap to put together. I often prepare the thick spread with Gorgonzola cheese and serve it with toasted pecans. —*Sandy Schneider, Naperville, Illinois*

- 1 package (8 ounces) cream cheese, softened
- 1/3 cup sour cream
- 1/2 teaspoon white pepper
- 1/4 to 1/2 teaspoon salt
- 1 cup (4 ounces) crumbled blue cheese
- 1/3 cup minced chives

Apple and pear slices *and/or* toasted pecan halves

In a small bowl, beat the cream cheese, sour cream, pepper and salt until blended. Fold in the blue cheese and chives. Serve with apple and pear slices and/or pecans. **Yield: 1-3/4 cups.**

Chunky Blue Cheese Dip

Granola Banana Sticks

Granola Banana Sticks

Prep/Total Time: 20 min.

My daughter and I won an award at our local fair for these peanut-butter-and-granola bananas. I like to assemble the ingredients ahead for my kids to whip up when they get home from school. Sometimes we substitute rice cereal as a crunchy alternative to the granola bars.

—*Diane Toomey, Allentown, Pennsylvania*

- 1/4 cup peanut butter
- 2 tablespoons plus 1-1/2 teaspoons honey
- 4-1/2 teaspoons brown sugar
- 2 teaspoons milk
- 3 medium firm bananas
- 6 Popsicle sticks
- 2 crunchy oat and honey granola bars, crushed

In a small saucepan, combine the peanut butter, honey, brown sugar and milk; cook until heated through, stirring occasionally.

Peel bananas and cut in half widthwise; insert a Popsicle stick into one end of each banana half. Spoon peanut butter mixture over bananas to coat completely. Sprinkle with granola. Serve immediately or place on a waxed paper-lined baking sheet and freeze. **Yield: 6 servings.**

Pesto Bruschetta

Prep/Total Time: 20 min.

My daughter came up with this recipe and I'm asked for a copy of it every time I make it. It's easy to switch up the flavor by using different types of pesto. —Shirley Dickstein, Parma, Idaho

- 1 loaf (1 pound) French bread, cut into slices
- 1 jar (7 ounces) prepared pesto
- 2 medium tomatoes, seeded and finely chopped
- 1 package (4 ounces) crumbled feta cheese

Arrange bread slices on an ungreased baking sheet. Spread with pesto; top with tomatoes and cheese. Broil 4 in. from the heat for 3-5 minutes or until edges are lightly browned. **Yield: 29 appetizers.**

Nutrition Facts: 1 appetizer equals 93 calories, 4 g fat (1 g saturated fat), 4 mg cholesterol, 196 mg sodium, 10 g carbohydrate, 1 g fiber, 4 g protein. Diabetic Exchanges: 1 fat, 1/2 starch.

Mini Apricot Cheesecakes

Prep: 10 min. | Bake: 20 min. + cooling

Vanilla wafers are used to create the no-fuss crusts for these darling bite-size cheesecake treats. For a different look and taste, vary the kind of preserves on top.
—Carol Twardzik, Spy Hill, Saskatchewan

- 24 vanilla wafers
- 2 packages (8 ounces each) cream cheese, softened
- 3/4 cup sugar
- 2 eggs, lightly beaten
- 1 tablespoon lemon juice
- 1 teaspoon vanilla extract
- 1 cup apricot preserves

Mini Apricot Cheesecakes

Sausage Wonton Stars

Place wafers flat side down in paper- or foil-lined muffin cups; set aside. In a large bowl, beat cream cheese and sugar until smooth. Add the eggs, lemon juice and vanilla; beat well. Fill muffin cups three-fourths full.

Bake at 375° for 17-20 minutes or until set. Cool on a wire rack for 20 minutes. Carefully remove from pans to cool completely. Top each cheesecake with 2 teaspoons preserves. Store in refrigerator. **Yield: 2 dozen.**

Sausage Wonton Stars

Prep/Total Time: 30 min.

These fancy-looking appetizers are ideal when entertaining large groups. The cute, crunchy cups are stuffed with a cheesy pork sausage filling that kids of all ages enjoy. We keep a few in the freezer so we can easily reheat them for late-night snacking.
—Mary Thomas, North Lewisburg, Ohio

- 1 package (12 ounces) wonton wrappers
- 1 pound bulk pork sausage
- 2 cups (8 ounces) shredded Colby cheese
- 1/2 medium green pepper, chopped
- 1/2 medium sweet red pepper, chopped
- 2 bunches green onions, sliced
- 1/2 cup ranch salad dressing

Lightly press wonton wrappers onto the bottom and up the sides of greased miniature muffin cups. Bake at 350° for 5 minutes or until edges are browned.

In a large skillet, cook sausage over medium heat until no longer pink; drain. Stir in the cheese, peppers, onions and salad dressing. Spoon a rounded tablespoonful into each wonton cup. Bake for 6-7 minutes or until heated through. **Yield: about 4 dozen.**

Cheese Puffs

Cheese Puffs

Prep: 15 min. | Bake: 15 min./batch

This recipe from one of my mother's cookbooks is updated by adding cayenne and mustard. These golden puffs go together in minutes and simply disappear at parties!

—Jamie Wetter, Boscobel, Wisconsin

1	cup water
2	tablespoons butter
1/2	teaspoon salt
1/8	teaspoon cayenne pepper
1	cup all-purpose flour
4	eggs
1-1/4	cups shredded Gruyere *or* Swiss cheese
1	tablespoon Dijon mustard
1/4	cup grated Parmesan cheese

In a large saucepan, bring water, butter, salt and cayenne to a boil. Add flour all at once and stir until a smooth ball forms. Remove from heat; let stand 5 minutes. Add eggs, one at a time, beating well after each addition. Continue beating until mixture is smooth and shiny. Stir in Gruyere and mustard.

Drop by rounded teaspoonfuls 2 in. apart onto greased baking sheets; sprinkle with cheese. Bake at 425° for 15-20 minutes or until golden. Serve warm or cold. **Yield: 4 dozen.**

Raspberry Ice Tea

Prep: 10 min. + chilling

Frozen raspberries lend fruity flavor and lovely color to this pretty iced tea. It calls for just a few common ingredients and offers make-ahead convenience. —Lois McGrady, Hillsville, Virginia

4	quarts water
1-1/2	cups sugar
1	package (12 ounces) frozen unsweetened raspberries
10	individual tea bags
1/4	cup lemon juice

In a large kettle or Dutch oven, bring water and sugar to a boil. Remove from the heat; stir until sugar is dissolved. Add the raspberries, tea bags and lemon juice. Cover and steep for 3 minutes. Strain; discard berries and tea bags.

Transfer tea to a large container or pitcher. Refrigerate until chilled. Serve over ice. **Yield: 16 servings (4 quarts).**

Sugar 'n' Spice Nuts

Prep/Total Time: 30 min.

My daughters, grandkids...everyone looks forward to this mouth-watering mix of crunchy nuts, spices and fruit when they're home for the holidays. And tucked in colorful tins, it makes a handy last-minute gift idea for busy hostesses or drop-in visitors.

—Joan Klinefelter, Utica, Illinois

1/4	cup packed brown sugar
1/2	teaspoon ground cinnamon
1/4	teaspoon cayenne pepper
1	egg white
1	cup salted cashews
1	cup pecan halves
1	cup dry roasted peanuts
1/2	cup dried cranberries

In a small bowl, combine the brown sugar, cinnamon and cayenne; set aside. In a large bowl, whisk the egg white; add nuts and cranberries. Sprinkle with sugar mixture and toss to coat. Spread in a single layer on a greased baking sheet.

Bake the pecans at 300° for 18-20 minutes or until golden brown, stirring once. Cool. Store in an airtight container. **Yield: 3-1/2 cups.**

Blue-Ribbon Beef Nachos

Sugar 'n' Spice Nuts

Blue-Ribbon Beef Nachos

Prep/Total Time: 20 min.

Try this tasty topper for tortilla chips. Chili powder and sassy salsa season a zesty mixture of ground beef and refried beans that is sprinkled with green onions, tomatoes and ripe olives.

—Diane Hixon, Niceville, Florida

1	pound ground beef
1	small onion, chopped
1	can (16 ounces) refried beans
1	jar (16 ounces) salsa
1	can (6 ounces) pitted ripe olives, chopped
1/2	cup shredded cheddar cheese
1	green onion, chopped
2	tablespoons chili powder
1	teaspoon salt

Tortilla chips
Sliced ripe olives, chopped green onions and tomatoes, optional

In a large skillet, cook the beef and onion over medium heat until meat is no longer pink; drain. Stir in the next seven ingredients; heat through. Serve over tortilla chips. Top with olives, onions and tomatoes if desired. **Yield: 6 servings.**

Where's the Beef?

Ground beef is labeled using the cut of meat that it's ground from, such as ground chuck or ground round. It can also be labeled according to the percentage of lean meat to fat, such as 85% or 90% lean. The higher the percentage, the leaner the meat. Select bright red beef in a tightly sealed package.

Hot Bacon Cheese Dip

Prep: 5 min. | Cook: 2 hours

I've tried several appetizers before, but this one is a surefire people-pleaser. The thick dip has lots of bacon flavor and keeps friends happily munching. I serve it with tortilla chips or sliced French bread. —*Suzanne Whitaker, Knoxville, Tennessee*

- 2 packages (8 ounces *each*) cream cheese, cubed
- 4 cups (16 ounces) shredded cheddar cheese
- 1 cup half-and-half cream
- 2 teaspoons Worcestershire sauce
- 1 teaspoon dried minced onion
- 1 teaspoon prepared mustard
- 16 bacon strips, cooked and crumbled

Tortilla chips *or* French bread slices

In a 1-1/2-qt. slow cooker, combine the first six ingredients. Cover and cook for 2 hours or until cheeses are melted, stirring occasionally. Just before serving, stir in bacon. Serve warm with tortilla chips or bread. **Yield: 4 cups.**

Hot Bacon Cheese Dip

S'more Drops

Prep: 20 min. + cooling

I first tried these gooey morsels in a sixth-grade home economics class. My friends and I would eat each mouth-watering drop so fast, they didn't have time to chill. We still reminisce about these indoor s'mores served with tall glasses of cold milk and times spent together. —*Diane Angell, Rockford, Illinois*

S'more Drops

- 4 cups Golden Grahams
- 1-1/2 cups miniature marshmallows
- 1 cup (6 ounces) semisweet chocolate chips
- 1/3 cup light corn syrup
- 1 tablespoon butter
- 1/2 teaspoon vanilla extract

In a large bowl, combine the cereal and marshmallows; set aside. Place the chocolate chips, corn syrup and butter in a 1-qt. microwave-safe dish.

Microwave, uncovered, on high for 1-2 minutes or until smooth, stirring every 30 seconds. Stir in vanilla. Pour over cereal mixture and mix well. Drop by tablespoonfuls onto waxed paper-lined baking sheets. Cool. **Yield: 2-1/2 dozen.**

Editor's Note: This recipe was tested in a 1,100-watt microwave.

Smoked Salmon Cucumbers

Prep/Total Time: 20 min.

This super-easy appetizer has pleased many guests at our house and is sure to be a hit at yours, too! The four-ingredient bites offer a light and refreshing taste any time of year. —*Cheryl Lama, Royal Oak, Michigan*

- 1 large English cucumber
- 1 carton (8 ounces) spreadable chive and onion cream cheese
- 7 to 8 ounces smoked salmon, chopped

Minced chives

With a fork, score cucumber peel lengthwise; cut into 1/4-in. slices. Pipe or spread cream cheese onto each slice; top with salmon. Sprinkle with chives. Refrigerate until serving. **Yield: about 3 dozen.**

Four-Layer Cheese Spread

Prep: 25 min. + chilling

Whenever I entertain, I always count on this streamlined cracker spread for a delicious party starter. To make it look extra special, I invert the chilled mold onto an attractive platter that is lined with baby spinach. It's impressive yet easy.

—Sherry Hulsman, Louisville, Kentucky

- 1   package (8 ounces) cream cheese, softened, *divided*
- 1/4   cup fresh baby spinach, chopped
- 4-1/2   teaspoons chutney
- 2   cups (8 ounces) shredded cheddar cheese
- 2/3   cup mayonnaise
- 1/2   cup chopped pecans
- 1/4   cup finely chopped onion

Dash hot pepper sauce
Additional fresh baby spinach
Assorted crackers and fresh vegetables

In a small bowl, combine 4 oz. cream cheese and chopped spinach. In another bowl, combine the chutney and remaining cream cheese. In a large bowl, combine the shredded cheddar cheese, mayonnaise, chopped pecans, onion and hot pepper sauce.

Line a 3-cup bowl with plastic wrap. Spread half of the cheddar cheese mixture into the prepared bowl. Layer with the baby spinach mixture and then with the chutney mixture. Top with the remaining cheddar cheese mixture. Cover and refrigerate overnight.

Unmold onto a serving plate; garnish with additional baby spinach. Serve with assorted crackers and vegetables. **Yield: about 3 cups.**

Tomato Bacon Cups

Prep: 20 min. | Bake: 10 min./batch

These savory biscuits have a flavorful tomato and bacon filling that is irresistible. I got the recipe at a friend's house one Thanksgiving and have made them ever since. They always disappear fast.   —Paige English, Saint Helens, Oregon

- 1   small tomato, finely chopped
- 1/2   cup mayonnaise
- 1/2   cup real bacon bits
- 1/2   cup shredded Swiss cheese
- 1   small onion, finely chopped
- 1   teaspoon dried basil
- 1   tube (12 ounces) refrigerated buttermilk biscuits, separated into 10 biscuits

In a small bowl, combine the chopped tomato, mayonnaise, bacon bits, shredded Swiss cheese, chopped onion and dried

basil; set aside. Split each refrigerated buttermilk biscuit into three layers; press each layer into an ungreased miniature muffin cup. Spoon the tomato mixture into the muffin cups. Bake at 450° for 8-10 minutes or until golden brown. Serve warm. **Yield: 2-1/2 dozen.**

Party Pesto Pinwheels

Prep/Total Time: 30 min.

I took a couple of my favorite recipes and combined them into these delicious hors d'oeuvres. The colorful snacks come together easily with refrigerated crescent roll dough, prepared pesto sauce and a jar of roasted red peppers.

—Kathleen Farrell, Rochester, New York

- 1   tube (8 ounces) refrigerated crescent rolls
- 1/3   cup prepared pesto sauce
- 1/4   cup roasted sweet red peppers, drained and chopped
- 1/4   cup grated Parmesan cheese
- 1   cup pizza sauce, warmed

Unroll the refrigerated crescent dough into two long rectangles; seal the seams and perforations. Spread each of the crescent dough rectangles with the prepared pesto; sprinkle with chopped red peppers and Parmesan cheese.

Roll each up jelly-roll style, starting with a short side. With a sharp knife, cut each roll into 10 slices. Place cut side down 2 in. apart on two ungreased baking sheets.

Bake at 400° for 8-10 minutes or until golden brown. Serve warm with pizza sauce. **Yield: 20 servings.**

Party Pesto Pinwheels

Cheese Spread Dice

Prep: 30 min. + chilling

You'll shake up your buffet table in an appetizing way with this delectable cracker spread. The novel cube of seasoned cream cheese is easily spotted with ripe olives.
—Taste of Home Test Kitchen, Greendale, Wisconsin

- 3 packages (8 ounces *each*) cream cheese, softened, *divided*
- 2 cups (8 ounces) shredded Italian cheese blend *or* part-skim mozzarella cheese
- 1 small onion, finely chopped
- 1 tablespoon Worcestershire sauce
- 1 tablespoon minced fresh parsley
- 1 teaspoon milk
- 8 medium pitted ripe olives

Assorted crackers

In a large bowl, beat two packages of cream cheese, shredded cheese, onion, Worcestershire sauce and parsley until blended. Press into a plastic wrap-lined 8-in. x 4-in. loaf pan. Cover and refrigerate overnight.

Remove cream cheese mixture from pan; cut in half widthwise. Stack one on top of the other on a serving plate. In a small bowl, beat milk and remaining cream cheese until smooth. Spread over cube. Cut olives in half; arrange on top and sides of dice. Serve with crackers. **Yield: 3 cups.**

Cheese Spread Dice

Cheeseburger Mini Muffins

Cheeseburger Mini Muffins

Prep: 20 min. | Bake: 15 min.

I invented these cute little muffins so I could enjoy the flavor of cheeseburgers without resorting to fast food. I often freeze a batch and reheat as many as I need. —Teresa Kraus, Cortez, Colorado

- 1/2 pound ground beef
- 1 small onion, finely chopped
- 2-1/2 cups all-purpose flour
- 1 tablespoon sugar
- 2 teaspoons baking powder
- 1 teaspoon salt
- 3/4 cup ketchup
- 3/4 cup milk
- 1/2 cup butter, melted
- 2 eggs
- 1 teaspoon prepared mustard
- 2 cups (8 ounces) shredded cheddar cheese

In a large skillet, cook beef and onion over medium heat until meat is no longer pink; drain.

In a small bowl, combine the flour, sugar, baking powder and salt. In another bowl, combine the ketchup, milk, butter, eggs and mustard; stir into the dry ingredients just until moistened. Fold in the beef mixture and cheese.

Fill greased miniature muffin cups three-fourths full. Bake at 425° for 15-18 minutes or until a toothpick comes out clean. Cool for 5 minutes before removing from pans to wire racks. Refrigerate leftovers. **Yield: 5 dozen.**

Editor's Note: Muffins may be baked in regular-size muffin cups for 20-25 minutes; recipe makes 2 dozen.

Mini Bagelizzas

Prep/Total Time: 25 min.

Garlic powder gives these speedy mini pizzas extra pizzazz. Not only are they a snap to put together, but best of all, the ingredient list is easy on your pocketbook. My husband loves them.
—Stephanie Klos-Kohr, Moline, Illinois

- 8   miniature bagels, split
- 1   cup spaghetti sauce with miniature meatballs
- 32 slices pepperoni
- 3/4 teaspoon garlic powder
- 2   cups (8 ounces) shredded part-skim mozzarella cheese

Spread the cut sides of the bagels with spaghetti sauce. Top each with two slices of pepperoni; sprinkle with the garlic powder and cheese.

Place the bagels on ungreased baking sheets. Bake at 350° for 15-20 minutes or until the cheese is melted and bubbly. **Yield: 8 servings.**

Nutty Cereal Crunch

Prep: 10 min. | Cook: 15 min. + cooling

This is one of my favorite snacks to take to large get-togethers. Cinnamon, brown sugar and butter create a lip-smacking coating for cereal and a variety of nuts in this change-of-pace party mix. One handful simply isn't enough!
—Grace Yaskovic, Lake Hiawatha, New Jersey

- 1   cup butter
- 1-1/3 cups packed brown sugar
- 1/2   teaspoon ground cinnamon
- 6   cups cornflakes
- 1   cup salted peanuts
- 1   cup salted cashews
- 1/2   cup almonds *or* macadamia nuts

In a Dutch oven or large saucepan, melt the butter; stir in the brown sugar and cinnamon until sugar is dissolved. Remove from the heat.

Combine cornflakes and nuts; add to sugar mixture and stir to coat. Spread onto two greased baking sheets. Cool; break apart. **Yield: 10 cups.**

Mini Bagelizzas

give me 5 or fewer

You'll be amazed at how just a handful of items can create such sensational and satisfying dishes. Every simple-to-make recipe in this chapter uses only five ingredients or less (not including the basic staples of salt, pepper and water).

Because these recipes don't use unusual items, you likely have most, if not all, of the necessary ingredients already in your kitchen cupboard! It's a cinch to whip up wholesome entrees, salads, sides and desserts that you and your family will love.

Tomato Salmon Bake
(recipe on p. 61)

No-Bake Cheesecake Pie

Ham 'n' Cheese Mashed Potatoes

Prep/Total Time: 25 min.

The way I dress up leftover ham and mashed potatoes is a surefire success in my house! Cheddar cheese and cream add richness to this casserole while garlic seasons it nicely. It's something my family looks forward to having on a regular basis.

—Debra Herlihy, Swedesboro, New Jersey

- 2 cups mashed potatoes
- 3/4 teaspoon garlic salt
- 1 cup diced fully cooked ham
- 1 cup (4 ounces) shredded cheddar cheese
- 1/2 cup heavy whipping cream, whipped

In a large bowl, combine potatoes and garlic salt. Spread into a greased 1-1/2-qt. baking dish. Sprinkle with ham. Fold cheese into whipped cream; spoon over ham.

Bake, uncovered, at 450° for 15 minutes or until golden brown. **Yield: 4-6 servings.**

Cherry Pie Dessert

Prep: 20 min. | Bake: 20 min. + cooling

A friend shared this recipe with me. It's an easy dessert with a shortbread-like crust that goes over great at get-togethers and that works equally well in casual and special occasions.

—Alisha Rice, Albany, Oregon

- 2 cups all-purpose flour
- 1/2 cup confectioners' sugar
- 1 cup cold butter
- 1 can (30 ounces) cherry pie filling
- 1 carton (12 ounces) frozen whipped topping, thawed

In a small bowl, combine flour and confectioners' sugar. Cut in butter until mixture resembles coarse crumbs. Press into an ungreased 13-in. x 9-in. baking dish.

Bake at 350° for 18-20 minutes or until lightly browned. Cool completely on a wire rack. Spoon pie filling over crust; spread with whipped topping. Store in the refrigerator. **Yield: 12-15 servings.**

No-Bake Cheesecake Pie

Prep: 15 min. + chilling

I came up with this creamy white chocolate cheesecake after remembering one evening that I needed to bring a treat to the office the next day. It was a tremendous hit.

—Geneva Mayer, Olney, Illinois

- 1 cup vanilla *or* white chips
- 2 packages (8 ounces *each*) cream cheese, cubed
- 1 carton (8 ounces) frozen whipped topping, thawed
- 1 graham cracker crust (9 inches)
- 1/3 cup English toffee bits *or* almond brickle chips

In a heavy saucepan, melt chips over medium-low heat; stir until smooth. Remove from the heat; stir in cream cheese until smooth. Fold in whipped topping. Pour into the crust.

Cover and refrigerate overnight or until set. Just before serving, sprinkle with toffee bits. **Yield: 6-8 servings.**

A Touch of Flavor

To add wonderful taste to frozen whipped topping, add a little vanilla extract. First, thaw an 8 ounce container of frozen topping, then stir in 1 teaspoon of vanilla extract. It gives a nice flavor boost!

Taco Puffs

Prep/Total Time: 30 min.

I received this recipe years ago and still serve these hot and cheesy sandwiches regularly for dinner.

—Jan Schmid, Hibbing, Minnesota

- 1 pound ground beef
- 1/2 cup chopped onion
- 1 envelope taco seasoning
- 2 tubes (16.3 ounces *each*) large refrigerated flaky biscuits
- 2 cups (8 ounces) shredded cheddar cheese

In a large skillet, cook beef and onion over medium heat until meat is no longer pink; drain. Add the taco seasoning and prepare according to package directions. Cool slightly.

Flatten half of the biscuits into 4-in. circles; place in greased 15-in. x 10-in. baking pans. Spoon 1/4 cup meat mixture onto each; sprinkle with 1/4 cup shredded cheese. Flatten the remaining biscuits; place on top and pinch edges to seal tightly. Bake at 400° for 15 minutes or until golden brown. **Yield: 8 servings.**

No-Fuss Meat Loaf

Prep: 15 min. | Bake: 1 hour 35 min.

Instant stuffing mix makes this meat loaf simple enough for even novice cooks to fix. I often combine the mixture in a resealable plastic bag, then toss the bag for easy cleanup. For a tender meat loaf, be sure not to overmix the raw meat mixture. If you like a touch of spice, add a bit of hot sauce to the ketchup.

—Betty Braswell, Elgin, Pennsylvania

- 2 eggs
- 1/2 cup water
- 1 package (6 ounces) instant stuffing mix
- 2 pounds ground beef

Ketchup

In a large bowl, beat the eggs and water. Stir in stuffing mix and contents of seasoning packet. Crumble the beef over mixture and mix well.

Press into an ungreased 9-in. x 5-in. loaf pan. Top with ketchup. Bake, uncovered, at 350° for 1-1/4 to 1-1/2 hours or until no pink remains and a meat thermometer reads 160°. **Yield: 6-8 servings.**

Taco Puffs

Smoked Chops with Cherry Sauce

Prep/Total Time: 20 min.

Grilling out? A sweet-but-spicy sauce is the secret to these moist pork chops. With a light touch of heat, they'll turn up the flavor on a summer night. Serve the chops with a fruity salad and a pitcher of iced tea or smoothies.

—Betty Kleberger, Florissant, Missouri

- 6   fully cooked smoked boneless pork chops (1 inch thick and 6 ounces *each*)
- 1   can (15 ounces) pitted dark sweet cherries, undrained
- 1   cup mild jalapeno pepper jelly
- 1/2   teaspoon ground coriander, optional

Grill pork chops, covered, over medium heat for 5-7 minutes on each side or until a meat thermometer reads 160°.

Meanwhile, in a small saucepan, combine the cherries, jelly and coriander if desired. Bring to a boil, stirring constantly. Serve with pork chops. **Yield: 6 servings.**

Pork Chops Galore

All pork chops cook the same, but go by a variety of names. The length of cooking primarily depends on the thickness of the chop.

Loin chops have a T-bone shape and include a lot of meat. Rib chops include some back and rib bone. Sirloin chops often include part of the hip bone. Top loin chops are T-bone chops, with boneless versions sometimes referred to as "America's Cut." Blade chops are often thicker and more marbled.

Pizza Cake

Prep: 15 min. | Bake: 20 min. + cooling

Our kids had a great time putting this together for a Cub Scout cake auction. A boxed cake mix forms the crust, prepared vanilla frosting tinted red makes the sauce, grated white chocolate is the cheese and fruit rolls cut into circles are the pepperoni. The recipe makes two cakes. —Caroline Simzisko, Cordova, Tennessee

- 1   package (18-1/4 ounces) yellow cake mix
- 1   cup vanilla frosting

Red liquid *or* paste food coloring

- 3   squares (1 ounce *each*) white baking chocolate, grated
- 2   strawberry Fruit Roll-Ups

Prepare the cake mix according to the package directions. Pour the batter into two greased and floured 9-in. round baking pans.

Bake at 350° for 20 minutes or until a toothpick inserted near the center comes out clean. Cool for 10 minutes before removing from pans to wire racks to cool completely.

Place each cake on a 10-in. serving platter. Combine the frosting and food coloring; spread over the top of each cake to within 1/2 in. of edges. Sprinkle with the grated white chocolate for cheese.

Unroll the Fruit Roll-Ups; use a 1-1/2-in. round cutter to cut into circles for pepperoni. Arrange on cakes. **Yield: 2 cakes (6-8 servings each).**

Pizza Cake

Savory Parmesan Sticks

chicken and feta cheese. Drizzle with dressing and toss to coat. **Yield: 9 servings.**

Onion Pork Tenderloins

Prep: 10 min. | Cook: 30 min.

This recipe came from my mom, and it's the easiest and fanciest entree I've found. Sometimes I add sliced fresh mushrooms to the skillet with the pork. Fix frozen mashed potatoes and a bagged salad, and you can pull together an entire meal with little effort.
—Stacie Blemings, Califon, New Jersey

2	pork tenderloins (1 to 1-1/4 pounds *each*)
2	tablespoons olive oil
1	envelope onion soup mix
1/2	cup white wine *or* chicken broth
1	tablespoon cornstarch
3/4	cup cold water

In a large skillet over medium-high heat, brown the tenderloins in olive oil on all sides. Sprinkle the soup mix over the meat; add wine or broth to the skillet. Reduce heat. Cover and simmer for 25-30 minutes or until a meat thermometer reads 160°, adding water to the skillet if needed. Remove tenderloins and keep warm.

Combine the cornstarch and water until smooth; gradually stir into pan juices. Bring to a boil; cook and stir for 2 minutes or until thickened. Serve with tenderloins. **Yield: 8-10 servings.**

Savory Parmesan Sticks

Prep/Total Time: 20 min.

I really like how easy this recipe is and how good these smell when baking. They look pretty on the table and can be eaten out of hand. Change up the herbs to your own tastes.
—Viki Ailport, West Lakeland, Minnesota

1	package (17.3 ounces) frozen puff pastry, thawed
1	egg, lightly beaten
1-1/2	cups grated Parmesan cheese
1	tablespoon dried rosemary, crushed

Brush one side of each puff pastry sheet with egg; sprinkle with cheese and rosemary. Cut each sheet into ten 1-in. strips. Place 1 in. apart on greased baking sheets.

Bake at 400° for 10-13 minutes or until golden brown. **Yield: 20 breadsticks.**

Fabulous Feta Salad

Prep/Total Time: 25 min.

On busy summer days I turn to this simple and pretty pasta salad for fast, flavorful side-dish flair. If you need a more filling entree, simply double the amount of chicken!
—Amy Adams, Ogden, Utah

2-1/2	cups uncooked bow tie pasta
4	cups torn romaine
1	cup cubed cooked chicken
1/2	cup crumbled feta cheese
1/2	cup Italian salad dressing

Cook pasta according to package directions; drain and rinse in cold water. In a large bowl, combine the pasta, romaine,

Onion Pork Tenderloins

Smoky Bacon Wraps

Smoky Bacon Wraps

Prep: 20 min. | Bake: 30 min.

These cute little sausage and bacon bites are finger-licking good. They have an irresistible sweet and salty taste that's fun for breakfast or as a dinner party appetizer. I like to take them to potlucks and other social functions because they travel well, look great and are very popular. They can't be beat!

—Cara Flora, Kokomo, Indiana

  1   pound sliced bacon
  1   package (16 ounces) miniature smoked sausage links
  1   cup packed brown sugar

Cut each bacon strip in half widthwise. Wrap one piece of bacon around each miniature sausage.

Place the bacon-wrapped sausages in a foil-lined 15-in. x 10-in. baking pan. Sprinkle with the brown sugar. Bake, uncovered, at 400° for 30-40 minutes or until the bacon is crisp and the smoked sausages are heated through. **Yield: about 3-1/2 dozen.**

Cherry Marble Cake

Prep: 15 min. | Bake: 30 min.

This recipe was given to me by a friend years ago. It's the perfect cake to mix up at the last minute. Choose any fruit pie filling, such as blueberry, peach or apple. If you use apple, sprinkle a little cinnamon on top.

—Tessa Downing, Doylestown, Pennsylvania

  1   package (18-1/4 ounces) yellow cake mix
  1/4 cup canola oil
  3   eggs
  1/2 cup water
  1   can (21 ounces) cherry pie filling

In a greased 13-in. x 9-in. baking pan, combine cake mix and oil. Combine eggs and water; stir into cake mix until blended. Drop tablespoons of pie filling into batter; cut through batter with a knife to swirl.

Bake at 350° for 30-35 minutes or until a toothpick inserted near the center comes out clean (top will have an uneven appearance). Cool on a wire rack. **Yield: 16-20 servings.**

Pina Colada Slush

Prep: 10 min. + freezing

For a special treat on a hot, steamy day, try this fruity cooler. I first had it when I was pregnant. It really hit the spot that summer and ever since! I'm asked to bring it to family gatherings all year long, so I always keep a batch or two in my freezer just waiting to be prepared. —Alisa Allred, Vernal, Utah

- 3 cans (6 ounces *each*) unsweetened pineapple juice
- 2 cups water
- 1 can (10 ounces) frozen non-alcoholic pina colada mix
- 1 tablespoon lime juice
- 1 tub sugar-free lemonade soft drink mix
- 6 cups lemon-lime soda, chilled

In a large bowl, combine the pineapple juice, water, pina colada mix, lime juice and soft drink mix; stir until drink mix is dissolved. Transfer to a 2-qt. freezer container. Freeze for 6 hours or overnight.

Remove from the freezer 45 minutes before serving. For each serving, combine 1/2 cup slush mixture with 1/2 cup lemon-lime soda. **Yield: 12 servings (3 quarts).**

Editor's Note: This recipe was tested with Crystal Light lemonade soft drink mix.

Taco Chicken Rolls

Pina Colada Slush

Taco Chicken Rolls

Prep: 15 min. | Bake: 35 min.

I keep the ingredients for this tender flavorful chicken on hand. The cheese-stuffed rolls are nice with a green salad or plate of fresh vegetables and Spanish rice.
—Kara de la Vega, Santa Rosa, California

- 1 cup finely crushed cheese-flavored crackers
- 1 envelope taco seasoning
- 6 boneless skinless chicken breast halves (4 ounces *each*)
- 2 ounces Monterey Jack cheese, cut into six 2-inch x 1/2-inch sticks
- 1 can (4 ounces) chopped green chilies

In a shallow dish, combine the cracker crumbs and taco seasoning; set aside. Flatten chicken between two sheets of waxed paper to 1/4-in. thickness. Place a cheese stick and about 1 tablespoon of chilies on each piece of chicken. Tuck ends of chicken in and roll up; secure with a toothpick.

Coat chicken with crumb mixture. Place in a greased 13-in. x 9-in. baking dish. Bake, uncovered, at 350° for 35-40 minutes or until chicken is no longer pink. Remove toothpicks. **Yield: 6 servings.**

Flattening Poultry

When cuts of poultry are flattened, it's best to put them inside a heavy-duty resealable plastic bag or between two sheets of heavy plastic wrap to prevent messy splatters. Use the smooth side of a meat mallet to gently pound them to the desired thickness. This will prevent the meat from shredding.

Savory Chicken Dinner
Prep: 10 min. | Bake: 45 min.

No one would guess that these moist chicken breasts and tender potatoes are seasoned with herb- and garlic-flavored soup mix. The meal-in-one is simple to assemble, and it all bakes in one dish so there's little cleanup.

—Leslie Adams, Springfield, Missouri

2 envelopes savory herb with garlic soup mix
6 tablespoons water
4 boneless skinless chicken breast halves (6 to 8 ounces *each*)
2 large red potatoes, cubed
1 large onion, halved and cut into small wedges

In a small bowl, combine soup mix and water; pour half into a large resealable plastic bag. Add chicken. Seal bag and toss to coat. Pour the remaining soup mix in another large resealable plastic bag. Add potatoes and onion. Seal bag and toss to coat.

Drain and discard marinade from chicken. Transfer to a greased 13-in. x 9-in. baking dish. Pour potato mixture with marinade over chicken.

Bake, uncovered, at 350° for 40-45 minutes or until vegetables are tender and a meat thermometer reads 170°, stirring vegetables occasionally. **Yield: 4 servings.**

Savory Chicken Dinner

Honey Grilled Shrimp

Honey Grilled Shrimp
Prep: 10 min. + marinating | Grill: 10 min.

My husband was given this super-simple recipe by a man who sold shrimp at the fish market. It's now become our family's absolute favorite shrimp recipe. We've even served it to company often...with great success. Enjoy!

—Lisa Blackwell, Henderson, North Carolina

1 bottle (8 ounces) Italian salad dressing
1 cup honey
1/2 teaspoon minced garlic
2 pounds uncooked medium shrimp, peeled and deveined

Combine the salad dressing, honey and garlic; set aside 1/2 cup. Pour the remaining marinade into a large resealable plastic bag; add the shrimp. Seal the bag and turn to coat; refrigerate for 30 minutes. Cover and refrigerate the reserved marinade for basting.

Coat grill rack with cooking spray before starting the grill. Drain and discard marinade. Thread shrimp onto eight metal or soaked wooden skewers. Grill, uncovered, over medium heat for 1 to 1-1/2 minutes on each side. Baste with reserved marinade. Grill 3-4 minutes longer or until shrimp turn pink, turning and basting frequently. **Yield: 8 servings.**

Nutrition Facts: 1 serving (1 each) equals 175 calories, 5 g fat (1 g saturated fat), 168 mg cholesterol, 383 mg sodium, 14 g carbohydrate, trace fiber, 18 g protein. Diabetic Exchanges: 3 very lean meat, 1 starch, 1 fat.

Sausage-Stuffed Squash

Prep/Total Time: 20 min.

I tuck a flavorful sausage mixture into colorful acorn squash halves. Cooking the squash in the microwave means this entree is done in minutes. I like to use maple-flavored bulk pork sausage.
—Mary Magner, Cedar Rapids, Iowa

 2   medium acorn squash
 1   pound bulk pork sausage
 1/2 cup finely chopped celery
 1/2 cup finely chopped onion
 1/3 cup sour cream

Cut squash in half; discard seeds. Cut a thin slice from bottom of squash with a sharp knife to allow it to sit flat. Place squash cut side down in a microwave-safe dish. Cover and microwave on high for 10-12 minutes or until tender.

Meanwhile, crumble sausage into a large skillet; add celery and onion. Cook over medium heat until meat is no longer pink; drain. Remove from the heat; stir in sour cream. Spoon into squash halves. Cover and microwave for 1 minute or until heated through. **Yield: 4 servings.**

Editor's Note: This recipe was tested in a 1,100-watt microwave.

Beefy Biscuit Cups

Prep/Total Time: 30 min.

On-the-go families will love these handheld pizzas. They're made in a wink with convenient refrigerated biscuits, ground beef, cheese and a jar of prepared spaghetti sauce.
—Kimberly Ledon, St. Marys, Georgia

 1   pound ground beef
 1   jar (14 ounces) spaghetti sauce
 2   tubes (8 ounces *each*) large refrigerated biscuits
 1   cup (4 ounces) shredded cheddar cheese

Beefy Biscuit Cups

Mexican Fried Ice Cream

In a large skillet, cook beef over medium heat until no longer pink; drain. Stir in the spaghetti sauce; cook over medium heat for 5-10 minutes or until heated through.

Press biscuits onto the bottom and up the sides of greased muffin cups. Spoon 2 tablespoons beef mixture into the center of each cup.

Bake at 375° for 15-17 minutes or until golden brown. Sprinkle with cheese; bake 3 minutes longer or until cheese is melted. **Yield: 8 servings.**

Mexican Fried Ice Cream

Prep: 25 min. + freezing

Fried ice cream is one of my favorite desserts to order from Mexican restaurants. When my sister and I found this recipe for preparing it at home, we knew it would be an impressive way to end a meal.
—Mandy Wright, Springville, Utah

 1/2 gallon French vanilla ice cream, softened
 3   cups crushed cornflakes
 4   teaspoons ground cinnamon
Oil for deep-fat frying
Honey and whipped topping, optional

Place nine 3-in. scoops of ice cream on a baking sheet. Freeze for 1 hour or until firm.

In a shallow bowl, combine cornflake crumbs and cinnamon. Roll ice cream balls in crumb mixture. Place on baking sheet; freeze overnight. Wrap each scoop in plastic wrap and place in a freezer bag. May be frozen for up to 2 months.

In an electric skillet or deep-fat fryer, heat oil to 375°. Unwrap ice cream; fry one scoop at a time for 8-10 seconds. Place in chilled bowls. Drizzle with honey and garnish with whipped topping if desired. **Yield: 9 servings.**

Heavenly Hash Bars

Prep: 25 min. + chilling

Chock-full of chips, nuts and mini marshmallows, these rich bars are a cinch to stir up. They make great Christmas treats, but I like to prepare them year-round. —Peg Wilson, Elm Creek, Nebraska

- 1 package (16 ounces) miniature marshmallows
- 1 can (11-1/2 ounces) mixed nuts
- 2 cups (12 ounces) semisweet chocolate chips
- 2 cups butterscotch chips
- 1 cup peanut butter

Sprinkle marshmallows and nuts in a greased 13-in. x 9-in. pan; set aside. In a small saucepan, melt chips and peanut butter over low heat, stirring constantly until smooth. Pour over marshmallows and nuts. Let stand for 8-10 minutes. Gently stir to coat marshmallows. Chill until set; cut into bars. **Yield: 2-1/2 dozen.**

Pecan Caramel Candies

Prep: 30 min. | Bake: 5 min. + cooling

These candies are fast and easy, but they look and taste like you did a lot of work. Make as many or as few as you want. They're great alongside other desserts for guests who want only a bite of something sweet. —Julie Wemhoff, Angola, Indiana

- 63 miniature pretzels
- 1 package (13 ounces) Rolo candies
- 63 pecan halves

Pecan Caramel Candies

Cherry-Nut Chocolate Pie

Line baking sheets with foil. Place pretzels on foil; top each pretzel with a candy.

Bake at 250° for 4 minutes or until candies are softened (candies will retain their shape). Immediately place a pecan half on each candy and press down so candy fills pretzel. Cool slightly. Refrigerate for 10 minutes or until set. **Yield: 63 candies (about 1-1/4 pounds).**

Cherry-Nut Chocolate Pie

Prep: 10 min. + freezing

I love chocolate and cherries, but couldn't find the flavor combination in any ice cream. So I came up with this rich dessert that has a nice crunch from nuts. This pie is handy to keep in the freezer for unexpected company.
—Diana Wilson Wing, Centerville, Utah

- 2 pints dark chocolate ice cream, softened
- 1 jar (10 ounces) maraschino cherries, drained and coarsely chopped
- 3/4 cup slivered almonds
- 1 chocolate crumb crust (8 inches)

Whipped topping

In a large bowl, combine the ice cream, cherries and almonds. Spoon into the crust. Cover and freeze overnight. Remove from the freezer 10 minutes before cutting. Garnish with whipped topping. **Yield: 6-8 servings.**

Pork Chops with Apples and Stuffing

Prep: 15 min. | Bake: 45 min.

The heartwarming taste of cinnamon and apples is the perfect accompaniment to these tender pork chops.
—Joan Hamilton, Worcester, Massachusetts

- 6 boneless pork loin chops (1 inch thick and 4 ounces *each*)
- 1 tablespoon canola oil
- 1 package (6 ounces) crushed stuffing mix
- 1 can (21 ounces) apple pie filling with cinnamon

In a large skillet, brown pork chops in oil over medium-high heat. Meanwhile, prepare stuffing according to package directions. Spread pie filling into a greased 13-in. x 9-in. baking dish. Place the pork chops on top; spoon stuffing over chops.

Cover and bake at 350° for 35 minutes. Uncover; bake 10 minutes longer or until a meat thermometer reads 160°. **Yield: 6 servings.**

Sweet and Savory Brisket

Prep: 10 min. | Cook: 8 hours

I like this recipe not only because it makes such tender and flavorful beef, but because it takes advantage of a slow cooker. It's wonderful to come home from work and have this mouth-watering dish waiting for you. —Chris Snyder, Boulder, Colorado

- 1 beef brisket (3 to 3-1/2 pounds), cut in half
- 1 cup ketchup
- 1/4 cup grape jelly
- 1 envelope onion soup mix
- 1/2 teaspoon pepper

Place half of the beef brisket in a 5-qt. slow cooker. In a bowl, combine the ketchup, jelly, soup mix and pepper; spread half over the meat. Top with the remaining meat and ketchup mixture.

Cover and cook on low for 8-10 hours or until the meat is tender. Slice the brisket; serve with cooking juices. **Yield: 8-10 servings.**

Editor's Note: This is a fresh beef brisket, not corned beef.

Pork Chops with Apples and Stuffing

Mint-Chocolate Ice Cream Cake

Prep: 15 min. + freezing

Frosty and impressive, this versatile ice cream cake is pretty enough for company or simple enough for a weeknight treat. Use food coloring to tint the whipped topping or use different flavors of ice cream, extracts and cookie or candy crumbs to suit different holidays or occasions!

—Kathy Morrow, Hubbard, Ohio

1	package (16 ounces) Suzy Q's
3	cups mint chocolate chip ice cream, softened
12	cream-filled chocolate sandwich cookies, crushed, *divided*
2	cups whipped topping
1/2	teaspoon mint extract, optional

Line an 8-in. x 4-in. loaf pan with plastic wrap. Place four Suzy Q's in pan, completely covering the bottom. Spread ice cream over Suzy Q's; sprinkle with half of the cookie crumbs. Press remaining Suzy Q's on top. Cover and freeze for at least 3 hours.

Just before serving, remove from the freezer and invert onto a serving plate. Remove the pan and plastic wrap. Combine whipped topping and extract if desired; frost the top and sides of cake. Sprinkle with the remaining cookie crumbs. **Yield:** 10 servings.

Savory Pork Roast

Prep: 5 min. | Bake: 80 min. + standing

I love this herbed roast so much that I make it as often as I can. It's wonderful for special occasions, particularly when served with sweet potatoes and corn muffins.

—Edie DeSpain, Logan, Utah

1	garlic clove, minced
2	teaspoons dried marjoram
1	teaspoon salt
1	teaspoon rubbed sage
1	boneless whole pork loin roast (4 pounds)

Combine the seasonings; rub over roast. Place on a rack in a shallow roasting pan.

Bake, uncovered, at 350° for 80 minutes or until a meat thermometer reads 160°. Let stand for 10-15 minutes before slicing. **Yield:** 9-12 servings (or 3-4 servings plus leftovers).

Swiss Onion Crescents

Prep/Total Time: 30 min.

I put a special spin on these golden crescents by filling them with Swiss cheese, green onions and Dijon mustard. They're a snap to prepare because I use refrigerated dough.

—Joy McMillan, The Woodlands, Texas

1	tube (8 ounces) refrigerated crescent rolls
3	tablespoons shredded swiss cheese, *divided*
2	tablespoons chopped green onion
1-1/2	teaspoons Dijon mustard

Unroll crescent dough and separate into eight triangles. Combine 2 tablespoons cheese, green onion and mustard; spread about 1 teaspoon over each triangle.

Roll up from the short side. Place point side down on an ungreased baking sheet and curve into a crescent shape. Sprinkle with remaining cheese. Bake at 375° for 11-13 minutes or until golden brown. **Yield:** 8 rolls.

Swiss Onion Crescents

Broccoli Waldorf Salad

Broccoli Waldorf Salad

Prep/Total Time: 15 min.

This salad is as easy to prepare as it is to eat! A colorful combination of apples, raisins and pecans jazzes up broccoli florets in this summery side dish. Its tangy-sweet flavor makes it a standout at company picnics and church potlucks.

—Vicki Roehrick, Chubbuck, Idaho

    6   cups fresh broccoli florets
    1   large red apple, chopped
    1/2 cup raisins
    1/4 cup chopped pecans
    1/2 cup coleslaw dressing

In a large serving bowl, combine the first four ingredients. Drizzle with dressing; toss to coat. Refrigerate leftovers. **Yield:** 10 servings.

Barbecued Turkey Chili

Prep: 5 min. | Cook: 4 hours

The first time I made this, it won first prize at a chili cook-off. It takes just minutes to mix together, and the slow cooker does the rest. It's often requested by friends and family.

—Melissa Webb, Ellsworth, South Dakota

    1   can (16 ounces) kidney beans, rinsed and drained
    1   can (15-1/2 ounces) hot chili beans
    1   can (15 ounces) turkey chili with beans
    1   can (14-1/2 ounces) diced tomatoes, undrained
    1/3 cup barbecue sauce

In a 3-qt. slow cooker, combine all of the ingredients. Cover and cook on high for 4 hours or until heated through and flavors are blended. **Yield:** 4-6 servings.

An Apple a Day

Everyone knows that "an apple a day keeps the doctor away." That's because apples are rich in vitamins A, B1, B2 and C. They also contain numerous minerals, such as calcium, phosphorous, magnesium and potassium. Although apples are available all year-round, they each have their own peak season. When purchasing apples, select ones that are firm and have a smooth, unblemished skin that is free from bruises.

S'more Tarts

Prep: 10 min. | Bake: 25 min.

Bring a fireside favorite indoors with the taste-tempting treats I fix for movie and game nights. Kids of all ages will gobble up the individual graham cracker tarts filled with a fudgy brownie and golden marshmallows before asking, "Can I have s'more?"

—Trish Quinn, Cheyenne, Wyoming

    1   package fudge brownie mix (13-inch x 9-inch pan size)
    12   individual graham cracker shells
    1-1/2 cups miniature marshmallows
    1   cup milk chocolate chips

Prepare the brownie batter according to package directions. Place the graham cracker shells on a baking sheet and fill with the brownie batter.

Bake at 350° for 20-25 minutes or until a toothpick inserted in the center comes out with moist crumbs. Immediately sprinkle with marshmallows and chocolate chips. Bake 3-5 minutes longer or until marshmallows are puffed and golden brown. **Yield:** 1 dozen.

S'more Tarts

Garlic Potatoes and Ham

Garlic Potatoes and Ham

Prep: 10 min. | Cook: 35 min.

Not even my finicky little eaters can resist the delicious veggies in this main dish when they're seasoned with full-flavored soup mix. I sometimes replace the ham with cooked kielbasa or smoked sausage for a change of pace.

—*Melody Williamson, Blaine, Washington*

- 8   small red potatoes, cut into wedges
- 1   tablespoon canola oil
- 1   package (16 ounces) frozen broccoli cuts, partially thawed
- 1   cup cubed fully cooked ham
- 1   envelope herb with garlic soup mix

In a large skillet, cook the potatoes in canola oil over medium-high heat for 10 minutes or until lightly browned. Stir in the broccoli, ham and dry soup mix. Reduce the heat; cover and cook for 25 minutes or until potatoes are tender. **Yield: 4 servings.**

Editor's Note: This recipe was tested with Lipton Recipe Secrets Savory Herb with Garlic soup mix.

Berries 'n' Cream Brownies

Prep: 15 min. + chilling | Bake: 25 min. + cooling

If you like chocolate-covered strawberries, you'll love this sweet treat that's an ideal ending to summer meals. A fudgy brownie, whipped topping and fresh fruit make this a no-fuss feast for the eyes as well as the taste buds.

—*Anna Lapp, New Holland, Pennsylvania*

- 1   package fudge brownie mix (13-inch x 9-inch pan size)
- 1   carton (8 ounces) frozen whipped topping, thawed
- 4   cups quartered fresh strawberries
- 1/3   cup chocolate hard-shell ice cream topping

Prepare and bake brownies according to package directions, using a greased 13-in. x 9-in. baking pan. Cool completely on a wire rack.

Spread the whipped topping over brownies. Arrange the strawberries cut side down over top. Drizzle with chocolate topping. Refrigerate for at least 30 minutes before serving. **Yield: 12-15 servings.**

Tortellini Soup

Prep/Total Time: 30 min.

This soup is fast, flavorful and good for you. Packaged cheese tortellini meets colorful summer squash, fresh spinach and shredded carrots in every eye-appealing bowl.

—Chris Snyder, Boulder, Colorado

- 5 cups chicken *or* vegetable broth
- 3-1/2 cups shredded carrots (about 10 ounces)
- 1 cup chopped yellow summer squash
- 3 cups torn fresh spinach
- 1 package (9 ounces) refrigerated cheese tortellini

In a large saucepan, combine the broth, shredded carrots and squash. Bring to a boil. Reduce the heat; simmer, uncovered, for 3 minutes.

Return to a boil. Stir in the spinach and tortellini. Cover and cook for 7-9 minutes or until the tortellini is tender. **Yield: 7 servings.**

Cherry Cheese Danish

Prep/Total Time: 30 min.

Here is a quick Sunday breakfast I like to whip up before going to church. I created it when trying to duplicate a favorite Danish from the bakery where I worked. I like to make it with prepared apple pie filling, too.   —Melanie Schrock, Monterey, Tennessee

- 1 tube (8 ounces) refrigerated crescent rolls
- 4 tablespoons cream cheese, softened
- 1 cup cherry pie filling
- 1/2 cup vanilla frosting

Cherry Cheese Danish

Macaroon Ice Cream Torte

Separate the crescent dough into four rectangles. Place on an ungreased baking sheet; seal perforations. Spread 1 tablespoon cream cheese onto each rectangle. Top each with 1/4 cup cherry pie filling.

Bake at 375° for 10-12 minutes or until edges are golden brown. Cool for 5 minutes.

Place frosting in a small microwave-safe bowl; heat on high for 15-20 seconds. Drizzle over warm pastries. Serve warm. Refrigerate leftovers. **Yield: 4 servings.**

Macaroon Ice Cream Torte

Prep: 15 min. + freezing

My family loves any frozen dessert. I often make this recipe for special occasions. I found it in a ladies' club cookbook, where it was called "the girdlebuster."

—Barbara Carlucci, Orange Park, Florida

- 24 macaroon cookies, crumbled
- 1 quart coffee ice cream, softened
- 1 quart chocolate ice cream, softened
- 1 cup milk chocolate toffee bits *or* 4 (1.4 ounces each) Heath candy bars, coarsely chopped

Hot fudge topping, warmed

Sprinkle a third of the cookies into an ungreased 9-in. springform pan. Top with 2 cups coffee ice cream, a third of the cookies, 2 cups chocolate ice cream and 1/2 cup toffee bits. Repeat layers. Cover and freeze until firm. May be frozen for up to 2 months.

Remove from the freezer 10 minutes before serving. Remove sides of pan. Cut into wedges; drizzle with hot fudge topping. **Yield: 12-16 servings.**

Spicy Ground Beef Stew

Prep/Total Time: 15 min.

I don't remember how I came up with the recipe for this swift stew, but it's so simple. It has good flavor from the spicy tomatoes with green chilies. My co-workers love it!

—Kelly Tyras, Houston, Texas

- 1 pound ground beef
- 2 cans (10-1/2 ounces *each*) condensed vegetable beef soup, undiluted
- 1 can (10 ounces) diced tomatoes with green chilies, undrained

In a large saucepan, cook the beef over medium heat until no longer pink; drain. Stir in soup and tomatoes; heat through. **Yield: 5 servings.**

Peanut Butter Cookie Cups

Prep: 35 min. | Bake: 15 min.

I'm a busy schoolteacher and pastor's wife who always looks for shortcuts. I wouldn't dare show my face at a church dinner or bake sale without these tempting peanut butter treats. They're such time-savers and always a hit.

—Kristi Tackett, Banner, Kentucky

- 1 package (17-1/2 ounces) peanut butter cookie mix
- 36 miniature peanut butter cups, unwrapped

Prepare the cookie mix according to package directions. Roll the dough into 1-in. balls. Place in greased miniature muffin cups. Press the dough evenly onto bottom and up sides of each cup.

Bake at 350° for 11-13 minutes or until set. Immediately place a peanut butter cup in each cookie cup; press down gently. Cool for 10 minutes; carefully remove from pans. **Yield: 3 dozen.**

Peanut Butter Cookie Cups

Creamy Lemonade Pie

Creamy Lemonade Pie

Prep: 20 min. + chilling

This luscious lemon pie looks quite elegant for a special holiday dinner, yet it requires little effort. Guests will never suspect they're eating a five-ingredient dessert.

—Carolyn Griffin, Macon, Georgia

- 1 can (5 ounces) evaporated milk
- 1 package (3.4 ounces) instant lemon pudding mix
- 2 packages (8 ounces *each*) cream cheese, softened
- 3/4 cup lemonade concentrate
- 1 graham cracker crust (9 inches)

In a large bowl, combine milk and pudding mix; beat on low speed for 2 minutes (mixture will be thick). In another large bowl, beat cream cheese until light and fluffy, about 3 minutes. Gradually beat in lemonade concentrate. Gradually beat in pudding mixture.

Pour into crust. Cover and refrigerate for at least 4 hours or until set. **Yield: 6-8 servings.**

Extra Evaporated Milk

Leftover evaporated milk should be transferred from the can to another container for storage. If stored in a covered container in the refrigerator, it can be used safely within 3 days. To avoid wasting the rest of the milk, pour it into ice cube trays specifically used for that purpose. Once frozen, the cubes store nicely in a resealable freezer bag. When needed, remove whatever evaporated milk is needed for a recipe, thaw and use accordingly.

Chicken with Stuffing

Prep: 5 min. | Cook: 4 hours

You need only five ingredients to create this comforting home-style meal of chicken topped with corn bread stuffing. I sometimes add two cans of soup so there's more sauce.

—Susan Kutz, Stillman Valley, Illinois

- 4 boneless skinless chicken breast halves (4 ounces *each*)
- 1 can (10-3/4 ounces) condensed cream of chicken soup, undiluted
- 1-1/4 cups water
- 1/4 cup butter, melted
- 1 package (6 ounces) corn bread stuffing mix

Place chicken in a greased 3-qt. slow cooker. Top with soup. In a bowl, combine the water, butter and stuffing mix; spoon over the chicken. Cover and cook on low for 4 hours or until a meat thermometer reads 170°. **Yield: 4 servings.**

Picante Chicken

Prep: 10 min. | Bake: 30 min.

My husband used to claim this entree as his specialty until I made it and discovered how quick and easy it is. Our two sons love the juicy chicken while my husband and I enjoy the twist that brown sugar and mustard give the picante sauce.

—Karen Stattelman, Effingham, Kansas

- 4 boneless skinless chicken breast halves (4 ounces *each*)
- 1 jar (16 ounces) picante sauce
- 3 tablespoons brown sugar
- 1 tablespoon prepared mustard

Hot cooked rice, optional

Picante Chicken

Tomato Salmon Bake

Place chicken in a greased shallow 2-qt. baking dish. Combine the picante sauce, brown sugar and mustard; pour over chicken.

Bake, uncovered, at 400° for 30-35 minutes or until a meat thermometer reads 170°. Serve with cooked rice if desired. Yield: 4 servings.

Tomato Salmon Bake

Prep/Total Time: 30 min.

I was looking for a healthy alternative to beef and chicken when I found this recipe and decided to personalize it. My husband doesn't usually like fish unless it's fried, but he loves the Italian flavor in this baked dish. Serve it with a green salad for a great meal any time of year.   —Lacey Parker, Gainesville, Virginia

- 4 salmon fillets (6 ounces *each*)
- 1 can (14-1/2 ounces) diced tomatoes, drained
- 1/2 cup sun-dried tomato salad dressing
- 2 tablespoons shredded Parmesan cheese

Hot cooked rice

Place salmon in a greased 13-in. x 9-in. baking dish. Combine tomatoes and salad dressing; pour over salmon. Sprinkle with Parmesan cheese.

Bake, uncovered, at 375° for 20-25 minutes or until fish flakes easily with a fork. Serve with rice. **Yield: 4 servings.**

Rosemary Romano Bread

In a shallow bowl, combine the bread crumbs and jerk seasoning; set aside. Combine the chutney, salt and pepper; spread over both sides of the lamb chops. Coat with the crumb mixture.

Place lamb chops on a rack coated with cooking spray in a shallow baking pan. Bake at 450° for 20-25 minutes or until meat reaches desired doneness (for medium-rare, a meat thermometer should read 145°; medium, 160°; well-done, 170°). **Yield: 4 servings.**

Rosemary Romano Bread
Prep/Total Time: 30 min.

Our 8-year-old son just loves this delicious bread. It's a perfect addition to a green salad or pasta dinner. Or for a hearty appetizer, dip slices in pizza or spaghetti sauce.
—Lois Dykeman, Olmstead, Kentucky

1/2	cup butter, cubed
1/2	cup grated Romano cheese
1	garlic clove, minced
1	teaspoon minced fresh rosemary
1	loaf (1 pound) French bread, halved lengthwise

In a microwave, melt butter. Stir in the Romano cheese, garlic and rosemary. Spread over cut side of bread.

Place cut side up on an ungreased baking sheet. Bake at 400° for 15 minutes or until lightly browned. Slice and serve warm. **Yield: 14-16 servings.**

Caribbean Chutney-Crusted Chops
Prep/Total Time: 30 min.

I like to impress my guests with delicious meals, and these lamb chops are one of my best entrees. It all started with a jar of chutney I received as a gift. Folks think I fuss all day over these sophisticated chops, but they're done in 30 minutes flat!
—Josephine Piro, Easton, Pennsylvania

1	cup soft bread crumbs
1-1/2	teaspoons Caribbean jerk seasoning
1/4	cup mango chutney
1/2	teaspoon salt
1/2	teaspoon pepper
4	lamb loin chops (2 inches thick and 8 ounces *each*)

Cran-Orange Turkey Bagel
Prep/Total Time: 15 min.

I adapted the recipe for this tasty turkey sandwich from a deli where I worked. To make it easier to eat, we often dip each bite into the cranberry mixture instead of spreading it inside.
—Tanya Smeins, Washington, North Carolina

1	can (11 ounces) mandarin oranges, drained
1	can (16 ounces) whole-berry cranberry sauce
6	tablespoons cream cheese, softened
6	onion bagels *or* flavor of your choice, split and toasted
1	pound thinly sliced cooked turkey

In a bowl, mash mandarin oranges with a fork. Stir in cranberry sauce. Spread cream cheese over the bottom of each bagel; top with turkey and cran-orange sauce. Replace bagel tops. **Yield: 6 servings.**

Cran-Orange Turkey Bagel

Strawberry Tossed Salad

Prep/Total Time: 10 min.

A neighbor served this wonderful salad at a summer barbecue. I've since experimented with many ingredient combinations, but this one draws the most compliments. I took it to a baby shower, and not a strawberry or sunflower seed was left in the bowl.

—Lisa Lesinki-Topp, Menomonee Falls, Wisconsin

  6   cups torn mixed salad greens
  1   pint fresh strawberries, sliced
  1   package (4 ounces) crumbled feta cheese
 1/4 cup sunflower kernels
Balsamic vinaigrette

In a large salad bowl, combine the salad greens, strawberries, feta cheese and sunflower kernels. Drizzle with vinaigrette and toss to coat. **Yield: 4-6 servings.**

Horseradish Crab Dip

Prep/Total Time: 10 min.

I depend on this mildly seasoned crab dip when hosting parties. It's a terrific time-saver because it gives me time to get other appetizers ready or mingle with my guests.

—Kathleen Snead, Lynchburg, Virginia

  1   package (8 ounces) cream cheese, softened
  2   to 3 tablespoons picante sauce
  1   to 2 tablespoons prepared horseradish
  1   can (6 ounces) crabmeat, drained, flaked and cartilage removed
Celery sticks

In a large bowl, beat the cream cheese, picante sauce and horseradish until blended. Stir in crab. Serve with celery. **Yield: about 1-1/2 cups.**

10 minutes
to the table

When you have to find a way to put dinner on the table, stopping at a fast-food restaurant may seem like your only option. But it's not! This chapter is the solution, because it's chock-full of recipes that take only 10 minutes or less to prepare from start to finish.

You'll find everything from mouth-watering main courses and side dishes to delicious desserts and appetizers. Whether you need a speedy supper for your family, an after-school snack for your kids or appetizers for a special occasion, you can have home-cooked dishes that take only minutes out of your day, but that look like you fussed!

Two-Cheese Quesadillas
(recipe on p. 78)

Corny Chicken Wraps

Prep/Total Time: 10 min.

My girls love these tortilla roll-ups—they ask for them practically every week. Tender chicken combines with canned corn and salsa for a fast-to-fix main dish. —Sue Seymour, Valatie, New York

- 2 cups cubed cooked chicken breast
- 1 can (11 ounces) whole kernel corn, drained
- 1 cup salsa
- 1 cup (4 ounces) shredded cheddar cheese
- 8 flour tortillas (6 inches), warmed

In a large saucepan, combine the chicken, corn and salsa. Cook over medium heat until heated through.

Sprinkle cheese over tortillas. Place about 1/2 cup chicken mixture down the center of each tortilla; roll up. Secure with toothpicks. **Yield: 4 servings.**

Nutty Apple Dip

Prep/Total Time: 10 min.

For a tempting after-school snack or anytime treat, serve this delightful dip with fresh apple slices. You need just five ingredients to blend together the sweet, nutty mixture. —Jean Morgan, Roscoe, Illinois

- 1 package (8 ounces) cream cheese, softened
- 3/4 cup packed brown sugar
- 1/4 cup sugar
- 1 teaspoon vanilla extract
- 1 cup chopped pecans

Apple slices *or* wedges

In a small bowl, beat the cream cheese, sugars and vanilla extract until smooth. Stir in pecans. Serve with apples. **Yield: about 2 cups.**

Corny Chicken Wraps

10-Minute Taco Salad

Angel Food Torte

Prep/Total Time: 10 min.

I use a few simple ingredients to transform prepared angel food cake into an impressive dessert. It can be whipped up in 10 minutes and adds a festive look to your table.

—Jane Lynn, Duncansville, Pennsylvania

- 1/2 cup cold milk
- 1 package (3.4 ounces) instant vanilla pudding mix
- 1 can (8 ounces) crushed pineapple, undrained
- 1 carton (8 ounces) frozen whipped topping, thawed
- 1 prepared angel food cake (16 ounces)
- 1/2 cup flaked coconut

Maraschino cherries

In a large bowl, whisk milk and pudding mix for 2 minutes. Let stand for 2 minutes or until soft-set. Stir in pineapple. Fold in whipped topping.

Split cake horizontally into three layers. Place the bottom layer on a serving plate; spread with 1-1/3 cups pineapple mixture. Repeat. Place top layer on cake; spread with remaining pineapple mixture. Sprinkle with coconut; garnish with cherries. **Yield: 12 servings.**

10-Minute Taco Salad

Prep/Total Time: 10 min.

My mom often made this hearty main-dish salad for my three brothers and me when we were growing up. Now it's one of my husband's favorite meals! I also frequently prepare it on the weekend for guests. —Cindy Stephan, Owosso, Michigan

- 2 cans (16 ounces *each*) chili beans, undrained
- 1 package (10-1/2 ounces) corn chips
- 2 cups (8 ounces) shredded cheddar cheese
- 4 cups chopped lettuce
- 2 small tomatoes, chopped
- 1 small onion, chopped
- 1 can (2-1/4 ounces) sliced ripe olives, drained
- 1-1/4 cups salsa
- 1/2 cup sour cream

In a small saucepan or microwave-safe bowl, heat the beans. Place corn chips on a large platter. Top with the beans, cheese, lettuce, tomatoes, onion, olives, salsa and sour cream. Serve immediately. **Yield: 8 servings.**

Jazz It Up

To make the 10-Minute Taco Salad even heartier, add shredded rotisserie chicken to the mix. You can also add some pizzazz by using a variety of toppings, including store-bought guacamole, chopped green onions or minced cilantro or parsley.

Angel Food Torte

Chilled Berry Soup

🍎 Chilled Berry Soup
Prep: 10 min. + chilling

I sampled a cool strawberry soup while visiting Walt Disney World. I enjoyed it so much that the restaurant gave me the recipe, but I eventually found this combination, which I like even better. The ginger ale adds a special zing.
—Lisa Watson, Sparta, Michigan

1	quart fresh strawberries, hulled
1/3	cup ginger ale
1/4	cup milk
1/3	cup sugar
1	tablespoon lemon juice
1	teaspoon vanilla extract
1	cup (8 ounces) sour cream

Place strawberries in a food processor or blender; cover and process until smooth. Add ginger ale, milk, sugar, lemon juice and vanilla; cover and process until blended.

Pour into a large bowl; whisk in sour cream until smooth. Cover and refrigerate until thoroughly chilled, about 2 hours. **Yield: 4 servings.**

Nutrition Facts: 1 cup equals 189 calories, 5 g fat (4 g saturated fat), 19 mg cholesterol, 55 mg sodium, 32 g carbohydrate, 3 g fiber, 5 g protein. Diabetic Exchanges: 1-1/2 fruit, 1 fat-free milk.

Strawberry Sense

Purchase strawberries that are shiny, firm and fragrant. Refrigerate and wash just before using. Use a huller or the tip of a serrated spoon to remove the stem/hull. Insert the tip of the spoon into the strawberry next to the stem, then cut around the stem.

Garden Squash Ravioli
Prep/Total Time: 10 min.

I created this dish to make the most of an overabundance of yellow squash and zucchini from our garden. It was a hit with the whole family. —Teri Christensen, West Jordan, Utah

1	package (24 ounces) frozen miniature cheese ravioli
1	medium yellow summer squash, cut into 1/2-inch pieces
1	medium zucchini, cut into 1/2-inch pieces
2	cans (one 15 ounces, one 8 ounces) tomato sauce
1	teaspoon garlic salt
1	teaspoon dried minced onion
1	teaspoon dried oregano
1	teaspoon dried basil
1/2	teaspoon sugar
1/2	teaspoon chili powder
1/4	teaspoon pepper

In a large saucepan, cook the cheese ravioli according to package directions.

Meanwhile, in a 1-1/2-qt. microwave-safe dish, combine the squash, zucchini, tomato sauce and seasonings. Cover and cook on high for 4-6 minutes or until vegetables are tender. Drain ravioli; top with sauce. **Yield: 6 servings.**

Editor's Note: This recipe was tested in a 1,100-watt microwave.

Garden Squash Ravioli

Tangy Poppy Seed Dressing

Prep/Total Time: 5 min.

My sister-in-law was kind enough to share her recipe for this deliciously tangy salad dressing. A super homemade mixture, it stirs up in a jiffy. —Michele Prendergast, Kingston, New York

- 1/2   cup canola oil
- 1/4   cup white wine vinegar
- 1   tablespoon honey
- 1   teaspoon Dijon mustard
- 1   teaspoon poppy seeds
- 1/8   teaspoon garlic powder
- 1/8   teaspoon salt

Mixed salad greens

In a jar with tight-fitting lid, combine the first seven ingredients and shake well. Serve with salad greens. **Yield:** 3/4 cup.

Chocolate Caramel Fondue

Prep/Total Time: 10 min.

It's easy to keep the ingredients for this wonderfully rich fondue on hand in case unexpected company drops by. I serve the thick sauce in punch cups, so guests can carry it on a dessert plate alongside their choice of fruit, pretzels and other dippers. —Cheryl Arnold, Lake Zurich, Illinois

- 1   can (14 ounces) sweetened condensed milk
- 1   jar (12 ounces) caramel ice cream topping
- 3   squares (1 ounce *each*) unsweetened chocolate

Assorted fresh fruit *and/or* pretzels

In a large saucepan, combine the milk, caramel topping and chocolate. Cook over low heat until chocolate is melted. Transfer to a fondue pot and keep warm. Serve with fruit and/or pretzels. **Yield:** 2-1/2 cups.

Chocolate Caramel Fondue

Fiery Chicken Spinach Salad

Fiery Chicken Spinach Salad
Prep/Total Time: 10 min.

This hearty and colorful main-course salad is easy to throw together when I get home from work, because it uses canned black beans and Mexicorn and packaged chicken breast strips. I sometimes add a can of ripe olives and fresh cherry tomatoes from our garden. —Kati Spencer, Taylorsville, Utah

  6   frozen breaded spicy chicken breast strips, thawed
  1   package (6 ounces) fresh baby spinach
  1   medium tomato, cut into 12 wedges
1/2 cup chopped green pepper
1/2 cup fresh baby carrots
  1   can (15 ounces) black beans, rinsed and drained
  1   can (11 ounces) Mexicorn, drained
  3   tablespoons salsa
  3   tablespoons barbecue sauce
  3   tablespoons prepared ranch salad dressing
  2   tablespoons shredded Mexican cheese blend

Heat the chicken strips in a microwave according to package directions. Meanwhile, arrange the baby spinach on individual plates; top with tomato wedges, green pepper, carrots, beans and corn.

In a small bowl, combine the salsa, barbecue sauce and ranch dressing. Place chicken over salads. Drizzle with dressing; sprinkle with cheese. **Yield: 6 servings.**

Editor's Note: This recipe was tested in a 1,100-watt microwave.

Salmon Chowder
Prep/Total Time: 10 min.

I made up this quick creamy chowder one winter afternoon. I like to use a can of red sockeye salmon for the best flavor. The soup also can be seasoned with tarragon instead of dill.
        —Tom Bailey, Golden Valley, Minnesota

    3   cans (10-3/4 ounces *each*) condensed cream of potato soup, undiluted
2-2/3 cups half-and-half cream
    1   can (14-3/4 ounces) salmon, drained, bones and skin removed
    1   teaspoon dill weed
  1/2 teaspoon salt
  1/4 teaspoon white pepper
  1/4 teaspoon crushed red pepper flakes

In a large saucepan, combine all of the ingredients. Cook and stir over medium heat until chowder is heated through. Yield: 7 servings.

Salmon Bones

Some people like to remove the bones from canned salmon...but they are edible and can add calcium to your diet. If you don't like the texture, mash the drained salmon in a bowl with the back of a spoon. The bones will become undetectable in seconds.

Black Bean Burritos

Prep/Total Time: 10 min.

My neighbor and I discovered these delicious low-fat burritos a few years ago. I never get frazzled on busy nights knowing I can have a satisfying supper on the table in minutes.
—Angela Studebaker, Goshen, Indiana

- 3 tablespoons chopped onion
- 3 tablespoons chopped green pepper
- 1 can (15 ounces) black beans, rinsed and drained
- 4 flour tortillas (8 inches), warmed
- 1 cup (4 ounces) shredded Mexican cheese blend
- 1 medium tomato, chopped
- 1 cup shredded lettuce

Salsa, optional

In a nonstick skillet coated with cooking spray, saute onion and green pepper until tender. Stir in beans; heat through.

Spoon about 1/2 cup bean mixture off center of each tortilla. Sprinkle with the cheese, tomato and lettuce. Fold sides and ends over filling and roll up. Serve with salsa if desired.
Yield: 4 servings.

Rocky Ford Chili

Prep/Total Time: 10 min.

Try this recipe the next time your busy schedule won't allow you to slave over chili simmering on the stove. Your family will never guess this tasty version takes just minutes to make.
—Karen Golden, Phoenix, Arizona

- 2 cans (14.3 ounces *each*) chili with beans
- 1 package (10 ounces) frozen corn
- 4 cups corn chips
- 1 cup shredded lettuce
- 1 cup (4 ounces) shredded Mexican cheese blend

Rocky Ford Chili

Frosty Peanut Butter Pie

- 1 can (2-1/4 ounces) sliced ripe olives, drained
- 1/4 cup sour cream
- 1/4 cup salsa

In a large microwave-safe bowl, microwave chili and corn on high for 2-4 minutes or until heated through. Place corn chips in four large soup bowls; top with chili mixture, lettuce, cheese, olives, sour cream and salsa.

In a large microwave-safe bowl, microwave chili and corn on high for 2-4 minutes. Yield: 4 servings.

Editor's Note: This recipe was tested in a 1,100-watt microwave.

Frosty Peanut Butter Pie

Prep: 10 min. + freezing

With only a handful of ingredients, this creamy, make-ahead pie promises to deliver well-deserved compliments. Whenever I bring it to get-togethers, I'm asked for the recipe.
—Christi Gillentine, Tulsa, Oklahoma

- 4 ounces cream cheese, softened
- 1/4 cup peanut butter
- 1/4 cup sugar
- 1 teaspoon vanilla extract
- 1 package (8 ounces) frozen whipped topping, thawed
- 1 chocolate crumb crust (8 inches)
- 2 teaspoons chocolate syrup

In a large bowl, beat the cream cheese, peanut butter, sugar and vanilla until smooth. Fold in the whipped topping. Spoon into the crust. Drizzle with chocolate syrup. Cover and freeze for 4 hours or until set.

Remove pie from the freezer 30 minutes before serving.
Yield: 6 servings.

Apple-Curry Tuna Melts

Prep/Total Time: 10 min.

You'll want to make plenty of these delicious open-faced sandwiches because your family will come back for seconds. Curry powder puts a twist on traditional tuna salad, adding a colorful appearance and delightful taste.

—Edie DeSpain, Logan, Utah

1/2	cup diced apple
1/4	cup mayonnaise
1	tablespoon chopped green onion
1	teaspoon Dijon mustard
1/2	teaspoon curry powder
1	can (6 ounces) tuna, drained and flaked
4	slices bread, toasted
1/4	cup chopped walnuts, toasted
4	slices cheddar cheese

In a bowl, combine the first five ingredients; stir in the tuna until well coated.

Spread 1/4 cup on each slice of toast; sprinkle with walnuts. Top with a slice of cheese. Broil 5 in. from the heat until cheese is melted. **Yield: 4 servings.**

Blueberry Angel Dessert

Prep: 10 min. + chilling

Make the most of angel food cake, pie filling and whipped topping by creating this light, impressive dessert that doesn't keep you in the kitchen for hours. It's the perfect way to end a summer meal. I frequently get requests for the recipe.

—Carol Johnson, Tyler, Texas

Blueberry Angel Dessert

Easy Cheesy Nachos

1	package (8 ounces) cream cheese, softened
1	cup confectioners' sugar
1	carton (8 ounces) frozen whipped topping, thawed
1	prepared angel food cake (16 ounces), cut into 1-inch pieces
2	cans (21 ounces *each*) blueberry pie filling

In a large bowl, beat cream cheese and sugar until smooth; fold in whipped topping and cake cubes. Spread evenly into an ungreased 13-in. x 9-in. dish; top with pie filling. Cover and refrigerate for at least 2 hours before cutting into squares. **Yield: 12-15 servings.**

Easy Cheesy Nachos

Prep/Total Time: 10 min.

There's no need to brown ground beef when fixing this satisfying snack. I top crunchy chips with warm canned chili and melted cheese, then sprinkle it all with chopped tomato and onion for fresh flavor and color. *—Laura Jirasek, Howell, Michigan*

1	package (14-1/2 ounces) tortilla chips
2	cans (15 ounces *each*) chili without beans
1	pound process cheese (Velveeta), cubed
4	green onions, sliced
1	medium tomato, chopped

Divide chips among six plates; set aside. In a saucepan, warm chili until heated through.

Meanwhile, in another saucepan, heat cheese over medium-low heat until melted, stirring frequently. Spoon chili over chips; drizzle with cheese. Sprinkle with onions and tomato. **Yield: 6 servings.**

Almond Sole Fillets

Prep/Total Time: 10 min.

My husband is a real fish lover. This buttery treatment is his favorite way to prepare sole, perch or halibut. It cooks quickly in the microwave, so it's perfect for a busy weekday.
—Erna Farnham, Marengo, Illinois

1/3	cup butter, cubed
1/4	cup slivered almonds
1	pound sole fillets
2	tablespoons lemon juice
1/2	teaspoon dill weed
1/4	teaspoon salt
1/4	teaspoon pepper
1/4	teaspoon paprika

In a microwave-safe bowl, combine butter and almonds. Microwave, uncovered, on high for 1-1/2 minutes or until almonds are golden brown.

Place the fillets in a greased microwave-safe 11-in. x 7-in. dish. Top with almond mixture.

In a small bowl, combine the lemon juice, dill, salt and pepper; drizzle over fish. Sprinkle with paprika. Cover and microwave on high for 4-5 minutes or until fish flakes easily with a fork. **Yield: 4 servings.**

Editor's Note: This recipe was tested in a 1,100-watt microwave.

Almond Sole Fillets

Italian Steak Sandwiches

Italian Steak Sandwiches

Prep/Total Time: 10 min.

My sister came up with these quick sandwiches which use minced garlic and other seasonings to bring pizzazz to deli roast beef. Add some carrot sticks or a simple tomato salad for a fantastic lunch in minutes.   *—Maria Regakis, Somerville, Massachusetts*

2	garlic cloves, minced
1/8	teaspoon crushed red pepper flakes
2	tablespoons olive oil
16	slices deli roast beef
1/2	cup beef broth
2	tablespoons red wine *or* additional beef broth
2	teaspoons dried parsley flakes
2	teaspoons dried basil
1/4	teaspoon salt
1/4	teaspoon dried oregano
1/8	teaspoon pepper
4	sandwich rolls, split
4	slices provolone cheese

In a large skillet, saute garlic and pepper flakes in oil. Add the roast beef, broth, wine or additional broth and seasonings; heat through. Place beef slices on rolls; drizzle with the broth mixture. Top with cheese. **Yield: 4 servings.**

Leftover Roast Beef

To use up leftover roast beef, grind it in a food processor and add to scrambled eggs along with leftover potatoes. Or saute slices of beef in butter with minced garlic until browned. Add some Worcestershire sauce and ground mustard; serve over noodles.

Frosty Tiramisu

Frosty Tiramisu

Prep/Total Time: 10 min.

Tiramisu is a family favorite, but time-consuming to make, so I created an easy everyday version to serve during the week. This rich, creamy blender dessert can be whipped up in minutes.
—Margee Berry, Trout Lake, Washington

- 3 tablespoons brewed coffee
- 6 ladyfingers
- 1 quart vanilla ice cream, softened
- 1 container (8 ounces) Mascarpone cheese
- 1 cup chocolate milk
- 2 tablespoons baking cocoa
Whipped cream and chocolate curls

Brush coffee over ladyfingers; set aside. In a large bowl, beat the ice cream, cheese and milk until smooth.

Divide among six parfait glasses or serving dishes. Sprinkle with cocoa. Place a ladyfinger in each glass. Top with whipped cream and chocolate curls. **Yield: 6 servings.**

Microwave Red Snapper

Prep/Total Time: 10 min.

We fish a lot, so when I tried this recipe at a microwave cooking class, I knew it was a keeper. My husband requests it several times a month. —Evelyn Gavin, Cayucos, California

- 4 red snapper fillets (6 ounces *each*)
- 3/4 cup sour cream
- 1/4 cup mayonnaise
- 3 tablespoons milk
- 1 tablespoon prepared mustard
- 1-1/2 teaspoons dill weed
Hot cooked rice

Cut fish into serving-size pieces; place in an ungreased shallow microwave-safe dish. Cover and microwave on high for 3 minutes. Drain liquid.

Meanwhile, combine the sour cream, mayonnaise, milk, mustard and dill; drizzle 1/2 cup over the fish. Microwave, uncovered, on high for 3 minutes or until the fish flakes easily with a fork. Serve with rice and remaining sauce. **Yield: 6 servings.**

Black Bean Pineapple Salad

Prep/Total Time: 10 min.

I created this when I had little left in the fridge and needed something healthy and fast. The black beans and pineapple go well together, and it's so easy to make!
—Julie Muccillo, Chicago, Illinois

- 6 cups fresh baby spinach
- 1 can (15-1/2 ounces) unsweetened pineapple chunks, drained
- 1 can (15 ounces) black beans, rinsed and drained
- 1/2 cup *each* chopped sweet red and orange peppers
- 1/2 cup crumbled feta cheese
- 1/4 cup prepared balsamic vinaigrette

In a large bowl, combine the spinach, pineapple, beans, peppers and cheese. Drizzle with vinaigrette; toss to coat. Serve with a slotted spoon. **Yield: 6 servings.**

Nutrition Facts: 2/3 cup equals 149 calories, 3 g fat (1 g saturated fat), 5 mg cholesterol, 338 mg sodium, 23 g carbohydrate, 5 g fiber, 6 g protein. Diabetic Exchanges: 1 lean meat, 1 vegetable, 1/2 starch, 1/2 fruit.

Black Bean Pineapple Salad

Chicken Salad Clubs

Prep/Total Time: 10 min.

Mondays have always been soup and sandwich night at our house. One evening, I embellished a regular chicken salad sandwich with some unusual ingredients including rye bread and honey-mustard dressing. The results were delicious.

—Sarah Smith, Edgewood, Kentucky

8	bacon strips
4	lettuce leaves
8	slices rye *or* pumpernickel bread
1	pound prepared chicken salad
4	slices Swiss cheese
8	slices tomato
1/3	cup honey mustard salad dressing

In a large skillet, cook bacon over medium heat until crisp. Remove to paper towels to drain. Place lettuce on four slices of bread; layer each with chicken salad, two bacon strips, one cheese slice and two tomato slices. Spread salad dressing on one side of remaining bread; place over tomatoes. **Yield: 4 servings.**

Open-Faced Crab Melts

Prep/Total Time: 10 min.

Over the years, I've seen these versatile sandwiches please guests at occasions from fancy teas to last-minute suppers. To serve them as appetizers, I add some chili sauce and a little prepared horseradish to the crab mixture.

—Florence McClelland, Fredonia, New York

4	English muffins, split
1	can (6 ounces) crabmeat, drained, flaked and cartilage removed
1/3	cup mayonnaise
1	tablespoon lemon juice
1/2	teaspoon pepper
1/4	teaspoon dried tarragon
1	cup (4 ounces) shredded cheddar cheese

Broil the English muffins 4-6 in. from the heat for 2-3 minutes or until golden brown. In a large bowl, combine the mayonnaise, lemon juice, pepper and tarragon; stir in the crab. Spread over each muffin half; sprinkle with cheddar cheese. Broil for 2-3 minutes or until the cheese is melted. **Yield: 4 servings.**

Chicken Salad Clubs

Parmesan Party Mix

Prep/Total Time: 10 min.

This is our favorite mix. The combination of seasonings gives it just the right flavor, and it's a snap to toss together.

—Karen Smith, Thornton, Colorado

7	cups Crispix
2	cups cheese-flavored snack crackers
1	cup pretzel sticks
3	tablespoons olive oil
1	teaspoon Italian seasoning
1/4	teaspoon fennel seed, crushed
1/8	teaspoon hot pepper sauce
1/2	cup grated Parmesan *or* Romano cheese

In a 2-gal. resealable plastic bag, combine the cereal, crackers and pretzels. In a small bowl, combine the oil, Italian seasoning, fennel seed and hot pepper sauce. Pour over cereal mixture; seal bag and toss to coat. Add Parmesan cheese; seal bag and toss to coat. Store in an airtight container. **Yield: 8 cups.**

Peppy Parmesan Pasta

Prep/Total Time: 10 min.

When my husband and I needed to round out dinner in a hurry, we came up with this flavorful pasta dish.

—Debbie Horst, Phoenix, Arizona

8	ounces angel hair pasta
1	large tomato, chopped
1	package (3 ounces) sliced pepperoni
1	can (2-1/4 ounces) sliced ripe olives, drained
1/4	cup grated Parmesan cheese
3	tablespoons olive oil
1/2	teaspoon salt *or* salt-free seasoning blend, optional
1/4	teaspoon garlic powder

Cook the pasta according to package directions. Meanwhile, in a serving bowl, combine the tomato, pepperoni, olives, Parmesan cheese, olive oil, salt if desired and garlic powder. Drain pasta; add to the tomato mixture and toss to coat. **Yield: 4 servings.**

Peppy Parmesan Pasta

Watermelon Smoothies

Watermelon Smoothies
Prep/Total Time: 10 min.

This is so good to sip on a hot day. The simple summer beverage is a snap to blend up. —Sandi Pichon, Slidell, Louisiana

- 6 cups coarsely chopped seedless watermelon
- 1 cup lemon sherbet
- 12 ice cubes

Place half of the watermelon in a blender; cover and process until smooth. Add half of the sherbet and ice; cover and process until smooth. Repeat. Pour into chilled glasses; serve immediately. **Yield: 6 servings.**

*Nutrition Facts: 1 cup equals 83 calories, 1 g fat (trace saturated fat), 1 mg cholesterol, 15 mg sodium, 18 g carbohydrate, 1 g fiber, 1 g protein. **Diabetic Exchange:** 1 fruit.*

Curried Tuna Sandwiches
Prep/Total Time: 10 min.

If you're looking for a change from traditional tuna sandwiches, try this recipe I developed. It includes my favorite ingredients from a few different tuna salad recipes, including apples, raisins and curry. The first time I combined them, I loved the results! —Lorene Corbett, Tryon, Nebraska

- 1/4 cup chopped apple
- 2 tablespoons raisins
- 2 tablespoons mayonnaise
- 1/4 teaspoon onion salt
- 1/8 teaspoon curry powder
- 1 can (6 ounces) tuna, drained and flaked
- 2 sandwich rolls, split

Additional mayonnaise, optional
Lettuce leaves

In a bowl, combine the first five ingredients; add the tuna and mix well. Spread rolls with additional mayonnaise if desired; top each with 1/2 cup tuna mixture and lettuce leaves. **Yield: 2 servings.**

*Nutrition Facts: 1 sandwich (prepared with low-sodium tuna and fat-free mayonnaise; calculated without roll) equals 170 calories, 1 g fat (0 saturated fat), 15 mg cholesterol, 375 mg sodium, 15 g carbohydrate, 0 fiber, 26 g protein. **Diabetic Exchanges:** 3 very lean meat, 1 fruit.*

Beef Soup in a Hurry
Prep/Total Time: 10 min.

All you need is a few canned goods to stir up this comforting microwave mixture. I call this "throw-together" soup. Serve it with a green salad and hot bread or rolls. You can also simmer this soup in a slow cooker. —Loellen Holley, Topock, Arizona

- 1 can (24 ounces) beef stew
- 1 can (14-1/2 ounces) stewed tomatoes, cut up
- 1 can (10-3/4 ounces) condensed vegetable beef soup, undiluted
- 1 can (8-3/4 ounces) whole kernel corn, drained
- 1/8 teaspoon hot pepper sauce

Combine all ingredients in a microwave-safe bowl. Cover and microwave on high for 2-3 minutes or until heated through, stirring once. **Yield: 6 servings.**

Editor's Note: This recipe was tested in a 1,100-watt microwave.

Beef Soup in a Hurry

Two-Cheese Quesadillas

Two-Cheese Quesadillas

Prep/Total Time: 10 min.

When we have to eat on the run, I turn to this tasty recipe because it comes together in a snap. Best of all, I can customize the ingredients to satisfy each member of my family. If someone doesn't care for onions, I simply omit them from their quesadilla.
—*Sharron Kemp, High Point, North Carolina*

    4   flour tortillas (8 inches), warmed
    1   cup (4 ounces) shredded cheddar cheese
    1   cup (4 ounces) shredded part-skim mozzarella cheese
    2   small tomatoes, finely chopped
  1/2   cup finely chopped green pepper
  1/4   cup chopped onion
Salsa and sour cream

Place tortillas on a griddle. Sprinkle each tortilla with cheeses, tomatoes, green pepper and onion. Fold in half and press edges lightly to seal. Cook over low heat for 1-2 minutes on each side or until cheese is melted. Serve with salsa and sour cream. **Yield: 2-4 servings.**

In-a-Hurry Curry Soup

Prep/Total Time: 10 min.

Curry makes this speedy soup so delicious. I just open a few cans, and I have a quick, hearty meal in minutes. The wonderful aroma brings my family to the table before I even call them.
—*Denise Elder, Hanover, Ontario*

    1   cup chopped onion
  3/4   teaspoon curry powder
    2   tablespoons butter
    2   teaspoons chicken bouillon granules
    1   cup hot water
    1   can (14-1/2 ounces) diced tomatoes, undrained
    1   can (10-3/4 ounces) condensed cream of celery soup, undiluted
    1   cup half-and-half cream
    1   can (5 ounces) white chicken, drained

In a 3-qt. saucepan, saute onion and curry powder in butter until onion is tender. Dissolve bouillon in water; add to the saucepan. Stir in remaining ingredients; heat through. **Yield: about 5 servings.**

Creole Rice

Prep/Total Time: 10 min.

I've found a fast and fantastic way to turn leftover rice into a spectacular side dish. I spice it up with Creole seasoning and pepper to give it a boost of flavor, then sprinkle it with paprika for color. Rest assured that no one will figure out the zippy combination is a "second-day" dish.

—Sundra Hauck, Bogalusa, Louisiana

1/4 cup butter, cubed
1 teaspoon Creole seasoning
1/8 teaspoon pepper
2 cups cooked long grain rice

In a small saucepan, melt butter; add Creole seasoning and pepper. Cook over medium heat for 3 minutes. Stir in rice. Cover and heat through. **Yield: 4 servings.**

Editor's Note: The following spices may be substituted for 1 teaspoon Creole seasoning: 1/4 teaspoon each salt, garlic powder and paprika; and a pinch each of dried thyme, ground cumin and cayenne pepper.

Sweet and Sour Pork Chops

Brownie Sundaes

Prep/Total Time: 10 min.

With prepared brownies, I can fix this treat in a flash. For extra flair, roll the ice cream scoops in pecans before placing them on top of the brownies. It's a perfect finish to a mouth-watering meal.

—Ruth Lee, Troy, Ontario

3/4 cup semisweet chocolate chips
1/2 cup evaporated milk
2 tablespoons brown sugar

Brownie Sundaes

2 teaspoons butter
1/2 teaspoon vanilla extract
6 prepared brownies (3 inches square)
6 scoops vanilla *or* chocolate fudge ice cream
1/2 cup chopped pecans

In a large saucepan, combine the chocolate chips, milk and brown sugar. Cook and stir over medium heat for 5 minutes or until chocolate is melted and sugar is dissolved. Remove from the heat; stir in butter and vanilla until smooth.

Spoon about 2 tablespoons warm chocolate sauce onto each dessert plate. Top with a brownie and a scoop of ice cream. Drizzle with additional chocolate sauce if desired. Sprinkle with pecans. **Yield: 6 servings.**

Sweet and Sour Pork Chops

Prep/Total Time: 10 min.

It's hard to believe that the flavorful sauce for these tender pork chops calls for only a handful of items. They're nice enough for company. —Deborah Anderson, Spooner, Wisconsin

8 boneless pork loin chops (1/4 inch thick and 4 ounces *each*)
3 tablespoons chili sauce
3 tablespoons honey
2 tablespoons soy sauce

In a small bowl, combine the chili sauce, honey and soy sauce. Brush over both sides of pork. Broil 4-6 in. from the heat for 3-4 minutes on each side, or until a meat thermometer reaches 160°. **Yield: 4 servings.**

Roast Beef Barbecue

8   cups torn romaine
1   cup fresh raspberries
1/2 cup sliced almonds, toasted
1/2 cup seedless raspberry jam
1/4 cup white wine vinegar
1/4 cup honey
2   tablespoons plus 2 teaspoons vegetable oil

In a salad bowl, combine the romaine, raspberries and almonds. In a blender, combine the remaining ingredients; cover and process until smooth. Serve with salad. **Yield: 10 servings.**

Pesto Cheese Tarts
Prep/Total Time: 10 min.

Whether I make these savory tarts for a special occasion or a simple family gathering, everyone always raves about them. You can mix the filling the night before to save assembly time before your event. —Jean Kern, Charlotte, North Carolina

2/3 cup chopped tomatoes
1/3 cup mayonnaise
1/4 cup shredded part-skim mozzarella cheese
3   tablespoons shredded Parmesan cheese
2   teaspoons prepared pesto
1/8 teaspoon pepper
1   package (1.9 ounces) frozen miniature phyllo tart shells

In a small bowl, combine the chopped tomatoes, mayonnaise, cheeses, pesto and pepper. Spoon heaping teaspoonfuls into the tart shells. Place on an ungreased baking sheet. Bake at 350° for 8 minutes or until lightly browned. **Yield: 15 appetizers.**

Pesto Cheese Tarts

Roast Beef Barbecue
Prep/Total Time: 10 min.

When I'm in a hurry and want something good, this sandwich fills the bill. It tastes great with a salad and pork and beans on the side. Instead of using ketchup, I occasionally use barbecue sauce with a little Tabasco for extra zip.
—Agnes Ward, Stratford, Ontario

2/3 pound thinly sliced deli roast beef
1/2 cup water
1/4 cup ketchup
1   tablespoon brown sugar
1/2 teaspoon prepared mustard
1/4 teaspoon hot pepper sauce
1/8 teaspoon salt
1/8 teaspoon pepper
1/8 teaspoon chili powder
4   hamburger buns, split

In a small saucepan, combine the first nine ingredients. Cook over medium-high heat for 4-6 minutes or until heated through. Serve on buns, using a slotted spoon. **Yield: 4 servings.**

Almond-Raspberry Tossed Salad
Prep/Total Time: 10 min.

My husband and I helped prepare this summery salad for a weekend retreat. The recipe served 60 to 80 people, so I modified it to use at home. The sweet-tart dressing is wonderful over romaine with toasted almonds and fresh raspberries.
—Jennifer Long, St. Peters, Missouri

Sausage Bean Stew

Easy Chicken Barbecue

Prep/Total Time: 10 min.

I have my family over for Sunday dinner once a month, so I'm always looking for new and different recipes to prepare. These simple sandwiches are fuss-free and taste delicious.
—Connie Perrone, Rockford, Illinois

1/4	cup *each* chopped celery, green pepper and onion
1	tablespoon butter
2/3	cup barbecue sauce
1	can (10 ounces) chunk white chicken, drained
3	sandwich rolls, split

In a saucepan, saute the celery, green pepper and onion in butter until tender. Stir in barbecue sauce and chicken; heat through. Serve on rolls. **Yield: 3 servings.**

Tossed Salad with Pine Nuts

Prep/Total Time: 10 min.

This wonderful 5-ingredient recipe has lots of blue cheese flavor and crunch from pine nuts. Topped with raspberry vinaigrette dressing, it couldn't be much easier to toss together on a busy weeknight. Adding grilled chicken breast turns it into a fabulous main dish.
—Alice Tremont, Rochester Hills, Michigan

5	cups spring mix salad greens
1	small red onion, thinly sliced
1	cup (4 ounces) crumbled blue cheese
1/2	cup pine nuts, toasted
1/4	to 1/3 cup raspberry vinaigrette

In a large salad bowl, combine greens and onion. Sprinkle with blue cheese and pine nuts. Drizzle with vinaigrette; toss to coat. **Yield: 6-7 servings.**

Sausage Bean Stew

Prep/Total Time: 10 min.

I made this colorful, robust stew often when our three kids were living at home. Since it calls for lots of canned vegetables, it stirs up in a jiffy. It's versatile, too—you can substitute cubed turkey, chicken, ham or beef for the sausage. Plus, you can replace the beans with other vegetables of your choice.
—Barb Schutz, Pandora, Ohio

1	pound fully cooked smoked sausage, halved and cut into 1/4-inch slices
2	cans (10 ounces *each*) diced tomatoes with green chilies, undrained
1	can (15-1/2 ounces) great northern beans, rinsed and drained
1	can (15-1/4 ounces) whole kernel corn, drained
1	can (15 ounces) lima beans, drained
1	can (15 ounces) black beans, rinsed and drained
1/2	teaspoon salt
1/8	teaspoon pepper

Hot cooked rice, optional

In a large saucepan, combine the first eight ingredients. Heat through. Serve with hot cooked rice if desired. **Yield: 6-8 servings (2 quarts).**

Easy Garlic Bread

Crusty garlic bread goes great with Sausage Bean Stew. Take a sliced loaf of bread, or hot dog or hamburger buns, spread cut sides with butter or margarine, then sprinkle with garlic salt and Parmesan. Broil until they're golden and the cheese is melted.

Tossed Salad with Pine Nuts

Pesto Pasta

Prep/Total Time: 10 min.

Add crusty bread and a salad to this easy pasta dish to make a complete meal in mere minutes. The creamy sauce with fresh tomatoes and basil is a pleasant change from traditional tomato-based sauces. —Irene Smoliga, Harrisburg, Pennsylvania

- 8   ounces uncooked angel hair pasta
- 6   tablespoons olive oil
- 2   packages (3 ounces *each*) cream cheese, cubed
- 2   garlic cloves, minced
- 16 fresh basil leaves
- 2   plum tomatoes, chopped
- 3   tablespoons shredded mozzarella cheese
- 2   tablespoons grated Parmesan cheese

Cook pasta according to package directions. Meanwhile, for pesto, in a blender, combine the oil, cream cheese, garlic and basil; cover and process until smooth.

Drain the pasta and transfer to a serving bowl. Top with tomatoes and pesto; sprinkle with mozzarella and Parmesan cheeses. **Yield: 4 servings.**

Enchilada Chicken Soup

Prep/Total Time: 10 min.

Canned soups, bottled enchilada sauce and a few other convenience items make this recipe one of my fast-to-fix favorites. Use mild green chilies if they suit your tastes, or try a spicier variety to give the soup more kick.

—Cristin Fischer, Bellevue, Nebraska

Enchilada Chicken Soup

Chocolate Ice Cream Pie

- 1   can (11 ounces) condensed fiesta nacho cheese soup, undiluted
- 1   can (10-3/4 ounces) condensed cream of chicken soup, undiluted
- 2-2/3 cups milk
- 1   can (10 ounces) chunk white chicken, drained
- 1   can (10 ounces) enchilada sauce
- 1   can (4 ounces) chopped green chilies

Sour cream

In a large saucepan, combine the soups, milk, chicken, enchilada sauce and chilies. Cook until heated through. Serve with sour cream. **Yield: 7 servings.**

Chocolate Ice Cream Pie

Prep: 10 min. + freezing

I keep the ingredients for these frosty chocolate pies on hand during the summer. They're so quick to assemble. My husband and kids love them. —Wendy Bognar, Sparks, Nevada

- 2   quarts vanilla ice cream, melted
- 1   package (5.9 ounces) instant chocolate pudding mix
- 2   graham cracker crusts (10 inches *each*)

Whipped topping, optional

In a large bowl, whisk melted ice cream and pudding mix for 2 minutes. Pour into crusts. Freeze until firm.

Pies may be frozen for up to 2 months. Remove from the freezer 10 minutes before serving. Garnish with whipped topping if desired. **Yield: 2 pies (6-8 servings each).**

Split-Second Shrimp

Prep/Total Time: 10 min.

I use my microwave to hurry along preparation of this super-fast shrimp scampi, which is buttery and full of garlic flavor. Serve it as an elegant entree or special-occasion appetizer.

—Jalayne Luckett, Marion, Illinois

2	tablespoons butter
1-1/2	teaspoons minced garlic
1/8	to 1/4 teaspoon cayenne pepper
2	tablespoons white wine *or* chicken broth
5	teaspoons lemon juice
1	tablespoon minced fresh parsley
1/2	teaspoon salt
1	pound uncooked large shrimp, peeled and deveined

In a 9-in. microwave-safe pie plate, combine the butter, garlic and cayenne. Cover and microwave on high for 1 minute or until butter is melted. Stir in the wine or broth, lemon juice, parsley and salt. Add shrimp; toss to coat.

Cover and microwave on high for 2-1/2 to 3-1/2 minutes or until shrimp turn pink. Stir before serving. **Yield: 6 servings.**

Nutrition Facts: 1 serving (prepared with reduced-fat butter) equals 79 calories, 3 g fat (2 g saturated fat), 119 mg cholesterol, 349 mg sodium, 1 g carbohydrate, trace fiber, 12 g protein. Diabetic Exchange: 2 very lean meat.

Whipping Cream

Before making whipped cream, refrigerate a deep bowl and beaters for about 30 minutes. Pour the cream into the chilled bowl and whip according to the recipe directions. For Candy Store Pudding, whip the cream until soft peaks form.

Candy Store Pudding

Prep/Total Time: 10 min.

This rich and creamy pudding will appeal to kids of all ages. For variety, I substitute miniature chocolate chips, pecans, gumdrops or whatever else I have on hand for the peanuts and mini marshmallows. —*Sue Thomas, Casa Grande, Arizona*

1	cup cold milk
1	package (3.9 ounces) instant chocolate pudding mix
1	cup heavy whipping cream, whipped
1/2	to 1 cup miniature marshmallows
1/4	to 1/2 cup chopped salted peanuts

In a large bowl, whisk milk and pudding mix for 2 minutes. Let stand for 2 minutes or until soft-set. Fold in the whipped cream, marshmallows and peanuts. Spoon into individual dessert dishes. Refrigerate until serving. **Yield: 4 servings.**

Split-Second Shrimp

snappy
soups
& sandwiches

Sometimes the perfect solution to a lunch or dinner dilemma is a steaming batch of hearty soup or a platter of super sandwiches. Not only are they delicious and satisfying, they can be put together in a snap. So they're perfect for speedy suppers and in-a-rush lunches, as well as parties, potlucks and take-along meals.

Quickly create delightful menus with recipes such as heartwarming Pumpkin Soup, White Chili with Chicken, Lasagna Sandwiches and The Ultimate Grilled Cheese. All of these simple-yet-satisfying dishes are great tasting and surprisingly filling.

Mushroom Salsa Chili
(recipe on p. 91)

Barley Chicken Chili

Prep/Total Time: 25 min.

I was looking for a new recipe for chicken when I discovered a dish I thought my husband might like. After making a few changes and additions to fit our preferences, I had this zesty chili simmering on the stovetop. It was delicious, and leftovers store well in the freezer. —Kayleen Grew, Essexville, Michigan

1	cup chopped onion
1/2	cup chopped green pepper
1	teaspoon olive oil
2-1/4	cups water
1	can (15 ounces) tomato sauce
1	can (14-1/2 ounces) chicken broth
1	can (10 ounces) diced tomatoes and green chilies, undrained
1	cup quick-cooking barley
1	tablespoon chili powder
1/2	teaspoon ground cumin
1/4	teaspoon garlic powder
3	cups cubed cooked chicken

In a large saucepan, saute onion and green pepper in oil until tender. Add the water, tomato sauce, broth, tomatoes, barley, chili powder, cumin and garlic powder; bring to a boil. Reduce heat; cover and simmer for 10 minutes. Add chicken. Cover and simmer for 5 minutes longer or until barley is tender. **Yield: 9 servings (about 2 quarts).**

Barley Chicken Chili

Easy Baked Potato Soup

Easy Baked Potato Soup

Prep/Total Time: 30 min.

I came up with this comforting soup when I was crunched for time and wanted to use up extra baked potatoes. Since then, it has become a mealtime staple. Its wonderful aroma always gets cheers from my husband when he arrives home from work. —Julie Smithouser, Colorado Springs, Colorado

3	to 4 medium baking potatoes, baked
5	bacon strips, diced
2	cans (10-3/4 ounces *each*) condensed cream of potato soup, undiluted
1	can (10-3/4 ounces) condensed cheddar cheese soup, undiluted
3-1/2	cups milk
2	teaspoons garlic powder
2	teaspoons Worcestershire sauce
1/2	teaspoon onion powder
1/4	teaspoon pepper

Dash Liquid Smoke, optional

1	cup (8 ounces) sour cream

Shredded cheddar cheese

Peel and dice the baked potatoes; set aside. In a Dutch oven or soup kettle, cook the bacon over medium heat until crisp. Using a slotted spoon, remove to paper towels. Drain, reserving 1-1/2 teaspoons drippings.

Add the soups, milk, garlic powder, Worcestershire sauce, onion powder, pepper, Liquid Smoke if desired and reserved potatoes to the drippings. Cook, uncovered, for 10 minutes or until heated through, stirring occasionally. Stir in the sour cream; cook for 1-2 minutes or until heated through (do not boil). Garnish with the cheddar cheese and bacon. **Yield: 10 servings (2-1/2 quarts).**

Boston Subs

Prep/Total Time: 20 min.

My mother has been making these satisfying sandwiches since she left her hometown of Boston many years ago. They're quick to prepare and travel well if tightly wrapped in plastic wrap. The recipe is great for parties if you use a loaf of French or Italian bread instead of the individual rolls.

—Sue Erdos, Meriden, Connecticut

- 1/2 cup mayonnaise
- 12 submarine sandwich buns, split
- 1/2 cup Italian salad dressing, *divided*
- 1/4 pound *each* thinly sliced bologna, deli ham, hard salami, pepperoni and olive loaf
- 1/4 pound thinly sliced provolone cheese
- 1 medium onion, diced
- 1 medium tomato, diced
- 1/2 cup diced dill pickles
- 1 cup shredded lettuce
- 1 teaspoon dried oregano

Spread mayonnaise on inside of buns. Brush with half of the salad dressing. Layer deli meats and cheese on bun bottoms. Top with onion, tomato, pickles and lettuce. Sprinkle with oregano and drizzle with remaining dressing. Replace bun tops. **Yield: 12 servings.**

Hearty Hamburger Soup

Prep: 10 min. | Cook: 30 min.

At family get-togethers, our children always request this soup with fresh homemade bread and tall glasses of milk. It has robust flavor, plenty of fresh-tasting vegetables and is easy to make.

—Barbara Brown, Janesville, Wisconsin

- 1 pound ground beef
- 4 cups water
- 1 can (14-1/2 ounces) diced tomatoes, undrained
- 3 medium carrots, sliced
- 2 medium potatoes, peeled and cubed
- 1 medium onion, chopped
- 1/2 cup chopped celery
- 4 teaspoons beef bouillon granules
- 1-1/2 teaspoons salt
- 1/4 teaspoon pepper
- 1/4 teaspoon dried oregano
- 1 cup cut fresh *or* frozen green beans

In a large saucepan, brown the beef; drain. Add the next 10 ingredients; bring to a boil.

Reduce heat; cover. Simmer 15 minutes or until potatoes and carrots are tender; add beans. Cover; simmer 15 minutes or until the beans are tender. **Yield: 8 servings (2 quarts).**

Boston Subs

Garden Turkey Burgers

Seafood Bisque

Prep/Total Time: 30 min.

We live on the Gulf Coast, where fresh seafood is plentiful. I adapted several recipes to come up with this rich bisque. It's great as a first course or an entree, and it can be made with just shrimp or crabmeat. —Pat Edwards, Dauphin Island, Alabama

- 2 cans (10-3/4 ounces *each*) condensed cream of mushroom soup, undiluted
- 1 can (10-3/4 ounces) condensed cream of celery soup, undiluted
- 2-2/3 cups milk
- 4 green onions, chopped
- 1/2 cup finely chopped celery
- 1 garlic clove, minced
- 1 teaspoon Worcestershire sauce
- 1/4 teaspoon hot pepper sauce
- 1-1/2 pounds uncooked medium shrimp, peeled and deveined
- 1 can (6 ounces) crabmeat, drained, flaked and cartilage removed
- 1 jar (4-1/2 ounces) whole mushrooms, drained
- 3 tablespoons Madeira wine *or* chicken broth
- 1/2 teaspoon salt
- 1/2 teaspoon pepper
Minced fresh parsley

In a Dutch oven or soup kettle, combine the first eight ingredients. Bring to a boil. Reduce heat; add the shrimp, crab and mushrooms. Simmer, uncovered, for 10 minutes. Stir in the wine or broth, salt and pepper; cook 2-3 minutes longer. Garnish with minced parsley. **Yield: 10 servings (2-1/2 quarts).**

Garden Turkey Burgers
Prep/Total Time: 30 min.

These moist burgers get plenty of color and flavor from onion, zucchini and red pepper. I often make the mixture ahead of time and put it in the refrigerator. Later, I can put the burgers on the grill while whipping up a salad or side dish.
—Sandy Kitzmiller, Unityville, Pennsylvania

- 1 cup old-fashioned oats
- 3/4 cup chopped onion
- 3/4 cup finely chopped sweet red *or* green pepper
- 1/2 cup shredded zucchini
- 1/4 cup ketchup
- 2 garlic cloves, minced
- 1/4 teaspoon salt, optional
- 1 pound ground turkey
- 6 whole wheat hamburger buns, split and toasted

Coat the grill rack with cooking spray before starting the grill. In a bowl, combine the first seven ingredients. Crumble the ground turkey over oats mixture and mix well. Shape into six 1/2-in.-thick patties.

Grill, covered, over indirect medium heat for 6 minutes on each side or until a meat thermometer reads 165° and juices run clear. Serve on buns. **Yield: 6 servings.**

Nutrition Facts: 1 serving (prepared with lean ground turkey and without salt; calculated without the bun) equals 156 calories, 2 g fat (0 saturated fat), 37 mg cholesterol, 174 mg sodium, 15 g carbohydrate, 0 fiber, 21 g protein. Diabetic Exchanges: 2 very lean meat, 1 starch.

Seafood Bisque

Bacon-Tomato Bagel Melts

Prep/Total Time: 10 min.

My husband introduced me to this open-faced sandwich shortly after we got married, and it quickly became an all-time favorite. It's good made with plain or onion bagels.

—Lindsay Orwig, Grand Terrace, California

- 2 bagels, split and toasted
- 8 tomato slices
- 8 cooked bacon strips
- 1 cup (4 ounces) shredded part-skim mozzarella cheese

Ranch salad dressing

Place bagel halves cut side up on a baking sheet. Top each half with two tomato slices and two cooked bacon strips. Sprinkle with cheese.

Broil 4-6 in. from the heat for 1-2 minutes or until the mozzarella cheese begins to brown. Serve with ranch dressing. **Yield: 4 sandwiches.**

Bacon-Tomato Bagel Melts

Acorn Squash Soup

Prep/Total Time: 30 min.

The recipe for this thick and creamy soup was given to me by a friend who also likes squash. This elegant, golden soup is especially enjoyable during the cool nights of Indian summer, but it's good any time of year.

—Dorrene Butterfield, Chadron, Nebraska

- 1 small onion
- 1/4 cup chopped celery
- 2 tablespoons butter
- 2 tablespoons all-purpose flour
- 1 teaspoon chicken bouillon granules
- 1/2 teaspoon dill weed
- 1/4 teaspoon curry powder

Dash cayenne pepper

- 2 cups chicken broth
- 1 can (12 ounces) evaporated milk
- 3 cups mashed cooked acorn squash

Salt and pepper to taste

- 5 bacon strips, cooked and crumbled

In a large saucepan, saute the onion and celery in butter. Stir in the flour, chicken bouillon, dill, curry and cayenne until blended. Gradually add the broth and milk. Bring to a boil; cook and stir for 2 minutes. Add the squash, salt and pepper; heat through.

In a blender, process the soup in batches until smooth. Pour into serving bowls; sprinkle with the cooked and crumbled bacon. **Yield: 6 servings.**

Spinach Tortellini Soup

Prep/Total Time: 30 min.

Tortellini, spinach and tomatoes are a pleasing combination in this tasty soup. Don't forget the sprinkle of Parmesan cheese—it adds a special touch! *—Cindy Politowicz, Northville, Michigan*

- 3/4 cup chopped onion
- 1 teaspoon minced garlic
- 1 tablespoon olive oil
- 2 cans (14-1/2 ounces *each*) reduced-sodium chicken broth
- 2 cups water
- 1 teaspoon sugar
- 1/4 teaspoon salt
- 1/4 teaspoon pepper
- 1 package (9 ounces) refrigerated cheese tortellini
- 1 can (14-1/2 ounces) diced tomatoes, undrained
- 1 package (10 ounces) frozen chopped spinach, thawed
- 3 tablespoons shredded Parmesan cheese

In a large saucepan, saute the onion and garlic in oil until tender. Add the broth, water, sugar, salt and pepper. Bring to a boil. Add the cheese tortellini; cook for 7-9 minutes or until tender, stirring occasionally.

Reduce heat. Stir in the tomatoes and spinach; heat through. Just before serving, sprinkle with Parmesan cheese. **Yield: 6 servings (about 2 quarts).**

*Nutrition Facts: 1-1/2 cups equals 206 calories, 7 g fat (3 g saturated fat), 20 mg cholesterol, 782 mg sodium, 28 g carbohydrate, 4 g fiber, 11 g protein. **Diabetic Exchanges:** 2 vegetable, 1-1/2 lean meat, 1 starch.*

Pumpkin Soup

Pumpkin Soup

Prep/Total Time: 20 min.

While it looks elegant and is an appealing addition to a holiday meal, this creamy soup is so simple to make. My husband was skeptical at first, but after one bowl, he asked for seconds.
—Elizabeth Montgomery, Taylorville, Illinois

- 1/2 cup finely chopped onion
- 2 tablespoons butter
- 1 tablespoon all-purpose flour
- 2 cans (14-1/2 ounces *each*) chicken broth
- 1 can (15 ounces) solid-pack pumpkin
- 1 teaspoon brown sugar
- 1/4 teaspoon salt
- 1/8 teaspoon pepper
- 1/8 teaspoon ground nutmeg
- 1 cup heavy whipping cream

In a large saucepan, saute onion in butter until tender. Remove from the heat; stir in flour until smooth. Gradually stir in broth, pumpkin, brown sugar, salt, pepper and nutmeg; bring to a boil. Reduce heat and simmer for 5 minutes. Add cream; cook for 2 minutes or until heated through. **Yield: 6 servings.**

Giant Sandwich

Prep: 25 min. | Bake: 15 min.

This lovely layered loaf is definitely not your everyday sandwich. Piled high with a variety of fillings, the wedges are great for a special occasion when served warm from the oven.
—Mildred Sherrer, Fort Worth, Texas

- 1 unsliced round loaf (1-1/2 pounds) rye bread
- 1 tablespoon prepared horseradish
- 1/4 pound sliced deli roast beef
- 2 tablespoons mayonnaise
- 4 to 6 slices Swiss cheese
- 2 tablespoons prepared mustard
- 1/4 pound sliced deli ham
- 6 bacon strips, cooked
- 6 slices process American cheese
- 1 medium tomato, thinly sliced
- 4 slices red onion, separated into rings
- 1 tablespoon butter, softened

Cut bread horizontally into six slices. Spread bottom slice with horseradish; top with roast beef. Place the next slice of bread over beef; spread with mayonnaise and top with Swiss cheese. Add next slice of bread; spread with mustard and top with ham. Add the next slice of bread; top with bacon and American cheese. Add the next slice of bread; top with tomato slices and onion.

Spread butter on cut side of bread top; cover sandwich. Place on a baking sheet; loosely tent with heavy-duty foil. Bake at 400° for 12-14 minutes or until heated through. Carefully slice into wedges. **Yield: 6-8 servings.**

Freezing Horseradish

A great way to preserve the zippy flavor of prepared horseradish is to freeze it. Place mounds, about one tablespoon each, onto a waxed paper-lined baking sheet and freeze. Transfer to a resealable plastic bag and store in the freezer. Thaw before using.

Mushroom Salsa Chili

Prep: 10 min. | Cook: 8 hours

Green, red and yellow peppers give this hearty chili a splash of color. I often fix it for my grandsons. They don't like spicy chili, so I use mild salsa, but try it with a hotter variety if you prefer.

—Richard Rundels, Waverly, Ohio

 1 pound ground beef
 1 pound bulk pork sausage
 2 cans (16 ounces *each*) kidney beans, rinsed and drained
 1 jar (24 ounces) chunky salsa
 1 can (14-1/2 ounces) diced tomatoes, undrained
 1 large onion, chopped
 1 can (8 ounces) tomato sauce
 1 can (4 ounces) mushroom stems and pieces, drained
 1/2 cup *each* chopped green pepper, sweet red and yellow pepper
 1/2 teaspoon dried oregano
 1/4 teaspoon garlic powder
 1/8 teaspoon dried thyme
 1/8 teaspoon dried marjoram

Shredded cheddar cheese, sour cream and thinly sliced green onions, optional

In a large skillet, cook the ground beef and pork sausage over medium heat until the meat is no longer pink; drain. Transfer to a 5-qt. slow cooker.

Stir in the beans, salsa, tomatoes, onion, tomato sauce, mushrooms, bell peppers and seasonings. Cover and cook on low for 8 hours or until the flavors are blended. Garnish with cheddar cheese, sour cream and green onions if desired. **Yield: 8 servings.**

Mushroom Salsa Chili

Pizza Hoagies

Pizza Hoagies

Prep: 30 min. | Bake: 15 min.

My husband and three sons love these crispy sandwiches filled with a moist, pizza-flavored mixture. They're so popular, I often make them on a weekend and double the recipe.

—Barbara Mery, Bothell, Washington

 1 pound ground beef
 1/2 cup chopped onion
 1 can (15 ounces) pizza sauce
 1/4 cup chopped ripe olives
 2 teaspoons dried basil
 1 teaspoon dried oregano
 8 hoagie *or* submarine sandwich buns *or* French rolls
 2 cups (8 ounces) shredded part-skim mozzarella cheese

In a skillet, cook beef and onion over medium heat until meat is no longer pink; drain. Stir in pizza sauce, olives, basil and oregano. Cook for 10 minutes or until heated through.

Cut 1/4 in. off the top of each roll; set aside. Carefully hollow out bottom of roll, leaving a 1/4-in. shell (discard removed bread or save for another use). Sprinkle 2 tablespoons cheese inside each shell. Fill each with about 1/2 cup meat mixture. Sprinkle with remaining cheese, gently pressing down to flatten. Replace bread tops.

Individually wrap four sandwiches tightly in foil; freeze for up to 3 months. Place remaining sandwiches on a baking sheet. Bake at 375° for 15 minutes or until heated through.

To use frozen: Place foil-wrapped sandwiches on baking sheets. Bake at 375° for 60-70 minutes or until heated through. **Yield: 8 servings.**

Pizza Soup

Prep: 5 min. | Cook: 40 min.

This robust soup is a family favorite, and it's a big hit with my canasta group as well. I top each bowl with a slice of toasted bread and cheese, but you can have fun incorporating other pizza toppings such as cooked sausage.

—Jackie Brossard, Kitchener, Ontario

    2   cans (14-1/2 ounces *each*) diced tomatoes
    2   cans (10-3/4 ounces *each*) condensed tomato
        soup, undiluted
2-1/2   cups water
    1   package (3-1/2 ounces) sliced pepperoni,
        quartered
    1   medium sweet red pepper, chopped
    1   medium green pepper, chopped
    1   cup sliced fresh mushrooms
    2   garlic cloves, minced
  1/2   teaspoon rubbed sage
  1/2   teaspoon dried basil
  1/2   teaspoon dried oregano
Salt and pepper to taste
   10   slices French bread, toasted
1-1/2   cups (6 ounces) shredded part-skim
        mozzarella cheese

In a Dutch oven or soup kettle, bring the tomatoes, soup and water to a boil. Reduce heat; cover and simmer for 15 minutes. Mash with a potato masher. Add the pepperoni, red and green peppers, mushrooms, garlic, sage, basil, oregano, salt and pepper. Cover and simmer for 10 minutes or until vegetables are tender.

Ladle soup into ovenproof bowls. Top each with a slice of bread and sprinkle with cheese. Broil 4 in. from the heat until the cheese is melted and bubbly. **Yield: 10 servings (about 2-1/2 quarts).**

Pita Pocket Chicken Salad

Prep/Total Time: 15 min.

We wanted something cool for lunch one summer day, so I tossed together whatever I had in the refrigerator. This wonderful salad was the result. Guests enjoy the sweet grapes, tender chicken and crunchy almonds...and they always ask for the recipe.

—Natasha Randall, Austin, Texas

    2   cups cubed cooked chicken
1-1/2   cups seedless red grapes, halved
    1   cup chopped cucumber
  3/4   cup sliced almonds
  3/4   cup shredded part-skim mozzarella cheese
  1/2   cup poppy seed salad dressing
    6   pita breads (6 inches), halved
Leaf lettuce, optional

In a large bowl, combine the chicken, grapes, cucumber, almonds and mozzarella cheese. Drizzle with dressing and toss to coat. Line pita breads with lettuce if desired; fill with chicken salad. **Yield: 6 servings.**

Pita Pocket Chicken Salad

Italian Peasant Soup

Mexican Chicken Sandwiches

Prep/Total Time: 25 min.

These sandwiches are so comforting with grilled bread and savory melted cheese. They come together in less than 30 minutes!
—Samantha Anhalt, Redford Township, Michigan

3	tablespoons olive oil
4	teaspoons chili powder
1/2	teaspoon garlic powder
1/4	to 1/2 teaspoon cayenne pepper
4	boneless skinless chicken breast halves (4 ounces *each*)
1-1/2	cups (6 ounces) shredded taco *or* Mexican cheese blend, *divided*
1/3	cup mayonnaise
8	slices sourdough bread
1/2	cup salsa

Combine oil and seasonings; rub over both sides of chicken. Grill, covered, over medium for 6-8 minutes on each side or until a meat thermometer reaches 170° and juices run clear.

Meanwhile, combine 1 cup cheese and mayonnaise; set aside. Grill bread slices on one side until lightly browned. Spread with cheese mixture; grill until cheese is melted.

Place chicken on four slices of bread; top with salsa, remaining cheese and remaining bread, cheese side down.
Yield: 4 servings.

Editor's Note: Reduced-fat or fat-free mayonnaise is not recommended for this recipe.

 # Italian Peasant Soup

Prep/Total Time: 25 min.

My father shared this recipe with me, and I use it when I need a hearty, healthy meal. It's my son's favorite. Loaded with sausage, chicken, beans and spinach, the quick soup is nice for special occasions, too.   —Kim Knight, Hamburg, Pennsylvania

1	pound Italian sausage links, casings removed and cut into 1-inch slices
2	medium onions, chopped
6	garlic cloves, chopped
1	pound boneless skinless chicken breasts, cut into 1-inch cubes
2	cans (15 ounces *each*) cannellini *or* white kidney beans, rinsed and drained
2	cans (14-1/2 ounces *each*) chicken broth
2	cans (14-1/2 ounces *each*) diced tomatoes
1	teaspoon dried basil
1	teaspoon dried oregano
6	cups fresh spinach leaves, chopped

Shredded Parmesan cheese, optional

In a Dutch oven or soup kettle, cook sausage over medium heat until no longer pink; drain. Add onions and garlic; saute until tender. Add chicken; cook and stir until no longer pink.

Stir in the beans, broth, tomatoes, basil and oregano. Cook, uncovered, for 10 minutes. Add the spinach leaves and heat just until wilted. Serve with Parmesan cheese if desired.
Yield: 11 servings (2-3/4 quarts).

Mexican Chicken Sandwiches

Creamy Swiss Onion Soup

Creamy Swiss Onion Soup
Prep: 40 min. | Broil: 5 min.

It was a cool spring day when I came up with this sweet and creamy variation of traditional baked French onion soup. I top individual bowls with toasty buttered croutons and a sprinkling of Swiss cheese, then pop them under the broiler. The rich results are delicious and delightful!

—I. MacKay Starr, North Saanich, British Columbia

7	tablespoons butter, *divided*
1-1/2	cups cubed day-old bread
3	large onions, quartered and thinly sliced
1-1/2	cups water
4-1/2	teaspoons chicken bouillon granules
1/4	cup all-purpose flour
1-3/4	cups milk, *divided*
1-1/2	cups (6 ounces) shredded Swiss cheese, *divided*

Pepper to taste
Fresh minced chives *or* parsley

Melt 3 tablespoons of butter; toss with bread cubes. Place on a lightly greased baking sheet. Bake at 350° for 7 minutes; turn and bake 7 minutes longer or until toasted.

Meanwhile, in a large saucepan, saute onions in remaining butter until lightly browned, about 12 minutes. Stir in water and bouillon; bring to a boil. Reduce heat; cover and simmer for 15 minutes.

Combine flour and 1/2 cup milk until smooth; gradually stir into onion mixture. Stir in remaining milk. Bring to a boil; boil for 2 minutes, stirring until thickened. Reduce heat to low; stir in 3/4 cup Swiss cheese and pepper.

Ladle into four ovenproof bowls; sprinkle with reserved croutons and remaining cheese. Broil 4 in. from the heat until cheese is melted and bubbly. Garnish with chives. **Yield: 4 servings.**

State Fair Subs
Prep: 20 min. | Bake: 20 min.

My college roommate and I first ate these meaty sandwiches at the Iowa State Fair. After a little experimenting, we re-created the recipe. We ate the subs often because they were fast to fix between classes and didn't break our next-to-nothing grocery budget. They're priced just right, too.

—Christi Ross, Mill Creek, Oklahoma

1	unsliced loaf (1 pound) French bread
2	eggs
1/4	cup milk
1/2	teaspoon pepper
1/4	teaspoon salt
1	pound bulk Italian sausage
1-1/2	cups chopped onion
2	cups (8 ounces) shredded part-skim mozzarella cheese

Cut bread in half lengthwise; carefully hollow out top and bottom of loaf, leaving a 1-in. shell. Cube removed bread. In a large bowl, beat the eggs, milk, pepper and salt. Add bread cubes and toss to coat; set aside.

In a skillet over medium heat, cook sausage and onion until the meat is no longer pink; drain. Add to the bread mixture. Spoon filling into bread shells; sprinkle with cheese. Wrap each in foil. Bake at 400° for 20-25 minutes or until cheese is melted. Cut into serving-size slices. **Yield: 6 servings.**

Lasagna Sandwiches
Prep/Total Time: 10 min.

These cheesy grilled sandwiches really taste like lasagna. They're perfect for a quick evening meal—our children loved them with vegetable soup and crunchy potato sticks.

—Gail Rotheiser, Highland Park, Illinois

1/4	cup sour cream
2	tablespoons chopped onion
1/2	teaspoon dried oregano
1/4	teaspoon seasoned salt
8	slices Italian *or* other white bread
8	bacon strips, halved and cooked
8	slices tomato
4	slices part-skim mozzarella cheese
2	to 3 tablespoons butter

Combine the first four ingredients; spread on four slices of bread. Layer each with four strips of bacon, two tomato slices and a slice of cheese; top with remaining bread.

In a large skillet or griddle, melt 2-3 tablespoons butter. Toast sandwiches until bread is lightly browned on both sides, adding butter if necessary. **Yield: 4 servings.**

Curry Chicken Salad Wraps

Prep/Total Time: 25 min.

With curry powder and mango chutney, these scrumptious sandwiches offer a twist on traditional chicken salad. The fresh mint leaves and creamy from-scratch dressing make them ideal for a warm night's dinner or a special lunch.

—Robyn Cavallaro, Easton, Pennsylvania

- 1/2 cup mayonnaise
- 1/2 cup sour cream
- 1/4 cup finely chopped green onions
- 2 tablespoons curry powder
- 1 tablespoon mango chutney
- 1/2 teaspoon salt
- 1/2 teaspoon pepper
- 1 package (10 ounces) ready-to-serve roasted chicken breast strips
- 1 cup seedless red grapes, halved
- 1/2 cup julienned carrot
- 6 tablespoons chopped pecans, toasted
- 1/4 cup thinly sliced onion
- 6 lettuce leaves
- 6 flour tortillas (10 inches), room temperature
- 3/4 cup fresh mint leaves (about 24)

For dressing, in a small bowl, combine the first seven ingredients. Set aside 1-1/2 cups for serving. In a large bowl, combine the chicken, grapes, carrot, pecans and onion. Stir in the remaining dressing.

Place a lettuce leaf on each tortilla; top with 2/3 cup chicken salad and 4 mint leaves. Roll up. Serve with reserved dressing. **Yield: 6 servings.**

Sausage Potato Soup

Prep/Total Time: 30 min.

After a full day of teaching and coaching, I'm often too tired to spend a lot of time preparing dinner. So I rely on this deliciously thick and chunky soup blend that I can have on the table in 30 minutes. The whole family enjoys the wonderful flavor of the vegetables and smoked sausage.

—Jennifer LeFevre, Hesston, Kansas

- 1/2 pound smoked kielbasa, diced
- 6 medium potatoes, peeled and cubed
- 2 cups frozen corn
- 1-1/2 cups chicken broth
- 1 celery rib, sliced
- 1/4 cup sliced carrot
- 1/2 teaspoon garlic powder
- 1/2 teaspoon onion powder
- 1/2 teaspoon salt
- 1/4 teaspoon pepper
- 1-1/2 cups milk
- 2/3 cup shredded cheddar cheese
- 1 teaspoon minced fresh parsley

In a large saucepan, brown the smoked kielbasa; drain. Remove sausage from pan and set aside. In the same pan, combine the potatoes, corn, chicken broth, celery, carrot and seasonings. Bring to a boil.

Reduce the heat; cover and simmer for 15 minutes or until the vegetables are tender. Add the milk, cheddar cheese, minced parsley and kielbasa. Cook and stir over low heat until the cheese is melted and the soup is heated through. **Yield: 6 servings.**

Curry Chicken Salad Wraps

Turkey Meatball Soup

Prep: 25 min. | Cook: 30 min.

You don't need to cook the tender homemade meatballs or boil the egg noodles separately, so you can easily stir up this savory soup in no time. I usually double the recipe for our family of seven.
—Carol Losier, Baldwinsville, New York

    2   cans (14-1/2 ounces *each*) chicken broth
    1   celery rib with leaves, thinly sliced
    1   medium carrot, thinly sliced
  1/4   cup chopped onion
    1   tablespoon butter
    1   egg, lightly beaten
  1/2   cup dry bread crumbs
    2   tablespoons dried parsley flakes
    1   tablespoon Worcestershire sauce
  1/4   teaspoon pepper
  1/2   pound lean ground turkey
    1   cup uncooked egg noodles

In a large saucepan, bring the broth, celery and carrot to a boil. Reduce heat; cover and simmer for 10 minutes.

Meanwhile, in a small skillet, saute onion in butter until tender. Transfer to a large bowl. Add the egg, bread crumbs, parsley, Worcestershire sauce and pepper. Crumble turkey over mixture and mix well. Shape into 1-in. balls.

Add meatballs to the simmering broth. Bring to a boil. Reduce heat; cover and simmer for 15 minutes or until meat is no longer pink. Add noodles. Cover and simmer for 5 minutes or until noodles are tender. **Yield: 5 servings.**

The Ultimate Grilled Cheese

Turkey Meatball Soup

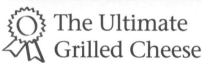 # The Ultimate Grilled Cheese

Prep/Total Time: 15 min.

These gooey grilled cheese sandwiches, subtly seasoned with garlic, taste great for lunch with sliced apples. And they're really fast to whip up, too. To save seconds, I soften the cream cheese in the microwave, then blend it with the rest of the ingredients in the same bowl. That makes cleanup a breeze.
—Kathy Norris, Streator, Illinois

    1   package (3 ounces) cream cheese, softened
  3/4   cup mayonnaise
    1   cup (4 ounces) shredded part-skim mozzarella cheese
    1   cup (4 ounces) shredded cheddar cheese
  1/2   teaspoon garlic powder
  1/8   teaspoon seasoned salt
   10   slices Italian bread (1/2 inch thick)
    2   tablespoons butter, softened

In a large bowl, beat cream cheese and mayonnaise until smooth. Stir in cheeses, garlic powder and seasoned salt. Spread five slices of bread with the cheese mixture, about 1/3 cup on each. Top with remaining bread.

Butter the outsides of the sandwiches. In a skillet over medium heat, toast sandwiches for 4-5 minutes on each side or until the bread is lightly browned and the cheese is melted. **Yield: 5 servings.**

Vegetarian Chili

Prep: 10 min. | Cook: 30 min.

Hominy and garbanzo beans are interesting additions to the zippy chili I stir up using canned goods from my cupboard. I often serve it with corn bread or flour tortillas for a speedy meal.
—Karen Hunt, Bellvue, Colorado

2 cans (15 ounces *each*) pinto beans, rinsed and drained
1 can (28 ounces) crushed tomatoes
1 can (16 ounces) kidney beans, rinsed and drained
1 can (15-1/2 ounces) hominy, rinsed and drained
1 can (15 ounces) garbanzo beans *or* chickpeas, rinsed and drained
1 can (6 ounces) tomato paste
1 can (4 ounces) chopped green chilies, undrained
2 small zucchini, halved and thinly sliced
1 medium onion, chopped
1-1/2 to 2 cups water
1 to 2 tablespoons chili powder
1 teaspoon ground cumin
1 teaspoon salt, optional
1/2 teaspoon garlic powder
1/2 teaspoon sugar
1/2 cup shredded Monterey Jack cheese

In a large kettle or Dutch oven, combine the first 15 ingredients. Bring to a boil. Reduce heat; cover and simmer for 30-35 minutes. Sprinkle with cheese. **Yield: 12 servings (about 3 quarts).**

Tortilla Turkey Sandwiches

Prep/Total Time: 20 min.

As my kids learned how to cook, this was always one of their favorite lunches to fix. We all love the creamy blend of flavors. The original recipe came from my husband, but I tweaked it a bit to make it even easier. —Leslie Heath, Salt Lake City, Utah

4 ounces cream cheese, softened
2 tablespoons mayonnaise
1-1/2 teaspoons prepared pesto
4 flour tortillas (8 inches), room temperature
1 cup shredded lettuce
1/2 pound sliced deli smoked turkey
3/4 cup chopped tomato
1 can (2-1/4 ounces) sliced ripe olives, drained
1 cup (4 ounces) shredded Colby-Monterey Jack cheese

In a small bowl, beat the cream cheese, mayonnaise and pesto until blended. Spread about 2 tablespoons over each tortilla. Layer with lettuce, turkey, tomato, olives and cheese; roll up. Secure with toothpicks. **Yield: 4 servings.**

Mushroom Crab Melts

Prep/Total Time: 30 min.

I received this recipe from my grandmother. The rich open-faced treats are great with a green salad, but I've also cut them into quarters to serve as hors d'oeuvres. To save time, make the crab-mushroom topping early in the day and store it in the refrigerator.
—Jean Bevilacqua, Rohdodendron, Oregon

3 bacon strips, diced
1 cup sliced fresh mushrooms
1/4 cup chopped onion
1 can (6 ounces) crabmeat, drained, flaked and cartilage removed *or* 1 cup chopped imitation crabmeat
1 cup (4 ounces) shredded Swiss cheese
1/2 cup mayonnaise
1/3 cup grated Parmesan cheese
2 tablespoons butter, softened
6 English muffins, split
Dash *each* cayenne pepper and paprika

In a skillet, cook bacon over medium heat until crisp; remove to paper towels. Drain, reserving 2 tablespoons drippings. Saute mushrooms and onion in drippings until tender. In a large bowl, combine the crab, Swiss cheese, mayonnaise, mushroom mixture, Parmesan cheese and bacon.

Spread butter over muffin halves. Top with crab mixture; sprinkle with cayenne and paprika. Place on an ungreased baking sheet. Bake at 400° for 10-15 minutes or until lightly browned. **Yield: 6 servings.**

Mushroom Crab Melts

Toasted Zippy Beef Sandwiches

Toasted Zippy Beef Sandwiches

Prep/Total Time: 20 min.

These yummy broiled sandwiches taste just like they came from a delicatessen. With sliced roast beef, provolone cheese, fresh vegetables and a simple homemade dressing, they're comforting and refreshing with a slight kick.

—Theresa Young, McHenry, Illinois

1/4	cup mayonnaise
4-1/2	teaspoons Western salad dressing
1	tablespoon prepared horseradish
4	whole wheat sandwich buns, split
1/2	pound sliced deli roast beef
4	slices provolone cheese
4	slices Swiss cheese
4	slices tomato
4	slices onion
1	small sweet yellow pepper, sliced
4	large lettuce leaves

In a small bowl, combine the mayonnaise, salad dressing and prepared horseradish; set aside. Place bun bottoms cut side up on an ungreased baking sheet; top with the sliced beef and cheeses. Broil 4 in. from the heat for 4-5 minutes or until cheese is melted.

Place bun tops cut side up on another baking sheet. Broil for 1-2 minutes or until golden brown. Meanwhile, layer the tomato, onion, yellow pepper and lettuce on bun bottoms. Spread mayonnaise mixture over bun tops; place over lettuce. **Yield: 4 sandwiches.**

White Chili with Chicken

Prep/Total Time: 30 min.

Folks who enjoy a change from traditional tomato-based chilies will enjoy this version. The flavorful blend has tender chunks of chicken, white beans and just enough zip.

—Christy Campos, Richmond, Virginia

1	medium onion, chopped
1	jalapeno pepper, seeded and chopped, optional
2	garlic cloves, minced
1	tablespoon canola oil
4	cups chicken broth
2	cans (15-1/2 ounces *each*) great northern beans, rinsed and drained
2	tablespoons minced fresh parsley
1	tablespoon lime juice
1	to 1-1/4 teaspoons ground cumin
2	tablespoons cornstarch
1/4	cup cold water
2	cups cubed cooked chicken

In a large saucepan, cook the onion, jalapeno if desired and garlic in oil until tender. Stir in the broth, beans, parsley, lime juice and cumin; bring to a boil. Reduce heat; cover and simmer for 10 minutes, stirring occasionally.

Combine cornstarch and water until smooth; gradually stir into chili. Add chicken. Bring to a boil; cook and stir for 2 minutes or until thickened. **Yield: 6 servings.**

Editor's Note: When cutting hot peppers, disposable gloves are recommended. Avoid touching your face.

Onion Cheese Soup

Prep/Total Time: 25 min.

I made a few adjustments to this savory soup recipe, so now it's rich, buttery and cheesy. —Janice Pogozelski, Cleveland, Ohio

1	large onion, chopped
3	tablespoons butter
3	tablespoons all-purpose flour
1/2	teaspoon salt

Pepper to taste

4	cups milk
2	cups (8 ounces) shredded Colby-Monterey Jack cheese

Seasoned salad croutons
Grated Parmesan cheese, optional

In a large saucepan, saute the onion in butter. Stir in the flour, salt and pepper until blended. Gradually add milk. Bring to a boil; cook and stir for 2 minutes or until thickened. Stir in cheese until melted. Serve with croutons and Parmesan cheese if desired. **Yield: 6 servings.**

Curried Chicken Pitas

Prep/Total Time: 15 min.

These zesty pitas are very different from your usual chicken sandwiches. They're a cinch to prepare and are perfect for a meal or a snack. —Marilou Robinson, Portland, Oregon

1/2	cup mayonnaise
1	tablespoon honey
1	teaspoon curry powder
2	cups cubed cooked chicken
1	cup halved green grapes
1/2	cup chopped pecans
4	green onions, chopped
4	pita breads, halved, warmed
8	lettuce leaves

In a bowl, combine mayonnaise, honey and curry powder. Stir in the chicken, grapes, pecans and onions. Line pita halves with lettuce; spoon 1/2 cup chicken mixture into each. **Yield: 4 servings.**

Say, "Cheese"

For a bolder tasting cheese soup, substitute half or all of the cheese with sharp cheddar. Refrigerate shredded cheese in an airtight container or freeze for up to 6 months. When adding cheese to a soup or sauce, stir it in at the end of cooking to avoid over-heating.

Pronto Taco Soup

Prep/Total Time: 30 min.

When out-of-state friends dropped by, I invited them to stay for dinner, knowing that I could put together this mild, chili-flavored soup in a jiffy. I served it with cornmeal muffins and a crisp salad for a filling meal everyone loved. My guests even asked for the recipe before leaving!
—Priscilla Gilbert, Indian Harbour Beach, Florida

1	pound ground beef
1	medium onion, chopped
2	garlic cloves, minced
2	cans (14-1/2 ounces *each*) beef broth
1	can (14-1/2 ounces) diced tomatoes, undrained
1-1/2	cups picante sauce
1	cup uncooked spiral *or* small shell pasta
1	medium green pepper, chopped
2	teaspoons chili powder
1	teaspoon dried parsley flakes

Shredded cheddar cheese and tortilla chips

In a large saucepan, cook the beef, onion and garlic until meat is no longer pink; drain. Add the broth, tomatoes, picante sauce, pasta, green pepper, chili powder and parsley. Bring to a boil, stirring occasionally.

Reduce heat; cover and simmer for 10-15 minutes or until pasta is tender. Garnish with cheese and tortilla chips. **Yield: 8 servings (2 quarts).**

Pronto Taco Soup

Raspberry Grilled Cheese

Prep/Total Time: 15 min.

My favorite appetizer is a raspberry-glazed cheese ball, so I used similar ingredients to dress up a plain grilled cheese sandwich. The quick combination was unique but delicious, and it became a popular request in my house.

—Jane Beers, Siloam Springs, Arkansas

- 2 tablespoons seedless red raspberry preserves
- 4 slices sourdough bread
- 2 tablespoons chopped pecans
- 1 to 2 tablespoons sliced green onion
- 4 slices Muenster *or* baby Swiss cheese
- 3 tablespoons butter, softened

Spread preserves on two slices of bread; top with the pecans, onion and cheese. Top with remaining bread; butter outsides of bread. Toast on a hot griddle for 3-4 minutes on each side or until golden brown. **Yield: 2 servings.**

Turkey Sloppy Joes

Prep/Total Time: 25 min.

This is a wonderful sandwich for family meals or parties. Once the meat is browned, the mixture simmers for just 10 minutes, so it's perfect for spur-of-the-moment backyard picnics.

—Sue Ann O'Buck, Sinking Spring, Pennsylvania

- 1 pound lean ground turkey
- 1/4 cup chopped onion
- 1/2 cup no-salt-added ketchup
- 3 tablespoons barbecue sauce
- 1 tablespoon white vinegar
- 1 tablespoon prepared mustard
- 1-1/2 teaspoons Worcestershire sauce
- 1/2 teaspoon celery seed
- 1/4 teaspoon pepper
- 6 whole wheat hamburger buns, split

Turkey Sloppy Joes

In a nonstick skillet, cook turkey and onion over medium heat until meat is no longer pink. Stir in the ketchup, barbecue sauce, vinegar, mustard, Worcestershire sauce, celery seed and pepper. Bring to a boil. Reduce heat; simmer, uncovered, for 10 minutes, stirring occasionally. Serve on buns. **Yield: 6 servings.**

Nutrition Facts: 1 serving equals 236 calories, 364 mg sodium, 37 mg cholesterol, 29 gm carbohydrate, 23 gm protein, 3 gm fat. Diabetic Exchanges: 2-1/2 very lean meat, 2 starch.

Beefy Tomato Pasta Soup

Prep: 15 min. | Cook: 45 min.

If you're a fan of Italian fare, you'll like this chunky combination. I enjoy this satisfying soup, and it's easier to fix than lasagna.

—Nancy Rollag, Kewaskum, Wisconsin

- 1 pound ground beef
- 2 medium green peppers, cut into 1-inch chunks
- 1 medium onion, cut into chunks
- 2 garlic cloves, minced
- 5 to 6 cups water
- 2 cans (14-1/2 ounces *each*) Italian diced tomatoes, undrained
- 1 can (6 ounces) tomato paste
- 1 tablespoon brown sugar
- 2 to 3 teaspoons Italian seasoning
- 1 teaspoon salt
- 1/4 teaspoon pepper
- 2 cups uncooked spiral pasta

Croutons, optional

In a Dutch oven, cook the ground beef, green peppers, onion and garlic over medium heat until meat is no longer pink; drain. Add the water, tomatoes, tomato paste, brown sugar, Italian seasoning, salt and pepper. Bring to a boil. Add the pasta. Cook for 10-14 minutes or until the pasta is tender, stirring occasionally. Serve with croutons if desired. **Yield: 10 servings (about 2-1/2 quarts).**

Perfect Pasta

To cook pasta more evenly and prevent it from sticking together, always cook it in a large pot. It's best to cook no more than 2 pounds at a time. For 8 ounces of pasta, bring 3 quarts of water plus 1 tablespoon salt to a rolling boil. Add the pasta and return to a boil. Cook, uncovered, stirring occasionally, according to the package directions until "al dente," or firm yet tender. Test often while cooking to avoid overcooking, which can result in pasta with a soft or mushy texture.

Cheeseburger Chowder

Prep/Total Time: 25 min.

I dressed up a can of cheese soup to see if I could capture the same flavors I tasted in a restaurant chowder. I then took it a step further by adding chilies and Southwestern spices. Now it's one of my favorite heartwarming meals!

—Lori Risdal, Sioux City, Iowa

1/2	pound ground beef
1	can (10-3/4 ounces) condensed cheddar cheese soup, undiluted
1-3/4	cups milk
1	cup frozen shredded hash brown potatoes
1	can (4 ounces) chopped green chilies
1	tablespoon taco seasoning
1	tablespoon dried minced onion
1/2	teaspoon chili powder

Coarsely crushed corn chips, shredded Monterey Jack cheese and chopped green onions, optional

In a large saucepan, cook beef over medium heat until no longer pink; drain. Stir in the soup, milk, potatoes, chilies, taco seasoning, onion and chili powder until blended. Bring to a boil. Reduce heat; simmer, uncovered, for 5 minutes or until heated through. Garnish with corn chips, cheese and green onions if desired. **Yield: 4 servings.**

 # Tasty Reuben Soup

Prep/Total Time: 25 min.

As a working mom with limited time to spend in the kitchen, I'm always looking for quick recipes. With the flavors of a Reuben sandwich, this delicious and speedy soup gets compliments from everyone who tries it. —Terry Ann Brandt, Tobias, Nebraska

4	cans (14-1/2 ounces each) chicken broth
4	cups shredded cabbage
2	cups uncooked medium egg noodles
1	pound fully cooked kielbasa, halved and cut into 1-inch slices
1/2	cup chopped onion
1	teaspoon caraway seeds
1/4	teaspoon garlic powder
1	cup (4 ounces) shredded Swiss cheese

In a large saucepan, combine the first seven ingredients; bring to a boil. Reduce heat; cover and simmer for 15 minutes or until cabbage and noodles are tender. Sprinkle with cheese. **Yield: 10 servings (2-1/2 quarts).**

Nutrition Facts: 1 cup serving (prepared with reduced-sodium chicken broth, reduced-fat turkey kielbasa and reduced-fat cheese) equals 125 calories, 5 g fat (0 saturated fat), 41 mg cholesterol, 455 mg sodium, 9 g carbohydrate, 0 fiber, 12 g protein. **Diabetic Exchanges:** *1 meat, 1 vegetable, 1/2 starch.*

Chilled Cantaloupe Soup

Prep: 10 min. + chilling

A friend in New York shared the recipe for this chilled melon soup that's pleasantly spiced with cinnamon. Most people are skeptical when I describe it, but after one spoonful, they're hooked.

—*M. McNeil, Germantown, Tennessee*

- 1 medium cantaloupe, peeled, seeded and cubed
- 2 cups orange juice, *divided*
- 1 tablespoon lime juice
- 1/4 to 1/2 teaspoon ground cinnamon

Fresh mint, optional

Place cantaloupe and 1/2 cup orange juice in a blender or food processor; cover and process until smooth.

Transfer to a large bowl; stir in lime juice, cinnamon and remaining orange juice. Cover and refrigerate for at least 1 hour. Serve with mint if desired. **Yield: 6 servings.**

Nutrition Facts: One 3/4-cup serving equals 70 calories, trace fat (0 saturated fat), 0 cholesterol, 9 mg sodium, 17 g carbohydrate, 0 fiber, 1 g protein. **Diabetic Exchange:** *1 fruit.*

Prosciutto Provolone Panini

Prep/Total Time: 25 min.

For a quick lunch or supper, try this fancy, "uptown" take on grilled cheese sandwiches. They're fast and easy but sophisticated enough for entertaining. I sometimes replace the fresh sage with one tablespoon of Italian seasoning for a tasty variation.

—*Candy Summerhill, Alexander, Arkansas*

- 8 slices white bread
- 8 slices provolone cheese
- 4 thin slices prosciutto
- 3 tablespoons olive oil
- 3 tablespoons minced fresh sage

On four slices of bread, layer a slice of provolone cheese, a slice of prosciutto and a second slice of cheese. Top with remaining bread.

Brush both sides of the prepared sandwiches with olive oil; sprinkle with minced sage. Cook in a panini maker or indoor grill until the bread is toasted and the cheese is melted. **Yield: 4 servings.**

Prosciutto Provolone Panini

Veggie Chowder

Prep/Total Time: 30 min.

This healthy and brothy soup features potatoes, carrots, mushrooms and corn for a delightful entree. Since it's not too heavy, it pairs well with salads or sandwiches.

—Vicki Kerr, Portland, Maine

- 2 cups reduced-sodium chicken broth
- 2 cups cubed peeled potatoes
- 1 cup chopped carrots
- 1/2 cup chopped onion
- 1 can (14-3/4 ounces) cream-style corn
- 1 can (12 ounces) fat-free evaporated milk
- 3/4 cup shredded reduced-fat cheddar cheese
- 1/2 cup sliced fresh mushrooms
- 1/4 teaspoon pepper
- 2 tablespoons real bacon bits

In a large saucepan, combine the broth, potatoes, carrots and onion. Bring to a boil. Reduce heat; simmer, uncovered, for 10-15 minutes or until vegetables are tender.

Add the corn, milk, cheese, mushrooms and pepper. Cook and stir 4-6 minutes longer or until heated through. Sprinkle with bacon. **Yield: 7 servings.**

Nutrition Facts: 1 cup equals 178 calories, 3 g fat (2 g saturated fat), 12 mg cholesterol, 554 mg sodium, 29 g carbohydrate, 2 g fiber, 11 g protein. Diabetic Exchanges: 2 starch, 1/2 fat.

Comforting Chicken Noodle Soup

Prep/Total Time: 25 min.

This rich, comforting soup is so simple to fix. I like to give a pot of it, along with the recipe, to new mothers so they don't have to worry about dinner.

—Joanna Sargent, Sandy, Utah

- 2 quarts water
- 8 teaspoons chicken bouillon granules
- 6-1/2 cups uncooked wide egg noodles
- 2 cans (10-3/4 ounces *each*) condensed cream of chicken soup, undiluted
- 3 cups cubed cooked chicken
- 1 cup (8 ounces) sour cream

Minced fresh parsley

In a large saucepan, bring the water and chicken bouillon to a boil. Add the egg noodles; cook, uncovered, until tender, about 10 minutes. Do not drain. Add the soup and cooked chicken; heat through.

Remove from the heat; stir in the sour cream. Sprinkle with minced parsley. **Yield: 10-12 servings (about 2-1/2 quarts).**

Veggie Chowder

Ham and Swiss Stromboli

Prep: 15 min. | Bake: 30 min.

This pretty swirled sandwich loaf is fast, easy and versatile. Fill it with anything your family likes. My family likes sliced pepperoni and provolone cheese, or try anchovies and ripe olives if you're feeling adventurous.

—Pat Raport, Gainesville, Florida

- 1 tube (11 ounces) refrigerated crusty French loaf
- 6 ounces thinly sliced deli ham
- 6 green onions, sliced
- 8 bacon strips, cooked and crumbled
- 1-1/2 cups (6 ounces) shredded Swiss cheese

Unroll dough on a greased baking sheet. Place ham over dough to within 1/2 in. of edges; sprinkle evenly with onions, bacon and cheese. Roll up jelly-roll style, starting with a long side. Pinch seams to seal and tuck ends under. Place seam side down on baking sheet.

With a sharp knife, cut several 1/4-in.-deep slits on top of loaf. Bake at 350° for 26-30 minutes or until golden brown. Cool slightly before slicing. Serve warm. **Yield: 8 servings.**

Sauces for Stromboli

Ham and Swiss Stromboli tastes great with honey mustard sauce. It's easy to make: whisk together 1/2 cup Dijon mustard, 1/2 cup honey, 4 teaspoons soy sauce and 2 teaspoons sugar. Or, simply heat a bowl of storebought marinara sauce in the microwave.

speedy sides, salads &breads

Sometimes the perfect way to round out a meal is with a tasty side dish, refreshing salad, fresh-baked bread or all of the above! Thanks to convenience items and quick cooking methods, it's a cinch to whip up easy supper accompaniments such as Southwestern Spuds, Summer Spinach Salad and Multigrain Bread.

Many of these quick recipes take just 30 minutes to arrive at the table, while others require only 15 minutes of preparation. One thing is for sure...adding any of these recipes to your menu makes meal planning a snap!

Au Gratin Potatoes
(recipe on p. 124)

Marmalade Monkey Bread

Marmalade Monkey Bread

Prep: 15 min. | Bake: 30 min.

We love this pretty pull-apart bread, and drop-in company just raves about it. Because it uses refrigerated biscuits, it's so easy and quick to fix. You can try whatever jam you have on hand in place of the marmalade.

—Delia Kennedy, Deer Park, Washington

- 2/3 cup orange marmalade
- 1/2 cup chopped pecans *or* walnuts
- 1/4 cup honey
- 2 tablespoons butter, melted
- 2 tubes (7-1/2 ounces *each*) refrigerated buttermilk biscuits

In a small bowl, combine the marmalade, pecans, honey and butter. Cut each biscuit into four pieces. Layer half of the pieces in a greased 10-in. tube pan; top with half of the marmalade mixture. Repeat.

Bake at 375° for 27-30 minutes or until golden brown. Cool in pan for 5 minutes before inverting onto a serving plate. Serve warm. **Yield: 8 servings.**

Pourable Honey

If honey is crystallized, heating it is the only way to dissolve the crystals. Place the jar in warm water and stir until the crystals dissolve. Or transfer the honey to a microwave-safe container and microwave on high, stirring every 30 seconds, until the crystals dissolve.

Pumpkin Chocolate Loaf

Prep: 15 min. | Bake: 55 min. + cooling + freezing

These moist chocolate loaves, with a hint of pumpkin and spice, have been a family favorite for years. They can be sliced to serve as snacks or dessert, or be given as gifts during the holidays.

—Kathy Gardner, Rockville, Maryland

- 3-3/4 cups all-purpose flour
- 3-1/2 cups sugar
- 1-1/2 teaspoons salt
- 1-1/2 teaspoons baking powder
- 1-1/4 teaspoons baking soda
- 1-1/4 teaspoons ground cinnamon
- 1 to 1-1/4 teaspoons ground cloves
- 1/2 teaspoon ground nutmeg
- 3 eggs
- 1 can (29 ounces) solid-pack pumpkin
- 1-1/4 cups canola oil
- 3 squares (1 ounce *each*) unsweetened chocolate, melted and cooled
- 1-1/2 teaspoons vanilla extract
- 2 cups (12 ounces) semisweet chocolate chips

In a large bowl, combine the flour, sugar, salt, baking powder, baking soda and ground cinnamon, cloves and nutmeg. In another large bowl, whisk the eggs, pureed pumpkin, canola oil, melted chocolate and vanilla extract. Stir into the dry ingredients just until moistened. Fold in the chocolate chips.

Transfer to three greased 9-in. x 5-in. loaf pans. Bake at 350° for 55-65 minutes or until a toothpick inserted near the center comes out clean. Cool for 10 minutes before removing from pans to wire racks. Wrap and freeze for up to 6 months if desired. **Yield: 3 loaves.**

Garlic Herb Twists

Prep/Total Time: 25 min.

I'm a busy wife, mother and grandmother who also works full time as an accounts payable clerk. So I need quick dinner ideas. These three-ingredient breadsticks are good for church meetings and potlucks or to accompany any dinner entree.

—Peggy Rosamond, Jacksonville, Texas

- 1 tube (8 ounces) refrigerated crescent rolls
- 1/3 cup sour cream
- 1 to 2 tablespoons herb with garlic soup mix

Unroll the crescent dough into one long rectangle; seal seams and perforations. Combine the sour cream and soup mix; spread over the dough. Cut into 1-in. strips. Loosely twist strips and place on an ungreased baking sheet. Bake at 375° for 11-13 minutes or until golden brown. Serve warm. **Yield: 1 dozen.**

Cheddar-Almond Lettuce Salad

Prep/Total Time: 30 min.

Sugared almonds and a honey-mustard dressing make this salad a real standout. In fact, I keep slivered almonds in my freezer just so I can whip it up for those spur-of-the-moment special occasions! I sometimes add broccoli and tomatoes.
— Julia Musser, Lebanon, Pennsylvania

1/2	cup slivered almonds
3	tablespoons sugar
9	cups torn romaine
2	hard-cooked eggs, sliced
1	cup (4 ounces) shredded cheddar cheese

HONEY-MUSTARD DRESSING:

1/4	cup sugar
2	tablespoons white vinegar
2	tablespoons honey
1	tablespoon lemon juice
1/2	teaspoon onion powder
1/2	teaspoon celery seed
1/2	teaspoon ground mustard
1/2	teaspoon paprika
1/4	teaspoon salt
1/2	cup canola oil

In a small heavy skillet, combine almonds and sugar. Cook and stir over medium heat for 5-6 minutes or until nuts are coated and golden. Spread onto foil to cool. Divide romaine among salad plates; top with eggs and cheese.

In a blender, combine the sugar, vinegar, honey, lemon juice, onion powder, celery seed, mustard, paprika and salt. While processing, gradually add oil in a steady stream. Drizzle over salads; sprinkle with almonds. **Yield: 9 servings.**

Herbed Rice

Prep/Total Time: 15 min.

My mom shared this recipe. It requires almost no preparation and makes a delicious addition to just about any main course. Try it with beef bouillon instead of chicken bouillon if that's a better fit with your meal.
— Valerie Meldrum, Taylorsville, Utah

1-1/2	cups water
2	teaspoons chicken bouillon granules
1	teaspoon dried minced onion
1/2	teaspoon dried thyme
1/2	teaspoon dried marjoram
1/4	teaspoon dried rosemary, crushed
1-1/2	cups uncooked instant rice

In a large saucepan, bring water to a boil. Add the bouillon, onion, thyme, marjoram and rosemary; stir until the bouillon is dissolved. Stir in the rice. Cover and remove from the heat; let stand for 5 minutes. Fluff with a fork. **Yield: 3 servings.**

Cheddar-Almond Lettuce Salad

Tempting Tomato Cups

Prep/Total Time: 15 min.

For as long as I can remember, I've eaten this pretty salad in the summer when fresh tomatoes are so wonderful. Brimming with a crunchy filling, it makes a terrific light lunch or can replace a green salad at dinner.

—Carla Browning, Fort Walton Beach, Florida

3	large tomatoes
1/2	cup crushed saltines (about 15 crackers)
1/3	cup chopped celery
1/3	cup chopped green pepper
1/4	cup chopped onion
1/4	cup mayonnaise
1/2	teaspoon garlic salt, optional
1/8	teaspoon pepper

Sliced ripe olives, optional

Cut a thin slice from the top of each tomato. Leaving a 1/4-in.-thick shell, scoop out pulp (discard pulp or save for another use). Invert tomatoes onto paper towels to drain.

In a large bowl, combine the cracker crumbs, celery, green pepper, onion, mayonnaise, garlic salt if desired and pepper; mix well. Spoon into tomatoes. Refrigerate until serving. Garnish with olives if desired. **Yield: 3 servings.**

Nutrition Facts: 1 serving (prepared with low-sodium saltines and fat-free mayonnaise and without garlic salt and olives) equals 129 calories, 284 mg sodium, 0 cholesterol, 25 g carbohydrate, 3 g protein, 2 g fat. Diabetic Exchanges: 1 starch, 1 vegetable, 1/2 fat.

Pull-Apart Bacon Bread

Tempting Tomato Cups

Pull-Apart Bacon Bread

Prep: 20 min. + rising | Bake: 20 min.

I stumbled across this recipe while looking for something different to take to a brunch. Boy, am I glad I did! Everyone asked for the recipe and could not believe it only called for five ingredients. It's the perfect item to bake for an informal get-together.

—Traci Collins, Cheyenne, Wyoming

12	bacon strips, diced
1	loaf (1 pound) frozen bread dough, thawed
2	tablespoons olive oil, *divided*
1	cup (4 ounces) shredded part-skim mozzarella cheese
1	envelope (1 ounce) ranch salad dressing mix

In a skillet, cook bacon over medium heat for 5 minutes or until partially cooked; drain on paper towels. Roll out dough to 1/2-in. thickness; brush with 1 tablespoon of oil. Cut into 1-in. pieces; place in a large bowl. Add the bacon, cheese, dressing mix and remaining oil; toss to coat.

Arrange pieces in a 9-in. x 5-in. oval on a greased baking sheet, layering as needed. Cover and let rise in a warm place for 30 minutes or until doubled.

Bake at 350° for 15 minutes. Cover with foil; bake 5-10 minutes longer or until golden brown. **Yield: 1 loaf.**

Ginger Garlic Linguine

Prep/Total Time: 25 min.

While this recipe's ginger sauce was designed for pasta, it's also good over green beans, pierogies or salmon. I've often tripled the sauce, then froze the extra so I can whip up this dish even faster on busy nights.
—Julie Miske, Acworth, Georgia

- 12 ounces uncooked linguine
- 1/2 cup butter
- 4 green onions, finely chopped
- 2 tablespoons minced fresh gingerroot
- 2 teaspoons minced garlic
- 1 teaspoon dried basil
- 1/4 teaspoon cayenne pepper
- 1/4 cup grated Parmesan cheese

Cook linguine according to package directions. Meanwhile, in a large skillet, saute the onions, ginger, garlic, basil and cayenne in butter for 3-4 minutes or until onions are tender. Drain the linguine; add to skillet and toss to coat. Sprinkle with the Parmesan cheese. **Yield: 6 servings.**

Mexican Bread

Prep: 15 min. | Bake: 3-4 hours

Chopped green chilies and red pepper flakes provide flecks of color in every slice of this loaf. Slightly spicy with ground cumin, it's great for sandwiches or as an accompaniment to mild soups.
—Loni McCoy, Blaine, Minnesota

- 1 cup plus 2 tablespoons water (70° to 80°)
- 1/2 cup shredded Monterey Jack cheese
- 1 can (4 ounces) chopped green chilies
- 1 tablespoon butter, softened
- 2 tablespoons sugar
- 1 to 2 tablespoons crushed red pepper flakes
- 1 tablespoon nonfat dry milk powder
- 1 tablespoon ground cumin
- 1-1/2 teaspoons salt
- 3-1/4 cups bread flour
- 2-1/2 teaspoons active dry yeast

Mexican Bread

Summer Spinach Salad

In a bread machine pan, place all ingredients in order suggested by manufacturer. Select basic bread setting. Choose crust color and loaf size if available.

Bake according to bread machine directions; (check dough after 5 minutes of mixing; add 1 to 2 tablespoons of water or flour if needed). **Yield: 1 loaf (about 2 pounds).**

Editor's Note: We recommend you do not use a bread machine's time-delay feature for this recipe.

 # Summer Spinach Salad

Prep/Total Time: 20 min.

Guests always request the recipe for this fabulous spinach salad. Tossed with ripe banana chunks, fresh strawberries and toasted almonds, it looks and tastes special enough for company. The tangy poppy seed dressing is a snap to combine in the blender.
— Callie Berger, Diamond Springs, California

- 1/2 cup canola oil
- 1/4 cup chopped onion
- 2 tablespoons plus 2 teaspoons red wine vinegar
- 2 tablespoons plus 2 teaspoons sugar
- 1-1/2 teaspoons ground mustard
- 1/2 teaspoon salt
- 1-1/2 teaspoons poppy seeds
- 8 cups torn fresh spinach
- 3 green onions, sliced
- 2 pints fresh strawberries, sliced
- 3 large ripe bananas, cut into 1/2-inch slices
- 1/2 cup slivered almonds, toasted

In a blender, combine the first six ingredients. Cover and process until the sugar is dissolved. Add the poppy seeds; process just until blended.

In a salad bowl, combine the remaining ingredients. Drizzle with dressing; toss to coat. **Yield: 14 servings.**

Buffalo Chicken Lettuce Wraps

Buffalo Chicken Lettuce Wraps

Prep/Total Time: 25 min.

These homemade buffalo chicken wraps work great as an easy lunch or light dinner salad. Honey and lime juice help tone down the hot wing sauce for a refreshing zip. They're perfect with a tall glass of ice-cold lemonade.

—Priscilla Gilbert, Indian Harbour Beach, Florida

1/3	cup crumbled blue cheese
1/4	cup mayonnaise
2	tablespoons milk
4-1/2	teaspoons lemon juice
1	tablespoon minced fresh parsley
1	teaspoon Worcestershire sauce
1	pound boneless skinless chicken breasts, cubed
1	teaspoon salt
1	tablespoon canola oil
1/4	cup lime juice
1/4	cup Louisiana-style hot sauce
1/4	cup honey
1	small cucumber, halved lengthwise, seeded and thinly sliced
1	celery rib, thinly sliced
3/4	cup julienned carrots
8	Bibb *or* Boston lettuce leaves

For dressing, in a small bowl, combine the first six ingredients. Cover and refrigerate until serving.

Sprinkle the chicken with salt. In a large skillet, cook chicken in oil until no longer pink. Combine the lime juice, hot sauce and honey; pour over the chicken. Bring to a boil. Reduce the heat; simmer, uncovered, for 2-3 minutes or until heated through. Remove from the heat; stir in the cucumber, celery and carrots.

Spoon 1/2 cup chicken mixture onto each lettuce leaf; fold sides over filling and secure with a toothpick. Serve with blue cheese dressing. **Yield: 8 servings.**

Cukes and Carrots

Prep: 15 min. + chilling

Carrots and green peppers bring extra color and crunch to this light and tasty cucumber salad. The sweet dressing creates an ideal match for crisp summer produce.

—Karla Hecht, Plymouth, Minnesota

5	medium cucumbers, thinly sliced
4	medium carrots, thinly sliced
1	medium onion, halved and thinly sliced
1	small green pepper, chopped
2	teaspoons canning salt
1-1/2	cups sugar
1/2	cup white vinegar

In a large bowl, combine cucumbers, carrots, onion and green pepper. Sprinkle with salt; toss to coat. Cover and refrigerate for 2 hours. Combine sugar and vinegar. Pour over vegetables; toss to coat. Cover and refrigerate for at least 1 hour. Serve with a slotted spoon. **Yield: 12 servings.**

Lemon Blueberry Muffins

Prep/Total Time: 30 min.

When my sister and I spent the night at our grandmother's house, we often requested these muffins for breakfast. Today, I bake them for my kids. The very aroma is a trip down memory lane.
—Kris Michels, Walled Lake, Michigan

2	cups biscuit/baking mix
1/2	cup plus 2 tablespoons sugar, *divided*
1	egg
1	cup (8 ounces) sour cream
1	cup fresh *or* frozen blueberries
2	teaspoons grated lemon peel

In a large bowl, combine the biscuit mix and 1/2 cup sugar. Whisk together the egg and sour cream; stir into dry ingredients just until moistened. Fold in blueberries.

Fill greased or paper-lined muffin cups half full. Combine lemon peel and remaining sugar; sprinkle over batter. Bake at 400° for 20-25 minutes or until a toothpick comes out clean. Cool for 5 minutes before removing from pan to a wire rack. Serve warm. **Yield: 1 dozen.**

Nutrition Facts: 1 muffin (prepared with reduced-fat baking mix and reduced-fat sour cream) equals 154 calories, 3 g fat (2 g saturated fat), 24 mg cholesterol, 251 mg sodium, 28 g carbohydrate, 1 g fiber, 3 g protein. Diabetic Exchanges: 1 starch, 1 fruit, 1/2 fat.

Editor's Note: If using frozen blueberries, do not thaw before adding to batter.

Lemon Blueberry Muffins

Orient Express Chicken Salad

Orient Express Chicken Salad

Prep: 25 min. + marinating | Grill: 10 min.

This always-popular salad makes use of lots of convenience items, but it's still healthy and nutritious. I created it one Mother's Day and received rave reviews. It's perfect for a fancy lunch and comes together in no time flat! —Sara Dziadosz, Olathe, Kansas

4	boneless skinless chicken breast halves (4 ounces *each*)
1	cup sesame ginger marinade
1/2	cup balsamic vinaigrette
2	tablespoons brown sugar
1	tablespoon reduced-sodium soy sauce
1/2	teaspoon ground ginger
1/4	teaspoon crushed red pepper flakes, optional
1	package (5 ounces) spring mix salad greens
1	cup chow mein noodles
1/2	cup sliced green onions
1/2	cup shredded Parmesan cheese
1/3	cup dried cranberries
1	tablespoon sesame seeds, toasted
1	can (11 ounces) mandarin oranges, drained
1/4	cup slivered almonds, toasted

Place chicken in a large resealable plastic bag; add marinade. Seal bag and turn to coat; refrigerate for at least 30 minutes. For dressing, in a small bowl, whisk the vinaigrette, brown sugar, soy sauce, ginger and red pepper flakes if desired. Cover and refrigerate until serving.

Drain and discard the marinade. Grill the chicken, covered, over indirect medium heat or broil 4 in. from the heat source for 5-6 minutes on each side or until a meat thermometer reads 170°.

In a large bowl, toss the salad greens, noodles, onions, Parmesan cheese, cranberries and sesame seeds. Divide among four plates. Top with oranges and almonds. Cut chicken into diagonal slices; arrange over each salad. Serve with dressing. **Yield: 4 servings.**

Watermelon Tomato Salad

1 pound sliced bacon, cut into 1-inch pieces
1/4 cup butter, cubed
4 slices white bread, crusts removed and cut into 1-inch cubes
1/2 cup mayonnaise
3 to 5 tablespoons minced fresh basil
2 tablespoons red wine vinegar
1/2 teaspoon pepper
1/2 teaspoon minced garlic
6 cups torn romaine
1-1/2 cups grape tomatoes

In a large skillet, cook the bacon over medium heat until crisp. Using a slotted spoon, remove to paper towels; drain, reserving 2 tablespoons of the drippings. Set the bacon and drippings aside.

In another large skillet, melt the butter. Add the bread cubes; cook over medium heat for 4-5 minutes or until golden brown, stirring frequently. Remove to paper towels; cool.

For the dressing, in a small bowl, whisk the mayonnaise, basil, vinegar, pepper, garlic and reserved drippings. In a large bowl, combine the romaine, tomatoes and bacon. Drizzle with the dressing and toss to coat. Top with the croutons. **Yield: 8 servings.**

Watermelon Tomato Salad

Prep/Total Time: 25 min.

Watermelon and tomatoes may seem an unlikely pair, but they team up to make a winning combination in this eye-catching salad dressed with parsley, basil and fresh-squeezed lime. Slice up leftover watermelon for summery snacks.

—Matthew Denton, Seattle, Washington

10 cups cubed seedless watermelon
2 pints yellow grape *or* pear tomatoes
1 medium red onion, chopped
1/2 cup minced fresh parsley
1/2 cup minced fresh basil
1/4 cup lime juice

In a large bowl, combine the watermelon, tomatoes and onion. In a small bowl, combine the parsley, basil and lime juice. Pour over watermelon mixture and toss to coat. Refrigerate until serving. **Yield: 16-18 servings.**

Nutrition Facts: 3/4 cup equals 33 calories, trace fat (trace saturated fat), 0 cholesterol, 7 mg sodium, 10 g carbohydrate, 1 g fiber, 1 g protein. Diabetic Exchange: 1/2 fruit.

BLT Salad

Prep/Total Time: 25 min.

In my family of six, it's hard to find a vegetable or salad that everyone will eat, but they all rave about this one. With garden-fresh basil, this salad is easy, but mouth-watering.

—Susie Clayton, South St. Paul, Minnesota

Au Gratin Garlic Potatoes

Prep: 10 min. | Cook: 6 hours

Cream cheese and a can of condensed cheddar cheese soup turn ordinary sliced potatoes into a rich side dish that is a perfect accompaniment to almost any meal. It may just turn into your own family's favorite potato recipe!

—Tonya Vowels, Vine Grove, Kentucky

1/2 cup milk
1 can (10-3/4 ounces) condensed cheddar cheese soup, undiluted
1 package (8 ounces) cream cheese, cubed
1 garlic clove, minced
1/4 teaspoon ground nutmeg
1/8 teaspoon pepper
2 pounds potatoes, peeled and sliced
1 small onion, chopped
Paprika, optional

In a saucepan, heat the milk over medium heat until bubbles form around the side of the saucepan. Remove from the heat. Add the soup, cream cheese, garlic, nutmeg and pepper; stir until smooth.

Place the sliced potatoes and chopped onion in a 3-qt. slow cooker. Pour the milk mixture over the potato mixture and mix well. Cover and cook on low for 6-7 hours or until the potatoes are tender. Sprinkle potatoes with paprika if desired. **Yield: 6-8 servings.**

Italian Veggie Skillet

Prep/Total Time: 25 min.

Although I'm retired, I like recipes that are fast to prepare. This side dish is ready in no time and incorporates vegetables and herbs from our garden for a refreshing taste.

—Josephine Piro, Easton, Pennsylvania

1	medium yellow summer squash, cut into 1/4-inch slices
1/2	cup sliced fresh mushrooms
1	tablespoon olive oil
1	cup cherry tomatoes, halved
1/2	teaspoon salt
1/2	teaspoon minced garlic
2	tablespoons minced fresh parsley
1-1/2	teaspoons minced fresh rosemary *or* 1/2 teaspoon dried rosemary, crushed
1-1/2	teaspoons minced fresh thyme *or* 1/2 teaspoon dried thyme
1-1/2	teaspoons plus 2 tablespoons minced fresh basil, *divided*
2	tablespoons sliced green onion
2	tablespoons grated Parmesan cheese

In a large skillet, saute squash and mushrooms in oil for 4-5 minutes or until tender. Add the tomatoes, salt and garlic. Reduce heat; simmer, uncovered, for 6-8 minutes.

Stir in the parsley, rosemary, thyme and 1-1/2 teaspoons basil; cook 1-2 minutes longer or until heated through. Transfer to a serving bowl. Sprinkle with onion and remaining basil; lightly toss. Sprinkle with Parmesan cheese. **Yield:** 2-3 servings.

Poppy Seed Biscuit Ring

Prep/Total Time: 30 min.

It takes just a few simple ingredients to dress up refrigerated biscuits and form this pretty ring. My daughter Robin first brought these rolls to a family celebration. Now they're a must at special occasions and family get-togethers.

—Elnora Willhite, Ontario, California

1/3	cup butter, melted
1	teaspoon dried minced onion
1	teaspoon poppy seeds
1/2	teaspoon dried minced garlic
2	tubes (12 ounces *each*) refrigerated buttermilk biscuits

In a shallow bowl, combine the butter, onion, poppy seeds and garlic. Separate each tube of biscuits into 10 biscuits; dip in butter mixture and stand up on end in a lightly greased 10-in. fluted tube pan.

Bake at 400° for 14-16 minutes or until golden brown. Immediately invert onto a serving plate. Serve warm. **Yield:** 10-15 servings.

Italian Veggie Skillet

Salsa Pasta 'n' Beans

Prep/Total Time: 25 min.

This warm side dish is well-seasoned with cumin, cilantro and salsa, so it adds a little zip to dinnertime. For people who like more spice, change the salsa to a medium or hot variety.

—Laura Perry, Chester Springs, Pennsylvania

8	ounces uncooked bow tie pasta
1/2	cup chopped onion
1	medium sweet yellow pepper, chopped
1	tablespoon olive oil
2	teaspoons minced garlic
1	can (16 ounces) red beans, rinsed and drained
3/4	cup vegetable broth
3/4	cup salsa
2	teaspoons ground cumin
1/3	cup minced fresh cilantro

Cook pasta according to package directions. Meanwhile, in a large skillet, saute onion and yellow pepper in oil for 3-4 minutes or until crisp-tender. Add garlic; cook 1-2 minutes longer or until tender.

Stir in the beans, broth, salsa and cumin. Bring to a boil. Reduce heat; simmer, uncovered, for 5-6 minutes or until heated through. Drain pasta; stir into bean mixture. Sprinkle with cilantro. **Yield: 4 servings.**

Creamy Parmesan Spinach

Prep/Total Time: 20 min.

This recipe combines fresh baby spinach with a tasty, creamy Parmesan cheese sauce. Crushed croutons top it off and give the side dish a wonderful crunch.

—Priscilla Gilbert, Indian Harbour Beach, Florida

Creamy Parmesan Spinach

Red, White and Bleu Slaw

2	packages (6 ounces *each*) fresh baby spinach, coarsely chopped
2	tablespoons water
2	teaspoons butter
1/2	cup heavy whipping cream
2	teaspoons grated lemon peel
1/2	teaspoon minced garlic
1/8	teaspoon crushed red pepper flakes
1/2	cup grated Parmesan cheese
2/3	cup onion and garlic salad croutons, crushed

Place the chopped spinach and water in a Dutch oven or large saucepan; cover and cook for 3 minutes or until wilted. Drain and set aside.

In the same pan, melt butter. Stir in the cream, lemon peel, garlic and pepper flakes; bring to a gentle boil. Reduce heat; simmer, uncovered, for 5 minutes or until slightly reduced. Stir in the Parmesan cheese and spinach; heat through. Sprinkle with croutons. **Yield: 3 servings.**

Red, White and Bleu Slaw

Prep/Total Time: 10 min.

One of my all-time favorite recipes is this refreshing salad perfect for Fourth of July celebrations—or any time at all. The blend of flavors is wonderful. I use this recipe as often as I can...it's simply the best! —*Bonnie Hawkins, Elkhorn, Wisconsin*

6	cups angel hair coleslaw
12	cherry tomatoes, halved
3/4	cup coleslaw salad dressing
3/4	cup crumbled blue cheese, *divided*
1/2	cup real bacon bits

In a large bowl, combine the coleslaw, tomatoes, salad dressing and 1/2 cup blue cheese. Cover and refrigerate until serving. Just before serving, sprinkle with bacon bits and remaining cheese. **Yield: 6 servings.**

Skillet Sausage Stuffing

Prep/Total Time: 25 min.

I dressed up a package of stuffing mix with pork sausage, mushrooms, celery and onion to make this filling. It impressed my in-laws at a family gathering and has since become a popular side dish with my husband and children.

—Jennifer Lynn Cullen, Taylor, Michigan

1	pound bulk pork sausage
1-1/4	cups chopped celery
1/2	cup chopped onion
1/2	cup sliced fresh mushrooms
1-1/2	teaspoons minced garlic
1-1/2	cups reduced-sodium chicken broth
1	teaspoon rubbed sage
1	package (6 ounces) stuffing mix

In a large skillet, cook the sausage, celery, onion, mushrooms and garlic over medium heat until meat is no longer pink; drain. Stir in broth and sage. Bring to a boil. Stir in stuffing mix. Cover and remove from the heat; let stand for 5 minutes. Fluff with a fork. **Yield: 8 servings.**

Dilly Veggie Pasta Salad

Prep/Total Time: 30 min.

My sister shared the recipe for this fresh, crunchy salad seasoned with dill. It's handy because you can assemble and eat it right away...or cover and refrigerate it to take to a picnic or potluck the next day. The longer it chills, the more tangy it is.

—Anna Emory Royal, Murfreesboro, Tennessee

2-3/4	cups uncooked medium shell pasta
1	cup halved cherry tomatoes
1	cup sliced green pepper
1	cup (4 ounces) shredded cheddar cheese
1/2	cup chopped green onions
1/2	cup sliced ripe olives

DRESSING:

1/4	cup olive oil
2	tablespoons lemon juice
2	tablespoons white wine vinegar
1	teaspoon dill weed
1	teaspoon dried oregano
1	teaspoon salt
1/8	teaspoon pepper

A Little Extra Dressing

If you like, double or triple the dressing recipe above and store the extra in a glass jar with a tight-fitting lid. It will keep in the refrigerator for up to 2 weeks.

Cook pasta according to package directions; drain and rinse in cold water. Place in a large bowl. Add tomatoes, green pepper, cheese, onions and olives.

In a small bowl, whisk together the dressing ingredients. Pour over salad and toss to coat. Cover and refrigerate until serving. **Yield: 8 servings.**

Paradise Buns

Prep: 20 min. + rising | Bake: 15 min.

I think frozen bread dough should be called magic dough because there is so much you can do with it. These flavorful knots are delicious with soup or salad.

—Liz Lazenby, Victoria, British Columbia

1	loaf (1 pound) frozen bread dough, thawed
1	cup (4 ounces) shredded cheddar cheese
1/4	cup *each* diced mushrooms, broccoli and sweet red and yellow pepper
1	tablespoon chopped green onion
1	garlic clove, minced
1/2	teaspoon garlic powder

Divide bread dough into eight pieces. In a shallow bowl, combine the cheese, vegetables, garlic and garlic powder. Roll each piece of dough into an 8-in. rope. Roll in cheese mixture, pressing mixture into dough. Tie into a knot and press vegetables into dough; tuck ends under.

Place 2 in. apart on greased baking sheets. Cover and let rise until doubled about 30 minutes. Bake at 375° for 15-20 minutes or until golden brown. **Yield: 8 servings.**

Nutrition Facts: 1 bun (prepared with reduced fat cheddar cheese) equals 198 calories, 5 g fat (2 g saturated fat), 8 mg cholesterol, 403 mg sodium, 31 g carbohydrate, 2 g fiber, 10 g protein. Diabetic Exchanges: 2 starch, 1 fat.

Paradise Buns

Pecan Spinach Salad

Pecan Spinach Salad

Prep/Total Time: 10 min.

My family thinks this refreshing salad is sensational. Coated with a pleasant vinaigrette dressing and topped with toasted pecans and blue cheese, it has an impressive look and taste. Though it can be prepared in 10 minutes or less, don't tell my family because they'd never believe it!

—Karen Robinson, Calgary, Alberta

3	cups fresh baby spinach
1/2	cup chopped pecans, toasted
1/3	cup real bacon bits
1/4	cup crumbled blue cheese

DRESSING:

1/3	cup olive oil
2	tablespoons cider vinegar
2	teaspoons brown sugar
1/2	teaspoon dried thyme
1/2	teaspoon minced garlic
1/4	teaspoon salt

In a large salad bowl, combine the fresh spinach, toasted pecans, bacon bits and crumbled blue cheese. In a jar with a tight-fitting lid, combine the dressing ingredients; shake well. Drizzle over the salad; toss to coat. **Yield: 4 servings.**

Cheddar Sausage Muffins

Prep: 20 min. Bake: 20 min.

Handy biscuit mix and cheese soup hurry along these hearty muffins. The golden muffins are great at breakfast, brunch or a soup lunch. They even make fun treats after school.

—Melissa Vannoy, Childress, Texas

1	pound bulk pork sausage
1	can (10-3/4 ounces) condensed cheddar cheese soup, undiluted
1	cup (4 ounces) shredded cheddar cheese
2/3	cup water
3	cups biscuit/baking mix

In a skillet over medium heat, cook sausage until no longer pink; drain. In a bowl, combine soup, cheese and water. Stir in biscuit mix until blended. Add sausage. Fill greased muffin cups three-fourths full.

Bake at 350° for 20-25 minutes or until a toothpick inserted near the center comes out clean. Cool for 5 minutes before removing from pans to wire racks. Serve warm. **Yield: about 1-1/2 dozen.**

Spanish Rice

Prep/Total Time: 15 min.

Instant rice and convenient canned goods simplify the stovetop preparation of this tangy side dish. Its traditional taste makes it a perfect accompaniment to any Mexican-style entree. I like to make extras for lunch the next day.

—*Flo Burtnett, Gage, Oklahoma*

1	cup chopped onion
1/2	cup chopped green pepper
1	tablespoon canola oil
1	cup uncooked instant rice
1	can (14-1/2 ounces) stewed tomatoes
3/4	cup tomato juice
1/2	teaspoon prepared mustard

In a large skillet, saute onion and green pepper in oil until tender. Stir in the remaining ingredients. Bring to a boil; reduce heat. Simmer, uncovered, for 5 minutes or until rice is tender and liquid is absorbed. **Yield: 6 servings.**

Mandarin-Cashew Tossed Salad

Prep/Total Time: 20 min.

Mandarin oranges and chopped red onion add a touch of color to mixed greens and sweet roasted cashews in this special salad. You're sure to be handing out the recipe once friends and family get a taste of the tangy honey dressing.

—*Sheri Shaffer, Northfield, Ohio*

5	cups torn red leaf lettuce
5	cups torn iceberg lettuce
3	cups torn Boston lettuce
2	cans (11 ounces *each*) mandarin oranges, well drained
3/4	cup chopped green pepper
1	celery rib, thinly sliced
1/4	cup chopped red onion

HONEY LIME DRESSING:

1/4	cup canola oil
1/4	cup honey
1/2	teaspoon ground mustard
1/2	teaspoon grated lime peel
1/4	teaspoon paprika
1/8	teaspoon salt

Dash white pepper

1	cup honey roasted cashews

In a large salad bowl, combine the lettuces, oranges, green pepper, celery and onion.

In a small bowl, combine oil, honey, mustard, lime peel, paprika, salt and pepper. Drizzle over salad. Add cashews; toss to coat. **Yield: 10-12 servings.**

Savory Italian Rounds

Prep/Total Time: 30 min.

A friend gave me the recipe for these cheesy golden rounds years ago. Her dad used to make them for her when she was little. Because they're a snap to put together, I frequently fix them for my family during the week and for company on the weekends.

—*Donna Ebert, Richfield, Wisconsin*

2/3	cup grated Parmesan cheese
1/2	cup mayonnaise
1/4	teaspoon dried basil
1/8	teaspoon garlic powder
1/8	teaspoon garlic salt
1/8	teaspoon dried oregano

Dash onion salt

1	tube (12 ounces) refrigerated buttermilk biscuits

In a small bowl, combine the first seven ingredients. Separate biscuits and place on two ungreased baking sheets. Let stand for 5 minutes.

Flatten the biscuits into 4-in. circles. Spread about 1 tablespoon of the mayonnaise mixture over each circle to within 1/2 in. of edge.

Bake at 400° for 10-13 minutes or until golden brown. Serve warm. **Yield: 10 servings.**

Editor's Note: Reduced-fat or fat-free mayonnaise is not recommended for this recipe.

Savory Italian Rounds

Southwestern Spuds

Prep/Total Time: 30 min.

I came up with this attractive side dish when my best friend unexpectedly stayed for dinner. While my husband grilled pork chops, I perked up potatoes with tasty taco fixings. The results received rave reviews. This recipe is even quicker to fix with leftover baked potatoes. —Penny Dykstra, Porterville, California

3	medium potatoes

Salt and pepper to taste

1	cup (4 ounces) shredded cheddar cheese
1	cup (4 ounces) shredded pepper Jack cheese
3	green onions, chopped
1	can (2-1/4 ounces) sliced ripe olives, drained

Sour cream and salsa, optional

Pierce potatoes; place on a microwave-safe plate. Microwave on high for 6-8 minutes or until almost tender. Cool slightly; peel and cut into 1/8-in. slices.

Arrange half of the potatoes in a greased microwave-safe 9-in. pie plate. Season with salt and pepper. Sprinkle with half of the cheeses. Repeat layers. Top with onions and olives.

Microwave, uncovered, for 7-8 minutes or until cheese is melted and potatoes are tender. Serve with sour cream and salsa if desired. **Yield: 4-6 servings.**

Editor's Note: This recipe was tested in a 1,100-watt microwave.

Vegetable Macaroni Salad

Prep/Total Time: 20 min.

This salad is so easy, versatile and tasty. The combination of pasta with seasonings, mayonnaise and vegetables is always a big success. The celery and radishes add a wonderfully crunchy texture. Even the leftovers taste great the next day! —Mary Kay Dillingham, Overland Park, Kansas

1	cup uncooked elbow macaroni
1/2	cup mayonnaise
1/4	cup sliced celery
1/4	cup chopped pitted green olives
1/4	cup sliced green onions
1/4	cup shredded cheddar cheese
2	tablespoons sliced radishes
1	tablespoon minced fresh parsley
1	tablespoon white vinegar
1	teaspoon prepared mustard
1/4	to 1/2 teaspoon salt
1/4	teaspoon celery seed

Dash pepper

Cook the macaroni according to package directions. Meanwhile, in a large bowl, combine the remaining ingredients. Drain macaroni and rinse in cold water. Add macaroni to mayonnaise mixture; toss to coat. Chill until serving. **Yield: 4 servings.**

Southwestern Spuds

Honey Wheat Breadsticks

Raspberry Cream Muffins

Prep: 15 min. | Bake: 25 min.

It took me a couple of batches to perfect these muffins but my family thinks this version is the best! Gently stir the raspberries into the batter, so they don't break apart.
—*Stephanie Moon-Martin, Silverdale, Washington*

1	cup fresh raspberries
3/4	cup plus 2 tablespoons sugar, *divided*
1/4	cup butter, softened
1	egg
1/2	teaspoon almond extract
1/2	teaspoon vanilla extract
2-1/4	cups all-purpose flour
3	teaspoons baking powder
1/2	teaspoon salt
1	cup half-and-half cream
1	cup finely chopped vanilla *or* white chips
2	tablespoons brown sugar

In a small bowl, toss the raspberries with 1/4 cup sugar; set aside. In a large bowl, cream the butter and 1/2 cup sugar until light and fluffy. Beat in egg and extracts. Combine the flour, baking powder and salt; add to creamed mixture alternately with cream, just until moistened. Stir in chips and reserved raspberries.

Fill greased or paper-lined muffin cups three-fourths full. Combine brown sugar and remaining sugar; sprinkle over batter. Bake at 375° for 25-30 minutes or until a toothpick comes out clean. Cool for 5 minutes before removing from pan to a wire rack. Serve warm. **Yield: 1 dozen.**

Honey Wheat Breadsticks

Prep: 30 min. + rising | Bake: 10 min.

Not only are these breadsticks delicious, but they come together very easily. Whole wheat flour and a little honey help give them a wholesome taste and keep them on the healthy side.
—*Ted Van Schoick, Jersey Shore, Pennsylvania*

1-1/3	cups water (70° to 80°)
3	tablespoons honey
2	tablespoons canola oil
1-1/2	teaspoons salt
2	cups bread flour
2	cups whole wheat flour
3	teaspoons active dry yeast

In bread machine pan, place all ingredients in order suggested by manufacturer. Select dough setting (check dough after 5 minutes of mixing; add 1 to 2 tablespoons of water or flour if needed).

When cycle is completed, turn the dough onto a lightly floured surface. Divide into 16 portions; shape each into a ball. Roll each ball into an 8-in. rope. Place 2 in. apart on greased baking sheets.

Cover and let rise in a warm place until doubled, about 30 minutes. Bake at 375° for 10-12 minutes or until golden brown. Remove to wire racks. **Yield: 16 breadsticks.**

Nutrition Facts: 1 breadstick equals 131 calories, 2 g fat (trace saturated fat), 0 cholesterol, 222 mg sodium, 25 g carbohydrate, 2 g fiber, 4 g protein. Diabetic Exchange: 1-1/2 starch.

Editor's Note: We recommend you do not use a bread machine's time-delay feature for this recipe.

Raspberry Cream Muffins

Colorful Corn 'n' Bean Salad

Colorful Corn 'n' Bean Salad

Prep/Total Time: 15 min.

This quick recipe couldn't be easier...the liquid from the corn relish makes the fuss-free dressing! And because there's no mayo, it's a perfect salad to bring along on summer outings.

—TerryAnn Moore, Haddon Township, New Jersey

1	can (15 ounces) black beans, rinsed and drained
1	jar (13 ounces) corn relish
1/2	cup canned kidney beans, rinsed and drained
1/2	cup quartered cherry tomatoes
1/2	cup chopped celery
1/4	cup chopped sweet orange pepper
1/4	cup sliced pimiento-stuffed olives
2	teaspoons minced fresh parsley

In a large bowl, combine all ingredients. Cover and refrigerate until serving. **Yield: 12 servings.**

Nutrition Facts: 1/2 cup equals 80 calories, 1 g fat (trace saturated fat), 0 cholesterol, 217 mg sodium, 16 g carbohydrate, 2 g fiber, 2 g protein. Diabetic Exchange: 1 starch.

Pull-Apart Caramel Coffee Cake

Prep: 10 min. | Bake: 25 min.

The first time I made this delightful breakfast treat for a brunch party, it was a huge hit. Now I get requests every time family or friends do anything around the breakfast hour! I always keep the four simple ingredients on hand.

—Jaime Keeling, Keizer, Oregon

2	tubes (12 ounces *each*) refrigerated flaky buttermilk biscuits
1	cup packed brown sugar
1/2	cup heavy whipping cream
1	teaspoon ground cinnamon

Cut each biscuit into four pieces; arrange evenly in a 10-in. fluted tube pan coated with cooking spray. Combine the brown sugar, cream and cinnamon; pour over biscuits.

Bake at 350° for 25-30 minutes or until golden brown. Cool for 5 minutes before inverting onto a serving platter. **Yield: 12 servings.**

Bacon Mashed Potatoes

Prep/Total Time: 25 min.

Featuring cheddar cheese, bacon and chives, these rich and hearty potatoes go well with anything. For a slightly different twist, add some chopped parsley.

—Pat Mathison, Meadowlands, Minnesota

2-1/2	cups cubed peeled potatoes (3/4 pound)
1/4	cup milk
1/4	cup mayonnaise
4-1/2	teaspoons minced chives
1/8	teaspoon garlic powder
1/8	teaspoon pepper
1/2	cup shredded cheddar cheese
3	bacon strips, cooked and crumbled

Place potatoes in a large saucepan and cover with water. Bring to a boil. Reduce heat; cover and cook for 15-20 minutes or until tender. Drain.

Transfer to a large bowl. Add the milk, mayonnaise, chives, garlic powder and pepper; mash potatoes. Stir in cheese and bacon. **Yield: 3 servings.**

Bacon Mashed Potatoes

Multigrain Bread

Prep: 10 min. | Bake: 3-4 hours

Cornmeal and wheat germ give this bread a wonderful texture and nutty flavor. —Michele MacKinlay, Madoc, Ontario

1	cup water (70° to 80°)
2	tablespoons canola oil
2	egg yolks
1/4	cup molasses
1	teaspoon salt
1-1/2	cups bread flour
1	cup whole wheat flour
1/2	cup rye flour
1/2	cup nonfat dry milk powder
1/4	cup quick-cooking oats
1/4	cup toasted wheat germ
1/4	cup cornmeal
2-1/4	teaspoons active dry yeast

In bread machine pan, place all ingredients in order suggested by manufacturer. Select basic bread setting. Choose crust color and loaf size if available.

Bake according to bread machine directions (check dough after 5 minutes of mixing; add 1 to 2 tablespoons water or flour if needed). **Yield: 1 loaf (2 pounds).**

Editor's Note: We recommend you do not use a bread machine's time-delay feature for this recipe.

Ranch Beans

Prep: 10 min. | Cook: 3 hours

This sweet and tangy side dish uses convenient canned goods, so it's a snap to throw together. It's nice to serve at a group picnic. —Barbara Gordon, Roswell, Georgia

1	can (16 ounces) kidney beans, rinsed and drained
1	can (15-3/4 ounces) pork and beans, undrained
1	can (15 ounces) lima beans, rinsed and drained
1	can (14-1/2 ounces) cut green beans, drained
1	bottle (12 ounces) chili sauce
3/4	cup packed brown sugar
1	small onion, chopped

In a 3-qt. slow cooker, combine all ingredients. Cover and cook on high for 3-4 hours or until heated through. **Yield: 8-10 servings.**

Slow Cooker Wisdom

When preparing the Ranch Beans, be sure to choose the correct size slow cooker. Your slow cooker should be from half to three-quarters full. And refrain from lifting the lid while the beans are cooking, because loss of steam can add 15 to 30 minutes of cooking each time you lift the lid!

Apple Streusel Muffins

Prep: 20 min. | Bake: 15 min.

I was looking for something warm to make for my daughter before school on a rainy morning. So I jazzed up a boxed muffin mix with a chopped apple, walnuts, brown sugar and a fast-to-fix vanilla glaze. The tasty results really hit the spot.

—Elizabeth Calabrese, Yucaipa, California

1	package (6-1/2 ounces) apple cinnamon muffin mix
1	large tart apple, peeled and diced
1/3	cup chopped walnuts
3	tablespoons brown sugar
4-1/2	teaspoons all-purpose flour
1	tablespoon butter, melted

GLAZE:

3/4	cup confectioners' sugar
1/2	teaspoon vanilla extract
1	to 2 tablespoons milk

Prepare muffin mix according to package directions; fold in apple. Fill greased muffin cups three-fourths full. In a small bowl, combine the walnuts, brown sugar, flour and butter; sprinkle over batter.

Bake at 400° for 15-20 minutes or until a toothpick comes out clean. Cool for 5 minutes before removing from pan to a wire rack. Combine the glaze ingredients; drizzle over warm muffins. **Yield: 6 muffins.**

Swiss Tossed Salad

Apple Streusel Muffins

Swiss Tossed Salad

Prep/Total Time: 30 min.

This simple, green salad requires just a few ingredients, yet its blend of flavors and combination of textures make it seem special. You can toss all the ingredients with the basic dressing or dollop it over individual servings.

—Sherian Peterson, High Ridge, Missouri

12	bacon strips, diced
1	bunch red leaf lettuce, torn (about 10 cups)
1	small red onion, julienned
1	block (8 ounces) Swiss cheese, cubed
1/4	cup sliced ripe olives
1/3	cup mayonnaise
1/3	cup sour cream

In a skillet over medium heat, cook bacon until crisp. Remove to paper towels to drain. In a large bowl, combine lettuce, onion, cheese, olives and bacon. In a small bowl, combine mayonnaise and sour cream. Serve with the salad. **Yield: 8-10 servings.**

Crisp Lettuce Greens

For crisp lettuce, wash greens in cold water and drain. Use a "salad spinner" or pat dry with paper towels. Store in a resealable plastic bag or airtight container with a paper towel in the bottom to absorb moisture. (Be certain to replace the towel if it gets wet.)

Creamy Vegetable Casserole

Prep: 15 min. | Bake: 25 min.

Searching for a different way to prepare vegetables? Look no further. I have a fussy eater in my house who absolutely loves this medley. It can be assembled in a snap, leaving time to fix the main course, set the table or just sit back and relax.

—Tami Kratzer, West Jordan, Utah

- 1 package (16 ounces) frozen broccoli, carrots and cauliflower
- 1 can (10-3/4 ounces) condensed cream of mushroom soup, undiluted
- 1 carton (8 ounces) spreadable garden vegetable cream cheese
- 1/2 to 1 cup seasoned croutons

Prepare the vegetables according to package directions; drain and place in a large bowl. Stir in soup and cream cheese. Transfer to a greased 1-qt. baking dish. Sprinkle with croutons. Bake, uncovered, at 375° for 25 minutes or until bubbly. **Yield: 6 servings.**

Blue Cheese Green Beans

Prep/Total Time: 20 min.

Bacon, blue cheese and chopped nuts make this my mom's favorite way to enjoy green beans. I always prepare this side dish when she's coming for dinner.

—Kate Hilts, Grand Rapids, Michigan

- 6 bacon strips, diced
- 1 pound fresh green beans, cut into 2-inch pieces
- 1/2 cup crumbled blue cheese
- 1/3 cup chopped pecans

Pepper to taste

In a large skillet, cook bacon over medium heat until crisp. Using a slotted spoon, remove to paper towels. Drain, reserving 2 tablespoons drippings.

In the bacon drippings, cook and stir the beans for 8-10 minutes or until crisp-tender. Add the blue cheese, pecans, pepper and bacon. Cook for 2 minutes or until heated through. **Yield: 6 servings.**

Creamy Vegetable Casserole

Au Gratin Potatoes

Au Gratin Potatoes

Prep: 15 min. | Bake: 30 min.

This is one of my favorite ways to fix potatoes. Slices are coated with a cheesy sauce and topped with golden crumbs. We often serve it with baked ham on New Year's Day.

—Lois Gelzer, Oak Bluffs, Massachusetts

2	cups Basic White Sauce (see recipe at right)
1-1/4	cups shredded cheddar cheese
1-1/2	teaspoons salt
1/4	teaspoon pepper
6	medium potatoes, peeled, cooked and cut into 1/4-inch slices
1/2	cup soft bread crumbs
2	tablespoons butter, melted

In a saucepan, prepare a double recipe of the white sauce. Stir in cheese, salt and pepper; cook and stir until cheese is melted. Gently stir in the potatoes until coated.

Transfer to a greased 2-qt. baking dish. Toss bread crumbs and butter; sprinkle over potatoes. Cover and bake at 350° for 20 minutes. Uncover; bake 10 minutes longer or until crumb topping is golden brown. **Yield: 8 servings.**

Basic White Sauce

Prep/Total Time: 10 min.

For years, I have used this smooth sauce to make many dishes. The recipe can easily be doubled.

—Lois Gelzer, Oak Bluffs, Massachusetts

2	tablespoons butter
2	tablespoons all-purpose flour
1/8	teaspoon salt
Dash white pepper	
1	cup milk

In a saucepan, melt butter over medium heat. Whisk in the flour, salt and pepper until smooth. Gradually whisk in the milk. Bring to a boil; cook and stir for 2 minutes or until thickened. Use immediately or refrigerate. **Yield: 1 cup.**

White Pepper Primer

Although white pepper comes from the same plant as black pepper, it's lighter in color and milder in flavor than black pepper. It's still spicy, so use sparingly.

Crunchy Romaine Strawberry Salad

Prep/Total Time: 30 min.

This impressive salad has been a hit at every get-together we've ever brought it to. In addition to being pretty and colorful, it's a snap to make. And the mouth-watering combination of tastes and textures seems to please every palate.

—Leslie Lancaster, Zachary, Louisiana

1	package (3 ounces) ramen noodles
1	cup chopped walnuts
1/4	cup butter
1/4	cup canola oil
1/4	cup sugar
2	tablespoons red wine vinegar
1/2	teaspoon soy sauce
8	cups torn romaine
1/2	cup chopped green onions
2	cups fresh strawberries, sliced

Discard seasoning packet from ramen noodles or save for another use. Break noodles into small pieces. In a small skillet, saute noodles and walnuts in butter for 8-10 minutes or until golden; cool.

For dressing, in a jar with a tight-fitting lid, combine the oil, sugar, vinegar and soy sauce; shake well. Just before serving, combine the romaine, onions, strawberries and noodle mixture in a large bowl. Drizzle with dressing and toss gently. **Yield: 12 servings.**

Crunchy Romaine Strawberry Salad

Bacon-Wrapped Green Beans

Bacon-Wrapped Green Beans

Prep/Total Time: 30 min.

Fresh green beans are wrapped in bacon and covered in a sweet sauce in this fast and simple side dish. Every time I take these green bean bundles to a luncheon or family dinner, people always beg me for the recipe. —Julie Hewitt, Union Mills, Indiana

3/4	pound fresh green beans
4	bacon strips
3	tablespoons butter, melted
1/4	cup packed brown sugar
1/4	teaspoon garlic salt
1/8	teaspoon soy sauce

Place beans in a large saucepan and cover with water. Bring to a boil. Cook, uncovered, for 8 minutes or until crisp-tender. Meanwhile, in a skillet, cook bacon over medium heat until cooked but not crisp, about 3 minutes. Remove to paper towels.

Drain beans; place about 12 beans on each bacon strip. Wrap bacon around beans and secure with a toothpick. Place on an ungreased baking sheet.

In a small bowl, combine the melted butter, brown sugar, garlic salt and soy sauce; brush over the green bean bundles. Bake at 400° for 10-15 minutes or until the bacon is crisp. **Yield: 4 servings.**

Garden-Fresh Green Beans

When purchasing fresh green beans, choose ones with slender green pods that are free of bruises or brown spots. Store unwashed fresh green beans in a resealable plastic bag for up to 4 days. Wash just before using, removing strings and ends if necessary.

stovetop
suppers

The secret to success in the kitchen is often convenience, especially when folks have very little time on their hands. That's why busy cooks are sure to appreciate the supper sensations in this chapter.

Stirring up speedy fare on the stovetop is one of the easiest ways to put dinner on the table pronto. Just pull out a skillet to whip up delicious, family-pleasing meals like Ginger Beef Stir-Fry, Chicken with Spicy Fruit or Au Gratin Sausage Skillet. Before you know it, you'll have dinner in hand!

Flank Steak Pinwheels
(recipe on p. 132)

Pork Kiev

Prep/Total Time: 25 min.

This dish provides the same great flavors of traditional chicken Kiev, but in a lot less time. This recipe is so easy and always a big hit. And it tastes terrific!

—Jeanne Barney, Saratoga Springs, New York

- 4 teaspoons butter, softened
- 2 teaspoons minced chives
- 2 teaspoons dried parsley flakes
- 1 teaspoon minced garlic
- 1/2 teaspoon pepper
- 4 boneless pork loin chops (4 ounces *each*)
- 1 egg
- 1 teaspoon water
- 1/2 cup all-purpose flour
- 1/2 cup dry bread crumbs
- 2 tablespoons canola oil

In a small bowl, combine the butter, chives, parsley, garlic and pepper. Cut a pocket in each pork chop. Fill with butter mixture; secure with toothpicks.

In a shallow bowl, beat egg and water. Place flour and bread crumbs in separate shallow bowls. Dip chops in flour, then in egg mixture; coat with bread crumbs.

In a large skillet over medium heat, cook the chops in oil for 6-8 minutes on each side or until meat juices run clear. **Yield:** 4 servings.

Pork Kiev

Simmered Swiss Steak

Prep: 20 min. | Cook: 1 hour

My husband and I are beef lovers, and we truly enjoy the flavor of this round steak. It's simple to make, but it tastes like it took several hours. —Cindy Stewart, Deshler, Ohio

- 1/4 cup mashed potato flakes
- 1-1/4 teaspoons garlic powder, *divided*
- 1/4 teaspoon onion powder
- 1/4 teaspoon pepper
- 1 pound boneless beef round steak
- 2 tablespoons canola oil
- 1 cup chopped onion
- 1 can (14-1/2 ounces) diced tomatoes, undrained
- 1/2 cup beef broth

In a small bowl, combine the potato flakes, 1/4 teaspoon garlic powder, onion powder and pepper; sprinkle over steak. Pound with a mallet to tenderize. In a large skillet over medium heat, brown steak in oil on both sides. Remove and set aside. In the same skillet, saute onion and remaining garlic powder until onion is tender. Return steak to the pan; add tomatoes and broth. Cover and simmer for 1 hour or until meat is tender. **Yield:** 4 servings.

Crunchy Cashew Pork

Prep/Total Time: 30 min.

I enjoy the crunchiness of the cashews and fresh veggies in this colorful medley. Besides being quick to fix, it's pretty enough to serve company. —Myra Innes, Auburn, Kansas

- 2 teaspoons cornstarch
- 1/2 cup chicken broth
- 1/4 cup red wine vinegar
- 2 tablespoons soy sauce
- 2 teaspoons plus 2 tablespoons canola oil, *divided*
- 3/4 pound boneless pork, cut into thin strips
- 1 cup thinly sliced carrots
- 1 cup fresh broccoli florets
- 3 green onions, thinly sliced
- 1/2 cup cashews

Hot cooked rice

In a small bowl, combine the cornstarch, broth, vinegar, soy sauce and 2 teaspoons oil until smooth; set aside.

In a large skillet or wok, stir-fry pork in 1 tablespoon oil until meat is no longer pink; remove and keep warm.

Heat remaining oil; stir-fry carrots and broccoli until crisp-tender. Stir broth mixture; stir into skillet along with the green onions. Bring to a boil; cook and stir for 2 minutes or until thickened. Return meat to pan and heat through. Stir in cashews. Serve with rice. **Yield:** 4 servings.

Pepper Jack Chicken Pasta

Ginger Beef Stir-Fry

Prep/Total Time: 30 min.

This quick stir-fry is so colorful and tasty. Vary the recipe by substituting chicken or other vegetables you have on hand. For extra ease, I pick up prepared veggies from our grocery store's salad bar. —Linda Murray, Allenstown, New Hampshire

I	teaspoon cornstarch
1/4	cup cold water
1/4	cup plum sauce
I	tablespoon grated fresh gingerroot
I	tablespoon soy sauce
1/4	teaspoon crushed red pepper flakes
I	pound boneless beef sirloin steak, cut into thin 2-inch strips
I	to 2 tablespoons canola oil
I	medium sweet red pepper, julienned
1-1/2	cups fresh broccoli florets
2	medium carrots, thinly sliced
4	green onions, chopped
I	teaspoon minced garlic
3	tablespoons salted peanuts, chopped

Hot cooked rice, optional

2	tablespoons sesame seeds, toasted

In a small bowl, whisk cornstarch and cold water until smooth. Stir in the plum sauce, ginger, soy sauce and pepper flakes; set aside. In a large skillet or wok, stir-fry beef in oil until no longer pink; remove and keep warm.

In the same pan, stir-fry the red pepper, broccoli, carrots, onions and garlic until tender. Return beef to the pan. Whisk the plum sauce mixture; stir into skillet. Cook and stir until slightly thickened. Stir in peanuts. Serve with rice if desired. Sprinkle with sesame seeds. **Yield: 4 servings.**

Pepper Jack Chicken Pasta

Prep/Total Time: 25 min.

My wife, Jennie, is a wonderful cook who's generally skeptical about my kitchen experiments. But she likes this recipe well enough to give me temporary kitchen privileges...and even encouraged me to enter a contest! If you can't find the soup called for here, nacho or cheese soup can be used.
—Mike Kirschbaum, Cary, North Carolina

3	cups uncooked mostaccioli
1/4	cup chopped onion
1/4	cup chopped sweet red pepper
1/2	teaspoon minced garlic
I	tablespoon canola oil
I	can (10-3/4 ounces) condensed Southwest style pepper Jack soup, undiluted
I	package (9 ounces) ready-to-use Southwestern chicken strips
3/4	cup water
I	can (15 ounces) black beans, rinsed and drained
1/4	cup shredded Monterey Jack cheese, optional

Cook mostaccioli according to package directions. Meanwhile, in a large skillet, saute the onion, red pepper and garlic in oil until tender. Stir in the soup, ready-to-use chicken and water. Bring to a boil. Reduce the heat; cover and simmer for 8 minutes.

Stir in beans; heat through. Drain mostaccioli; transfer to a serving bowl. Top with chicken mixture. Sprinkle with cheese if desired. **Yield: 6 servings.**

Ginger Beef Stir-Fry

Smothered Chicken Breasts

Smothered Chicken Breasts

Prep/Total Time: 30 min.

After trying this delicious chicken dish in a restaurant, I decided to recreate it at home. Topped with bacon, caramelized onions and zippy shredded cheese, it comes together in no time with ingredients I usually have on hand. Plus, it cooks in one skillet, so it's a cinch to clean up!

—Brenda Carpenter, Warrensburg, Missouri

4	boneless skinless chicken breast halves (6 ounces *each*)
1/4	teaspoon salt
1/4	teaspoon lemon-pepper seasoning
1	tablespoon canola oil
8	bacon strips
1	medium onion, sliced
1/4	cup packed brown sugar
1/2	cup shredded Colby-Monterey Jack cheese

Sprinkle the chicken with salt and lemon-pepper seasoning. In a large skillet, cook chicken in oil for 6-7 minutes on each side or until a meat thermometer reads 170°; remove and keep warm.

In the same skillet, cook bacon over medium heat until crisp. Using a slotted spoon, remove to paper towels; drain, reserving 2 tablespoons drippings.

In the drippings, saute onion and brown sugar until onion is tender and golden brown. Place two bacon strips on each chicken breast half; top with caramelized onions and cheese. **Yield: 4 servings.**

Saucy Skillet Lasagna

Prep/Total Time: 30 min.

Thanks to no-cook lasagna noodles, this dish makes a fresh, filling, flavorful and fast entree for any Italian meal. All you need to round out the dinner is warm bread and a tossed green salad.

—Meghan Crihfield, Ripley, West Virginia

1	pound ground beef
1	can (14-1/2 ounces) diced tomatoes, undrained
2	eggs, lightly beaten
1-1/2	cups ricotta cheese
4	cups Italian baking sauce
1	package (9 ounces) no-cook lasagna noodles
1	cup (4 ounces) shredded part-skim mozzarella cheese, optional

In a large skillet, cook beef over medium heat until no longer pink; drain. Transfer to a large bowl; stir in tomatoes. In a small bowl, combine eggs and ricotta cheese.

Return 1 cup meat mixture to the skillet; spread evenly. Layer with 1 cup ricotta mixture, 1-1/2 cups sauce and half of the noodles. Repeat layers. Top with remaining sauce.

Bring to a boil. Reduce heat; cover and simmer for 15-17 minutes or until noodles are tender. Remove from the heat. Sprinkle with mozzarella cheese if desired; let stand for 2 minutes or until cheese is melted. Serve immediately. **Yield: 6-8 servings.**

Editor's Note: This recipe was tested with Barilla Al Forno Italian Baking Sauce.

Pork Slaw Skillet

Prep/Total Time: 20 min.

Tender, moist slices of pork tenderloin and crispy slaw combine in this delicious recipe. I've been serving it to family and friends for nearly 30 years, and it's still a hit.

—Jerry Harrison, St. Mary's, Georgia

2	pork tenderloins (about 3/4 pound *each*) cut into 1/4-inch slices
2	tablespoons canola oil

Salt and pepper to taste
SLAW:

1	tablespoon all-purpose flour
1/2	cup water
2	tablespoons cider vinegar
1	tablespoon sugar
1	tablespoon prepared mustard
2	teaspoons Worcestershire sauce
1	teaspoon salt
1/2	to 1 teaspoon celery seed

Dash pepper

7	cups shredded cabbage
1-1/2	cups shredded carrots
1	medium onion, chopped
1	cup chopped green pepper, optional

In a large skillet, cook pork in oil over medium heat for 2-3 minutes on each side or until lightly browned. Season with salt and pepper. Remove and keep warm.

For the slaw, in a large bowl, combine the flour and water until smooth. Stir in the cider vinegar, sugar, mustard, Worcestershire sauce, salt, celery seed and pepper; pour into the skillet. Add vegetables.

Cook and stir over medium heat until mixture comes to a boil. Cook and stir for 2 minutes or until thickened and vegetables are crisp-tender. Top with pork; cover and cook until a meat thermometer reaches 160°. **Yield: 4 servings.**

Hamburger Rice Skillet

Prep/Total Time: 25 min.

Onion soup mix mildly flavors this kid-pleasing blend of ground beef, instant rice and fresh vegetables. It can be served as either a main course or a hearty side dish.

—Suzanne Dolata, Ripon, Wisconsin

1	pound ground beef
3	cups water
2	medium carrots, cut into 1/4-inch slices
1	celery rib, chopped
1	envelope onion soup mix
2	cups uncooked instant rice

In a large skillet, cook beef over medium heat until no longer pink; drain. Stir in the water, carrots, celery and soup mix. Bring to a boil. Reduce heat; cover and simmer for 8 minutes or until vegetables are tender.

Return to a boil; add the rice. Remove from the heat; let stand for 5 minutes or until rice is tender. **Yield: 4 servings.**

Chicken Artichoke Pasta

Prep/Total Time: 25 min.

Here's a simple main course my whole family likes, including the kids! Similar to a restaurant favorite, it uses canned artichokes and olives and a jar of sun-dried tomatoes.

—Beth Washington, Ayer, Massachusetts

8	ounces uncooked bow tie pasta
1-1/2	pounds boneless skinless chicken breasts, cubed
1/2	teaspoon dried oregano
1/4	teaspoon salt
1/4	teaspoon pepper
3	tablespoons olive oil
1	to 2 tablespoons minced garlic
2	cans (14 ounces *each*) water-packed artichoke hearts, rinsed, drained and quartered
1	jar (8-1/2 ounces) oil-packed sun-dried tomatoes, quartered
1	can (2-1/4 ounces) sliced ripe olives, drained

Shredded Parmesan cheese

Cook pasta according to package directions. Meanwhile, sprinkle chicken with the oregano, salt and pepper. In a large skillet, saute chicken in oil until no longer pink. Add garlic; saute 1 minute longer. Stir in the artichokes, tomatoes and olives; heat through. Drain pasta; toss with chicken mixture. Sprinkle with Parmesan cheese. **Yield: 6 servings.**

Chicken Artichoke Pasta

Flank Steak Pinwheels

Grill, covered, over medium heat for 5-7 minutes on each side or until meat reaches desired doneness (for medium-rare, a meat thermometer should read 145°; medium, 160°; well-done, 170°). Discard toothpicks.

In a small saucepan, combine the cream cheese, milk, butter and pepper. Cook and stir over low heat just until smooth (do not boil). Stir in blue cheese. Serve with pinwheels. **Yield: 4 servings.**

Editor's Note: This recipe was tested in a 1,100-watt microwave.

 Sweet 'n' Spicy Chicken
Prep/Total Time: 20 min.

My husband and children love this tender chicken that has a spicy sauce. Peach preserves add just a touch of sweetness, while taco seasoning and salsa give this dish some kick. Add more zip to this entree with additional taco seasoning and spicier salsa.
—*Sheri White, Higley, Arizona*

1	pound boneless skinless chicken breasts, cut into 1/2-inch cubes
3	tablespoons taco seasoning
1	to 2 tablespoons canola oil
1	jar (11 ounces) chunky salsa
1/2	cup peach preserves

Hot cooked rice

Place taco seasoning in a large resealable plastic bag; add chicken and toss to coat.

In a large skillet, brown chicken in oil until no longer pink. Combine salsa and preserves; stir into skillet. Bring to a boil. Reduce heat; cover and simmer for 2-3 minutes or until heated through. Serve with rice. **Yield: 4 servings.**

Flank Steak Pinwheels
Prep: 30 min. | Grill: 10 min.

The secret to these pretty flank steak pinwheels lies in their butterfly treatment. Because the steaks are flattened, marinade isn't needed to tenderize. Instead, they're filled with a colorful stuffing of red pepper and spinach and draped with a flavorful, homemade blue cheese sauce.
—*Taste of Home Test Kitchen, Greendale, Wisconsin*

8	bacon strips
1	beef flank steak (1-1/2 pounds)
4	cups fresh baby spinach
1	jar (7 ounces) roasted sweet red peppers, drained

CREAM CHEESE SAUCE:

1	package (3 ounces) cream cheese, softened
1/4	cup milk
1	tablespoon butter
1/4	teaspoon pepper
1/2	cup crumbled blue cheese

Place the bacon strips on a microwave-safe plate lined with microwave-safe paper towels. Cover with another paper towel; microwave on high for 2-3 minutes or until the bacon is partially cooked.

Meanwhile, cut the steak horizontally from a long side to within 1/2 in. of opposite side. Open the meat so it lies flat; cover with plastic wrap. Flatten to 1/4-in. thickness. Remove plastic. Place the spinach over steak to within 1 in. of edges; top with red peppers. With the grain of the meat going from left to right, roll up jelly-roll style. Wrap the bacon strips around beef; secure with toothpicks. Slice beef across the grain into eight slices.

Sweet 'n' Spicy Chicken

Shrimp Creole
Prep/Total Time: 30 min.

I give a mild Creole flavor to convenient cooked shrimp in this skillet supper that has been part of my recipe collection for years. It's quick and very good. —W. Florence Johns, Houston, Texas

- 1/2 cup chopped onion
- 1/2 cup chopped green pepper
- 1 celery rib, chopped
- 1 teaspoon minced garlic
- 2 tablespoons canola oil
- 2 cans (8 ounces *each*) tomato sauce
- 1 teaspoon chili powder
- 1/2 teaspoon sugar
- 1/4 teaspoon cayenne pepper
- 1 pound frozen peeled cooked small shrimp, thawed

Hot cooked rice, optional

In a large skillet, saute the onion, green pepper, celery and garlic in oil for 6 minutes. Stir in the tomato sauce, chili powder, sugar and cayenne. Bring to a boil. Reduce heat; simmer, uncovered, for 10 minutes. Add shrimp; cook and stir until shrimp turn pink. Serve with rice if desired. **Yield: 4 servings.**

Nutrition Facts: 3/4 cup (calculated without rice) equals 220 calories, 8 g fat (1 g saturated fat), 221 mg cholesterol, 791 mg sodium, 10 g carbohydrate, 2 g fiber, 26 g protein. Diabetic Exchanges: 3 lean meat, 2 vegetable.

Parmesan Chicken
Prep/Total Time: 20 min.

I like to make this yummy recipe when I have extra spaghetti sauce on hand. The herbed coating on the tender chicken gets nice and golden. —Margie Eddy, Ann Arbor, Michigan

- 1/2 cup seasoned bread crumbs
- 1/2 cup grated Parmesan cheese, *divided*
- 1-1/2 teaspoons dried oregano, *divided*
- 1/2 teaspoon dried basil
- 1/2 teaspoon salt
- 1/4 teaspoon pepper
- 1 egg
- 1 tablespoon water
- 4 boneless skinless chicken breast halves (4 ounces *each*)
- 2 tablespoons butter
- 2 cups meatless spaghetti sauce
- 1/2 teaspoon garlic salt
- 1 cup (4 ounces) shredded part-skim mozzarella cheese

Hot cooked fettuccine *or* pasta of your choice

Parmesan Chicken

In a shallow bowl, combine the bread crumbs, 1/4 cup Parmesan cheese, 1 teaspoon oregano, basil, salt and pepper. In another shallow bowl, combine the egg and water. Dip chicken in egg mixture, then coat with crumb mixture.

In a large skillet, cook chicken in butter on both sides until a meat thermometer reads 170°.

Meanwhile, in a large saucepan, combine the spaghetti sauce, garlic salt and remaining oregano; cook over medium heat until heated through. Spoon over chicken; sprinkle with mozzarella cheese and remaining Parmesan cheese. Serve with pasta. **Yield: 4 servings.**

Skillet Steak and Corn
Prep: 10 min. | Cook: 30 min.

This skillet dish combines canned vegetables and meat in a savory sauce. The thin strips of steak cook up in minutes. If you like, you can use slices of chicken breast for the steak. —Ruth Taylor, Greeneville, Tennessee

- 1 pound boneless beef top round steak, cut into strips
- 1 medium onion, cut into 1/4-inch wedges
- 1/2 teaspoon dried thyme
- 2 tablespoons canola oil
- 3/4 cup red wine *or* beef broth
- 1 can (14-1/2 ounces) diced tomatoes, undrained
- 2 cans (11 ounces *each*) Mexicorn, drained

Hot cooked rice

In a large skillet, cook the steak, onion and thyme over medium-high heat in oil until meat is no longer pink; drain. Add wine; simmer, uncovered, for 10 minutes or until the liquid has evaporated. Stir in tomatoes; cover and simmer 15 minutes longer. Add the corn and heat through. Serve with rice. **Yield: 4 servings.**

Steak and Onions

Steak and Onions

Prep/Total Time: 30 min.

Sweet caramelized onions add great flavor to these rosemary-rubbed steaks. Serve them with baked potatoes and a Caesar salad. Or complement the entree with steamed carrots and warm apple pie with vanilla ice cream.

—Taste of Home Test Kitchen, Greendale, Wisconsin

1	large onion, halved and sliced
2	tablespoons butter
1/3	cup white wine *or* chicken broth
1	garlic clove, minced
1/2	teaspoon dried rosemary, crushed
1/4	teaspoon salt
1/4	teaspoon pepper
2	beef tenderloin steaks (1-1/2 to 2 inches thick and 8 ounces *each*)

In a large skillet, cook onion in butter over medium heat for 15-20 minutes or until onion is golden brown, stirring frequently. Stir in wine or broth and garlic. Bring to a boil. Reduce heat; simmer, uncovered, for 3-4 minutes or until liquid has evaporated.

Meanwhile, combine the rosemary, salt and pepper; rub over steaks. Broil 4 in. from the heat for 7-9 minutes on each side or until meat reaches desired doneness (for medium-rare, a meat thermometer should read 145°; medium, 160°; well-done, 170°). Serve with caramelized onions. **Yield: 2 servings.**

Lamb Ratatouille

Prep: 30 min. | Cook: 20 min.

Based on the classic French dish, this quick-and-easy recipe is a great way to use up leftover lamb. With the tomatoes, zucchini, mushrooms and more, it's truly a well-rounded meal. I also make it with beef. —Maxine Cenker, Weirton, West Virginia

1	package (6.8 ounces) beef-flavored rice and vermicelli mix
2	tablespoons butter
2-1/2	cups water
3	medium tomatoes, peeled, seeded and chopped
1	medium zucchini, sliced
1-1/2	cups sliced fresh mushrooms
1	small onion, chopped
6	green onions, sliced
3	garlic cloves, minced
2	tablespoons olive oil
1	pound cooked lamb *or* beef, cut into thin strips

Set rice seasoning packet aside. In a large skillet, saute the rice mix in butter until browned. Stir in water and contents of seasoning packet; bring to a boil. Reduce heat; cover and simmer for 15 minutes.

Meanwhile, in another skillet, saute the vegetables in olive oil until crisp-tender. Add the lamb and vegetables to the rice. Cover and simmer for 5-10 minutes or until the meat is well heated and the rice is tender. **Yield: 6 servings.**

Teriyaki Mushroom Chicken

Prep/Total Time: 25 min.

Fresh mushrooms and onions top this savory skillet chicken with a rich, teriyaki sauce. I enjoy serving this dish over chicken-flavored rice, but regular white rice works fine, too.

—Cheri Casolari, Rinard, Illinois

4	boneless skinless chicken breast halves (6 ounces *each*)
5	tablespoons butter, *divided*
4	cups sliced fresh mushrooms
1	cup sliced onion
1/4	cup water
1/4	cup honey teriyaki marinade

In a large skillet over medium heat, cook the chicken breasts in 1 tablespoon butter for 5-7 minutes on each side or until a meat thermometer reads 170°. Remove from the skillet and keep warm.

In the same skillet, saute mushrooms and onion in remaining butter until tender, adding the water and marinade during the last 2 minutes. Return the chicken to the pan; heat through. **Yield: 4 servings.**

Honey-Ginger Chicken Stir-Fry

Prep/Total Time: 25 min.

When I was first married, we didn't have a working oven or grill, so I had to use the stovetop for everything. After a few months of the same thing, I needed some new ideas and developed this simple chicken and veggie stir-fry.

—April Walcher, Hutchinson, Kansas

1/4	cup honey
3	to 4 teaspoons soy sauce
1-1/2	teaspoons lemon juice
1	teaspoon ground ginger
1-1/4	pounds boneless skinless chicken breasts, cut into 1/4-inch slices
1/2	teaspoon salt
1/4	teaspoon pepper
1	tablespoon canola oil
1	package (16 ounces) frozen stir-fry vegetable blend
1	can (8 ounces) sliced water chestnuts, drained
4	to 6 cups hot cooked rice

In a small bowl, combine the honey, soy sauce, lemon juice and ginger; set aside.

Sprinkle the chicken with salt and pepper. In a large skillet or wok, stir-fry the chicken slices in the oil for 3-4 minutes or until lightly browned. Add the vegetables and water chestnuts; stir-fry 3-4 minutes longer or until the vegetables are crisp-tender.

Stir honey mixture and stir into chicken mixture. Cook for 3-5 minutes or until heated through and chicken is no longer pink. Serve with rice. **Yield: 4 servings.**

Chicken with Spicy Fruit

Prep/Total Time: 30 min.

This speedy entree is special enough for company, yet easy enough for everyday. The chicken gets wonderful flavor from a sauce made with strawberry jam, dried cranberries and pineapple juice. I serve it with rice pilaf, peas, a garden salad and rolls.

—Kathy Rairigh, Milford, Indiana

1-1/4	cups unsweetened pineapple juice
1/4	cup dried cranberries
2	garlic cloves, minced
1/8	to 1/4 teaspoon crushed red pepper flakes
4	boneless skinless chicken breast halves (4 ounces *each*)
1/4	cup strawberry spreadable fruit
1	teaspoon cornstarch
2	green onions, thinly sliced

In a large skillet, combine the pineapple juice, cranberries, garlic and red pepper flakes; bring to a boil. Add chicken. Reduce heat; cover and simmer for 10 minutes or until a meat thermometer reaches 170°. Remove chicken to a platter and keep warm.

Bring cooking liquid to a boil; cook for 5-7 minutes or until liquid is reduced to 3/4 cup. Combine spreadable fruit and cornstarch until blended; add to the skillet. Boil and stir for 1 minute or until thickened. Spoon over chicken. Sprinkle with onions. **Yield: 4 servings.**

Nutrition Facts: 1 chicken breast half equals 248 calories, 3 g fat (0 saturated fat), 73 mg cholesterol, 66 mg sodium, 26 g carbohydrate, 1 g fiber, 27 g protein. **Diabetic Exchanges:** *4 very lean meat, 1-1/2 fruit.*

Chicken with Spicy Fruit

Creamed Chicken 'n' Biscuits

Prep/Total Time: 25 min.

We have a dairy farm and three young children, so I'm always on the lookout for easy, hearty meals like this one. Using leftover or canned chicken, I can whip up this entree in minutes.

—Shari Zimmerman, Deford, Michigan

BISCUITS:

2	cups all-purpose flour
1	tablespoon baking powder
1	teaspoon salt
2/3	cup milk
1/3	cup canola oil

CREAMED CHICKEN:

1/4	cup finely chopped onion
1/4	cup butter
1/4	cup all-purpose flour
1/4	to 1/2 teaspoon salt
1/8	teaspoon pepper
2	cups milk *or* chicken broth
2	cups chopped cooked chicken

Minced fresh parsley

In a large bowl, combine the flour, baking powder and salt; add the milk and oil. Stir until the dough forms a ball. On a lightly floured surface, knead 8-10 times or until smooth.

Roll or pat the biscuit dough into a 6-in. square that is about 1 in. thick. Cut into six rectangles. Place on a lightly greased baking sheet. Bake at 450° for 10-12 minutes or until golden brown.

Meanwhile, in a large skillet, saute the onion in butter until tender. Stir in the flour, salt and pepper until blended. Gradually add the milk; bring to a boil. Reduce the heat; cook and stir for 1-2 minutes or until the sauce is thickened. Stir in the cooked chicken and parsley; cook until heated through. Split the biscuits; top with the creamed chicken. **Yield:** 6 servings.

Creamed Chicken 'n' Biscuits

Sweet-Sour Chicken Nuggets

Prep/Total Time: 30 min.

Everyone loves this meal, particularly our grandchildren. Frozen breaded chicken and canned pineapple make this dish a snap to prepare, and the sweet tangy taste keeps them asking for more.

—Arlene Best, East Ridge, Tennessee

1	medium green pepper, cut into chunks
1	large onion, cut into wedges
1	to 2 tablespoons canola oil
1	can (14-1/2 ounces) chicken broth
1/2	cup pancake syrup
1/4	cup cider vinegar
1	tablespoon soy sauce
1	can (8 ounces) pineapple chunks
2	to 3 tablespoons cornstarch
20	pieces breaded chicken nuggets, thawed

Hot cooked rice

In a large skillet, saute the green pepper and onion in oil until crisp-tender; remove and keep warm. Add the chicken broth, pancake syrup, cider vinegar and soy sauce to the skillet; bring to a boil.

Drain pineapple, reserving juice; set pineapple aside. Combine cornstarch and juice until smooth; gradually add to broth mixture. Bring to a boil; cook and stir for 2 minutes or until thickened.

Add chicken nuggets; cook for 2 minutes. Stir in the pineapple and sauteed vegetables; heat through. Serve over rice. **Yield:** 4 servings.

White vs. Cider Vinegar

When recipes don't call for a specific type of vinegar, use one that fits the dish. If sharpness is desired, use white vinegar. If a milder flavor is desired, use cider vinegar. White vinegar has a strong, clean flavor and is often used for pickling. Cider vinegar, made from apples, has a faint fruity flavor and is used in foods where a milder flavor is preferred.

Pasta Primavera with Shrimp

Pasta Primavera with Shrimp

Prep/Total Time: 30 min.

I added shrimp to a simple, easy primavera, and the result was a timely and fabulous dinner bursting with flavor in every bite. This dish capitalizes on summer's bounty with five different types of fresh vegetables in a dish that's perfect for summer.

—Kimberly Wagner, Castle Rock, Colorado

1	package (16 ounces) linguine
1	pound uncooked medium shrimp, peeled and deveined
2	cups chopped fresh broccoli
1	cup sliced fresh carrots
1	cup fresh green beans, cut into 2-inch pieces
1	medium zucchini, cut into 1/4-inch slices
1	medium sweet red pepper, julienned
2	tablespoons all-purpose flour
1-1/4	cups heavy whipping cream
3/4	cup chicken broth
1/4	cup grated Parmesan cheese
3/4	teaspoon salt
1/2	teaspoon pepper

In a Dutch oven, cook the linguine according to package directions, adding the shrimp and vegetables during the last 4 minutes.

Meanwhile, in a small saucepan, combine the flour, cream and broth until smooth. Add the Parmesan cheese, salt and pepper. Bring to a boil over medium heat; cook and stir for 2 minutes or until thickened. Drain linguine mixture and return to the pan. Add cream sauce; toss to coat. **Yield: 6 servings.**

Italian Chicken Noodle Skillet

Prep/Total Time: 25 min.

This saucy, cheesy pasta and chicken dish is so good, you'll want to lick the plate clean! My husband loves it.

—Mary Jones, St. Louis, Missouri

1-3/4	cups uncooked egg noodles
1/2	cup sliced fresh mushrooms
1	can (14-1/2 ounces) diced tomatoes in sauce
1	can (10-3/4 ounces) reduced-fat reduced-sodium condensed cream of chicken soup, undiluted
2	cups cubed cooked chicken breast
1/4	cup shredded Parmesan cheese
1	teaspoon Italian seasoning
1/3	cup shredded part-skim mozzarella cheese

Cook noodles according to package directions. Meanwhile, in a large nonstick skillet coated with cooking spray, saute mushrooms for 2-4 minutes or until tender. Stir in tomatoes and soup until blended. Stir in the chicken, Parmesan cheese and Italian seasoning.

Bring to a boil. Reduce heat; simmer, uncovered, for 5-8 minutes or until heated through.

Drain noodles; stir into skillet. Sprinkle with mozzarella cheese; cover until cheese is melted. **Yield: 4 servings.**

Italian Chicken Noodle Skillet

Broccoli Shrimp Alfredo

 ## Broccoli Shrimp Alfredo
Prep/Total Time: 30 min.

After tasting fettuccine Alfredo at a restaurant, I duplicated it at home. You can't imagine how pleased I was when I came up with this delicious version. My family loves the creamy dish, and my husband prefers it to the one at the restaurant.

—Rae Natoli, Kingston, New York

1	package (16 ounces) fettuccine
1	pound uncooked medium shrimp, peeled and deveined
3	garlic cloves, minced
1/2	cup butter, cubed
1	package (8 ounces) cream cheese, cubed
1	cup milk
1/2	cup shredded Parmesan cheese
1	package (10 ounces) frozen broccoli florets
1/2	teaspoon salt

Dash pepper

Cook the fettuccine according to package directions. Meanwhile, in a large skillet, saute the shrimp and garlic in butter until shrimp turn pink. Remove and keep warm. In the same skillet, combine the cream cheese, milk and Parmesan cheese; cook and stir until the cheeses are melted and the mixture is smooth.

Place 1 in. of water in a saucepan; add broccoli. Bring to a boil. Reduce heat; cover and simmer for 6-8 minutes or until tender. Drain. Stir the broccoli, shrimp, salt and pepper into cheese sauce; cook until heated through. Drain fettuccine; top with shrimp mixture. **Yield: 4 servings.**

Herbed Chicken Fettuccine
Prep: 25 min. | Cook: 15 min.

Savory seasonings add zip to these moist chicken strips tossed with pasta. For variety, add steamed broccoli and glazed carrots.
—Kathy Kirkland, Denham Springs, Louisiana

1	to 2 teaspoons salt-free seasoning blend
1	teaspoon poultry seasoning
1	pound boneless skinless chicken breasts, cut into 1-inch strips
2	tablespoons olive oil
4	tablespoons butter, *divided*
2/3	cup water
2	tablespoons teriyaki sauce
2	tablespoons onion soup mix
1	envelope savory herb and garlic soup mix, *divided*
8	ounces uncooked fettuccine *or* pasta of your choice
2	tablespoons grated Parmesan cheese
1	tablespoon Worcestershire sauce

Combine seasoning blend and poultry seasoning; sprinkle over chicken. In a large skillet, saute chicken in oil and 2 tablespoons butter for 5 minutes or until chicken is no longer pink. Add the water, teriyaki sauce, onion soup mix and 2 tablespoons herb and garlic soup mix. Bring to a boil. Reduce heat; cover and simmer for 15 minutes.

Meanwhile, cook fettuccine according to package directions. Drain; add to chicken mixture. Stir in the cheese, Worcestershire sauce, remaining butter, and remaining herb and garlic soup mix; toss to coat. **Yield: 4 servings.**

Chicken Cacciatore

Prep/Total Time: 15 min.

Not only is this satisfying main dish easy to fix, it tastes fantastic. And it has plenty of nicely spiced sauce.
—Susan Adair, Somerset, Kentucky

1-1/2   pounds boneless skinless chicken breasts, cut into 1/2-inch strips
1   medium onion, sliced and separated into rings
1   medium green pepper, julienned
2   tablespoons canola oil
1   can (15 ounces) tomato sauce
1   can (14-1/2 ounces) stewed tomatoes
2   teaspoons garlic powder
1/2   teaspoon dried oregano
1/2   teaspoon salt
1/2   teaspoon pepper
Hot cooked rice

In a large skillet, cook the chicken, onion and green pepper in the oil until the chicken is lightly browned and the vegetables are tender. Add tomato sauce, stewed tomatoes and seasonings; bring to a boil.

Reduce heat; simmer, uncovered, for 5 minutes or until chicken juices run clear. Serve with rice. **Yield: 6 servings.**

Pineapple Chicken Lo Mein

Prep/Total Time: 30 min.

The perfect supper to serve on busy weeknights, this speedy lo mein combines tender chicken and colorful veggies with a tangy sauce. Quick-cooking spaghetti and canned pineapple make it a cinch to throw together when time is short.
—Linda Stevens, Madison, Alabama

1   can (20 ounces) unsweetened pineapple chunks
1   pound boneless skinless chicken breasts, cut into 1-inch cubes
2   garlic cloves, minced
3/4   teaspoon ground ginger *or* 1 tablespoon minced fresh gingerroot
3   tablespoons canola oil, *divided*
2   medium carrots, julienned
1   medium green pepper, julienned
4   ounces spaghetti, cooked and drained
3   green onions, sliced
1   tablespoon cornstarch
1/3   cup soy sauce

Drain pineapple, reserving 1/3 cup juice (discarding remaining juice or save for another use); set pineapple aside.

In a large skillet, cook the chicken, garlic and ginger over medium heat in 2 tablespoons oil for 6 minutes or until

chicken is no longer pink. Stir in the carrots, green pepper and pineapple. Cover and cook for 2-3 minutes or until vegetables are crisp-tender. Stir in spaghetti and onions.

In a small bowl, combine the cornstarch, soy sauce, reserved pineapple juice and remaining oil until smooth. Gradually add to chicken mixture. Bring to a boil; cook and stir for 2 minutes or until thickened. **Yield: 4 servings.**

Santa Fe Supper

Prep/Total Time: 30 min.

This zesty skillet meal is a great way to bring a little variety to your dinnertime lineup. Green chilies spice up the rice, while salsa, zucchini, onion and cheddar cheese dress up the ground beef mixture.   *—Valerie Collier, Charleston, South Carolina*

1   cup uncooked long grain rice
1   pound ground beef
2   small zucchini, cut into 1/4-inch slices
1   large onion, halved and sliced
1-1/2   cups chunky salsa, *divided*
1/4   teaspoon salt
1/4   teaspoon pepper
1   cup (4 ounces) shredded pepper Jack cheese
1   can (4 ounces) chopped green chilies, drained
1   cup (4 ounces) shredded cheddar cheese

Cook rice according to package directions. Meanwhile, in a large skillet, cook beef over medium heat until no longer pink; drain. Stir in the zucchini, onion, 1 cup salsa, salt and pepper; cook until vegetables are crisp-tender.

Add pepper Jack cheese and chilies to the rice. Sprinkle cheddar cheese over beef mixture; serve with rice and remaining salsa. **Yield: 4 servings.**

Santa Fe Supper

Tuxedo Pasta

Prep/Total Time: 20 min.

With chicken and veggies, this pasta medley in a mild lemon and wine sauce is a complete meal-in-one that's a snap to assemble. I try to keep leftover chicken or turkey on hand so that I can fix this dish whenever I want. —Jackie Hannahs, Fountain, Michigan

2	cups uncooked bow tie pasta
2	cups cubed cooked chicken
1	medium zucchini, sliced
1-1/2	cups sliced fresh mushrooms
1/2	cup chopped sweet red pepper
3	tablespoons butter, *divided*
1/4	cup lemon juice
2	tablespoons white wine *or* chicken broth
3/4	cup shredded Parmesan cheese
3	tablespoons minced fresh basil *or* 1 tablespoon dried basil

Cook pasta according to package directions. Meanwhile, in a large skillet, saute the chicken, zucchini, mushrooms and red pepper in 2 tablespoons butter for 4-5 minutes or until vegetables are tender. Add the lemon juice and wine or broth. Bring to a boil. Reduce heat; cook and stir for 2 minutes or until heated through.

Drain the pasta; add to skillet. Stir in the Parmesan cheese, basil and remaining butter. **Yield: 6 servings.**

Steak Stir-Fry

Tuxedo Pasta

Steak Stir-Fry

Prep/Total Time: 25 min.

No one would guess this elegant entree is a cinch to prepare at the last minute. To save even more prep time, use frozen vegetables instead of fresh. Sometimes I substitute chicken, chicken bouillon and curry for the beef, beef bouillon and ginger. —Janis Plourde, Smooth Rock Falls, Ontario

1	teaspoon beef bouillon granules
1	cup boiling water
2	tablespoons cornstarch
1/3	cup soy sauce
1	pound boneless sirloin steak, cut into thin strips
1	garlic clove, minced
1	teaspoon ground ginger
1/4	teaspoon pepper
2	tablespoons canola oil
1	large green pepper, julienned
1	cup sliced carrots *or* celery
5	green onions, cut into 1-inch pieces

Hot cooked rice

Dissolve bouillon in water. Combine the cornstarch and soy sauce until smooth; add to bouillon. Set aside. Toss beef with garlic, ginger and pepper. In a large skillet or wok over medium-high heat, stir-fry beef in 1 tablespoon oil until meat is no longer pink; remove and keep warm.

Heat remaining oil; stir-fry vegetables until crisp-tender. Stir soy sauce mixture and add to the skillet; bring to a boil. Cook and stir for 2 minutes. Return meat to pan and heat through. Serve with rice. **Yield: 4 servings.**

Spicy Pepper Penne

Prep/Total Time: 30 min.

Bring a bit of Sicily to the table with this zesty combination of pepperoni, pasta and peppers!

—Candace Greene, Columbiana, Ohio

1	package uncooked penne pasta
1/2	teaspoon minced fresh rosemary *or* 1/8 teaspoon dried rosemary, crushed
2	packages (3-1/2 ounces *each*) sliced pepperoni, halved
1/2	cup sliced pepperoncinis
1	jar (7 ounces) roasted sweet red peppers, drained and chopped
3-1/2	cups boiling water
1/2	cup heavy whipping cream
1/2	cup grated Parmesan cheese

In a large skillet, layer the pasta, rosemary, pepperoni, pepperoncinis and red peppers. Add water; bring to a boil. Reduce heat; cover and simmer for 12 minutes or until pasta is tender. Add cream and Parmesan cheese; toss to coat. **Yield: 8 servings.**

Editor's Note: Look for pepperoncinis (pickled peppers) in the pickle and olive section of your grocery store.

Fruited Chicken Curry

Prep: 15 min. | Cook: 45 min.

The curry lovers in your house will certainly take to this juicy chicken that's served over a bed of hot rice. Dried fruits and toasted almonds make it a wonderful change-of-pace entree.

—Bernadine Dirmeyer, Harpster, Ohio

4	bone-in chicken breast halves (8 ounces *each*)
1	tablespoon butter
1/4	cup chopped onion
2	teaspoons curry powder
1/2	teaspoon salt
1/8	teaspoon pepper
1	cup dried mixed fruit (such as apples, apricots and prunes)
3/4	cup hot water
1	tablespoon sugar
1	teaspoon lemon juice

Hot cooked rice
1/4	cup slivered almonds, toasted

In a large skillet, brown the chicken in butter on each side; remove and keep warm. In the drippings, cook the onion, curry, salt and pepper until onion is tender. Stir in the fruit, water, sugar and lemon juice.

Return chicken to pan. Bring to a boil. Reduce heat; cover and simmer for 25-30 minutes or until a meat thermometer reaches 170°. Serve with rice; sprinkle with toasted almonds. **Yield: 4 servings.**

Chicken in Basil Cream

Prep/Total Time: 25 min.

When I first read this recipe, I thought it looked difficult. But because I had all the ingredients readily at hand, I gave it a try. Am I glad I did! It's simple to prepare and delicious.

—Judy Baker, Craig, Colorado

1/4	cup milk
1/4	cup dry bread crumbs
4	boneless skinless chicken breast halves (4 ounces *each*)
3	tablespoons butter
1/2	cup chicken broth
1	cup heavy whipping cream
1	jar (4 ounces) sliced pimientos, drained
1/2	cup grated Parmesan cheese
1/4	cup minced fresh basil
1/8	teaspoon pepper

Place milk and bread crumbs in separate shallow bowls. Dip chicken in milk, then coat with crumbs. In a skillet over medium-high heat, cook chicken in butter for about 5 minutes on each side or until a meat thermometer reads 170°. Remove and keep warm.

Add broth to the skillet. Bring to a boil over medium heat; stir to loosen browned bits. Stir in the cream and pimientos; boil and stir for 1 minute. Reduce heat. Add Parmesan cheese, basil and pepper; cook and stir until heated through. Serve with chicken. **Yield: 4 servings.**

Chicken in Basil Cream

Shrimp Taco Salad

vinegar, green pepper, garlic, coriander and sugar; shake well and set aside.

In a skillet, stir-fry the tortilla strips in the remaining oil; drain on paper towels. Sprinkle with remaining taco seasoning. In the same skillet, saute shrimp for 8-10 minutes or until shrimp turn pink.

In a large bowl, combine the greens, tomato, beans, shrimp and tortilla strips. Just before serving, shake dressing and pour over salad; sprinkle with cheese and toss to coat. **Yield: 6-8 servings.**

Sesame Chicken
Prep/Total Time: 30 min.

My mother passed down the recipe for this tasty chicken stir-fry, which is so quick and easy to make. Served with wild rice and vegetables, it's a wholesome meal in minutes. It's also a lot more affordable than ordering takeout!

—Elizabeth Limestahl, Port Clinton, Ohio

1-1/4	pounds boneless skinless chicken breasts, cubed
2	tablespoons canola oil
1/4	cup soy sauce
1/4	cup sesame seeds
1	large onion, sliced
2	jars (4-1/2 ounces *each*) sliced mushrooms, drained *or* 2 cups sliced fresh mushrooms

In a large skillet, cook chicken in oil until no longer pink. Stir in the soy sauce and sesame seeds. Cook and stir over medium heat for 5 minutes.

Remove chicken with a slotted spoon; set aside and keep warm. In the same skillet, saute onion and mushrooms until onion is tender. Return chicken to pan; heat through. **Yield: 5 servings.**

Nutrition Facts: 1 serving (made with reduced-sodium soy sauce and fresh mushrooms) equals 272 calories, 13 g fat (0 saturated fat), 73 mg cholesterol, 474 mg sodium, 8 g carbohydrate, 2 g fiber, 31 g protein. **Diabetic Exchanges:** *4 very lean meat, 2 fat, 1 vegetable.*

Shrimp Taco Salad
Prep/Total Time: 30 min.

I created this main-dish salad to satisfy our family's love of shrimp. It has lots of contrasting textures, including firm taco-seasoned shrimp, crispy tortilla strips and hearty black beans. A convenient bag of salad greens cuts down on prep time, so I can have this meal ready in half an hour.

—Ellen Morrell, Hazleton, Pennsylvania

1	pound uncooked large shrimp, peeled and deveined
1	envelope taco seasoning, *divided*
1/2	cup plus 3 tablespoons olive oil, *divided*
1	small onion, finely chopped
3	tablespoons cider vinegar
2	tablespoons diced green *or* sweet red pepper
6	garlic cloves, minced
1/2	teaspoon ground coriander
1/4	teaspoon sugar
3	corn tortillas (6 inches), cut into 1/4-inch strips
1	package (8 ounces) ready-to-serve salad greens
1	medium tomato, chopped
1	can (8 ounces) black beans, rinsed and drained
2	cups (8 ounces) finely shredded Colby-Monterey Jack cheese

Remove the shrimp tails if desired. Place the shrimp in a bowl; sprinkle with half of the taco seasoning. Set aside. In a jar with a tight-fitting lid, combine 1/2 cup olive oil, onion,

Toasting Sesame Seeds

These little seeds, which come in both black and white varieties, add loads of flavor to traditional Asian dishes and stir-frys. To toast sesame seeds, heat them in a dry skillet over medium heat for 10-15 minutes or until lightly browned, stirring occasionally. You can also bake sesame seeds on an ungreased baking sheet at 350° for 10-15 minutes or until lightly browned. Watch them closely to avoid scorching.

Hearty Fajitas

Prep/Total Time: 30 min.

When I need to get dinner on the table fast for my husband and three children, I fix these filling fajitas. With beef, chicken and shrimp, they satisfy everyone's tastes. They're wonderful with Spanish rice. —Elaine Keith, Mineral Wells, West Virginia

- 1/2   pound boneless beef top round steak, cut into strips
- 1/4   pound boneless skinless chicken breast, cut into strips
- 2   to 3 tablespoons canola oil
- 1/2   pound uncooked medium shrimp, peeled and deveined
- 1   medium green pepper, thinly sliced
- 1   medium sweet red pepper, thinly sliced
- 2   small onions, thinly sliced
- 2   to 3 medium tomatoes, cut into wedges
- 2   teaspoons chili powder
- 1   teaspoon salt
- 1   can (16 ounces) refried beans
- 1/2   cup shredded part-skim mozzarella cheese
- 14   flour tortillas (8 inches), warmed

In a large skillet, stir-fry the steak and chicken in the oil. Add the shrimp, peppers, onions, tomatoes, chili powder and salt; cook until the meat juices run clear and the vegetables are crisp-tender.

Meanwhile, in a large saucepan, cook refried beans and cheese until cheese is melted. Spoon over tortillas; top with meat mixture. **Yield: 14 fajitas.**

Almond Chicken Stir-Fry

Prep/Total Time: 30 min.

Almonds and water chestnuts add crunch to this tasty, convenient and speedy supper. To make it even quicker, you can use frozen and thawed stir-fry vegetables instead of the fresh. —Denise Uhlenhake, Ossian, Iowa

- 1-1/2   pounds boneless skinless chicken breasts, cut into strips
- 3   tablespoons canola oil
- 1-1/2   cups fresh cauliflowerets
- 1-1/2   cups fresh broccoli florets
- 3/4   cup julienned carrots
- 1/2   cup chopped celery
- 1/4   cup chopped sweet red pepper
- 1   can (8 ounces) sliced water chestnuts, drained
- 3   cups chicken broth
- 3   tablespoons soy sauce
- 1/3   cup cornstarch
- 1/2   cup cold water

Hot cooked rice, optional
- 1/3   to 1/2 cup slivered almonds, toasted

In a large skillet or wok, stir-fry the chicken strips in the oil until no longer pink. Stir in the vegetables, chicken broth and soy sauce. Bring to a boil. Reduce the heat to low; cover and cook until the vegetables are crisp-tender. Combine the cornstarch and water until smooth; stir into the chicken mixture. Bring to a boil; cook and stir for 2 minutes or until thickened. Serve with the rice if desired. Sprinkle with slivered almonds. **Yield: 6 servings.**

Hearty Fajitas

Chicken with Mushroom Sauce

Prep: 15 min. | Cook: 35 min.

This is a fast but special treatment for chicken. Chicken breasts are browned to juicy perfection, then topped with a buttery sauce of fresh mushrooms and green onions.

—Patsy Jenkins, Tallahassee, Florida

8	bone-in chicken breast halves (8 ounces *each*)
2	tablespoons olive oil
2	cups sliced fresh mushrooms
2	green onions, chopped
1	cup white wine *or* chicken broth
3	tablespoons butter
1/2	teaspoon salt
1/4	teaspoon pepper
1	tablespoon cornstarch
2	tablespoons cold water

In a large skillet, brown chicken over medium heat in oil. Cover and cook for about 20 minutes or until a meat thermometer reaches 170°. Remove chicken; keep warm. In the same skillet, saute mushrooms and onions until tender. Stir in the wine or broth, butter, salt and pepper.

In a small bowl, combine the cornstarch and water until smooth; add to skillet. Bring to a boil; cook and stir for 2 minutes or until thickened. Return chicken to skillet; heat through. **Yield:** 8 servings.

Chicken with Mushroom Sauce

Spinach Penne Toss

Spinach Penne Toss

Prep/Total Time: 25 min.

Spinach provides a delicious base for all the wonderful flavor combinations found in this hearty salad. It's perfect for so many different occasions, including when company comes to visit.

—Kierste Wade, Midland, Michigan

2	cups uncooked penne pasta
1	medium sweet red pepper, julienned
1	medium onion, sliced
1	tablespoon plus 1/4 cup olive oil, *divided*
1	package (6 ounces) fresh baby spinach
3/4	cup crumbled cooked bacon
1/2	cup crumbled feta cheese
1/2	cup oil-packed sun-dried tomatoes, chopped
2	tablespoons cider vinegar
1/4	teaspoon pepper
1/8	teaspoon salt

Cook pasta according to package directions. Meanwhile, in a large skillet, saute red pepper and onion in 1 tablespoon oil for 3-4 minutes or until tender.

Drain pasta and place in a serving bowl. Add the red pepper mixture, spinach, bacon, feta cheese and tomatoes. In a jar with a tight-fitting lid, combine the vinegar, pepper, salt and remaining oil; shake well. Drizzle over pasta mixture; toss to coat. **Yield:** 10 servings.

A Bit about Feta Cheese

Feta is a white, salty, semi-firm cheese. Traditionally made from sheep's or goat's milk, it's also made with cow's milk. When being made, feta is formed in a mold, sliced into pieces, salted and brined. "Feta" comes from the Italian "fette", meaning slice of food.

Polynesian Sausage Supper

Prep/Total Time: 30 min.

When my sister first served us this unique medley, I couldn't believe how good it was because she had thrown it together so quickly. Sweet pineapple really adds to the taste.

—Laura McCarthy, Butte, Montana

1	pound smoked sausage, cut into 1/2-inch slices
1	medium onion, chopped
1	medium green pepper, cut into 1-inch chunks
1	can (14-1/2 ounces) diced tomatoes, undrained
1/2	cup beef broth
1	tablespoon brown sugar
1/4	teaspoon garlic powder
1/4	teaspoon pepper
1	can (20 ounces) unsweetened pineapple chunks
2	tablespoons cornstarch

Hot cooked rice

In a large skillet, cook the sausage, onion and green pepper until the vegetables are tender; drain. Add the tomatoes, broth, brown sugar, garlic powder and pepper. Drain pineapple, reserving juice. Stir pineapple into sausage mixture. Bring to a boil; cook, uncovered, for 5 minutes.

Combine cornstarch and reserved pineapple juice until smooth; gradually add to sausage mixture. Bring to a boil; cook and stir for 2 minutes or until thickened. Serve with rice. **Yield: 6 servings.**

Festive Spaghetti 'n' Meatballs

Prep/Total Time: 30 min.

When I don't have enough time to make spaghetti sauce from scratch, I dress up a store-bought jar with fresh vegetables and frozen meatballs. A touch of wine makes it special.

—Mary Ann Kosmas, Minneapolis, Minnesota

1/2	pound sliced fresh mushrooms
1	large green pepper, julienned
1	large onion, halved and sliced
2	tablespoons olive oil
1/4	cup red wine *or* water
1	jar (26 ounces) meatless spaghetti sauce
1	package (12 ounces) frozen fully cooked Italian meatballs, thawed

Hot cooked spaghetti

In a large saucepan, saute the mushrooms, green pepper and onion in oil until crisp-tender; stir in wine or water. Bring to a boil; cook for 2 minutes. Stir in spaghetti sauce and meatballs. Return to a boil. Reduce heat; simmer, uncovered, for 10-15 minutes or until meatballs are heated through.

Serve meatballs and sauce with spaghetti. **Yield: 4 servings.**

Au Gratin Sausage Skillet

Prep: 15 min. | Cook: 30 min.

Using frozen vegetables and a package of au gratin potatoes, I can get this satisfying stovetop supper on the table in no time. Even our oldest daughter, who can be a picky eater, loves it—and it is an excellent way of getting her to eat her vegetables.

—Penny Greene, Lancaster, Ohio

1	pound smoked kielbasa *or* Polish sausage, halved and sliced 1/2 inch thick
2	tablespoons canola oil
1	package (4.9 ounces) au gratin potatoes
2-1/2	cups water
1	package (8 ounces) frozen California-blend vegetables
1	to 2 cups (4 to 8 ounces) shredded cheddar cheese

In a large skillet, cook sausage in oil until lightly browned; drain. Add potatoes with contents of sauce mix and water. Cover and cook over medium heat for 18-20 minutes or until the potatoes are almost tender, stirring occasionally.

Add vegetables; cover and cook for 8-10 minutes or until potatoes and vegetables are tender. Sprinkle with cheese. Remove from the heat; cover and let stand for 2 minutes or until the cheese is melted. **Yield: 4 servings.**

Au Gratin Sausage Skillet

slow cooker, casseroles & oven entrees

These days, convenience is the key ingredient for folks who don't have a lot of extra time to spend cooking. That's what makes the recipes in this chapter so appealing.

Whether you choose from the variety of quick-to-fix slow-cooked dishes, easy meal-in-one casseroles or delicious oven entrees, you'll find dozens of satisfying suppers in the pages ahead. A small sample of some of the hearty and family-pleasing recipes include Orange-Glazed Cornish Hens, Pizza Tot Casserole and Wild Rice Turkey Dinner.

Saucy Apricot Chicken
(recipe on p. 158)

Beef Burgundy

Beef Burgundy

Prep: 10 min. | Cook: 5-1/2 hours

I trim meat, cut up vegetables and store them in separate containers the night before. The next day, I toss all of the ingredients into the slow cooker in minutes. Shortly before dinnertime, I cook the noodles and bake some cheesy garlic toast to complete this meal. —Mary Jo Nikolaus, Mansfield, Ohio

1-1/2	pounds beef stew meat, cut into 1-inch cubes
1/2	pound whole fresh mushrooms, halved
4	medium carrots, chopped
1	can (10-3/4 ounces) condensed golden mushroom soup, undiluted
1	large onion, cut into thin wedges
1/2	cup Burgundy wine *or* beef broth
1/4	cup quick-cooking tapioca
1/2	teaspoon salt
1/4	teaspoon dried thyme
1/4	teaspoon pepper

Hot cooked egg noodles

In a 5-qt. slow cooker, combine the first 10 ingredients. Cover and cook on low for 5-1/2 to 6-1/2 hours or until meat is tender. Serve with noodles. **Yield: 6 servings.**

Pizza Rigatoni

Prep: 15 min. | Cook: 4 hours

I turn my slow cooker into a pizzeria with this zesty slow-cooked casserole. It's loaded with cheese, sausage, pepperoni and pasta. —Marilyn Cowan, North Manchester, Indiana

1-1/2	pounds bulk Italian sausage
3	cups uncooked rigatoni *or* large tube pasta
4	cups (16 ounces) shredded part-skim mozzarella cheese
1	can (10-3/4 ounces) condensed cream of mushroom soup, undiluted
1	small onion, chopped
2	cans (one 15 ounces, one 8 ounces) pizza sauce
1	package (3-1/2 ounces) sliced pepperoni
1	can (6 ounces) pitted ripe olives, drained and halved

In a skillet, cook sausage until no longer pink; drain. Cook pasta according to package directions; drain.

In a 5-qt. slow cooker, layer half of the sausage, pasta, cheese, soup, onion, pizza sauce, pepperoni and olives. Repeat the layers. Cover and cook on low for 4 hours. **Yield: 6-8 servings.**

Golden Corn Casserole

Prep: 10 min. | Bake: 35 min.

I combine corn bread mix, French onion dip and canned corn to make this super moist side dish. After serving it for Thanksgiving one year, it was so popular that it's now served at all of our holiday gatherings. —Marcia Braun, Scott City, Kansas

3	eggs
1	carton (8 ounces) French onion dip
1/4	cup butter, softened
1	package (8-1/2 ounces) corn bread/muffin mix
1/2	teaspoon salt
1/2	teaspoon pepper
1	can (15-1/4 ounces) whole kernel corn, drained
1	can (14-3/4 ounces) cream-style corn

In a large bowl, beat the eggs, dip, butter, corn bread mix, salt and pepper until combined. Stir in the corn.

Pour into a greased 11-in. x 7-in. baking dish. Bake, uncovered, at 350° for 35-40 minutes or until the edges are lightly browned and pull away from the sides of the dish. Yield: 8-10 servings.

Meaty Mac 'n' Cheese

Prep/Total Time: 20 min.

My husband is disabled and requires constant care. This doesn't leave me a lot of time to cook, so I came up with this tasty way to beef up a box of macaroni and cheese. The hearty mixture gets extra flavor from corn, ripe olives and zippy salsa. —Charlotte Kremer, Pahrump, Nevada

1	package (7-1/4 ounces) macaroni and cheese
1	pound ground beef
1/4	cup chopped onion
1-1/2	cups salsa
1/2	cup fresh *or* frozen corn
1	can (2-1/4 ounces) sliced ripe olives, drained
3	tablespoons diced pimientos

Shredded cheddar cheese

Chopped tomato

Set aside cheese sauce mix from macaroni and cheese; cook macaroni according to package directions.

Meanwhile, in a large saucepan, cook beef and onion over medium heat until meat is no longer pink; drain. Add the salsa, corn, olives and pimientos; cook until heated through.

Drain macaroni; add to beef mixture with contents of cheese sauce mix. Cook and stir until blended and heated through. Sprinkle with cheese and tomato. **Yield: 4-6 servings.**

Editor's Note: The milk and butter listed on the macaroni and cheese package are not used in this recipe.

Hearty Jambalaya

Prep: 15 min. | Cook: 6-1/4 hours

I love anything with Cajun spices, so I created this slow-cooker jambalaya that's just as good as that served in restaurants. If you can't find andouille sausage, hot links, smoked sausage or chorizo will also work. I like to serve it with warm corn bread and garnish it with sliced green onions. —Jennifer Fulk, Moreno Valley, California

1	can (28 ounces) diced tomatoes, undrained
1	pound fully cooked andouille sausage links, cubed
1/2	pound boneless skinless chicken breasts, cut into 1-inch cubes
1	can (8 ounces) tomato sauce
1	cup diced onion
1	small sweet red pepper, diced
1	small green pepper, diced
1	cup chicken broth
1	celery rib with leaves, chopped
2	tablespoons tomato paste
2	teaspoons dried oregano
2	teaspoons Cajun seasoning
1-1/2	teaspoons minced garlic
2	bay leaves
1	teaspoon Louisiana-style hot sauce
1/2	teaspoon dried thyme
1	pound cooked medium shrimp, peeled and deveined

Hot cooked rice

In a 5-qt. slow cooker, combine the first 16 ingredients. Cover and cook on low for 6-7 hours or until chicken juices run clear. Stir in shrimp. Cover and cook 15 minutes longer or until heated through. Discard bay leaves. Serve with rice. Yield: 8 servings.

Hearty Jambalaya

Lazy Man's Ribs

Lazy Man's Ribs

Prep: 20 min. | Cook: 5-1/2 hours

These ribs are finger-lickin' good and fall-off-the-bone tender! I've made them for a lot of my buddies—including my preacher—and some have even suggested that I try bottling my sauce and selling it to the public! —Allan Stackhouse Jr., Jennings, Louisiana

2-1/2   pounds pork baby back ribs, cut into eight pieces
2   teaspoons Cajun seasoning
1   medium onion, sliced
1   cup ketchup
1/2   cup packed brown sugar
1/3   cup orange juice
1/3   cup cider vinegar
1/4   cup molasses
2   tablespoons Worcestershire sauce
1   tablespoon barbecue sauce
1   teaspoon stone-ground mustard
1   teaspoon paprika
1/2   teaspoon garlic powder
1/2   teaspoon Liquid Smoke, optional
Dash salt
5   teaspoons cornstarch
1   tablespoon water

Rub ribs with Cajun seasoning. Layer ribs and onion in a 5-qt. slow cooker. In a small bowl, combine the ketchup, brown sugar, orange juice, vinegar, molasses, Worcestershire sauce, barbecue sauce, mustard, paprika, garlic powder, Liquid Smoke if desired and salt. Pour over ribs. Cover and cook on low for 5-1/2 to 6-1/2 hours or until meat is tender.

Remove the ribs and keep warm. Strain cooking juices and skim fat; transfer to a saucepan. Combine the cornstarch and water until smooth; stir into juices. Bring to a boil; cook and stir for 2 minutes or until thickened. Serve with the ribs.
Yield: 4 servings.

Pizza Loaf

Prep: 20 min. | Bake: 35 min.

This stromboli relies on frozen bread dough, so it comes together in no time. The golden loaf is stuffed with cheese, pepperoni, mushrooms, peppers and olives. I often add a few slices of ham. It's tasty served with warm pizza sauce for dipping.
—Jenny Brown, West Lafayette, Indiana

1   loaf (1 pound) frozen bread dough, thawed
2   eggs, *separated*
1   tablespoon grated Parmesan cheese
1   tablespoon olive oil
1   teaspoon minced fresh parsley
1   teaspoon dried oregano
1/2   teaspoon garlic powder
1/4   teaspoon pepper
8   ounces sliced pepperoni
2   cups (8 ounces) shredded part-skim mozzarella cheese
1   can (4 ounces) mushroom stems and pieces, drained
1/4   to 1/2 cup pickled pepper rings
1   medium green pepper, diced
1   can (2-1/4 ounces) sliced ripe olives
1   can (15 ounces) pizza sauce

On a greased baking sheet, roll out dough into a 15-in. x 10-in. rectangle. In a small bowl, combine the egg yolks, Parmesan cheese, oil, parsley, oregano, garlic powder and pepper. Brush over the dough.

Sprinkle with the pepperoni, mozzarella cheese, mushrooms, pepper rings, green pepper and olives. Roll up, jelly-roll style, starting with a long side; pinch seam to seal and tuck the ends under.

Place seam side down; brush with egg whites. Do not let the loaf rise. Bake at 350° for 35-40 minutes or until golden brown. Warm the pizza sauce; serve with the sliced loaf.
Yield: 10-12 slices.

Pizza Loaf

Zucchini Ricotta Bake

Prep: 15 min. | Bake: 1 hour + standing

I have made this lasagna-like zucchini casserole frequently over the years and shared the recipe with many people. Best of all, it's a little bit lighter than other layered casseroles, making it a great choice for anyone trying to eat right.

—Eleanor Hauserman, Huntsville, Alabama

- 2 pounds zucchini
- 1 carton (15 ounces) reduced-fat ricotta cheese
- 1/2 cup egg substitute
- 1/2 cup dry bread crumbs, *divided*
- 5 tablespoons grated Parmesan cheese, *divided*
- 1 tablespoon minced fresh parsley
- 1/4 teaspoon dried oregano
- 1/4 teaspoon dried basil
- 1/8 teaspoon pepper
- 1 jar (28 ounces) reduced-sodium meatless spaghetti sauce
- 1-1/2 cups (6 ounces) shredded reduced-fat mozzarella cheese

Cut zucchini lengthwise into 1/4-in. slices. Place in a basket over 1 in. of boiling water. Cover and steam for 5-6 minutes or until just tender. Drain; pat dry.

In a large bowl, combine the ricotta cheese, egg substitute, 3 tablespoons bread crumbs, 3 tablespoons Parmesan, parsley, oregano, basil and pepper; set aside.

Spread a third of the spaghetti sauce in a 13-in. x 9-in. baking dish coated with cooking spray. Sprinkle with 2 tablespoons bread crumbs. Cover with half of the zucchini, ricotta mixture and mozzarella. Repeat layers of sauce, zucchini, ricotta mixture and mozzarella. Cover with remaining sauce.

Combine remaining crumbs and Parmesan; sprinkle over top. Cover and bake at 350° for 45 minutes. Uncover; bake 15 minutes longer. Let stand 15 minutes before cutting. **Yield: 12 servings.**

Nutrition Facts: 1 serving equals 201 calories, 9 g fat (0 saturated fat), 21 mg cholesterol, 237 mg sodium, 18 g carbohydrate, 3 g fiber, 12 g protein. **Diabetic Exchanges:** *1 starch, 1 meat, 1 fat, 1/2 vegetable.*

Meatball Sub Casserole

Prep: 15 min. | Bake: 45 min.

If you like meatball subs, you'll love this tangy casserole—it has all the rich flavor of the popular sandwiches with none of the mess. Italian bread is spread with a cream cheese mixture, then topped with meatballs, spaghetti sauce and cheese. Served with a green salad, it's a hearty meal the whole family will enjoy.

—Gina Harris, Seneca, South Carolina

Meatball Sub Casserole

- 1/3 cup chopped green onions
- 1/4 cup seasoned bread crumbs
- 3 tablespoons grated Parmesan cheese
- 1 pound ground beef
- 1 loaf (1 pound) Italian bread, cut into 1-inch slices
- 1 package (8 ounces) cream cheese, softened
- 1/2 cup mayonnaise
- 1 teaspoon Italian seasoning
- 1/4 teaspoon pepper
- 2 cups (8 ounces) shredded part-skim mozzarella cheese, *divided*
- 1 jar (28 ounces) spaghetti sauce
- 1 cup water
- 2 garlic cloves, minced

In a bowl, combine the onions, crumbs and Parmesan cheese. Add beef and mix well. Shape into 1-in. balls; place on a greased rack in a shallow baking pan. Bake at 400° for 15-20 minutes or until no longer pink.

Meanwhile, arrange bread in a single layer in an ungreased 13-in. x 9-in. baking dish (all of the bread might not be used). Combine the cream cheese, mayonnaise, Italian seasoning and pepper; spread over the bread. Sprinkle with 1/2 cup mozzarella.

Combine the sauce, water and garlic; add meatballs. Pour over cheese mixture; sprinkle with remaining mozzarella. Bake, uncovered, at 350° for 30 minutes or until heated through. **Yield: 6-8 servings.**

Editor's Note: Reduced-fat or fat-free mayonnaise is not recommended for this recipe.

Meat Loaf Miniatures

Prep: 20 min. | Bake: 30 min.

I don't usually like meat loaf, but my family and I can't get enough of these little muffins topped with a sweet ketchup sauce. This recipe requires no chopping, so it's quick and easy to make a double batch and have extras for another day. They're great to give to new moms, too. —Joyce Wegmann, Burlington, Iowa

1	cup ketchup
3	to 4 tablespoons packed brown sugar
1	teaspoon ground mustard
2	eggs, lightly beaten
4	teaspoons Worcestershire sauce
3	cups Crispix cereal, crushed
3	teaspoons onion powder
1/2	to 1 teaspoon seasoned salt
1/2	teaspoon garlic powder
1/2	teaspoon pepper
3	pounds lean ground beef

In a large bowl, combine the ketchup, brown sugar and mustard. Remove 1/2 cup for topping; set aside. Add the eggs, Worcestershire sauce, cereal and seasonings to remaining ketchup mixture. Let stand for 5 minutes. Crumble beef over cereal mixture and mix well.

Press meat mixture into 18 muffin cups (about 1/3 cup each). Bake at 375° for 18-20 minutes. Drizzle with reserved ketchup mixture; bake 10 minutes longer or until meat is no longer pink and a meat thermometer reads 160°.

Serve the desired number of meat loaves. Cool the remaining loaves and freeze. Transfer to freezer bags; seal and freeze for up to 3 months.

To use frozen meat loaves: Completely thaw in the refrigerator. Place loaves in a greased baking dish. Bake at 350° for 30 minutes or until heated through, or cover and microwave on high for 1 minute or until heated through.
Yield: 1-1/2 dozen.

Tomato Bacon Pie

Tomato Bacon Pie

Prep: 15 min. | Bake: 30 min.

This simple but savory pie makes a tasty addition to brunch buffets and leisurely luncheons. I rely on a cheesy mixture for the pie's golden topping and a refrigerated pastry shell for easy preparation. —Gladys Gibson, Hodgenville, Kentucky

1	unbaked deep-dish pastry shell (9 inches)
3	medium tomatoes, cut into 1/4-inch slices
10	bacon strips, cooked and crumbled
1	cup (4 ounces) shredded cheddar cheese
1	cup mayonnaise

Bake pastry shell according to package directions; cool. Place tomatoes in the crust; sprinkle with bacon. In a small bowl, combine the cheese and mayonnaise. Spoon over bacon in the center of pie, leaving 1 in. around edge.

Bake at 350° for 30-40 minutes or until golden brown (cover the edges with foil if necessary to prevent over browning).
Yield: 6 servings.

Editor's Note: Reduced-fat or fat-free mayonnaise is not recommended for this recipe.

Meat Loaf Miniatures

Watermelon Spinach Salad

For a refreshing side salad, try this easy idea:

In a blender, combine 1/2 cup each of white wine vinegar and sugar, 1/2 teaspoon each of ground mustard and salt and 1/4 teaspoon onion powder. Process until sugar is dissolved. With the blender running, slowly add 1/2 cup canola oil. Add 1/2 cup chopped onion and 1 teaspoon poppy seeds. In a large salad bowl, combine 6 ounces fresh baby spinach, 2 cups cubed watermelon, 1 cup halved green grapes and 1 cup fresh raspberries. Sprinkle with 1/4 cup sliced almonds and the dressing.

Rich French Onion Soup

Prep: 10 min. | Cook: 5 hours

When entertaining guests, I bring out this hearty soup while we're waiting for the main course. It's a snap to make—just saute the onions early in the day and let the soup simmer until dinnertime. In winter, big bowls of it create a warm supper with a salad and biscuits. —Linda Adolph, Edmonton, Alberta

- 6 large onions, chopped
- 1/2 cup butter
- 6 cans (10-1/2 ounces *each*) condensed beef broth, undiluted
- 1-1/2 teaspoons Worcestershire sauce
- 3 bay leaves
- 10 slices French bread, toasted

Shredded Parmesan and shredded part-skim mozzarella cheese

In a large skillet, saute onions in butter until crisp-tender. Transfer to an ungreased 3-qt. slow cooker. Add the broth, Worcestershire sauce and bay leaves.

Cover and cook on low for 5-7 hours or until the onions are tender. Discard bay leaves. Top each serving with French bread and cheeses. **Yield:** 10 servings.

Pork with Apricot Sauce

Prep: 10 min. | Bake: 30 min.

Dress up pork tenderloin with a sweet apricot sauce mildly seasoned with ginger. It makes an impressive entree, yet leaves plenty of extra pork for meals later in the week. The sauce is also good on baked ham. —Kris Wells, Hereford, Arizona

- 4 pork tenderloins (1 pound *each*)
- 1 jar (12 ounces) apricot preserves
- 1/3 cup lemon juice
- 1/3 cup ketchup
- 1/4 cup sherry *or* chicken broth
- 3 tablespoons honey
- 1 tablespoon soy sauce
- 1/8 to 1/4 teaspoon ground ginger

Place tenderloins on a rack in a shallow roasting pan. Bake, uncovered, at 450° for 30-35 minutes or until a meat thermometer reads 160°. Meanwhile, in a saucepan, combine the remaining ingredients. Cook and stir until heated through.

Slice the pork; serve 1 1/2 pounds with the apricot sauce. Refrigerate or freeze remaining pork. **Yield:** 4-6 servings (2 cups sauce) plus 2-1/2 pounds leftover pork.

Pork with Apricot Sauce

Southwestern Veggie Bake

Southwestern Veggie Bake

Prep: 20 min. | Bake: 20 min.

Refrigerated corn bread twists create an appealing lattice top on this zippy main dish. The original recipe contained cooked chicken instead of kidney beans and celery, but my family prefers my meatless version, which is spicier, too. It's such a time-saver that I make it often!
                                    —Julie Zeager, Kent, Ohio

> 3 medium carrots, sliced
> 2 celery ribs, chopped
> 1 small onion, chopped
> 2 to 3 teaspoons chili powder
> 1 teaspoon ground cumin
> 1/4 teaspoon cayenne pepper
> 2 tablespoons butter
> 3 tablespoons all-purpose flour
> 1/2 cup milk
> 1 can (16 ounces) kidney beans, rinsed and drained
> 1 can (15 ounces) black beans, rinsed and drained
> 1 can (15-1/4 ounces) whole kernel corn, drained
> 1 can (14-1/2 ounces) diced tomatoes, undrained
> 1 can (4 ounces) chopped green chilies
> 1 tube (11-1/2 ounces) refrigerated corn bread twists

In a large skillet, saute the carrots, celery, onion and seasonings in butter until vegetables are crisp-tender. Stir in flour until blended. Gradually add the milk. Bring to a boil; cook and stir for 2 minutes or until thickened and bubbly.

Remove from the heat; add beans, corn, tomatoes and chilies. Spoon into an ungreased 13-in. x 9-in. baking dish. Separate corn bread twists; weave a lattice crust over filling.

Bake, uncovered, at 350° for 20-25 minutes or until corn bread is golden brown. **Yield: 8 servings.**

Taco-Filled Pasta Shells

Prep: 20 min. + chilling | Bake: 45 min.

I've been stuffing pasta shells with different fillings for years, but my family enjoys this version with taco-seasoned meat the most. I freeze the shells so I can take out only the number I need for a single-serving lunch or family dinner. Just add zippy taco sauce and bake.   —Marge Hodel, Roanoke, Illinois

> 2 pounds ground beef
> 2 envelopes taco seasoning
> 1 package (8 ounces) cream cheese, cubed
> 24 uncooked jumbo pasta shells
> 1/4 cup butter, melted
> ADDITIONAL INGREDIENTS (for each casserole):
> 1 cup salsa
> 1 cup taco sauce
> 1 cup (4 ounces) shredded cheddar cheese
> 1 cup (4 ounces) shredded Monterey Jack cheese
> 1-1/2 cups crushed tortilla chips
> 1 cup (8 ounces) sour cream
> 3 green onions, chopped

In a Dutch oven, cook beef over medium heat until no longer pink; drain. Add taco seasoning; prepare according to package directions. Add cream cheese; cook and stir for 5-10 minutes or until melted. Transfer to a bowl; chill for 1 hour.

Cook pasta according to package directions; drain. Gently toss with butter. Fill each shell with about 3 tablespoons of meat mixture. Place 12 shells in a freezer container. Cover and freeze for up to 3 months.

To prepare remaining shells, spoon salsa into a greased 9-in. square baking dish. Top with stuffed shells and taco sauce. Cover and bake at 350° for 30 minutes. Uncover; sprinkle with cheeses and chips. Bake 15 minutes longer or until heated through. Serve with sour cream and onions.

To use frozen shells: Thaw in the refrigerator for 24 hours (shells will be partially frozen). Spoon salsa into a greased 9-in. square baking dish; top with shells and taco sauce. Cover and bake at 350° for 40 minutes. Uncover and continue as above. **Yield: 2 casseroles (6 servings each).**

Taco-Filled Pasta Shells

Reuben Meat Loaf

Special Scallops and Chicken
Prep: 15 min. | Bake: 20 min.

I make this main course when I want to wow company. It tastes heavenly, and guests always love it.
—*Sheila Vail, Long Beach, California*

- 1/2   cup all-purpose flour
- 1/2   teaspoon salt
- 1/2   teaspoon pepper
- 6   boneless skinless chicken breast halves (4 ounces *each*)
- 1/2   pound bay scallops
- 1/4   cup olive oil
- 1-1/2   cups sliced fresh mushrooms
- 1   medium onion, chopped
- 1/4   cup white wine *or* chicken broth
- 2   teaspoons cornstarch
- 1/2   cup heavy whipping cream
- 1   teaspoon dried tarragon
- 1/2   cup shredded Swiss cheese

In a large resealable plastic bag, combine the flour, salt and pepper. Add chicken and scallops in batches; shake to coat. In a large skillet, saute chicken and scallops in oil until lightly browned. Transfer to a greased 13-in. x 9-in. baking dish.

In the pan drippings, saute mushrooms and onion. Add wine or broth. Bring to a boil; cook until the liquid is reduced to 2 tablespoons. Combine the cornstarch, cream and tarragon until blended; add to skillet. Bring to a boil; cook and stir for 1 minute or until thickened. Spoon over chicken and scallops. Sprinkle with cheese.

Bake, uncovered, at 375° for 18-20 minutes or until a meat thermometer reads 170°. **Yield: 6 servings.**

Reuben Meat Loaf
Prep: 15 min. | Bake: 55 min. + standing

This moist loaf is sure to become a favorite with sauerkraut lovers. I roll tangy kraut, Swiss cheese and Thousand Island salad dressing into well-seasoned ground beef for a delicious dinner.
—*Mary Alice Taylor, Downingtown, Pennsylvania*

- 1   egg, lightly beaten
- 1   medium onion, chopped
- 1/4   cup sweet pickle relish
- 1   tablespoon Worcestershire sauce
- 1   cup soft rye bread crumbs
- 1/2   teaspoon salt
- 1/4   teaspoon pepper
- 2   pounds lean ground beef
- 1/4   cup prepared Thousand Island salad dressing
- 1   can (8 ounces) sauerkraut, rinsed and drained
- 1   cup (4 ounces) shredded Swiss cheese, *divided*

In a large bowl, combine the first seven ingredients. Crumble beef over mixture and mix well. On a piece of heavy-duty aluminum foil, pat meat mixture into a 14-in. x 10-in. rectangle. Spread with salad dressing; top with sauerkraut and 1/2 cup Swiss cheese. Roll up, starting with a long side and peeling foil away while rolling; seal seams and ends.

Place in a greased 15-in. x 10-in. baking pan. Bake, uncovered, at 350° for 50-55 minutes or until the meat is no longer pink and a meat thermometer reads 160°; drain. Sprinkle with the remaining cheese. Bake 2 minutes longer or until cheese is melted. Let stand 10 minutes before slicing. **Yield: 8 servings.**

Special Scallops and Chicken

Pork Chop Potato Dinner

Pork Chop Potato Dinner
Prep: 10 min. | Cook: 2-1/2 hours

Tender chops cook on a bed of tasty potatoes in this all-in-one meal. It's a snap to assemble, thanks to frozen hash browns, canned soup, shredded cheese and french-fried onions.

—Dawn Huizinga, Owatonna, Minnesota

       6   bone-in pork loin chops (1/2 inch thick and
           8 ounces *each*)
       1   tablespoon canola oil
       1   package (30 ounces) frozen shredded hash
           brown potatoes, thawed
   1-1/2   cups (6 ounces) shredded cheddar cheese,
           divided
       1   can (10-3/4 ounces) condensed cream of celery
           soup, undiluted
     1/2   cup milk
     1/2   cup sour cream
     1/2   teaspoon seasoned salt
     1/8   teaspoon pepper
       1   can (2.8 ounces) french-fried onions,
           divided

In a large skillet, brown the chops in oil on both sides; set aside and keep warm. In a large bowl, combine the potatoes, 1 cup cheese, soup, milk, sour cream, seasoned salt and pepper. Stir in half of the onions.

Transfer to a greased 5-qt. slow cooker; top with pork chops. Cover and cook on high for 2-1/2 to 3 hours or until meat is tender. Sprinkle with remaining cheese and onions. Cover and cook 10 minutes longer or until cheese is melted. **Yield: 6 servings.**

Turkey Rice Casserole
Prep: 20 min. | Cook: 15 min.

The recipe for this creamy and comforting casserole came from my aunt as a way to use extra turkey. I love it so much, however, that I don't wait for leftovers to make it. The green chilies provide the memorable flavor.

—Tamy Baker, Kearney, Nebraska

       1   medium onion, chopped
       1   celery rib, chopped
       2   tablespoons butter
       2   cups milk
   1-1/4   cups uncooked instant rice
       2   cups diced cooked turkey
       1   can (10-3/4 ounces) condensed cream of
           mushroom soup, undiluted
       1   cup seasoned stuffing cubes
       1   can (4 ounces) chopped green chilies, drained
       1   cup (4 ounces) shredded cheddar cheese, *divided*

In a 2-qt. microwave-safe dish, combine the onion, celery and butter. Cover and microwave on high for 1-1/2 to 3 minutes or until butter is melted. Stir in milk. Cover and cook on high for 3-5 minutes or until milk is steaming (do not boil). Stir in rice. Cover and let stand for 2 minutes.

Add the turkey, soup, stuffing cubes, green chilies and 1/2 cup cheese. Cover and microwave on high for 3-6 minutes or until heated through, stirring once. Sprinkle with the remaining cheese. Cover and let stand for 5 minutes. **Yield: 6-8 servings.**

Editor's Note: This recipe was tested in a 1,100-watt microwave.

Colorful Chicken Stew

Prep: 10 min. | Cook: 8 hours

I rely on chili powder to spice up this hearty stew with chicken and fresh-tasting veggies. Since it's prepared in a slow cooker, it's wonderful to have it ready when you walk in the door.
—Ila Mae Alderman, Galax, Virginia

- 1 pound boneless skinless chicken breasts, cubed
- 1 can (14-1/2 ounces) Italian diced tomatoes, undrained
- 2 medium potatoes, peeled and cut into 1/2-inch cubes
- 5 medium carrots, chopped
- 3 celery ribs, chopped
- 1 large onion, chopped
- 1 medium green pepper, chopped
- 2 cans (4 ounces *each*) mushroom stems and pieces, drained
- 2 low-sodium chicken bouillon cubes

Artificial sweetener equivalent to 2 teaspoons sugar
- 1 teaspoon chili powder
- 1/4 teaspoon pepper
- 1 tablespoon cornstarch
- 2 cups cold water

In a 5-qt. slow cooker, combine the first 12 ingredients. In a small bowl, combine the cornstarch and water until smooth. Stir into the chicken mixture. Cover and cook on low for 8-10 hours or until the chicken is no longer pink and vegetables are tender. **Yield:** 10 servings.

Nutrition Facts: 1 cup serving equals 123 calories, 209 mg sodium, 25 mg cholesterol, 16 gm carbohydrate, 11 gm protein, 1 gm fat, 3 gm fiber. Diabetic Exchanges: 2 vegetable, 1 very lean meat, 1/2 starch.

Vegetable Beef Stew

Prep: 20 min. | Cook: 9 hours

Here's a great beef stew that simmers in a delicious gravy. Served with a loaf of crusty bread and a green salad, it's a tasty meal for grown-ups and kids alike. I think it's better the next day.
—Randee Eckstein, Commack, New York

- 5 medium red potatoes, peeled and cut into 1/2-inch chunks
- 2-1/2 cups sliced fresh mushrooms
- 4 medium carrots, sliced
- 2 celery ribs, thinly sliced
- 3 bacon strips, diced
- 1/4 cup all-purpose flour
- 3/4 teaspoon pepper, *divided*
- 1/2 teaspoon salt, *divided*
- 2 pounds beef stew meat, cut into 3/4-inch cubes
- 1 large onion, chopped

- 2 garlic cloves, minced
- 1 tablespoon canola oil
- 1 can (14-1/2 ounces) beef broth
- 1/2 cup dry red wine *or* additional beef broth
- 1 bay leaf
- 1/8 teaspoon dried thyme
- 1 can (10-3/4 ounces) condensed tomato soup, undiluted
- 1/3 cup water
- 2 tablespoons cornstarch
- 3 tablespoons cold water

Place the first four ingredients in a 5-qt. slow cooker. In a large skillet, cook the bacon over medium heat until crisp. Using a slotted spoon, remove bacon to paper towels to drain. Reserve drippings.

In a large resealable plastic bag, combine the flour, 1/4 teaspoon pepper and 1/4 teaspoon salt. Add meat, a few pieces at a time; seal and shake to coat. Brown the beef, onion and garlic in drippings and oil.

Transfer to slow cooker. Stir in the broth, wine or additional broth, bay leaf, thyme, reserved bacon and remaining salt and pepper. Cover and cook on low for 8-9 hours or until meat is tender. Discard bay leaf.

Combine soup and 1/3 cup water; add to slow cooker. Cover and cook on high for 30 minutes. Combine cornstarch and cold water; stir into slow cooker. Cover and cook for 30-40 minutes or until thickened. **Yield:** 7-8 servings.

Vegetable Beef Stew

Orange-Glazed Cornish Hens

Prep: 10 min. | Bake: 1-1/4 hours

This is a wonderfully elegant entree to serve at a dinner party for four. Your guests will think you spent hours in the kitchen preparing the tender hens and perfecting the full-flavored basting sauce. —Laurie Bartley, Lake Hiawatha, New Jersey

4	Cornish game hens (22 ounces *each*)
1/4	cup butter, melted
1	teaspoon salt
1/2	teaspoon pepper
3/4	cup orange juice
1/2	cup packed brown sugar
1/2	cup Madeira wine, sherry *or* chicken broth
2	tablespoons lemon juice
1	teaspoon ground mustard
1/4	teaspoon ground allspice

Tie the legs of each hen together; turn wing tips under backs. Place on a greased rack in a roasting pan. Brush with butter; sprinkle with salt and pepper. Bake, uncovered, at 350° for 1 hour.

In a saucepan, combine the remaining ingredients; bring to a boil. Reduce heat; simmer, uncovered, for 15 minutes. Spoon over hens. Bake 15 minutes longer or until a meat thermometer reads 180°. **Yield: 4 servings.**

Orange-Glazed Cornish Hens

Saucy Apricot Chicken

Saucy Apricot Chicken

Prep: 5 min. | Cook: 4 hours

Four ingredients are all you'll need for this tender chicken entree. The tangy glaze is just as wonderful with ham or turkey. Leftovers reheat nicely in the microwave. —Dee Gray, Kokomo, Indiana

6	boneless skinless chicken breast halves (4 ounces *each*)
2	jars (12 ounces *each*) apricot preserves
1	envelope onion soup mix

Hot cooked rice

Place chicken in a 3-qt. slow cooker. Combine the preserves and soup mix; spoon over chicken. Cover and cook on low for 4-5 hours or until a meat thermometer reads 170°. Serve with rice. **Yield: 6 servings.**

Cornish Hens

A Rock Cornish game hen, or Cornish hen as it's more commonly called, is actually a young chicken that is usually from 5 to 6 weeks of age and weighs no more than 2 pounds at the ready-to-cook stage. The name comes from the breed, which is a cross between a Cornish and Plymouth Rock chicken. Because their meat-to-bone ratio is so small, one Cornish hen is enough to serve one person. Roasting is the best way to cook Cornish hens, but they can also be sauteed and braised. When filling the cavities with stuffing, be sure not to stuff until just before you put them in the oven.

Soft Chicken Tacos

Prep: 30 min. | Cook: 5 hours

My family loves these tacos. The chicken filling cooks in the slow-cooker, so it's convenient to throw it together before I leave for work. At the end of the day, I just have to roll it up in a tortilla with the remaining ingredients and dinner's ready in minutes. The chicken also makes a great topping for salad.

—Cheryl Newendorp, Pella, Iowa

1	broiler/fryer chicken (3-1/2 pounds), cut up and skin removed
1	can (8 ounces) tomato sauce
1	can (4 ounces) chopped green chilies
1/3	cup chopped onion
2	tablespoons chili powder
2	tablespoons Worcestershire sauce
1/4	teaspoon garlic powder
10	flour tortillas (8 inches), warmed
1-1/4	cups shredded cheddar cheese
1-1/4	cups salsa
1-1/4	cups shredded lettuce
1	large tomato, chopped
3/4	cup sour cream, optional

Place the chicken in a 3-qt. slow cooker. In a small bowl, combine the tomato sauce, chilies, onion, chili powder, Worcestershire sauce and garlic powder; pour over chicken. Cover and cook on low for 5-6 hours or until chicken is tender and juices run clear.

Remove the chicken. Shred meat with two forks and return to the slow cooker; heat through. Spoon 1/2 cup chicken mixture down the center of each tortilla. Top with cheese, salsa, lettuce, tomato and sour cream if desired; roll up. **Yield: 5 servings.**

Ham and Cheese Loaf

Prep: 15 min. | Bake: 30 min.

This golden loaf relies on the convenience of refrigerated dough that's stuffed with ham and cheese. I created the recipe by experimenting with a few simple ingredients my family loves. It makes a delicious hot sandwich in no time.

—Gloria Lindell, Welcome, Minnesota

1	tube (13.8 ounces) refrigerated pizza crust
10	slices deli ham
1/4	cup sliced green onions
1	cup (4 ounces) shredded part-skim mozzarella cheese
1	cup (4 ounces) shredded cheddar cheese
4	slices provolone cheese
1	tablespoon butter, melted

Unroll dough onto a greased baking sheet; top with the ham, onions and cheeses. Roll up tightly jelly-roll style, starting with a long side; pinch seam to seal and tuck ends under. Brush with butter.

Bake at 350° for 30-35 minutes or until golden brown. Let stand for 5 minutes; cut into 1-in. slices. **Yield: 6 servings.**

Pizza Tot Casserole

Prep: 10 min. | Bake: 30 min.

This upside-down pizza casserole requires ground beef and six other easy ingredients. The Tater Tots make this simple supper a guaranteed kid-pleaser. —Chris Stukel, Des Plaines, Illinois

1	pound ground beef
1	medium green pepper, chopped
1	medium onion, chopped
1	can (10-3/4 ounces) condensed tomato soup, undiluted
1	jar (4-1/2 ounces) sliced mushrooms, drained
1	teaspoon Italian seasoning
2	cups (8 ounces) shredded part-skim mozzarella cheese
1	package (32 ounces) frozen Tater Tots

In a large skillet, cook the beef, pepper and onion over medium heat until meat is no longer pink; drain. Add soup, mushrooms and Italian seasoning.

Transfer to a greased 13-in. x 9-in. baking dish. Top with cheese and potatoes. Bake, uncovered, at 400° for 30-35 minutes or until golden brown. **Yield: 6-8 servings.**

Pizza Tot Casserole

Slow Cooker Beef Brisket

Slow Cooker Beef Brisket

Prep: 20 min. | Cook: 6 hours

This brisket is so easy to prepare and has been a family favorite for years. I added the fresh mushrooms to give it more flavor.
—*Mary Ann Lee, Clifton Park, New York*

1	fresh beef brisket (3 to 4 pounds)
1/2	pound sliced fresh mushrooms
2	bay leaves
2	cups crushed tomatoes
1	cup chopped onion
1/2	cup packed brown sugar
1/2	cup balsamic vinegar
1/2	cup ketchup
1/4	cup cornstarch
1/4	cup cold water

Cut brisket in half; place in a 5-qt. slow cooker. Add mushrooms and bay leaves. Combine the tomatoes, onion, brown sugar, vinegar and ketchup; pour over beef. Cover and cook on low for 6-7 hours or until meat is tender.

Remove beef and keep warm. Discard bay leaves. In a large saucepan, combine cornstarch and water until smooth. Gradually stir in cooking liquid. Bring to a boil; cook and stir for 2 minutes or until thickened. Slice meat across the grain; serve with gravy. **Yield: 6-8 servings.**

Editor's Note: This is a fresh beef brisket, not corned beef.

Leftover Brisket

A delicious way to use up leftover beef brisket is to use it for sandwiches. Saute some garlic, onion and bell peppers in a little olive oil. Layer the meat and vegetables on bread and top with your favorite cheese. Pop the sandwich under the broiler to melt the cheese.

Taco Lasagna

Prep: 20 min. | Bake: 25 min.

If you like foods with Southwestern flair, this just might become a new favorite. Loaded with cheese, meat and beans, the layered casserole comes together in a snap. There are never any leftovers when I take this dish to potlucks.
—*Terri Keenan, Tuscaloosa, Alabama*

1	pound ground beef
1/2	cup chopped green pepper
1/2	cup chopped onion
2/3	cup water
1	envelope taco seasoning
1	can (15 ounces) black beans, rinsed and drained
1	can (14-1/2 ounces) Mexican diced tomatoes, undrained
6	flour tortillas (8 inches)
1	can (16 ounces) refried beans
3	cups (12 ounces) shredded Mexican cheese blend

In a large skillet, cook the beef, green pepper and onion over medium heat until meat is no longer pink; drain. Add water and taco seasoning; bring to a boil. Reduce heat; simmer, uncovered, for 2 minutes. Stir in the black beans and tomatoes. Simmer, uncovered, for 10 minutes.

Place two tortillas in a greased 13-in. x 9-in. baking dish. Spread with half of the refried beans and beef mixture; sprinkle with 1 cup cheese. Repeat layers. Top with remaining tortillas and cheese.

Cover and bake at 350° for 25-30 minutes or until heated through and cheese is melted. **Yield: 9 servings.**

Taco Lasagna

Southwestern Pulled Pork

Prep: 5 min. | Cook: 8-1/4 hours

The best way to describe this tender pork recipe is "yummy"! Bottled barbecue sauce, canned green chilies and a few other kitchen staples make preparation fast and simple. We like to wrap the seasoned pork in flour tortillas.

—Jill Hartung, Colorado Springs, Colorado

2	cans (4 ounces *each*) chopped green chilies
1	can (8 ounces) tomato sauce
1	cup barbecue sauce
1	large sweet onion, thinly sliced
1/4	cup chili powder
1	teaspoon ground cumin
1	teaspoon dried oregano
1	boneless pork loin roast (2 to 2-1/2 pounds)

Flour tortillas

Toppings: sour cream, shredded lettuce and chopped tomatoes, optional

In a 3-qt. slow cooker, combine the chilies, tomato sauce, barbecue sauce, onion, chili powder, cumin and oregano. Cut pork in half; place on top of tomato sauce mixture. Cover and cook on low for 8-9 hours or until meat is tender.

Remove pork. When cool enough to handle, shred meat using two forks. Return to slow cooker and heat through. Spread on tortillas; top with sour cream, lettuce and tomatoes if desired. Roll up. **Yield: 6-8 servings.**

Garlic Chuck Roast

Prep: 15 min. | Bake: 2-1/4 hours + standing

Having never made a roast before, I experimented with a few ingredients to come up with this hearty all in one meal. Not only is it easy, but the tender entree gets terrific flavor from garlic, onion and bay leaves. —Janet Boyer, Nemacolin, Pennsylvania

1	boneless beef chuck roast (3 pounds)
15	garlic cloves, peeled
1	teaspoon salt
1/4	teaspoon pepper
2	tablespoons canola oil
5	bay leaves
1	large onion, thinly sliced
2	tablespoons butter, melted
1-1/2	cups water
1	pound baby carrots

With a sharp knife, cut 15 slits in roast; insert garlic into slits. Sprinkle meat with salt and pepper.

In a Dutch oven, brown meat in oil; drain. Place bay leaves on top of roast; top with onion slices. Drizzle with butter. Add water to pan. Cover and bake at 325° for 1-1/2 hours.

Baste the roast with pan juices; add carrots. Cover and bake 45-60 minutes longer or until meat and carrots are tender. Discard bay leaves. Let roast stand for 10 minutes before slicing. Thicken pan juices if desired. **Yield: 6-8 servings.**

Florentine Egg Bake

Prep: 30 min. | Bake: 50 min. + standing

This flavorful breakfast bake comes together quickly using handy convenience foods, including refrigerated hash browns, biscuit mix and store-bought pesto. For a seafood variation, replace the ham with crabmeat. —Patricia Harmon, Baden, Pennsylvania

1	package (20 ounces) refrigerated shredded hash brown potatoes
1	tablespoon olive oil
1	package (10 ounces) frozen chopped spinach, thawed and squeezed dry
4	ounces Swiss cheese, cubed
4	ounces thinly sliced deli ham, coarsely chopped
8	eggs
1/2	cup buttermilk
1	tablespoon prepared pesto
1	cup biscuit/baking mix
1/4	teaspoon salt
1/8	teaspoon pepper
1-1/2	cups shredded Asiago cheese
2	tablespoons minced fresh basil

In a large bowl, combine the hash browns and oil. Press into a 13-in. x 9-in. baking dish coated with cooking spray. Bake at 350° for 25-30 minutes or until edges are golden brown.

Combine the spinach and Swiss cheese; sprinkle over crust. Top with ham. In a large bowl, whisk the eggs, buttermilk and pesto. Combine the biscuit mix, salt and pepper; add to egg mixture. Stir in the Asiago cheese. Pour over ham.

Bake, uncovered, for 25-30 minutes or until a knife inserted near the center comes out clean. Let stand for 10-15 minutes before cutting. Sprinkle with basil. **Yield: 8 servings.**

Florentine Egg Bake

Herbed Chicken and Shrimp

Prep: 15 min. | Cook: 4 hours 20 min.

Tender chicken and shrimp make a flavorful combination that's easy to prepare, yet elegant enough to serve at a dinner party. While I clean the house, it practically cooks itself. I serve it over hot cooked rice with crusty bread and a green salad. —Diana Knight, Reno, Nevada

1	teaspoon salt
1	teaspoon pepper
1	broiler/fryer chicken (3 to 4 pounds), cut up and skin removed
1/4	cup butter
1	large onion, chopped
1	can (8 ounces) tomato sauce
1/2	cup white wine *or* chicken broth
1	garlic clove, minced
1	teaspoon dried basil
1	pound uncooked medium shrimp, peeled and deveined

Combine the salt and pepper; rub over the chicken pieces. In a skillet, brown the chicken on all sides in butter. Transfer to an ungreased 5-qt. slow cooker. In a bowl, combine the onion, tomato sauce, wine or broth, garlic and basil; pour over the chicken.

Cover and cook on low for 4-5 hours or until chicken juices run clear. Stir in the shrimp. Cover; cook on high for 20-30 minutes or until shrimp turn pink. **Yield: 4 servings.**

Mom's Oven-Barbecued Ribs

Prep: 10 min. | Bake: 2-3/4 hours

My mom made these tender ribs for special Sunday suppers when we were growing up. A few common ingredients are all you need to make the zesty sauce that coats them. My family's eyes light up when I bring these ribs to the table. —Yvonne White, Williamson, New York

3	to 4 pounds country-style pork ribs
1-1/2	cups water
1	cup ketchup
1/3	cup Worcestershire sauce
1	teaspoon salt
1	teaspoon chili powder
1/2	teaspoon onion powder
1/8	teaspoon hot pepper sauce

Place ribs in a greased roasting pan. Bake, uncovered, at 350° for 45 minutes. Meanwhile, in a saucepan, combine the remaining ingredients. Bring to a boil; cook for 1 minute. Drain ribs. Spoon sauce over ribs. Cover and bake for 1-1/2 hours. Uncover; bake 30 minutes longer, basting once. **Yield: 4-6 servings.**

Polish Kraut and Apples

1 pound bulk Italian sausage
2 cups (16 ounces) 4% cottage cheese
1 package (8 ounces) manicotti shells
1 jar (26 ounces) Italian baking sauce
1 cup (4 ounces) shredded part-skim mozzarella cheese

In a large bowl, combine the bulk Italian sausage and the cottage cheese. Stuff into the manicotti shells. Place in a greased 13-in. x 9-in. baking dish. Top with baking sauce.

Cover and bake the manicotti at 350° for 55-60 minutes or until a meat thermometer inserted into the center of a shell reads 160°.

Uncover; sprinkle with mozzarella cheese. Bake 8-10 minutes longer or until cheese is melted. Let stand for 5 minutes before serving. **Yield: 7 servings.**

Tips for Making Manicotti

Here are a couple of helpful hints when making the Sausage Manicotti:

When a recipe calls for Italian sausage, it is referring to sweet Italian sausage. Recipes using hot Italian sausage specifically call for that type. Spooning a cheesy filling into tubular manicotti shells can be time-consuming and messy. To avoid the trouble, put the filling into a cake decorating bag and easily pipe it into the pasta tubes.

Polish Kraut and Apples

Prep: 10 min. | Cook: 4 hours

My family loves this hearty, heartwarming meal on cold winter nights. The tender apples, brown sugar and smoked sausage give this dish fantastic flavor. I like making it because it's super easy to prepare and the prep time is short.

—Caren Markee, Crystal Lake, Illinois

1 can (14 ounces) sauerkraut, rinsed and well drained
1 package (16 ounces) smoked Polish sausage or kielbasa, cut into chunks
3 medium tart apples, peeled and cut into eighths
1/2 cup packed brown sugar
1/2 teaspoon caraway seeds, optional
1/8 teaspoon pepper
3/4 cup apple juice

Place half of the sauerkraut in an ungreased 3-qt. slow cooker. Top with sausage, apples, brown sugar, caraway seeds if desired and pepper. Top with remaining sauerkraut. Pour apple juice over all. Cover and cook on low for 4-5 hours or until apples are tender. **Yield: 4 servings.**

Sausage Manicotti

Prep: 15 min. | Bake: 65 min.

This classic Italian entree comes together in a snap but tastes like it took hours. Made with sausage, cheese and marinara sauce, it's so tasty and easy to fix. My family always enjoys it.

—Carolyn Henderson, Maple Plain, Minnesota

Sausage Manicotti

Cajun-Style Pot Roast

Cajun-Style Pot Roast

Prep: 15 min. | Cook: 6 hours

I make this zippy roast when expecting dinner guests. It gives me time to visit. Everyone enjoys it, even my friend who's a chef!
—Ginger Menzies, Oak Creek, Colorado

1	boneless beef chuck roast (2 to 3 pounds)
2	tablespoons Cajun seasoning
1	tablespoon olive oil
2	cans (10 ounces *each*) diced tomatoes with green chilies
1	medium sweet red pepper, chopped
1-1/2	cups chopped celery
3/4	cup chopped onion
1/4	cup quick-cooking tapioca
1-1/2	teaspoons minced garlic
1	teaspoon salt

Hot cooked rice

Cut the roast in half; sprinkle with Cajun seasoning. In a large skillet, brown roast in oil on all sides; drain. Transfer to a 5-qt. slow cooker.

Combine the tomatoes, red pepper, celery, onion, tapioca, garlic and salt; pour over roast. Cover and cook on low for 6-8 hours or until meat is tender. Slice and serve with rice. **Yield: 6 servings.**

Glazed Corned Beef Dinner

Prep: 20 min. | Cook: 8 hours 20 min.

This recipe is so tasty that it's the only way my family will eat corned beef. The glaze is the kicker!
—Shannon Strate, Salt Lake City, Utah

8	medium red potatoes, quartered
2	medium carrots, sliced
1	medium onion, sliced
1	corned beef brisket with spice packet (3 pounds)
1-1/2	cups water
4	orange peel strips (3 inches)
3	tablespoons orange juice concentrate
3	tablespoons honey
1	tablespoon Dijon mustard

Place the potatoes, carrots and onion in a 5-qt. slow cooker. Cut brisket in half; place over vegetables. Add the water, orange peel and contents of spice packet. Cover and cook on low for 8-9 hours or until meat and vegetables are tender.

Using a slotted spoon, transfer corned beef and vegetables to a 13-in. x 9-in. baking dish. Discard orange peel.

Combine the orange juice concentrate, honey and mustard; pour over meat. Bake, uncovered, at 375° for 20 minutes, basting occasionally. **Yield: 8 servings.**

Slow-Simmered Kidney Beans

Prep: 15 min. | Cook: 6 hours

My husband always puts us down for a side dish when we're invited to a potluck. Canned beans cut down on prep time yet get plenty of zip from bacon, apple, red pepper and onion. I like simmering this mixture in the slow cooker because it blends the flavors and I don't have to stand over the stove.

—Sheila Vail, Long Beach, California

6	bacon strips, diced
1/2	pound smoked Polish sausage *or* kielbasa
4	cans (16 ounces *each*) kidney beans, rinsed and drained
1	can (28 ounces) diced tomatoes, drained
2	medium sweet red peppers, chopped
1	large onion, chopped
1	cup ketchup
1/2	cup packed brown sugar
1/4	cup honey
1/4	cup molasses
1	tablespoon Worcestershire sauce
1	teaspoon salt
1	teaspoon ground mustard
2	medium unpeeled red apples, cut into 1/2-inch pieces

In a large skillet, cook bacon until crisp. Remove with a slotted spoon to paper towels. Add sausage to drippings; cook and stir for 5 minutes. Drain and set aside.

In a 5-qt. slow cooker, combine the beans, tomatoes, red peppers, onion, ketchup, brown sugar, honey, molasses, Worcestershire sauce, salt and mustard. Stir in the cooked bacon and sausage. Cover and cook on low for 4-6 hours. Stir in apples. Cover and cook 2 hours longer or until bubbly. **Yield:** 16 servings.

Cornish Hens with Potatoes

Prep: 20 min. | Cook: 6-8 hours

For a wonderful holiday meal with only a fraction of the work, consider this savory dish. This special slow-cooked dinner is delicious. I serve it with green beans and French bread.

—Deborah Randall, Abbeville, Louisiana

4	Cornish game hens (20 ounces *each*)
2	tablespoons vegetable oil
4	large red potatoes, cut into 1/8-inch slices
4	bacon strips, cut into 1-inch pieces

Lemon-pepper seasoning and garlic powder to taste
Minced fresh parsley

In a large skillet, brown hens in oil. Place the potatoes in a 5-qt. slow cooker. Top with the hens and bacon. Sprinkle with lemon-pepper and garlic powder.

Cover and cook on low for 6-8 hours or until a meat thermometer reads 180° and potatoes are tender. Thicken the cooking juices if desired. Sprinkle the hens with parsley. **Yield:** 4 servings.

Sweet 'n' Sour Ribs

Prep: 10 min. | Cook: 8 hours

If you're looking for a change from typical barbecue ribs, you'll enjoy this recipe my mom always prepared on birthdays and special occasions. The tender ribs have a slight sweet-and-sour taste that my family loves. I usually serve them with garlic mashed potatoes and a salad or coleslaw.

—Dorothy Voelz, Champaign, Illinois

3	to 4 pounds boneless country-style pork ribs
1	can (20 ounces) pineapple tidbits, undrained
2	cans (8 ounces *each*) tomato sauce
1/2	cup thinly sliced onion
1/2	cup thinly sliced green pepper
1/2	cup packed brown sugar
1/4	cup cider vinegar
1/4	cup tomato paste
2	tablespoons Worcestershire sauce
1	garlic clove, minced

Salt and pepper to taste

Place ribs in an ungreased 5-qt. slow cooker. In a large bowl, combine the remaining ingredients; pour over the ribs.

Cover and cook on low for 8-10 hours or until meat is tender. Thicken the sauce if desired. **Yield:** 8 servings.

Sweet 'n' Sour Ribs

Teriyaki Pork Roast

Cut roast in half; rub with brown sugar. Place in a 5-qt. slow cooker. Pour apple juice and soy sauce over roast. Sprinkle with salt and pepper. Cover and cook on low for 6 to 6-1/2 hours or until meat is tender.

Remove the roast; cover and let stand for 15 minutes. Meanwhile, strain the cooking juices and return to slow cooker. Combine cornstarch and cold water until smooth; gradually stir into juices. Cover and cook on high for 15 minutes or until thickened. Slice pork; serve with gravy. **Yield: 6-8 servings.**

Ravioli Casserole

Prep: 10 min. | Bake: 30 min.

The whole family will love the fun, cheesy flavor of this main dish that tastes like lasagna without all the fuss. Time-saving ingredients, including prepared spaghetti sauce and frozen ravioli, hurry the preparation along.

—*Mary Ann Rothert, Austin, Texas*

1   jar (28 ounces) spaghetti sauce
1   package (25 ounces) frozen cheese ravioli, cooked and drained
2   cups (16 ounces) 4% cottage cheese
4   cups (16 ounces) shredded mozzarella cheese
1/4   cup grated Parmesan cheese

Spread 1/2 cup of spaghetti sauce in an ungreased 13-in. x 9-in. baking dish. Layer with half of the ravioli, 1-1/4 cups of sauce, 1 cup cottage cheese and 2 cups mozzarella cheese. Repeat layers. Sprinkle with Parmesan cheese.

Bake the casserole, uncovered, at 350° for 30-40 minutes or until bubbly. Let stand for 5-10 minutes before serving. **Yield: 6-8 servings.**

Teriyaki Pork Roast

Prep: 10 min. | Cook: 6 hours + standing

How good is this dish? It's the only kind of meat my kids will eat and enjoy—other than hot dogs! It's also incredibly easy to make and simply delicious.   —*Debbie Dunaway, Kettering, Ohio*

1   boneless pork shoulder roast (3 to 4 pounds), trimmed
1   cup packed brown sugar
1/3   cup unsweetened apple juice
1/3   cup soy sauce
1/2   teaspoon salt
1/4   teaspoon pepper
2   tablespoons cornstarch
3   tablespoons cold water

Preparing Pork Roast

The amount of pork you need varies with the cut. For a boneless pork shoulder roast, 1 pound yields 3 to 4 servings. Unlike beef, cuts of pork vary little in tenderness. Use dry-heat cooking methods (broiling, grilling, pan-broiling, roasting and stir-frying) when a firm texture is desired. The moist-heat method of braising is used when a fork-tender texture is desired.

Ravioli Casserole

Vegetable Oven Pancake

Prep: 15 min. | Bake: 20 min.

*I clipped this recipe when I was first married, but my husband
was actually first to prepare it. The puffy pancake looked
beautiful and tasted even better. It wasn't until I made this dish
myself that I realized how simple it really is. We like to vary the
vegetables, depending on what's in season.*

—*Mirien Church, Aurora, Colorado*

    1   teaspoon butter
    1/2 cup all-purpose flour
    2   eggs, lightly beaten
    1/2 cup milk
    1/2 teaspoon salt, *divided*
    2   cups fresh broccoli florets
    1   cup chopped green pepper
    1   cup chopped tomato

    1/2   cup chopped red onion
    2   tablespoons water
    1/8   teaspoon pepper
    1-1/2 cups (6 ounces) shredded cheddar cheese

Place the butter in a 9-in. pie plate; heat in a 450° oven until
melted. Carefully tilt the pan to thoroughly coat the bottom
and sides of the pie plate. In a bowl, beat the flour, eggs,
milk and 1/4 teaspoon salt until smooth. Pour into the pie
plate. Bake for 14-16 minutes or until puffed around the
edges and golden brown.

Meanwhile, in a large skillet, cook the broccoli, green pepper,
tomato and onion in water for 8-10 minutes or until crisp-
tender; drain well. Add pepper and remaining salt.

Sprinkle 1/2 cup cheese over pancake; top with vegetables
and remaining cheese. Bake 3-4 minutes longer or until
cheese is melted. Cut into four wedges; serve immediately.
Yield: 4 servings.

Great Pork Chop Bake

Prep: 10 min. | Bake: 55 min.

A friend brought this hearty meat-and-potatoes dish to our home when I returned from the hospital with our youngest child. Since then, we have enjoyed it many times. It's a snap to throw together on a busy day, then pop in the oven to bake. The tender chops, potato wedges and golden gravy are simple and satisfying.
—Rosie Glenn, Los Alamos, New Mexico

- 6 bone-in pork loin chops (3/4 inch thick and 8 ounces *each*)
- 1 tablespoon canola oil
- 1 can (10-3/4 ounces) condensed cream of chicken soup, undiluted
- 3 tablespoons ketchup
- 2 tablespoons Worcestershire sauce
- 1/2 teaspoon salt
- 1/4 teaspoon pepper
- 4 medium potatoes, cut into 1/2-inch wedges
- 1 medium onion, sliced into rings

In a large skillet, brown pork chops in oil. Transfer to a greased 13-in. x 9-in. baking dish. In a bowl, combine the soup, ketchup, Worcestershire sauce, salt and pepper. Add potatoes and onion; toss to coat. Pour over the chops.

Cover and bake at 350° for 55-60 minutes or until a meat thermometer reads 160° and the potatoes are tender. **Yield: 6 servings.**

Taco Casserole

Great Pork Chop Bake

Taco Casserole

Prep: 15 min. | Bake: 30 min.

My preschooler doesn't eat ground beef unless it's taco flavored, so I came up with this casserole we all like. To make assembly easy, I prepare the taco meat and freeze several bags at a time. I also cook the noodles over the weekend for a timely supper later in the week. *—Kathy Wilson, Romeoville, Illinois*

- 3 cups uncooked bow tie pasta
- 1 pound ground beef
- 1/4 cup chopped onion
- 2 cups (8 ounces) shredded cheddar cheese
- 1 jar (16 ounces) salsa
- 1 can (14-1/2 ounces) diced tomatoes, undrained
- 1 envelope taco seasoning
- 2 cups nacho tortilla chips, crushed

Cook the pasta according to package directions. Meanwhile, in a large skillet, cook the beef and onion over medium heat until the meat is no longer pink; drain. Add the cheese, salsa, tomatoes and taco seasoning. Drain the pasta; stir into the beef mixture.

Transfer to a greased 11-in. x 7-in. baking dish. Cover and bake at 350° for 20 minutes. Uncover; sprinkle with the crushed tortilla chips. Bake 10 minutes longer or until heated through. **Yield: 7 servings.**

Chicken soup not just for sick day

EILEEN GOLTZ
For The Journal Gazette

For many, the concept of chicken soup is either tied to matzo balls or feeding a multitude of sick family and friends.

Let me suggest that we take a step back from what we think we know and talk about how almost every culture has a version they believe is the original one.

We know that all you really need to make chicken soup is a chicken and a liquid (usually water) of some kind to cook it in. What parts of the chicken make the best soup? Well, hold on to your collective cooking hats, because with all my research there isn't one part of the chicken (except the head and feathers) that one culture or another doesn't use in some recipe for chicken soup.

As for chicken soup being good for you, it is, but it's not a cure for the common cold. It's just a helpful, delicious feel-better supplement. You're supposed to drink plenty of liquids when you're sick, so chicken soup works.

So with the weather

SLICE OF LIFE

changing, and our need to start planning our fall menus, I offer the following chicken soup-with-a-twist recipes that can be served to anyone looking for the perfect comfort food.

Quick and Easy Chicken and Green Onion Soup

2 cups brown rice or orzo prepared according to the package
3 cups chicken broth
2 tablespoons sugar
3 tablespoons soy sauce
3 egg whites
1 large egg
2 large boneless, skinless chicken breasts cut into bite-size pieces
8 green onions, sliced thin

In a large saucepan combine the broth, sugar and soy sauce. Bring the mixture to a boil; reduce heat to a simmer. In a small bowl combine the egg and egg whites and whisk to combine. Add chicken to the simmering broth. Cook for 2 minutes then slowly pour in the egg mixture, but don't stir it. Scatter the chopped green onions on top. When the egg starts to firm up, after about 2 to 3 minutes, stir gently. When the chicken is done, the soup is ready. Divide the rice or noodles between eight bowls and spoon the soup on top. Serves 6 to 8.

Curried Chicken Soup

2 tablespoons butter or margarine
4 shallots or 6 green onions, thinly sliced
1 red bell pepper, diced small
2 teaspoons curry powder
4 to 5 cups chicken broth
1 head cauliflower, cut into florets
2 medium-sized potatoes, peeled and cut into small cubes
1 pound cooked chicken, shredded (leftovers work great)
1 15-ounce can chickpeas, rinsed
Salt and pepper
3 to 4 green onions, sliced for garnish
¾ cup plain yogurt

In a large saucepan sauté the green onions, pepper and curry powder in the butter. Cook for 3 to 4 minutes until the bell pepper pieces are starting to get soft. Add the chicken broth, cauliflower and potato and bring the soup to a boil. Lower to a simmer, cover and cook, 10 to 12 minutes. Add the shredded chicken and chickpeas. Mix to combine, and cook 2 to 3 more minutes. Season with salt and pepper. Remove from heat and whisk in the yogurt. Top with the sliced green onions just before serving. Serves 4 to 6.

Slice of Life is a food column that offers recipes, cooking advice and information on new food products. It appears Sundays. If you have a question about cooking or a food item, contact Eileen Goltz at ztlog@verizon.net or write The Journal Gazette, 600 W. Main St., Fort Wayne, IN 46802.

I also must advise you to be specific about your expectations when making a reservation because I made a reservation well in advance and was given the worst seat in the house – right around the corner from the host station where it was even noisier and a line of people constantly marched past throughout my meal.

Restaurant: Chop's
Address: 6421 W Jefferson Blvd.
Phone: 436-9115
Hours: 11 a.m. to 2 p.m. and 5 to 9 p.m. Monday through Thursday; 11 a.m. to 2 p.m. and 5 to 10 p.m. Friday; 5 to 10 p.m. Saturday
Cuisine: Steak & seafood

Handicapped accessible: Yes
Alcohol: Full bar
Credit cards: No
Kid-friendly: Not really
Menu: Beef egg rolls ($7.95), crab cakes ($9.95), smoked salmon ($12.95), goat cheese salad ($9.95), pork chop ($19.95), paella ($19.95), seafood manicotti ($19.95), NY Strip ($32.95), bread pudding ($5),
Rating breakdown:
Food: ★½ (3-star maximum);
atmosphere: ½ (1 maximum), **service:** ½ (1 maximum)
Note: Restaurants are categorized by price range: $ (less than $20 for three-course meal), $$ ($20-$29); $$$

($30-$39), $$$$ ($40-$49), $$$$$ ($50 and up).

Ryan DuVall is a restaurant critic for The Journal Gazette. This review is based on two unannounced visits. The Journal Gazette pays for all meals. Email him at rduvall@jg.net; call at 461-8130. DuVall's past reviews can be found at www.journalgazette.net. You can follow him on Twitter @ DiningOutDuVall.

Colorful Chicken and Rice

Prep: 20 min. | Bake: 25 min.

Topped with crushed corn chips, shredded lettuce and chopped tomatoes, this marvelous meal-in-one is as pretty as it is tasty. I serve it to company along with bread and dessert, and it always gets compliments. —Dana Wise, Quinter, Kansas

- 1 can (10-3/4 ounces) condensed cream of chicken soup, undiluted
- 1 cup (8 ounces) sour cream
- 1/2 cup 4% cottage cheese
- 1 package (3 ounces) cream cheese, cubed
- 3 cups cubed cooked chicken
- 3 cups cooked rice
- 1-1/2 cups (6 ounces) shredded Monterey Jack cheese
- 1 can (4 ounces) chopped green chilies
- 1 can (2-1/4 ounces) sliced ripe olives, drained
- 1/8 teaspoon garlic salt
- 1-1/2 cups crushed corn chips
- 2 cups shredded lettuce
- 2 medium tomatoes, chopped

In a blender, combine the soup, sour cream, cottage cheese and cream cheese; cover and process until smooth. Transfer to a large bowl. Stir in the chicken, rice, Monterey Jack cheese, chilies, olives and garlic salt.

Pour into a greased 2-qt. baking dish. Bake, uncovered, at 350° for 25-30 minutes or until heated through. Just before serving, top with the crushed corn chips, lettuce and tomatoes. **Yield: 6-8 servings.**

Lobster Newburg

Prep/Total Time: 25 min.

We live in Maine, so we like to use fresh lobster in this time-honored recipe. However, it can also be made with frozen, canned or imitation lobster. No matter how you prepare it, guests will think you fussed when you treat them to these rich individual seafood casseroles. —Wendy Cornell, Hudson, Maine

- 3 cups cooked lobster meat *or* canned flaked lobster meat *or* imitation lobster chunks
- 3 tablespoons butter
- 1/4 teaspoon paprika
- 3 cups heavy whipping cream
- 1/2 teaspoon Worcestershire sauce
- 3 egg yolks, lightly beaten
- 1 tablespoon sherry, optional
- 1/4 teaspoon salt
- 1/3 cup crushed butter-flavored crackers (about 8 crackers)

In a large skillet, saute the lobster in butter and paprika for 3-4 minutes; set aside. In a large saucepan, bring cream and Worcestershire sauce to a gentle boil. Meanwhile, in a bowl, combine egg yolks, sherry if desired and salt.

Remove cream from the heat; stir a small amount into egg yolk mixture. Return all to the pan, stirring constantly. Bring to a gentle boil; cook and stir for 5-7 minutes or until slightly thickened. Stir in the lobster.

Divide lobster mixture among four 10-oz. baking dishes. Sprinkle with cracker crumbs. Broil 6 in. from the heat for 2-3 minutes or until golden brown. **Yield: 4 servings.**

Lobster Newburg

Salmon with Dill Sauce

Beefy Jalapeno Corn Bake

Prep: 20 min. | Bake: 55 min.

You'll love digging into these squares of beefed-up corn bread. Loaded with cheese, corn and jalapenos, it's a filling main dish.
—James Coleman, Charlotte, North Carolina

1	pound ground beef
2	eggs
1	can (14-3/4 ounces) cream-style corn
1	cup milk
1/2	cup vegetable oil
1	cup cornmeal
3	tablespoons all-purpose flour
1-1/2	teaspoons baking powder
3/4	teaspoon salt
4	cups (16 ounces) shredded cheddar cheese, *divided*
1	medium onion, chopped
4	jalapeno peppers, seeded and chopped

In a large skillet, cook beef over medium heat until no longer pink; drain and set aside. In a large bowl, beat eggs, corn, milk and oil. Combine the cornmeal, flour, baking powder and salt; add to egg mixture and mix well.

Pour half of the batter into a greased 13-in. x 9-in. baking dish. Sprinkle with 2 cups cheese; top with the beef, onion and jalapenos. Sprinkle with remaining cheese; top with remaining batter.

Bake, uncovered, at 350° for 55-60 minutes or until a toothpick inserted into corn bread topping comes out clean. Serve warm. Refrigerate any leftovers. **Yield: 12 servings.**

Editor's Note: When cutting hot peppers, disposable gloves are recommended. Avoid touching your face.

🍎 Salmon with Dill Sauce

Prep/Total Time: 30 min.

This moist, tender salmon is a savory treat draped with a smooth, creamy dill sauce. When my daughter served this tempting main dish for dinner, I was surprised to learn how easy the recipe is.
—Janet Painter, Three Springs, Pennsylvania

1	salmon fillet (1 pound)
1-1/2	teaspoons dill weed, *divided*
1/2	cup reduced-fat plain yogurt
1/2	teaspoon sugar
1/2	teaspoon salt-free seasoning blend

Place the salmon in a 13-in. x 9-in. baking dish coated with cooking spray; sprinkle with 1/2 teaspoon dill. Cover and bake at 375° for 20-25 minutes or until the fish flakes easily with a fork.

Meanwhile, in a small saucepan, combine the yogurt, sugar, seasoning blend and remaining dill. Cook and stir over low heat until warmed. Serve with the salmon. **Yield: 4 servings.**

Nutrition Facts: 4 ounces equals 227 calories, 12 g fat (3 g saturated fat), 77 mg cholesterol, 76 mg sodium, 3 g carbohydrate, 0 fiber, 24 g protein. Diabetic Exchanges: 2-1/2 lean meat, 2 fat.

Cooking Salmon

Overcooked fish loses its flavor and becomes tough. As a general guideline, fish is cooked 10 minutes for every inch of thickness.

For fish fillets, check for doneness by inserting a fork at an angle into the thickest portion of the fish and gently parting the meat. When it is opaque and flakes into sections, it is cooked completely.

Beefy Jalapeno Corn Bake

Slow-Cooked Spaghetti Sauce

Slow-Cooked Spaghetti Sauce

Prep: 15 min. | Cook: 7 hours

I like to serve this dish to company. Not only is it delicious and a snap to prepare, but it's economical, too. I'd be lost without my slow cooker. —Shelley McKinney, New Castle, Indiana

I	pound ground beef *or* bulk Italian sausage
I	medium onion, chopped
2	cans (14-1/2 ounces *each*) diced tomatoes, undrained
I	can (8 ounces) tomato sauce
I	can (6 ounces) tomato paste
I	bay leaf
I	tablespoon brown sugar
4	garlic cloves, minced
I	to 2 teaspoons dried basil
I	to 2 teaspoons dried oregano
I	teaspoon salt
1/2	to I teaspoon dried thyme

Hot cooked spaghetti

In a large skillet, cook beef and onion over medium heat until meat is no longer pink; drain.

Transfer to a 3-qt. slow cooker. Add the next 10 ingredients. Cover and cook on low for 7-8 hours or until heated through. Discard bay leaf. Serve with spaghetti. **Yield: 6-8 servings**.

Sweet Potato Sausage Casserole

Prep: 20 min. | Bake: 25 min.

Most people never consider combining sweet potatoes with pasta and kielbasa, but I adapted this recipe from several others and I've received several compliments on it. You can add more cheese or sausage to suit your taste.
—Rickey Madden, Clinton, South Carolina

8	ounces uncooked spiral pasta
8	ounces smoked sausage, cut into 1/4-inch slices
2	medium sweet potatoes, peeled and cut into 1/2-inch cubes
I	cup chopped green pepper
1/2	cup chopped onion
I	teaspoon minced garlic
2	tablespoons olive oil
I	can (14-1/2 ounces) diced tomatoes, undrained
I	cup heavy whipping cream
1/4	teaspoon salt
1/4	teaspoon pepper
I	cup (4 ounces) shredded cheddar cheese

Cook pasta according to package directions. Meanwhile, in a large skillet, cook the sausage, sweet potatoes, green pepper, onion and garlic in oil over medium heat for 5 minutes or until vegetables are tender; drain.

Add the tomatoes, cream, salt and pepper. Bring to a boil; remove from the heat. Drain the pasta; stir into the sausage mixture. Transfer to a greased 13-in. x 9 in. baking dish. Sprinkle with cheddar cheese.

Bake, uncovered, at 350° for 25-30 minutes or until bubbly. Let stand for 5 minutes before serving. **Yield: 8 servings**.

Sweet Potato Sausage Casserole

Shrimp Marinara

Shrimp Marinara

Prep: 30 min. | Cook: 3 hours 20 min.

This wonderful marinara sauce simmers for most of the day. Then shortly before mealtime, I add cooked shrimp, which merely require being heated through. Served over spaghetti, it makes a delicious dressed-up main dish. —Sue Mackey, Galesburg, Illinois

1	can (14-1/2 ounces) Italian diced tomatoes, undrained
1	can (6 ounces) tomato paste
1/2	to 1 cup water
2	garlic cloves, minced
2	tablespoons minced fresh parsley
1	teaspoon salt
1	teaspoon dried oregano
1/2	teaspoon dried basil
1/4	teaspoon pepper
1	pound fresh *or* frozen shrimp, cooked, peeled and deveined
1	pound spaghetti, cooked and drained

Shredded Parmesan cheese, optional

In a 3-qt. slow cooker, combine the first nine ingredients. Cover and cook on low for 3-4 hours. Stir in shrimp. Cover and cook 20 minutes longer or just until shrimp turn pink. Serve with spaghetti. Sprinkle with Parmesan cheese if desired. **Yield: 6 servings.**

French Country Casserole

Prep: 10 min. | Bake: 1 hour

This flavorful dish is great for busy nights when you don't have much time to devote to dinner. It's a quick-to-fix version of a traditional French cassoulet that was an instant hit with my husband, who enjoys smoked sausage. Just mix everything together in a dish and bake. The heavenly aroma will draw your family to the table. —Kim Lowe, Coralville, Iowa

1	pound smoked kielbasa *or* Polish sausage, cut into 1/4 inch pieces
1	can (16 ounces) kidney beans, rinsed and drained
1	can (15-1/2 ounces) great northern beans, rinsed and drained
1	can (15 ounces) black beans, rinsed and drained
1	can (15 ounces) tomato sauce
3	medium carrots, thinly sliced
2	small onions, sliced into rings
1/2	cup dry red wine *or* beef broth
2	tablespoons brown sugar
2	garlic cloves, minced
1-1/2	teaspoons dried thyme

Combine all ingredients in a bowl; transfer to an ungreased 3-qt. baking dish. Cover and bake at 375° for 60-70 minutes or until the carrots are tender. **Yield: 9 servings.**

Saucy Chicken Thighs

Prep: 20 min. | Cook: 4 hours

Everyone raves about how sweet the sauce is for these slow-cooked chicken thighs. They're such a breeze because they simmer away while you do other things. They're ideal appetizers, but you can also add your favorite side for a nice meal.

—Kim Puckett, Reagan, Tennessee

9	bone-in chicken thighs (6 ounces *each*)
1/2	teaspoon salt
1/4	teaspoon pepper
1-1/2	cups barbecue sauce
1/2	cup honey
2	teaspoons prepared mustard
2	teaspoons Worcestershire sauce
1/8	to 1/2 teaspoon hot pepper sauce

Sprinkle the chicken with the salt and pepper. Place on a broiler pan. Broil 4-5 in. from the heat source for 6-8 minutes on each side or until a meat thermometer reads 180°. Transfer to a 5-qt. slow cooker.

In a small bowl, combine the barbecue sauce, honey, mustard, Worcestershire sauce and pepper sauce. Pour over chicken; stir to coat. Cover and cook on low for 4-5 hours or until heated through. **Yield: 9 servings.**

Buttermilk Pecan Chicken

Saucy Chicken Thighs

Buttermilk Pecan Chicken

Prep: 10 min. | Bake: 30 min.

My family enjoys chicken and always asks me to bake it this way. Sometimes I like to give this dish kid appeal by cutting the chicken into strips before coating with the nut mixture.

—Julie Jahn, Decatur, Indiana

1	cup ground pecans
1/4	cup sesame seeds, optional
1	tablespoon paprika
2	teaspoons salt
1/8	teaspoon pepper
1	cup all-purpose flour
1/2	cup buttermilk
6	boneless skinless chicken breast halves (4 ounces *each*)
2	tablespoons butter, melted
18	pecan halves

In a shallow bowl, combine the pecans, sesame seeds if desired, paprika, salt and pepper. Place flour and buttermilk in separate bowls. Coat chicken with flour, dip in buttermilk, then coat with pecan mixture.

Place in a greased 13-in. x 9-in. baking dish. Drizzle with butter. Top each with three pecan halves. Bake, uncovered, at 375° for 30-35 minutes or until a meat thermometer reads 170°. **Yield: 6 servings.**

Beef 'n' Rice Enchiladas

Beef 'n' Rice Enchiladas

Prep: 30 min. | Bake: 10 min.

With a toddler in the house, I look for foods that are a snap to make. Loaded with beef, cheese and a flavorful rice mix, these enchiladas come together without any fuss. But they're so good that guests think I spent hours in the kitchen.

—*Jennifer Smith, Colona, Illinois*

- 1   package (6.8 ounces) Spanish rice and vermicelli mix
- 1   pound ground beef
- 2   cans (10 ounces *each*) enchilada sauce, *divided*
- 10   flour tortillas (8 inches), warmed
- 4   cups (16 ounces) shredded cheddar cheese, *divided*

Prepare the rice mix according to package directions. Meanwhile, in a large skillet, cook beef over medium heat until no longer pink; drain. Stir in the Spanish rice and 1-1/4 cups enchilada sauce.

Spoon about 2/3 cup of the beef mixture down the center of each tortilla. Top each with 1/3 cup shredded cheddar cheese; roll up.

Place in an ungreased 13-in. x 9-in. baking dish. Top with the remaining enchilada sauce and cheese. Bake, uncovered, at 350° for 8-10 minutes or until the cheese is melted. **Yield: 10 enchiladas.**

Chicken Lasagna

Prep: 25 min. | Bake: 30 min. + standing

A friend served this to us one night and I just had to try it at home. It's quick, easy and so delicious! I love to serve it to guests with a Caesar salad and warm rolls. Also, it can be frozen and saved for a busy weeknight.

—*Janelle Rutrough, Callaway, Virginia*

- 2   cups (16 ounces) 2% cottage cheese
- 1   package (3 ounces) cream cheese, softened
- 4   cups cubed cooked chicken
- 1   can (10-3/4 ounces) condensed cream of chicken soup, undiluted
- 1   can (10-3/4 ounces) condensed cream of celery soup, undiluted
- 2/3 cup milk
- 1/2 cup chopped onion
- 1/2 teaspoon salt
- 6   lasagna noodles, cooked and drained
- 1   package (6 ounces) stuffing mix
- 1/2 cup butter, melted

In a small bowl, combine the cottage cheese and cream cheese. In a large bowl, combine the chicken, soups, milk, onion and salt.

Spread half of the chicken mixture into a greased 13-in. x 9-in. baking dish. Top with three noodles. Spread with half of the cheese mixture. Repeat layers. Toss stuffing mix with butter; sprinkle over casserole.

Bake, uncovered, at 350° for 30-40 minutes or until bubbly and golden brown. Let stand for 10 minutes before cutting. **Yield: 8 servings.**

Company Swordfish

Prep: 10 min. | Bake: 25 min.

This mouth-watering meal will have fish aficionados and novices alike asking for more. The tender swordfish is topped with artichokes, sun-dried tomatoes and shallots, adding color and lively flavor. Best of all, the tasty entree is easy to prepare and takes just over 30 minutes from start to finish!

—*Callie Berger, Diamond Springs, California*

- 4   swordfish *or* halibut steaks (7 ounces *each*)
- 2   jars (7-1/2 ounces *each*) marinated artichoke hearts, drained and chopped
- 1/2 cup oil-packed sun-dried tomatoes, drained and chopped
- 4   shallots, chopped
- 2   tablespoons butter, melted
- 1   teaspoon lemon juice

Place the swordfish or halibut in a greased 13-in. x 9-in. baking dish. In a small bowl, combine the marinated artichokes, sun-dried tomatoes and shallots; spread over the fish. Drizzle with melted butter and lemon juice.

Cover and bake at 425° for 20 minutes. Uncover; bake 5-7 minutes longer or until the fish flakes easily with a fork. **Yield: 4 servings.**

Time is of the essence for Karol Chandler-Ezell and her family in Nacogdoches, Texas. "I'm an anthropology professor," Karol explains. "And my husband, Alex, teaches high school science and has a long commute. I work late and rush to cook dinner quickly." Besides a busy life teaching, the pair has one child, a bundle of energy named Sasha. In spite of their hectic schedules, Karol and her husband have sit-down suppers seven days a week.

For a mouth-watering menu, Karol created this dinner that's a perfect fit for on-the-go lifestyles. For tasty *Tomato-Stuffed Avocados*, each attractive avocado is packed with chopped tomatoes, onion and basil for a flavorful start. Karol pairs them with mushroom-topped *Broiled Sirloin Steaks*, a family favorite. "A butcher gave me great advice on cooking different types of meat," she says. "Broiling works really well on lean cuts like this."

What goes better with steak than potatoes? *Twice-Baked Deviled Potatoes* is a delicious side dish flavored with bacon, cheddar and a hint of Dijon mustard for extra flavor. "The microwave makes them very quick to fix," Karol says.

Twice-Baked Deviled Potatoes

Prep/Total Time: 30 min.

    4   small baking potatoes
    1/4 cup butter, softened
    1/4 cup milk
    1   cup (4 ounces) shredded cheddar cheese
    1/3 cup real bacon bits
    2   green onions, chopped
    1   teaspoon Dijon mustard
Dash paprika

Scrub and pierce potatoes; place on a microwave-safe plate. Microwave, uncovered, on high for 7-10 minutes or until tender, turning once. Let stand for 5 minutes. Cut a thin slice off the top of each potato and discard. Scoop out pulp, leaving a thin shell.

In a large bowl, mash the pulp with butter and milk. Stir in the cheese, bacon, onions, mustard and paprika. Spoon into potato shells. Return to the microwave-safe plate. Microwave, uncovered, on high for 1-2 minutes or until cheese is melted. **Yield:** 4 servings.

Editor's Note: This recipe was tested in a 1,100-watt microwave.

Tomato-Stuffed Avocados

Prep/Total Time: 10 min.

    2   plum tomatoes, seeded and chopped
    3/4 cup thinly sliced red onion, quartered
    1   teaspoon fresh basil leaves, julienned
    1/2 teaspoon salt
    1/4 teaspoon pepper
    2   medium ripe avocados, halved and pitted
    2   teaspoons lime juice

In a large bowl, gently toss the tomatoes, onion, basil, salt and pepper. Spoon into avocado halves; drizzle with lime juice. **Yield:** 4 servings.

Broiled Sirloin Steaks

Prep/Total Time: 20 min.

    2   tablespoons lime juice
    1   teaspoon onion powder
    1   teaspoon garlic powder
    1/4 teaspoon ground mustard
    1/4 teaspoon dried oregano
    1/4 teaspoon dried thyme
    4   boneless beef sirloin steaks (5 ounces *each*)
    1   cup sliced fresh mushrooms

In a small bowl, combine the first six ingredients; rub over both sides of steaks. Broil 4 in. from the heat for 7 minutes. Turn steaks; top with mushrooms. Broil 7-8 minutes longer or until meat reaches desired doneness (for medium-rare, a meat thermometer should read 145°; medium, 160°; well-done, 170°) and mushrooms are tender. **Yield:** 4 servings.

Nutrition Facts: 1 steak with about 3 tablespoons mushrooms equals 187 calories, 7 g fat (3 g saturated fat), 80 mg cholesterol, 60 mg sodium, 3 g carbohydrate, trace fiber, 28 g protein
Diabetic Exchange: 3 lean meat.

About Avocados

To quickly ripen an avocado, place it in a paper bag with an apple. Poke the bag with a toothpick in several spots and leave at room temperature. The avocado should be ripe in 1 to 3 days. To pit an avocado, wash it and cut it in half lengthwise, cutting around the seed. Twist the halves in opposite directions and separate them. Slip a tablespoon under the seed to loosen it from the fruit and remove. Scoop out the half and chop or slice if desired.

She calls herself a silver-haired citizen, but Claudine Moffatt of Manchester, Missouri is much more than that. This mother, grandmother and great-grandmother is a woman with golden memories of an action-packed life.

After raising her family and dedicating years to a career in publishing hobby and craft magazines, Claudine retired. But she didn't slow down. These days, Claudine stays closer to home. She enjoys watching cooking shows on television, playing computer games and surfing the Internet.

But she remembers when everyday life didn't include today's modern conveniences. "When I was learning to cook, going out for chicken meant going to a poultry yard and picking out a chicken. In the time it takes to drive to a fast-food place, wait in line and drive home, I can make a healthier, tastier and less expensive meal," she assures.

For a stick-to-your-ribs dinner, Claudine might prepare Onion Salisbury Steak. "I've relied on this recipe for as long as I can remember," she shares. Ground beef patties, tender onion slices and a rich gravy top toasted bread to make this Depression-era favorite. To complement it, Claudine serves Carrots with Raisins. "You can fix this simple side dish in minutes," she says. "Just mix the ingredients, then microwave."

She tops off the meal with comforting Biscuit Apple Cobbler. The sweet treat requires only four ingredients but tastes like you fussed.

Carrots with Raisins

Prep/Total Time: 10 min.

4	medium carrots, julienned
1/4	cup water
1/4	cup raisins
2	tablespoons brown sugar
1/2	to 1 teaspoon salt
1/8	to 1/4 teaspoon pepper

In a microwave-safe bowl, combine all ingredients. Cover and microwave on high for 1-1/2 minutes. Stir; cook 1-2 minutes longer or until carrots are tender. **Yield: 4 servings.**

Editor's Note: This recipe was tested in a 1,100-watt microwave.

Onion Salisbury Steak

Prep/Total Time: 25 min.

1	pound lean ground beef
1/2	teaspoon salt
1/8	to 1/4 teaspoon pepper
2	medium onions, thinly sliced
4	slices bread, toasted
1/4	cup all-purpose flour
1-1/2	cups water
1	tablespoon beef bouillon granules

In a large bowl, combine the beef, salt and pepper; shape into four oval patties. In a large skillet, brown patties on one side. Turn and add onions. Cook until a meat thermometer reads 160° and juices run clear.

Place toast on serving plates. Top each with onions and a beef patty; keep warm.

Stir flour into skillet until blended. Gradually add water; stir in bouillon. Bring to a boil; cook and stir for 2 minutes or until thickened and bubbly. Serve with meat and onions. **Yield: 4 servings.**

Biscuit Apple Cobbler

Prep/Total Time: 20 min.

1	can (21 ounces) apple pie filling
1/2	teaspoon ground cinnamon
1	tube (7-1/2 ounces) refrigerated flaky buttermilk biscuits

Whipped topping and mint, optional

Place pie filling in an ungreased 9-in. pie plate. Sprinkle with cinnamon. Separate each biscuit into three layers and arrange over apples.

Bake at 400° for 12-14 minutes or until the biscuits are browned. Top with whipped topping and mint if desired. **Yield: 4-6 servings.**

Freezing Beef Patties

When ground beef goes on sale, it's a great time to take advantage of low prices and stock up. It's easy to freeze ground beef patties. Simply shape the ground beef into patties and place at least 1/2 inch apart on a baking sheet that is lightly coated with cooking spray. Place in the freezer until the patties are completely frozen, then transfer the individal patties to large resealable plastic bags and freeze.

Family comes first for Krista Collins of Concord, North Carolina. Married to husband Andy for many years, the former middle school teacher works part-time at a preschool so she can spend more time with children Jared and Olivia.

When planning dinner menus and preparing the food for her family, Krista always keeps several considerations in mind. "Andy works for an equipment rental company until late evening and looks forward to a warm meal every night," she relates. "So I need to cook dishes that remain delicious until he gets home. Also, our kids can be picky eaters, so whatever I cook must meet their tastes as well.

"We're on a budget," Krista adds. "Since it's more economical to cook at home than eat at a restaurant, I fix dinner at least 6 nights a week. I also try to incorporate items that are buy-one-get-one-free at the grocery store or beans or tomatoes that I canned over the summer."

The minute-saving menu that Krista shares here is inexpensive and enjoyed by the whole family. "I fix the salad first, the sandwiches next and the punch last, so it retains its fizz," she explains.

"I've made Ranch Pasta Salad for years—it's a recipe from a high school friend's mom. Any time I serve a sandwich meal like hamburgers, hot dogs or sloppy joes, I make this flavorful salad as an accompaniment," she notes.

Only ground beef and three other convenient ingredients are needed to make the filling for sure-to-please Salsa Sloppy Joes. "I created these sandwiches when I realized I did not have a can of sloppy joe sauce," Krista recalls. "The sweet brown sugar in this recipe complements the tangy salsa."

To round out the meal, Krista stirs up refreshing Strawberry Spritzers. "My grandma Naomi Beller served this tangy beverage in a punch bowl every year at Christmas, and we all looked forward to that tradition," she says. "It's great on hot summer days when the grill is fired up. Plus, it's a way to get my picky kids to eat their fruit...I have to be creative!"

Strawberry Spritzer
Prep/Total Time: 10 min.

1	package (10 ounces) frozen sweetened sliced strawberries, thawed
2	liters lemon-lime soda, chilled
1	can (12 ounces) frozen pink lemonade concentrate, thawed

Place the strawberries in a blender; cover and process until pureed. Pour into a pitcher; stir in the soda and lemonade concentrate. Serve immediately. **Yield: 2-1/2 quarts.**

Ranch Pasta Salad
Prep/Total Time: 25 min.

3	cups uncooked tricolor spiral pasta
1	cup chopped fresh broccoli florets
3/4	cup chopped seeded peeled cucumber
1/2	cup seeded chopped tomato
1	bottle (8 ounces) ranch salad dressing
1/2	cup shredded Parmesan cheese

Cook pasta according to package directions; drain and rinse in cold water. In a large bowl, combine the pasta, broccoli, cucumber and tomato. Drizzle with salad dressing; toss to coat. Sprinkle with Parmesan cheese. **Yield: 8 servings.**

Salsa Sloppy Joes
Prep/Total Time: 20 min.

1	pound ground beef
1	jar (11 ounces) salsa
1	can (10-3/4 ounces) condensed tomato soup, undiluted
1	tablespoon brown sugar
8	hamburger buns, split

In a large skillet, cook beef over medium heat until no longer pink; drain. Stir in the salsa, soup and brown sugar. Cover and simmer for 10 minutes or until heated through. Spoon 1/2 cup onto each bun. **Yield: 8 servings.**

Seeding Cucumbers

To seed a cucumber, peel or score the cucumber and cut lengthwise in half. Using the tip of a teaspoon or melon baller, gently scrape the seeds out and discard. Slice or chop the cucumber as desired.

For Dona Hoffman of Addison, Illinois, planning a fast and nutritious supper for her family of four is extremely important. "I currently work part-time so that I can complete my master's degree in health care administration," Dona explains. "Often, if I'm working into the dinner hours, my husband, Doug, is in control of the kitchen, which means we need something simple yet healthy."

To keep kitchen time to a minimum, Dona plans ahead, relying on her slow cooker for stress-free but satisfying menus on the days she works. She also likes to prepare a few extra servings so that she'll be sure to have leftovers to pack for an easy work lunch the next day.

When not working, Dona loves to bake and spend time with daughters Megan and Mia. "On evenings when I'm home, I look forward to having meals with everyone gathered together around the table, just as I did with my parents when I was growing up," Dona recalls.

The Italian-inspired menu she shares here makes supper time a breeze any night of the week. And, since it serves six, Dona is guaranteed to have a few extra lunches for work.

Dona starts the meal with Tomato Olive Salad. "My daughters love salad," Dona notes. "I try to have a different version for them." This amazingly simple dish features a sweet three-ingredient dressing that's ready in moments. I often top it with fresh mozzarella, feta or Parmesan," she adds. "To add color, I use red lettuce with leaf lettuce."

Speedy Minestrone makes a hearty entree on cold winter nights. Filled with veggies, sausage and beans, the flavorful soup counts on several convenience products, so it's a snap to assemble. As Dona explains, "Everything is precooked, so you're just chopping, combining and heating."

Ending the meal on a sweet note is easy with Mini Rum Cakes. Dona says, "Many rum cakes are dry, but these are moist. They use basic ingredients that are in your pantry. I serve them slightly warm with vanilla ice cream and a dollop of whipped cream."

Tomato Olive Salad
Prep/Total Time: 10 min.

      4   cups torn leaf lettuce
    1/2   cup cherry tomatoes
    1/3   cup sliced red onion
      1   can (2-1/4 ounces) sliced ripe olives, drained
DRESSING:
      2   tablespoons canola oil
      1   tablespoon red wine vinegar
      1   tablespoon brown sugar

In a large bowl, combine the torn leaf lettuce, cherry tomatoes, onion and olives. In a small bowl, whisk the dressing ingredients. Drizzle over salad and toss to coat. **Yield: 6 servings.**

Speedy Minestrone
Prep/Total Time: 25 min.

      2   cans (14-1/2 ounces *each*) beef broth
      1   package (24 ounces) frozen vegetable and pasta medley in garlic sauce
      1   pound smoked sausage, cut into 1/2-inch slices
      1   can (16 ounces) kidney beans, rinsed and drained
    1/4   cup chopped onion
      1   teaspoon dried basil
      1   teaspoon dried parsley flakes
Shredded Parmesan cheese

In a large saucepan, combine the first seven ingredients. Bring to a boil. Reduce heat; simmer, uncovered, for 10-15 minutes or until heated through. Sprinkle with Parmesan cheese. **Yield: 6 servings.**

Mini Rum Cakes
Prep/Total Time: 10 min.

      2   cups cold milk
      1   package (3.4 ounces) instant vanilla pudding mix
      1   teaspoon rum extract
      6   individual round sponge cakes
  1-1/2   cups whipped topping
Fresh *or* frozen raspberries

In a small bowl, whisk the cold milk and pudding mix for 2 minutes; stir in the rum extract. Let stand for 2 minutes or until soft-set.

Place the sponge cakes on dessert plates; top with the pudding. Garnish with the whipped topping and raspberries. **Yield: 6 servings.**

International flavor is right at home in Amy Corlew-Sherlock's kitchen. This full-time, special-ed teacher in Lapeer, Michigan manages to prepare sit-down suppers for her family of four at least five times a week...and even plans menus that have around-the-world appeal.

"To keep things interesting, I try to feature a variety of dishes that reflect different cultural influences and flavors," Amy explains. "Our household is always on the go, so fast meals are essential to our lifestyle." This classic Asian menu meets her family's needs on both counts and is a longtime favorite.

"We start with delicious Egg Drop Soup, which cooks in just minutes and requires only five simple ingredients. I got the recipe from Grandma's old cookbook," Amy recalls.

Her Instant Fried Rice is a tasty and fuss-free side dish. The recipe uses leftover cooked rice and a packet of seasoning mix to cut the prep time, while peas and onions add nutrition.

"But it's the main dish, Sweet-and-Sour Popcorn Chicken, that really shines," Amy notes. Frozen popcorn chicken coated in a homemade sweet-and-sour sauce is the secret to this quick entree.

For extra fun, purchase fortune cookies to munch on for dessert. They'll make the perfect ending for your family's Far East feast.

Egg Drop Soup

Prep/Total Time: 15 min.

- 3 cups chicken broth
- 1 tablespoon cornstarch
- 2 tablespoons cold water
- 1 egg, lightly beaten
- 1 green onion, sliced

In a large saucepan, bring broth to a boil over medium heat. Combine cornstarch and water until smooth; gradually stir into broth. Bring to a boil; cook and stir for 2 minutes or until thickened.

Reduce the heat. Drizzle the beaten egg into hot broth, stirring constantly. Remove from the heat; stir in onion. **Yield: 4 servings.**

Instant Fried Rice

Prep/Total Time: 20 min.

- 1 envelope fried rice seasoning
- 2 tablespoons water
- 2 green onions, chopped
- 2 tablespoons canola oil
- 1 egg, lightly beaten
- 3 cups cold cooked instant rice
- 1/2 cup peas

In a small bowl, combine the rice seasoning mix and water; set aside. In a large skillet or wok, stir-fry the green onions in the oil for 2-3 minutes. Add the lightly beaten egg; stir until scrambled.

Add rice and peas; stir-fry until heated through. Stir in seasoning mixture; stir-fry 3-4 minutes longer or until heated through. **Yield: 4 servings.**

Sweet-and-Sour Popcorn Chicken

Prep/Total Time: 25 min.

- 1 medium green pepper, cut into 1-inch pieces
- 1 small onion, thinly sliced
- 1 tablespoon canola oil
- 1 can (20 ounces) unsweetened pineapple chunks
- 3 tablespoons white vinegar
- 2 tablespoons soy sauce
- 2 tablespoons ketchup
- 1/3 cup packed brown sugar
- 2 tablespoons cornstarch
- 1 package (12 ounces) frozen popcorn chicken

In a large skillet or wok, stir-fry the green pepper and onion in oil for 3-4 minutes or until crisp-tender. Drain the pineapple, reserving the juice in a 2-cup measuring cup; set the pineapple aside. Add enough water to the pineapple juice to measure 1-1/3 cups; stir in the vinegar, soy sauce and ketchup.

In a large bowl, combine brown sugar and cornstarch. Stir in pineapple juice mixture until smooth. Gradually add to the skillet. Bring to a boil; cook and stir for 2 minutes or until thickened. Add pineapple. Reduce heat; simmer, uncovered, for 4-5 minutes or until heated through.

Meanwhile, microwave chicken according to package directions. Stir into pineapple mixture. Serve immediately. **Yield: 4 servings.**

Late afternoons and early evenings are busy times in Kristine Marra's home. "Even though things can get pretty hectic, I'm committed to having sit-down family dinners nearly every night of the week," she says. Located in Clifton Park, New York, the Marra family home is always bustling.

"My husband, Frank, and I have six children—Bryan, Stephen, Kyle, Brendan and twins Colin and Taryn," shares Kristine. "Getting meals on the table can be a challenge when you're trying to cook around homework needs and extracurricular activities," she explains. "My mother always had sit-down dinners. I'm determined to do the same."

In order to accommodate her lively schedule, the busy cook does as much preparation as possible before mealtime. Kristine depends on recipes that are fast and delicious, and Pepper Steak with Potatoes fits the bill nicely. "I added potatoes to an Asian favorite to create this well-rounded dish," she says.

To complement the main dish, Kristine tosses together Sweet Sesame Salad. She jazzes up salad greens with tomato, mandarin oranges and sesame seeds, then tops it off with a honey vinaigrette for a sweet and fruity sensation the whole family loves.

An old-fashioned favorite, Mayonnaise Chocolate Cake, often ends meals at the Marra home. "My aunt has made this moist, rich sheet cake for as long as I can remember," Kristine says. "Not only is it a cake I can quickly make from scratch, but it calls for ingredients I usually have in the pantry."

Sweet Sesame Salad

Prep/Total Time: 30 min.

1	package (10 ounces) ready-to-serve salad greens
1	medium tomato, cut into thin wedges
2/3	cup balsamic vinaigrette salad dressing
2	teaspoons honey
1	can (11 ounces) mandarin oranges, drained
1	teaspoon sesame seeds, toasted

In a large salad bowl, combine the salad greens and tomato; set aside. In a jar with a tight-fitting lid, combine the salad dressing and honey; shake well. Drizzle over the greens. Sprinkle with oranges and toasted sesame seeds; toss to coat. **Yield: 6 servings.**

Pepper Steak with Potatoes

Prep/Total Time: 30 min.

5	medium red potatoes, cut into 1/4-inch slices
1/2	cup water
1	pound boneless beef sirloin steak, thinly sliced
1	garlic clove, minced
2	tablespoons olive oil
1	medium green pepper, julienned
1	small onion, chopped
Pepper to taste	
4	teaspoons cornstarch
1	cup beef broth

Place the potatoes and water in a microwave-safe bowl; cover and microwave on high for 5-7 minutes or until tender.

Meanwhile, in a large skillet, saute beef and garlic in oil until meat is no longer pink. Remove and keep warm; drain drippings. In same skillet, saute green pepper and onion until crisp-tender. Add beef, potatoes and pepper; heat through.

In a small saucepan, mix cornstarch and broth until smooth. Bring to a boil; cook and stir for 2 minutes or until thickened. Drizzle over meat mixture; toss to coat. **Yield: 6 servings.**

Nutrition Facts: 1 cup is 277 calories, 10 g fat (2 g saturated fat), 55 mg cholesterol, 179 mg sodium, 27 g carbohydrate, 3 g fiber, 23 g protein. Diabetic Exchanges: 2 meat, 2 vegetable, 1 starch.

Editor's Note: This recipe was tested in a 1,100-watt microwave.

Mayonnaise Chocolate Cake

Prep: 15 min. | Bake: 20 min.

1	cup all-purpose flour
3/4	cup sugar
1/4	cup baking cocoa
1	teaspoon baking powder
1	teaspoon baking soda
1	cup mayonnaise
1	cup water
1	can (16 ounces) French vanilla *or* vanilla frosting

In a large bowl, combine the flour, sugar, cocoa, baking powder and baking soda. Beat in mayonnaise and water.

Pour into a greased 13-in. x 9-in. baking pan. Bake at 350° for 20-25 minutes or until a toothpick inserted near the center comes out clean. Cool on a rack; spread with the frosting. **Yield: 12-15 servings.**

Editor's Note: Reduced-fat or fat-free mayonnaise is not recommended for this recipe.

Fast and simple meals are a must for Elizabeth Tomlinson of Streetsboro, Ohio. "I'm a graduate assistant who sometimes takes night classes. My husband, Ed, is a business professor who occasionally teaches night classes. So it's important for us to get supper on the table quickly," she says.

When not working, the academic duo also has a young son, Ethan, who keeps them on their toes. "I like being able to do some food preparation while my son naps or plays," Elizabeth says, "but there are never any guarantees as to how much time I'll have, so quicker is always better!"

To make the most out of kitchen time, Elizabeth plans meals in advance. "I often use side dishes from convenience items and improve them by adding additional seasonings and toppings," she notes.

To accommodate her family's hectic lifestyle, Elizabeth created this delightful menu for an easy and impressive dinner in no time. For the main course, she serves Rosemary Lamb Chops. While the lamb chops may seem upscale, they're actually a super-fast entree. "I tend to make them for special occasions, but they're quick enough for a weeknight meal," she explains. Pair the lamb chops with Mediterranean Couscous. With garlic, tomatoes and Parmesan, it's a great side dish for any main course. "It relies on a boxed item to get started; then it's just a matter of adding a few ingredients," says Elizabeth.

Finish things off with warm and inviting Blueberry Crumble. This delicious dessert features sweet blueberries with a brown sugar, almond and oat topping that's especially nice with vanilla ice cream.

Mediterranean Couscous
Prep/Total Time: 15 min.

    2   tablespoons chopped onion
    3   teaspoons minced garlic
    2   tablespoons olive oil, *divided*
1-1/4   cups water
    1   package (5.6 ounces) couscous with toasted pine nuts
1-1/2   teaspoons chicken bouillon granules
  1/2   cup cherry tomatoes, halved
    2   tablespoons grated Parmesan cheese

In a small skillet, saute the onion and garlic in 1 tablespoon olive oil for 3-4 minutes or until tender. Meanwhile, in a large saucepan, combine the water, contents of seasoning packet from couscous mix, bouillon and remaining olive oil. Bring to a boil.

Stir in the onion mixture and couscous. Cover and remove from the heat; let stand for 5 minutes. Fluff with a fork. Stir in tomatoes and Parmesan cheese. **Yield: 4 servings.**

Rosemary Lamb Chops
Prep/Total Time: 20 min.

    2   teaspoons dried rosemary, crushed
    1   teaspoon dried thyme
  1/2   teaspoon salt
  1/4   teaspoon pepper
  1/4   cup olive oil
    8   lamb loin chops (1 inch thick and 6 ounces *each*)

Combine the rosemary, thyme, salt and pepper. Pour oil over both sides of chops; rub with spice mixture.

In a large skillet, cook chops over medium heat for 6-7 minutes on each side or until meat reaches desired doneness (for medium-rare, a meat thermometer should read 145°; medium, 160°; well-done, 170°). **Yield: 4 servings.**

Blueberry Crumble
Prep/Total Time: 15 min.

    3   cups fresh *or* frozen blueberries
    3   tablespoons sugar
    1   tablespoon cornstarch
  1/3   cup old-fashioned oats
  1/3   cup packed brown sugar
    3   tablespoons all-purpose flour
    2   tablespoons chopped almonds
  1/8   teaspoon ground cinnamon
    3   tablespoons cold butter
Vanilla ice cream

In a greased 9-in. microwave-safe pie plate, combine the blueberries, sugar and cornstarch. Cover and microwave on high for 7-8 minutes or until thickened, stirring twice.

Meanwhile, in a small bowl, combine the old-fashioned oats, brown sugar, flour, chopped almonds and cinnamon. Cut in the butter until mixture resembles coarse crumbs. Sprinkle over blueberry mixture.

Microwave, uncovered, on high for 2-3 minutes or until butter is melted. Serve with ice cream. **Yield: 4 servings.**

Editor's Note: This recipe was tested in a 1,100-watt microwave.

At her home in Union, Kentucky, preparing fast, simple meals is the norm for Renae Rossow. "My husband, Brian, and I are real estate agents," Renae explains. "We're on call for clients who often need to see homes in the evening, so dinner has to be quick and easy, yet appealing and satisfying."

The couple has four sons, Trevor, Nick, Brett and Ben, and one daughter, Kennedy. Although not all of their older children make it home for supper each night, Renae and Brian make a point of devoting supper time to the family. "We try to put everything aside to spend time together," Renae notes. "We ask each person at the table to tell us the high and low points of their day, so that we can share in each other's joys and sorrows."

The delicious dishes Renae shares here are perfect for the family yet special enough for company. Adapted from a recipe that her sister-in-law gave her, Renae came up with easy Alfredo Seafood Fettuccine. "Whenever I prepare this dish for guests, they say I shouldn't have worked so hard," she says. "I don't tell them what a breeze it is to assemble. The longest part of the recipe is cooking the pasta!"

As an accompaniment, Almond Strawberry Salad calls for just a few ingredients but is loaded with flavor. "Everyone loves it and says it's a great idea to use fruit in a dinner salad," she relates. "It's a nice complement to a rich main course."

For dessert, Renae whips up Peanut Butter Delights. The yummy parfaits require no cooking or baking, so they're ready in no time. "I've been making these for 17 years, so I do it by memory now," she notes. "Instead of sprinkling them with chocolate chips, try using chocolate syrup to create a gourmet design."

Almond Strawberry Salad
Prep/Total Time: 10 min.

3	cups fresh baby spinach
1/2	cup sliced fresh strawberries
1/4	cup sliced honey-roasted almonds
1	tablespoon cider vinegar
1	tablespoon honey
1-1/2	teaspoons sugar

In a large bowl, combine the spinach, strawberries and almonds. In a jar with a tight-fitting lid, combine the vinegar, honey and sugar; shake well. Drizzle over salad and toss to coat. **Yield: 4 servings.**

Nutrition Facts: 3/4 cup equals 74 calories, 4 g fat (trace saturated fat), 0 cholesterol, 98 mg sodium, 9 g carbohydrate, 1 g fiber, 2 g protein. **Diabetic Exchanges:** *2 vegetable, 1/2 fat.*

Alfredo Seafood Fettuccine
Prep/Total Time: 20 min.

8	ounces uncooked fettuccine
1	envelope Alfredo sauce mix
1	package (8 ounces) imitation crabmeat
6	ounces bay scallops
6	ounces uncooked medium shrimp, peeled and deveined
1	tablespoon plus 1-1/2 teaspoons butter
1/8	to 1/4 teaspoon garlic powder

Cook fettuccine according to package directions. Meanwhile, prepare Alfredo sauce according to package directions.

In a large skillet, saute the crabmeat, bay scallops and shrimp in butter for 2-3 minutes or until the scallops are opaque and the shrimp turn pink. Stir into the Alfredo sauce. Season with garlic powder. Cook and stir for 5-6 minutes or until thickened. Drain the fettuccine; top with seafood mixture. **Yield: 4 servings.**

Peanut Butter Delights
Prep/Total Time: 10 min.

2	ounces cream cheese, softened
6	tablespoons peanut butter
3/4	cup whipped topping, *divided*
1/2	cup plus 2 tablespoons graham cracker crumbs
1	tablespoon sugar
4-1/2	teaspoons butter, melted
1-1/4	cups miniature semisweet chocolate chips

In a small bowl, beat the softened cream cheese and peanut butter until smooth. Fold in 1/2 cup of the whipped topping; set aside.

In a small bowl, combine the graham cracker crumbs and sugar. Stir in butter until coarse crumbs form. Press 1 tablespoon of crumb mixture into each of four parfait glasses. Spoon about 2 tablespoons peanut butter mixture over crumbs; sprinkle with 2 tablespoons chocolate chips. Repeat layers. Top with remaining whipped topping and chocolate chips. **Yield: 4 servings.**

Even after Charlene Kalb leaves her job at the local high school cafeteria, she can't escape student life. "My husband, David, and our daughter, Anna, both take night classes at a community college," Charlene says from her Catonsville, Maryland home. "So I make a point to get a good dinner on the table fast, giving everyone plenty of time to eat before we all head out to class.

"I like the three of us to eat together as often as possible. But Anna's work at a theater sometimes causes her to miss dinner, so it's important that the recipes I prepare reheat well," she says.

"I love coming up with different ways to fix the foods my family likes. I'm always experimenting with new ways to cook chicken," she explains.

And Charlene found a surefire success in Creamy Tomato Chicken. Served over noodles, the effortless entree is great for weeknight meals yet tastes special enough for weekend company.

Frozen vegetables make for a fast and fabulous side dish in Charlene's Cinnamon Carrots.

Charlene likes to top off meals with a time-tested treat. "After Sunday dinners, my grandmother served her special Hot Fudge Sundaes," remembers Charlene. "The thick fudgy sauce comes together in no time and is terrific over ice cream. My whole family looks forward to this delicious dessert."

 Cinnamon Carrots

Prep/Total Time: 10 min.

- 1 package (16 ounces) frozen sliced carrots
- 1/4 cup honey
- 1 to 2 tablespoons butter
- 1/2 to 1 teaspoon ground cinnamon

Cook carrots according to package directions.

Meanwhile, in a saucepan, heat the honey, butter and cinnamon until the butter is melted; stir to blend. Drain carrots; place in a serving bowl. Drizzle with honey mixture. **Yield: 6 servings.**

Nutrition Facts: 1/2 cup serving (prepared with 1 tablespoon butter) equals 90 calories, 2 g fat (1 g saturated fat), 5 mg cholesterol, 65 mg sodium, 19 g carbohydrate, 3 g fiber, 1 g protein. Diabetic Exchanges: 1 vegetable, 1 fruit.

Creamy Tomato Chicken

Prep/Total Time: 20 min.

- 6 boneless skinless chicken breast halves (4 ounces *each*)
- 2 tablespoons canola oil
- 1 can (14-1/2 ounces) Italian diced tomatoes, undrained
- 1 can (10-3/4 ounces) condensed cream of chicken soup, undiluted
- 1/8 teaspoon ground cinnamon
- 6 slices slices part-skim mozzarella cheese

Hot cooked noodles

In a large skillet, cook chicken over medium heat in oil until a meat thermometer reads 170°. Remove and keep warm.

In a large bowl, combine the tomatoes, soup and cinnamon; add to the skillet. Cook and stir until heated through. Return chicken to skillet; top with cheese. Cover and cook until the cheese is melted. Serve with noodles. **Yield: 6 servings.**

Hot Fudge Sundaes

Prep/Total Time: 15 min.

- 3/4 cup sugar
- 6 tablespoons baking cocoa
- 1 can (5 ounces) evaporated milk
- 1/3 cup butter, cubed
- 3/4 cup miniature marshmallows
- 1 teaspoon vanilla extract

Vanilla ice cream

Nuts and maraschino cherries, optional

In a large saucepan, combine the sugar and baking cocoa; stir in the milk. Add the butter. Bring to a boil over medium heat; cook and stir until sugar is dissolved. Add marshmallows; cook until melted. Remove from the heat; stir in vanilla. Serve with ice cream. Top with the nuts and cherries if desired. **Yield: 2 cups hot fudge sauce.**

Sundae's Best

Here are some great suggestions to add some variety to your typical ice cream sundae. Drizzle chocolate sauce over strawberry ice cream and top with sliced berries and kiwi. Instead of chocolate sauce, top vanilla ice cream with warmed orange marmalade and a few fresh berries. Like s'mores? Dress up ice cream with chocolate sauce, mini marshmallows, whipped cream and graham cracker crumbs.

Whether it's for her husband, grandkids, children or others, Ruth Lee of Troy, Ontario has always enjoyed preparing tasty meals with a healthy twist. "Simplicity and variety are key elements in my cooking, but I always put nutrition first and use lots of fruits and vegetables," she says.

Ruth first learned to create new menus as a teenage nursing-home cook, and later honed those skills as a cook for a private school. "The diets of those at the nursing home were extremely varied due to health issues," she recalls. "At the school, we focused on creating nutrition-packed menus appealing to the eye."

These days, Ruth works part-time as a dog groomer and acts as a caregiver to her three youngest grandchildren. "I love my slow cooker because it allows me to prepare my main meal before my house fills up," she writes. "I also rely on dishes I've frozen for busy nights or to send with my husband, Doug, for work."

Besides feeding her husband and grandkids most days, Ruth organized a group of 19 to cook meals for the local Ronald McDonald House every Friday. "To save money, I plan menus around whatever is on sale at the store," she says. "I avoid convenience products and buy most of my produce at the local outdoor market."

The supper Ruth shares here is a favorite from her days as a school cook. Comforting Chicken a la King has a thick and creamy sauce that's perfect over biscuits or rice. "I've been making this for 30 years," says Ruth. "It's a wonderful way to create a quick lunch or dinner with leftover chicken."

For an easy and colorful salad, Ruth serves Tomatoes with Feta Cheese. "I make this no-fuss dish at least once a month," she writes. "It puts fresh summer tomatoes to great use and adds zip to winter tomatoes, too."

Black Forest Sundaes make a sweet ending to the meal, and best of all, they take just 5 minutes to prepare! "My husband and grandchildren just love them," Ruth says.

Tomatoes with Feta Cheese
Prep/Total Time: 5 min.

8	slices tomato
2	tablespoons crumbled feta cheese
1	tablespoon balsamic vinegar
2	tablespoons minced fresh basil

Pepper to taste

Arrange tomato slices on a serving plate. Sprinkle with feta cheese. Drizzle with vinegar; sprinkle with basil and pepper. **Yield:** 4 servings.

Nutrition Facts: 1 serving equals 20 calories, 1 g fat (trace saturated fat), 2 mg cholesterol, 38 mg sodium, 3 g carbohydrate, 1 g fiber, 1 g protein. **Diabetic Exchange:** *Free food.*

Chicken a la King
Prep/Total Time: 25 min.

4	individually frozen biscuits
1-3/4	cups sliced fresh mushrooms
1/4	cup chopped onion
1/4	cup chopped celery
1/3	cup butter, cubed
1/4	cup all-purpose flour
1/8	to 1/4 teaspoon salt
1	cup chicken broth
1	cup milk
2	cups cubed cooked chicken
2	tablespoons diced pimientos

Bake biscuits according to package directions. Meanwhile, in a large skillet, saute the mushrooms, onion and celery in butter until crisp-tender. Stir in flour and salt until blended. Gradually stir in broth and milk. Bring to a boil; cook and stir for 2 minutes or until thickened.

Add chicken and pimientos. Bring to a boil. Reduce heat; simmer, uncovered, for 4-6 minutes or until heated through. Serve with biscuits. **Yield:** 4 servings.

Black Forest Sundaes
Prep/Total Time: 5 min.

1/2	cup crushed cream-filled chocolate sandwich cookies
4	scoops vanilla ice cream
1	can (21 ounces) cherry pie filling

Whipped cream in a can
Chopped walnuts

Divide cookie crumbs among four dessert dishes; top each with ice cream and pie filling. Garnish with whipped cream and walnuts. Freeze until serving. **Yield:** 4 servings.

There is always someone coming or going at Brenda Jackson's home in Garden City, Kansas. Brenda's husband, Michael, works long hours as a physician, and the couple's daughter, Stephanie, stays on the run with her college classes.

"Michael, Stephanie and I come and go at different times of the day, but we always try to eat dinner together," says Brenda. *"There are usually just the three of us at the table, unless our son, Matthew, pays a visit."*

"I make an average of six sit-down dinners each week," says Brenda. *"Due to our varied schedules, I rarely prepare main courses that need to be served right away, because I don't always know when we'll all be home and ready to sit down to dinner."*

She enjoys preparing hearty Pasta Beef Soup. *"Convenient canned goods, tomato juice and a frozen pasta-vegetable medley make it flavorful and fast,"* she writes. *"But it's also flexible because you can use other ingredients, such as shredded zucchini or yellow squash,"* Brenda adds.

As the soup simmers, Brenda whips up Hard-Shell Ice Cream Sauce. *"I keep the ingredients for this chocolate sauce on hand so I can make it any time I need an easy dessert,"* she says. *"Once the sauce has cooled a bit, I transfer it to a microwave-safe container and set it in the refrigerator. When it's time for dessert, I just warm it up in the microwave."*

With the chocolate sauce complete, Brenda quickly creates Savory Cheese Bread. *"This golden bread is a recipe I made up years ago,"* she explains. *"These cheese-topped slices are perfect with chunky soup or most any entree."*

Savory Cheese Bread
Prep/Total Time: 10 min.

- 1/4 cup butter, softened
- 1/4 to 1/2 teaspoon lemon-pepper seasoning
- 1/4 teaspoon garlic powder
- 1/4 teaspoon dried basil
- 1/4 teaspoon dried oregano
- 12 slices French bread (1 inch thick)
- 2 cups (8 ounces) shredded Italian cheese blend

Combine the butter, lemon-pepper, garlic powder, basil and oregano. Spread over one side of each slice of bread.

Place butter-side up on ungreased baking sheet. Sprinkle with cheese. Broil 4 in. from heat for 2-3 minutes or until cheese is melted and edges are golden brown. **Yield: 6 servings.**

Pasta Beef Soup
Prep/Total Time: 25 min.

- 1 pound ground beef
- 2 cans (14-1/2 ounces *each*) beef broth
- 1 package (16 ounces) frozen pasta with broccoli, corn and carrots in garlic-seasoned sauce
- 1-1/2 cups tomato juice
- 1 can (14-1/2 ounces) diced tomatoes, undrained
- 2 teaspoons Italian seasoning
- 1/4 cup shredded Parmesan cheese, optional

In a large saucepan, cook beef over medium heat until no longer pink; drain. Add the broth, pasta with vegetables, tomato juice, tomatoes and Italian seasoning; bring to a boil. Reduce heat; cover and simmer for 10 minutes or until vegetables are tender. Serve with Parmesan cheese if desired. **Yield: 6 servings.**

Nutrition Facts: 1-1/2 cups has 253 calories (made with lean beef and reduced-sodium broth and tomato juice; calculated without Parmesan), 9 g fat (4 g saturated fat), 46 mg cholesterol, 680 mg sodium, 21 g carbohydrate, 3 g fiber, 20 g protein. Diabetic Exchanges: 2-1/2 lean meat, 1 vegetable, 1 starch.

Hard-Shell Ice Cream Sauce
Prep/Total Time: 15 min.

- 1 cup (6 ounces) semisweet chocolate chips
- 1/4 cup butter, cubed
- 3 tablespoons evaporated milk
  Vanilla ice cream
- 1/2 cup sliced almonds

In a heavy saucepan, combine chocolate chips, butter and milk. Cook and stir over low heat until chips are melted and mixture is smooth. Serve warm over ice cream (sauce will harden). Sprinkle with almonds. Refrigerate any leftovers. Sauce can be reheated in the microwave. **Yield: about 1 cup.**

Oh Nuts!

Nuts can turn rancid over time, so it's best to store them in the freezer. To toast them, spread on a baking sheet and bake at 350° for 5 to 10 minutes or until lightly toasted. Watch closely so they don't burn.

Stop by the Nevada, Ohio home of Tina Lust and you may find the energetic mom chasing after young son Clayton. "My husband, Tom, farms corn and soybeans with his dad, uncle and cousin," Tina says. "I help out when I'm not busy selling corn and soybean seeds to area farmers.

"I love to serve pork," says Tina. "Not only is it delicious, but it cooks up in no time. That's why Cranberry Pork Chops are popular in our house, particularly around the holidays." Speedy Spinach Salad is the perfect accompaniment to the moist pork chops. "I created this recipe to make the most of the fresh spinach from our garden," she explains.

Tina jazzes up refrigerated crescent rolls with sour cream and herbs to create Country Herb Croissants. "I keep the herbs on hand, but feel free to use dried cranberries, chopped walnuts and grated orange peel for rolls to serve with brunch," she says.

Tina tops off her meal with taste-tempting Pumpkin Pie Dessert, an easy alternative to the traditional treat served around the holidays. "It's particularly quick when you need a special dessert," she says. "It doesn't require baking, which frees up the oven for the rest of your meal."

Speedy Spinach Salad
Prep/Total Time: 10 min.

- 4 cups torn fresh spinach
- 1/2 cup shredded Monterey Jack cheese
- 1/2 cup coarsely crushed butter-flavored crackers (about 8)

Ranch salad dressing *or* dressing of your choice

Place spinach in a salad bowl; top with cheese and crackers. Serve with dressing. **Yield: 4 servings.**

Country Herb Croissants
Prep/Total Time: 25 min.

- 1 tube (8 ounces) refrigerated crescent rolls
- 1 tablespoon sour cream
- 1 tablespoon dried minced onion
- 1/2 teaspoon dried parsley flakes
- 1/2 teaspoon rubbed sage
- 1/4 teaspoon celery salt

Unroll crescent roll dough and separate into triangles. In a small bowl, combine the sour cream, onion, parsley, sage and celery salt; spread over dough.

Roll up from the wide end and place pointed side down 2 in. apart on greased baking sheets. Curve ends down to form crescent shape. Bake at 375° for 11-13 minutes or until golden brown. Serve warm. **Yield: 8 rolls.**

Cranberry Pork Chops
Prep/Total Time: 20 min.

- 4 boneless pork loin chops (6 ounces *each*)
- 1 tablespoon canola oil
- 1 can (16 ounces) whole-berry cranberry sauce
- 1 cup French salad dressing
- 4 teaspoons onion soup mix

In a large skillet, cook the boneless pork chops in the oil for 12-15 minutes on each side or until a meat thermometer reads 160°.

Meanwhile, in a microwave-safe bowl, combine the cranberry sauce, salad dressing and soup mix. Cover and microwave on high 1-1/2 to 2 minutes or until heated through. Serve with pork chops. **Yield: 4 servings.**

Editor's Note: This recipe was tested in a 1,100-watt microwave.

Pumpkin Pie Dessert
Prep: 20 min. + chilling

- 2-1/4 cups crushed butter-flavored crackers (about 50 crackers)
- 1/2 cup sugar
- 3/4 cup butter, melted
- 2 cups cold milk
- 2 packages (3.4 ounces *each*) instant vanilla pudding mix
- 1 can (15 ounces) solid-pack pumpkin
- 1 teaspoon pumpkin pie spice
- 1/2 teaspoon ground cinnamon
- 1/4 teaspoon ground ginger
- 1/4 teaspoon ground nutmeg

Whipped topping and chopped pecans

Combine the cracker crumbs, sugar and melted butter. Press into a greased 13-in. x 9-in. dish; set aside.

In a large bowl, whisk the milk and pudding mix for 2 minutes. Let stand for 2 minutes or until soft-set. Stir in pumpkin and spices. Spread over the crust. Refrigerate for 3 hours or until set. Garnish with whipped topping and nuts. **Yield: 12-15 servings.**

easy
half-hour
entrees

The mouth-watering dishes in this chapter have all the hearty and homemade quality of any recipe, but these flavor-packed, main dishes get to the table in a flash. From start to finish, each and every entree takes only 30 minutes to prepare...or less!

You'll find exceptional, family-pleasing recipes such as Chicago-Style Pan Pizza, Sloppy Joe Under a Bun, Mediterranean Chicken, Shrimp Cantonese and more. Fabulous, restaurant-style dishes like these that require just half-an-hour are perfect for today's busy cooks!

 Chicken in Lime Butter
(recipe on p. 213)

Italian Sausage with Bow Ties

Greek Pork Pockets

Prep/Total Time: 20 min.

For a nutritious, grab-and-go meal on busy summer days, I rely on these hefty handfuls for my family. They're so easy to make, and my kids prefer them to peanut butter and jelly any day.

—Diane Hixon, Niceville, Florida

1	pork tenderloin (1 pound), sliced
1/2	cup creamy Caesar salad dressing
1	teaspoon canola oil
2	pita breads (6 inches), halved
1/2	cup chopped cucumber
4	slices red onion, separated into rings
1/4	cup cucumber ranch salad dressing

Place the pork in a large resealable plastic bag; add the Caesar dressing. Seal the bag and turn to coat. In a large nonstick skillet, saute the pork in oil for 7-8 minutes or until meat is no longer pink.

Fill each pita half with pork, cucumber and onion; drizzle with cucumber dressing. **Yield: 4 servings.**

Microwave Mac 'n' Cheese

Prep/Total Time: 30 min.

My family prefers homemade macaroni and cheese over the kind you get out of the box. This recipe is an easy way to keep them happy. Whenever we have a family get-together, I bring this comforting, "from scratch" dish.

—Linda Gingrich, Freeburg, Pennsylvania

2	cups uncooked elbow macaroni
2	cups hot water
1/3	cup butter, cubed
1/4	cup chopped onion
3/4	teaspoon salt
1/4	teaspoon pepper
1/4	teaspoon ground mustard
1/3	cup all-purpose flour
1-1/4	cups milk
8	ounces process cheese (Velveeta), cubed

In a 2-qt. microwave-safe dish, combine the first seven ingredients. Cover and microwave on high for 3 minutes; stir. Cover and cook at 50% power for 3 minutes or until mixture comes to a boil.

Combine the flour and milk until smooth; gradually stir into the macaroni mixture. Add the cheese cubes. Cover and cook on high for 6-8 minutes or until the macaroni is tender and the cheese sauce is bubbly, stirring every 3 minutes. **Yield: 4 servings.**

Editor's Note: This recipe was tested in a 1,100-watt microwave.

Italian Sausage with Bow Ties

Prep/Total Time: 25 min.

Here's a family favorite that's requested monthly in our house. The Italian sausage paired with creamy tomato sauce tastes out of this world. Not only is this dish simple to make, it tastes like you slaved over a hot stove for hours!

—Janelle Moore, Federal Way, Washington

1	package (16 ounces) bow tie pasta
1	pound bulk Italian sausage
1/2	cup chopped onion
1-1/2	teaspoons minced garlic
1/2	teaspoon crushed red pepper flakes
2	cans (14-1/2 ounces *each*) Italian stewed tomatoes, drained and chopped
1-1/2	cups heavy whipping cream
1/2	teaspoon salt
1/4	teaspoon dried basil

Shredded Parmesan cheese

Cook pasta according to package directions. Meanwhile, in a Dutch oven, cook the sausage, onion, garlic and pepper flakes over medium heat for 4-5 minutes or until meat is no longer pink; drain.

Stir in the tomatoes, cream, salt and basil. Bring to a boil over medium heat. Reduce heat; simmer, uncovered, for 6-8 minutes or until thickened, stirring occasionally. Drain pasta; toss with sausage mixture. Garnish with Parmesan cheese. **Yield: 5 servings.**

Tangy Turkey Saute

Prep/Total Time: 30 min.

This recipe turns turkey breast slices into something extraordinary. With garlic, thyme and lots of fresh mushrooms, it really packs the flavor. But the really special aspect of it is the use of marsala wine. If you don't want to use the wine, feel free to substitute chicken broth.
—Amy Wenger, Severance, Colorado

- 1/4 cup all-purpose flour
- 8 turkey breast cutlets (2 ounces *each*)
- 3 tablespoons olive oil, *divided*
- 2 cups sliced fresh mushrooms
- 1/2 cup thinly sliced green onions
- 1/2 teaspoon minced garlic
- 1/2 cup chicken broth
- 1 cup marsala wine *or* additional chicken broth
- 1/2 teaspoon salt
- 1/4 teaspoon dried thyme
- 1 tablespoon minced fresh parsley

Place flour in a large resealable plastic bag. Add turkey, a few pieces at a time, and shake to coat. In a large skillet, saute turkey in 2 tablespoons oil in batches for 2 minutes on each side or until no longer pink; drain. Remove and keep warm.

In the same skillet, saute the mushrooms, onions and garlic in remaining oil for 3 minutes or until crisp-tender. Stir in the broth, wine or additional broth, salt and thyme. Bring to a boil; cook and stir for 3 minutes or until slightly thickened. Stir in parsley. Serve over turkey. **Yield: 4 servings.**

Southern Pecan Catfish

Prep/Total Time: 30 min.

For this super fast recipe, I coat catfish fillets in pecans, then top them with a thick, rich cream sauce. It looks like you spent all day on it, but it's actually so speedy to prepare. For pizzazz, garnish the fish with lemon wedges, parsley or chopped pecans.
—Mary Ann Griffin, Saginaw, Michigan

- 1 cup finely chopped pecans, *divided*
- 1/2 cup cornmeal
- 1 teaspoon salt, *divided*
- 1 teaspoon pepper, *divided*
- 4 catfish fillets (6 ounces *each*)
- 1/2 cup butter, *divided*
- 1/2 cup heavy whipping cream
- 2 tablespoons lemon juice
- 1 to 2 tablespoons minced fresh parsley

In a shallow bowl, combine 1/2 cup pecans, cornmeal, 1/2 teaspoon salt and 1/2 teaspoon pepper. Coat the catfish with pecan mixture. In a large skillet, melt 1/4 cup butter over medium-high heat; fry fillets for 6-7 minutes on each side or until the fish flakes easily with a fork. Remove and keep warm.

In the same skillet, melt remaining butter over medium heat. Add remaining pecans; cook and stir for 1 minute. Add the cream, lemon juice and remaining salt and pepper; cook and stir for 1 minute. Stir in the parsley. Serve with catfish. **Yield: 4 servings.**

Southern Pecan Catfish

Shrimp with Style

Prep/Total Time: 25 min.

I created this standout supper one busy day with items already in my refrigerator. My family craves this dish any time of year because it's so delicious and light. Enjoy!

—Cyndi McLaughlin, Pinon Pines, California

1	package (9 ounces) refrigerated angel hair pasta
1/2	pound sliced fresh mushrooms
1-1/2	teaspoons minced garlic
1	cup butter, cubed
1	pound uncooked medium shrimp, peeled and deveined
2	packages (3 ounces *each*) julienned sun-dried tomatoes (not packed in oil)
1	package (2-1/4 ounces) slivered almonds, toasted
1/2	cup crumbled feta cheese
1/2	cup minced fresh parsley
3	tablespoons white wine *or* chicken broth
2	teaspoons lemon juice
1/2	teaspoon salt
1/2	teaspoon pepper
1/2	cup shredded Parmesan cheese

Cook pasta according to package directions. Meanwhile, in a large skillet, saute mushrooms and garlic in butter for 2 minutes. Add shrimp; cook and stir for 5-7 minutes or until shrimp turn pink.

Stir in the tomatoes, almonds, feta cheese, parsley, wine or broth, lemon juice, salt and pepper; cook for 3-5 minutes or until heated through. Drain pasta and place in a serving bowl; top with shrimp mixture and Parmesan cheese. **Yield: 5 servings.**

Shrimp with Style

Chicago-Style Pan Pizza

Chicago-Style Pan Pizza

Prep: 20 min. | Bake: 30 min.

I developed a love for Chicago's unique deep-dish pizzas while attending college in the Windy City. This simple recipe relies on frozen bread dough, so I can indulge in the mouth-watering sensation without leaving home.

—Nikki MacDonald, Sheboygan, Wisconsin

1	loaf (1 pound) frozen bread dough, thawed
1	pound bulk Italian sausage
2	cups (8 ounces) shredded part-skim mozzarella cheese
1/2	pound sliced fresh mushrooms
1	small onion, chopped
2	teaspoons olive oil
1	can (28 ounces) diced tomatoes, drained
3/4	teaspoon dried oregano
1/2	teaspoon salt
1/2	teaspoon fennel seed, crushed
1/4	teaspoon garlic powder
1/2	cup grated Parmesan cheese

Press dough onto the bottom and up the sides of a greased 13-in. x 9-in. baking dish. In a large skillet, cook sausage over medium heat until no longer pink; drain. Sprinkle over dough. Top with mozzarella cheese.

In a large skillet, saute mushrooms and onion in oil until onion is tender. Stir in the tomatoes, oregano, salt, fennel seed and garlic powder.

Spoon over mozzarella cheese. Sprinkle with Parmesan cheese. Bake at 350° for 25-35 minutes or until crust is golden brown. **Yield: 6 slices.**

Thai Beef Stir-Fry

Prep/Total Time: 25 min.

The savory flavor of this stir-fry is very similar to restaurant-style Thai dishes. A pleasant peanut sauce coats the meat and vegetables, giving the entree a special flair.

—Janet Lowe, Kennewick, Washington

- 2 tablespoons cornstarch
- 3/4 cup water
- 2 tablespoons plus 1-1/2 teaspoons chunky peanut butter
- 4 tablespoons soy sauce, *divided*
- 1-1/2 pounds boneless beef top sirloin steak, thinly sliced
- 1-1/2 teaspoons minced garlic
- 1/4 teaspoon pepper
- 2 tablespoons olive oil
- 1 *each* medium green, sweet red and yellow pepper, julienned
- 1 can (8 ounces) bamboo shoots, drained
- 1/2 cup julienned carrot
- 1/2 teaspoon crushed red pepper flakes

Hot cooked rice

In a small bowl, combine cornstarch and water until smooth. Stir in peanut butter and 3 tablespoons soy sauce; set aside.

In a large skillet or wok, stir-fry the sliced beef, garlic, pepper and remaining soy sauce in olive oil until the meat is no longer pink; remove and keep warm. Add the peppers, bamboo shoots, carrot and pepper flakes; stir-fry for 2-3 minutes or until tender.

Stir cornstarch mixture; gradually add to the pan. Bring to a boil; cook and stir for 1 minute or until thickened. Return beef mixture to the pan. Serve with rice. **Yield: 6 servings.**

Thai Beef Stir-Fry

Chicken Pesto Pasta

Chicken Pesto Pasta

Prep/Total Time: 25 min.

This is one of my favorite recipes because it's so quick and easy, but it looks and tastes like I spent all day cooking it. And it has all of my favorite things in it!

—Barbara Christensen, Arvada, Colorado

- 1 package (16 ounces) bow tie pasta
- 1 cup cut fresh asparagus (1-inch pieces)
- 1-1/4 cups sliced fresh mushrooms
- 1 medium sweet red pepper, sliced
- 1-1/2 teaspoons minced garlic
- 2 tablespoons olive oil
- 2 cups cubed cooked chicken
- 1 can (14 ounces) water-packed artichoke hearts, rinsed and drained
- 2 jars (3-1/2 ounces *each*) prepared pesto
- 1 jar (7 ounces) oil-packed sun-dried tomatoes, drained and chopped
- 1 teaspoon salt
- 1/8 teaspoon crushed red pepper flakes
- 1 cup (4 ounces) shredded Parmesan cheese
- 2/3 cup pine nuts, toasted

Cook pasta according to package directions, adding asparagus during the last 3 minutes of cooking.

Meanwhile, in a large skillet, saute the mushrooms, red pepper and garlic in oil until tender. Reduce heat; stir in the chicken, artichokes, pesto, tomatoes, salt and pepper flakes. Cook 2-3 minutes longer or until heated through.

Drain pasta; toss with chicken mixture. Sprinkle with cheese and pine nuts. **Yield: 8 servings.**

Cranberry Turkey Cutlets

Prep/Total Time: 30 min.

When our son-in-law brought home some wild turkey one year, we turned to this recipe. He took care of the grilling while I made the sauce, and we all enjoyed this healthy entree.

—Marguerite Shaeffer, Sewell, New Jersey

1	cup thinly sliced onion
2	teaspoons canola oil
2	cups dried cranberries
2	cups orange juice
1-1/2	teaspoons balsamic vinegar
6	turkey cutlets (1/2-inch thick and 4 ounces *each*)
1/2	teaspoon salt
1/2	teaspoon pepper

In a large skillet, saute onion in oil for about 6 minutes or until lightly browned. Stir in the cranberries, orange juice and vinegar. Bring to a boil over medium heat; cook and stir until sauce begins to thicken. Set aside.

Coat grill rack with cooking spray before starting the grill. Sprinkle turkey cutlets with salt and pepper. Grill, covered, over indirect medium heat for 5-6 minutes on each side or until juices run clear. Top each cutlet with some of the cranberry sauce; grill 1-2 minutes longer. Serve with remaining cranberry sauce. **Yield: 6 servings.**

Sensational Sloppy Joes

Prep/Total Time: 30 min.

I've always liked sloppy joes but was feeling that my own recipe lacked character. Then a co-worker shared hers with me, and I guarantee I'll never go back! Grape jelly adds a hint of sweetness to this fun, flavorful mixture, but I often use more than called for because my husband likes his extra sweet.

—Jessica Mergen, Cuba City, Wisconsin

1	pound ground beef
1/2	cup chopped onion
1/2	cup condensed tomato soup, undiluted
1/2	cup ketchup
3	tablespoons grape jelly
1	tablespoon brown sugar
1	tablespoon cider vinegar
1	tablespoon prepared mustard
1/2	teaspoon salt
1/2	teaspoon celery seed
5	hamburger buns, split

In a large skillet, cook beef and onion over medium heat until meat is no longer pink; drain. Stir in the soup, ketchup, jelly, brown sugar, vinegar, mustard, salt and celery seed. Bring to a boil. Reduce heat; simmer, uncovered, for 10 minutes or until heated through. Serve on buns. **Yield: 5 servings.**

Cranberry Turkey Cutlets

Apricot Chicken

Chicken Pizza Packets
Prep: 15 min. | Grill: 20 min.

This speedy grilled supper is a tasty way to get little ones to eat their veggies. Basil, garlic, pepperoni and mozzarella give plenty of pizza flavor to chicken, green pepper, zucchini and cherry tomatoes in these individual foil dinners.
—Amber Zurbrugg, Alliance, Ohio

1	pound boneless skinless chicken breasts, cut into 1-inch pieces
2	tablespoons olive oil
1	small zucchini, thinly sliced
16	pepperoni slices
1	small green pepper, julienned
1	small onion, sliced
1/2	teaspoon dried oregano
1/2	teaspoon dried basil
1/4	teaspoon salt
1/4	teaspoon garlic powder
1/4	teaspoon pepper
1	cup halved cherry tomatoes
1/2	cup shredded part-skim mozzarella cheese
1/2	cup shredded Parmesan cheese

In a large bowl, combine the first 11 ingredients. Coat four pieces of heavy-duty foil (about 12 in. square) with cooking spray. Place a quarter of the chicken mixture in the center of each piece. Fold foil around mixture and seal tightly.

Grill, covered, over medium-hot heat for 15-18 minutes or until chicken is no longer pink.

Carefully open each packet. Sprinkle with tomatoes and cheeses. Seal loosely; grill 2 minutes longer or until cheese is melted. **Yield: 4 servings.**

Chicken Pizza Packets

Apricot Chicken
Prep/Total Time: 15 min.

This is one of my favorite ways to fix chicken in a hurry. Everybody loves it and leftovers are delicious the next day. For variation, use pork instead of chicken and add additional ingredients like pineapple, mandarin oranges, snow peas or broccoli.
— Vicki Ruiz, Twin Falls, Idaho

1/2	cup apricot preserves
2	tablespoons soy sauce
1	tablespoon chicken broth *or* sherry
1	tablespoon canola oil
1	tablespoon cornstarch
1	teaspoon minced garlic
1/4	teaspoon ground ginger
1	pound boneless skinless chicken breasts, cut into strips
1	medium green pepper, chopped
1/2	cup salted cashews

Hot cooked rice

In a large bowl, combine the first seven ingredients. Add chicken and toss to coat. Transfer to a shallow microwave-safe dish. Cover and microwave on high for 3 minutes, stirring once.

Add green pepper and cashews. Cover and microwave on high for 2-4 minutes or until chicken is no longer pink, stirring once. Let stand for 3 minutes. Serve with rice. **Yield: 4 servings.**

Dressed-Up Meatballs

Prep/Total Time: 20 min.

Frozen meatballs and a jar of sweet-and-sour sauce make this meal a lifesaver when racing against the clock. The flavorful sauce is dressed up with a hint of garlic and nicely coats the colorful mixture of meatballs, carrots, green pepper and onion.

—Ivy Eresmas, Dade City, Florida

2	pounds frozen fully cooked meatballs, thawed
1	small onion, sliced
2	medium carrots, julienned
1	small green pepper, julienned
1	garlic clove, minced
1	jar (10 ounces) sweet-and-sour sauce
4-1/2	teaspoons soy sauce

Hot cooked rice

Place the meatballs in a 3-qt. microwave-safe dish; top with the onion, carrots, green pepper and garlic. Combine the sauces; pour over meatballs.

Cover and microwave on high for 6-8 minutes or until vegetables are tender and meatballs are heated through, stirring twice. Serve with rice. **Yield: 8 servings.**

Editor's Note: This recipe was tested in a 1,100-watt microwave.

Dressed-Up Meatballs

Angel Hair with Walnuts

Prep/Total Time: 20 min.

I worked in an Italian restaurant that served pasta with olive oil, garlic and a sprinkling of walnuts. I enjoyed the medley so much that I developed this recipe. It was a huge hit!

—Nancy Beckman, Helena, Montana

8	ounces uncooked angel hair pasta
1-1/2	to 2 teaspoons minced garlic
1/4	cup olive oil
1/2	cup chopped walnuts
1/8	to 1/4 teaspoon crushed red pepper flakes
1/8	teaspoon salt
2	tablespoons minced fresh parsley
1/2	cup shredded Romano cheese

Cook pasta according to package directions. Meanwhile, in a large skillet, saute garlic in oil until tender. Stir in the walnuts, pepper flakes and salt. Cook for 2-3 minutes or until walnuts are toasted.

Remove from the heat; stir in parsley. Drain pasta; add to skillet. Add cheese; toss to coat. **Yield: 4 servings.**

Tortellini Alfredo

Prep/Total Time: 30 min.

I jazz up refrigerated tortellini with ham, mushrooms, peas and my homemade Alfredo sauce for a fast supper. When we're having company, I prepare the dinner shortly before guests arrive, put it in a casserole dish and keep it warm in the oven.

—Chris Snyder, Boulder, Colorado

2	packages (9 ounces *each*) refrigerated cheese tortellini
1/2	cup chopped onion
1/3	cup butter, cubed
1-1/2	cups frozen peas, thawed
1	cup thinly sliced fresh mushrooms
1	cup cubed fully cooked ham
1-3/4	cups heavy whipping cream
1/4	teaspoon coarsely ground pepper
3/4	cup grated Parmesan cheese

Shredded Parmesan cheese, optional

Cook the cheese tortellini according to package directions. Meanwhile, in a large skillet, saute the onion in butter until tender. Add the peas, mushrooms and ham; cook until the mushrooms are tender. Stir in the heavy cream and pepper; heat through. Add the grated Parmesan cheese and stir until melted.

Drain tortellini and place in a serving dish; add the sauce and toss to coat. Sprinkle with shredded Parmesan cheese if desired. **Yield: 4-6 servings.**

Sloppy Joe Under a Bun

Sloppy Joe Under a Bun

Prep/Total Time: 30 min.

I usually keep a can of sloppy joe sauce in the pantry, but sometimes don't have buns on hand. With this fun casserole, the bun-like top crust is made with biscuit mix, sprinkled with sesame seeds and baked until golden.

—Trish Bloom, Ray, Michigan

1-1/2 pounds ground beef
1 can (15-1/2 ounces) sloppy joe sauce
2 cups (8 ounces) shredded cheddar cheese
2 cups biscuit/baking mix
2 eggs, lightly beaten
1 cup milk
1 tablespoon sesame seeds

In a large skillet, cook beef over medium heat until no longer pink; drain. Stir in sloppy joe sauce. Transfer to a lightly greased 13-in. x 9-in. baking dish; sprinkle with cheese.

In a large bowl, combine the biscuit mix, eggs and milk just until blended. Pour over cheese; sprinkle with sesame seeds.

Nutty Pork Fried Rice

Prep/Total Time: 30 min.

Every time I made this versatile dish, I was told I should send it to a magazine to share with readers. So I did! It's quick, easy and tasty! Honeyed walnuts and water chestnuts add flavor and crunch. *—Becky Reilly, Cheney, Washington*

1 package (6.2 ounces) fried rice mix
1 cup chopped walnuts, *divided*
1 tablespoon honey

2 boneless pork loin chops (4 ounces *each*), cut into strips
2 tablespoons canola oil
1 can (8 ounces) sliced water chestnuts, drained
1 cup sliced celery
1 cup chopped green onions
1/2 teaspoon minced garlic
1 cup coleslaw mix
2 tablespoons sesame seeds, toasted, *divided*
1 tablespoon lemon juice
1/2 teaspoon sesame oil

Prepare rice according to package directions. Meanwhile, in a small skillet over medium heat, cook and stir the walnuts and honey for 4 minutes or until coated. Spread on foil to cool.

In a large skillet or wok, stir-fry pork in oil for 3-4 minutes or until no longer pink. Remove with a slotted spoon. Stir-fry the water chestnuts, celery, onions and garlic for 3-4 minutes or until vegetables are crisp-tender.

Add the coleslaw mix, 1 tablespoon sesame seeds, lemon juice, sesame oil, rice and 1/2 cup walnuts. Cook and stir for 2 minutes. Add pork; heat through. Sprinkle with remaining sesame seeds and walnuts. **Yield: 4 servings.**

Mushroom-Swiss Lamb Chops

Prep/Total Time: 30 min.

Looking for something fast but impressive to serve company on a busy weeknight? These lamb chops make a really nice, last-minute meal for guests. I pick up the ingredients on the way home from work and finish off the menu with a salad and new potatoes.

—Candy McMenamin, Lexington, South Carolina

4 lamb loin chops (2-inches thick and 8 ounces *each*)
1/2 teaspoon salt
1/2 teaspoon pepper
2 cups sliced fresh mushrooms
2 tablespoons butter
1/4 cup prepared Russian salad dressing
1/2 cup shredded Swiss cheese

Sprinkle both sides of the lamb chops with salt and pepper. Broil 4-6 in. from the heat for 10-15 minutes on each side or until the meat reaches desired doneness (for medium-rare, a meat thermometer should read 145°; medium, 160°; well-done, 170°).

Meanwhile, in a large skillet, saute mushrooms in butter for 5-6 minutes or until tender. Stir in salad dressing. Bring to a boil; cook until liquid is reduced by half.

Sprinkle cheese over lamb chops; broil 1-2 minutes longer or until cheese is melted. Serve with mushroom mixture. **Yield: 4 servings.**

Mediterranean Chicken

Mediterranean Chicken

Prep/Total Time: 25 min.

Moist and tender chicken is dressed in tomatoes, olives and capers for a knockout main dish. As special as it is simple, this delicious entree works well for a casual dinner or company.
—Mary Relyea, Canastota, New York

4	boneless skinless chicken breast halves (6 ounces *each*)
1/4	teaspoon salt
1/4	teaspoon pepper
3	tablespoons olive oil
I	pint grape tomatoes
16	pitted Greek *or* ripe olives, sliced
3	tablespoons capers, drained

Sprinkle the chicken with salt and pepper. In a large ovenproof skillet, cook chicken in oil over medium heat for 2-3 minutes on each side or until golden brown. Add the tomatoes, olives and capers.

Bake, uncovered, at 475° for 10-14 minutes or until a meat thermometer reads 170°. **Yield:** 4 servings.

Spicy Warm Chicken Salad

Prep/Total Time: 30 min.

This hearty main-dish salad makes a great cool-weather dish. It's colorful, delicious and filled with the kind of heat that's great after a chilly football game or hike. Best of all, you can have it on the table in half an hour! *—Iola Egle, Bella Vista, Arkansas*

I	envelope onion soup mix
4	boneless skinless chicken breast halves (4 ounces *each*)
2	tablespoons olive oil
I	can (15 ounces) pinto beans, rinsed and drained
I	cup frozen corn
1/2	cup picante sauce
I	can (4 ounces) chopped green chilies
1/4	cup chopped green onions
1/2	cup sour cream
1/2	cup jalapeno pepper jelly
I	tablespoon lemon juice
2	cups chopped iceberg lettuce
2	cups torn romaine
I	small sweet red pepper, thinly sliced
1/4	cup minced fresh cilantro
2	jalapeno peppers, seeded and chopped, optional

Rub the onion soup mix over both sides of the chicken breast halves. In a large skillet, cook the chicken in the olive oil over medium heat for 8-10 minutes on each side or until a meat thermometer reads 170°. Remove and keep warm.

In the same skillet, combine the pinto beans, corn and picante sauce. Cook and stir over medium heat for 2-3 minutes or until heated through. Stir in the chopped green chilies and green onions; set aside. Combine the sour cream, pepper jelly and lemon juice; set aside.

Toss the iceberg lettuce and romaine; divide among four salad plates. Slice the cooked chicken; arrange on the greens. Place the sweet red pepper slices and bean mixture around the chicken slices. Drizzle with the sour cream mixture; sprinkle with the minced cilantro. Serve with the chopped jalapenos if desired. **Yield:** 4 servings.

Editor's Note: When cutting hot peppers, disposable gloves are recommended. Avoid touching your face.

Cilantro (see-LAHN-troh)

With its slightly sharp yet aromatic flavor, cilantro (also known as Chinese parsley) gives a distinctive taste to Mexican, Latin American and Asian dishes. The dry spice coriander, which comes in both a whole seed as well as ground form, comes from the seed of the cilantro plant.

Like all fresh herbs, cilantro should be used as soon as possible, especially because fresh cilantro leaves are particularly delicate. For short-term storage, immerse the freshly cut stems in water about 2 inches deep. Cover leaves loosely with a plastic bag and refrigerate for several days. Wash just before using.

Turkey and Gravy Baskets

Prep/Total Time: 20 min.

Take advantage of convenience items to put a special main course on the table even when time is tight. A colorful mixture of fresh vegetables and packaged cooked turkey and gravy is spooned into puff pastry shells from the freezer section.
—Taste of Home Test Kitchen, Greendale, Wisconsin

1	package (10 ounces) frozen puff pastry shells
2	cups fresh broccoli florets
1/2	cup chopped onion
1/2	cup chopped sweet red pepper
4	teaspoons canola oil
1	package (18 ounces) refrigerated turkey breast slices in gravy
1/2	cup turkey gravy

Bake four puff pastry shells according to the package directions; save the remaining shells for another use. Meanwhile, in a large skillet, saute the broccoli florets, chopped onion and sweet red pepper in the canola oil for 5 minutes or until crisp-tender.

Cut turkey slices into bite-size pieces; add to skillet with gravy from package and additional gravy. Heat through. Serve in pastry shells. **Yield: 4 servings.**

Chicken in Lime Butter

Prep/Total Time: 20 min.

A few ordinary, on-hand ingredients make this moist and tender chicken something really extraordinary! The flavor of the rich and buttery sauce with lime juice is unmatched. It's been a hands-down winner at our house for 20 some years.
—Denise Segura, Draper, Utah

4	boneless skinless chicken breast halves (4 ounces *each*)
1/8	teaspoon salt
1/8	teaspoon pepper
2	tablespoons canola oil
1/4	cup butter
1	tablespoon lime juice
1/2	teaspoon dill weed
1/4	teaspoon minced chives

Sprinkle chicken with salt and pepper. In a large skillet, cook chicken in oil over medium heat for 5-7 minutes on each side or until a meat thermometer reaches 170°; drain. Remove and keep warm.

Add butter and lime juice to the skillet; cook and stir until butter is melted. Stir in dill and chives. Drizzle over chicken. **Yield: 4 servings.**

Chicken in Lime Butter

Blackened Chicken

Prep/Total Time: 25 min.

This spicy standout packs a one-two punch of flavor. The grilled chicken is basted with a simple peppery white sauce. Plus there's plenty of extra sauce for dipping.

—Stephanie Kenney, Falkville, Alabama

I	tablespoon paprika
4	teaspoons sugar, *divided*
1-1/2	teaspoons salt, *divided*
I	teaspoon garlic powder
I	teaspoon dried thyme
I	teaspoon lemon-pepper seasoning
I	teaspoon cayenne pepper
1-1/2	to 2 teaspoons pepper, *divided*
4	boneless skinless chicken breast halves (4 ounces *each*)
1-1/3	cups mayonnaise
2	tablespoons water
2	tablespoons cider vinegar

Combine the paprika, I teaspoon sugar, I teaspoon salt, garlic powder, dried thyme, lemon-pepper, cayenne and 1/2 to I teaspoon pepper; sprinkle over both sides of the chicken. Set aside.

In another bowl, combine the mayonnaise, water, vinegar and remaining sugar, salt and pepper; cover and refrigerate I cup for serving. Save remaining sauce for basting.

Grill chicken, covered, over indirect medium heat for 4-6 minutes on each side or until a thermometer reads 170°, basting frequently with remaining sauce. Serve with reserved sauce. **Yield: 4 servings.**

Blackened Chicken

Crab Cakes with Lime Sauce

Crab Cakes with Lime Sauce

Prep/Total Time: 25 min.

Reel in a breezy taste of the seashore with these delectable, crispy-coated crab cakes. A refreshing, lip-smacking lime sauce adds a delightful summery tang to this old-fashioned favorite.

—Marjie Gaspar, Oxford, Pennsylvania

2	cans (6 ounces *each*) crabmeat, drained, flaked and cartilage removed
I	green onion, chopped
I	tablespoon Dijon mustard
I	teaspoon Italian salad dressing mix
1-1/2	cups crushed butter-flavored crackers (about 37), *divided*
I	cup mayonnaise, *divided*
2	tablespoons lime juice, *divided*
1/4	cup canola oil
1/4	cup sour cream
1-1/2	teaspoons grated lime peel

Combine the crab, green onion, mustard, Italian dressing mix, I cup cracker crumbs, 1/2 cup mayonnaise and I tablespoon lime juice. Shape into six patties; coat with the remaining cracker crumbs.

In a large skillet, heat oil over medium heat. Cook crab cakes for 3-4 minutes on each side or until lightly browned.

For lime sauce, combine the sour cream, lime peel, and remaining mayonnaise and lime juice until blended. Serve with crab cakes. **Yield: 3 servings.**

Mushroom Salisbury Steak

Prep/Total Time: 30 min.

My family really looks forward to supper when these tasty beef patties are on the menu. I often bring it to covered-dish gatherings, and then I hand out the recipe.
—Louise Miller, Westminster, Maryland

1/4	cup cornstarch
2	cans (10-1/2 ounces *each*) condensed beef consomme, undiluted
1	jar (6 ounces) sliced mushrooms, drained
4	teaspoons Worcestershire sauce
1	teaspoon dried basil
1	egg, lightly beaten
1/2	cup soft bread crumbs
1	medium onion, finely chopped
1/2	to 1 teaspoon seasoned salt
1/4	teaspoon pepper, optional
1-1/2	pounds ground beef

Hot mashed potatoes *or* cooked noodles

In a large bowl, combine the cornstarch and consomme until smooth. Stir in mushrooms, Worcestershire sauce and basil; set aside.

In another large bowl, combine egg, bread crumbs, onion, seasoned salt and pepper if desired. Crumble beef over mixture and mix well. Shape into six oval patties; place in a shallow 1-1/2-qt. microwave-safe dish.

Cover and microwave on high for 3-5 minutes; drain. Turn patties, moving the ones in the center to the outside of dish. Pour consomme mixture over patties. Cover and microwave on high for 6-8 minutes or until a meat thermometer reads 160°. Let stand for 5 minutes. Serve with potatoes or noodles. **Yield: 6 servings.**

Editor's Note: This recipe was tested in a 1,100-watt microwave.

Pronto Prosciutto Pasta

Prep/Total Time: 15 min.

With lots of flavor from prosciutto, feta and seasonings, this impressive pasta is quick and easy. It's a tasty entree for a twosome's weeknight meal. Plus, it's a cinch to double for a crowd at special gatherings. *—Jill Conley, Chicago, Illinois*

5	ounces uncooked spaghetti
2	teaspoons minced garlic
1/4	cup olive oil
1/4	cup chopped prosciutto
1	tablespoon chopped ripe olives
1	teaspoon onion powder
1/2	teaspoon dried basil
1/2	teaspoon dried parsley flakes

Pronto Prosciutto Pasta

1/2	teaspoon pepper
1/8	teaspoon salt
1/4	cup crumbled feta cheese

Cook spaghetti according to package directions. Meanwhile, in a large skillet, saute garlic in oil until tender. Stir in the prosciutto, olives, onion powder, basil, parsley, pepper and salt. Cook, uncovered, over medium heat for 3-4 minutes or until heated through. Drain spaghetti; toss with prosciutto mixture. Sprinkle with feta cheese. **Yield: 2 servings.**

Savory Beer Pork Chops

Prep/Total Time: 30 min.

These tender chops are perfect for a hectic weeknight because they're so easy to prep. But they're also a real money-saver at the grocery store. *—Jana Christian, Farson, Wyoming*

4	boneless pork loin chops (3/4-inch thick and 4 ounces *each*)
1/2	teaspoon salt
1/2	teaspoon pepper
1	tablespoon canola oil
3/4	cup beer *or* nonalcoholic beer
3	tablespoons ketchup
2	tablespoons brown sugar

Sprinkle both sides of the pork chops with salt and pepper. In a large skillet, brown the pork in canola oil on both sides over medium heat.

Combine the beer, ketchup and brown sugar; pour over the pork. Bring to a boil. Reduce heat; simmer, uncovered, for 18-20 minutes or until a meat thermometer reads 160°. **Yield: 4 servings.**

Glazed Salmon

Glazed Salmon

Prep/Total Time: 20 min.

After I grilled this for my boss and her husband, I was swamped with calls asking for the recipe the next day at work. My boss said she'd never tasted such delicious salmon, and it takes only minutes to prepare! —Naomi Mahoney, Oakville, Ontario

1/2	cup olive oil
1/3	cup molasses
2	teaspoons minced garlic
1-1/2	teaspoons grated lemon peel
4	salmon fillets (6 ounces *each*)

Combine the oil, molasses, garlic and lemon peel; reserve half of the mixture for serving.

Coat grill rack with cooking spray before starting the grill. Grill salmon, uncovered, over medium heat for 6-8 minutes on each side or until fish flakes easily with a fork, basting frequently with molasses mixture. Serve with reserved molasses mixture. **Yield: 4 servings.**

Buffalo Chicken Pizza

Prep: 20 min. | Bake: 20 min.

If your family likes spicy chicken wings, they'll love this pizza made with bottled buffalo wing sauce and refrigerated pizza dough. Serve the blue cheese salad dressing on the side so you can drizzle it over each slice.

—Shari DiGirolamo, Newton, Pennsylvania

2	tubes (13.8 ounces *each*) refrigerated pizza crust
1	cup buffalo wing sauce, *divided*
1-1/2	cups (6 ounces) shredded cheddar cheese
1-1/2	cups (6 ounces) part-skim shredded mozzarella cheese
2	pounds boneless skinless chicken breasts, cubed
1/2	teaspoon *each* garlic salt, pepper and chili powder
2	tablespoons butter
1/2	teaspoon dried oregano

Celery sticks and blue cheese salad dressing

Unroll the pizza crusts into a lightly greased 15-in. x 10-in. baking pan; flatten the pizza dough and build up edges slightly. Bake at 400° for 7 minutes. Brush the dough with 3 tablespoons of the buffalo wing sauce. Combine the shredded cheddar and mozzarella cheeses; sprinkle a third over the crust. Set aside.

In a large skillet, cook the chicken, garlic salt, pepper and chili powder in butter until the chicken is browned. Add the remaining wing sauce; cook and stir over medium heat for about 5 minutes or until the chicken is no longer pink. Spoon over the cheese. Sprinkle with dried oregano and remaining cheese.

Bake for 18-20 minutes or until crust is golden brown and cheese is melted. Serve with celery and blue cheese dressing. **Yield: 8 slices, 4 servings.**

Editor's Note: This recipe was tested with Frank's Red Hot Buffalo Wing Sauce.

Fiesta Ravioli

Prep/Total Time: 20 min.

I adapted this recipe to suit our taste for spicy food. My family thinks that the beef-filled ravioli taste like mini enchiladas. For a complete meal, I serve them with a refreshing, Mexican-inspired salad and pineapple sherbet for dessert.

—Debbie Purdue, Westland, Michigan

- 1 package (25 ounces) frozen beef ravioli
- 1 can (10 ounces) enchilada sauce
- 1 jar (8 ounces) salsa
- 2 cups (8 ounces) shredded Monterey Jack cheese
- 1 can (2-1/4 ounces) sliced ripe olives, drained

Cook the beef ravioli according to the package directions. Meanwhile, in a large skillet, combine the enchilada sauce and salsa. Cook and stir over medium heat until completely heated through.

Drain the ravioli; add to the sauce and gently toss to coat. Top with the cheese and olives. Cover and cook over low heat for 3-4 minutes or until the cheese is melted. **Yield:** 4-6 servings.

Favorite Meat Loaf Cups

Prep/Total Time: 30 min.

My family enjoys meat loaf, but sometimes I can't spare the hour or more it takes to bake one in the traditional shape. An easy and quick alternative is to divide the meat mixture into regular-sized muffin cups. This way, convenient, individual servings of a down-home favorite are ready in less than 30 minutes.

—Sue Gronholz, Columbus, Wisconsin

- 2 eggs, lightly beaten
- 1/4 cup milk
- 1/4 cup ketchup
- 1/2 cup crushed cornflakes
- 4 tablespoons dried minced onion
- 1 teaspoon prepared mustard
- 1 teaspoon salt
- 1/4 teaspoon pepper
- 2 pounds lean ground beef

Additional ketchup, optional

In a large bowl, combine the first eight ingredients. Crumble beef over mixture and mix well.

Press into 12 foil-lined or greased muffin cups. Bake at 350° for 25 minutes or until a meat thermometer reaches 160°. Drain before serving. Drizzle with additional ketchup if desired. **Yield:** 6 servings.

Speedy Weeknight Chili

Prep/Total Time: 30 min.

Super-easy and great-tasting, this chili makes a big batch so it's terrific for parties. I use my food processor to chop up the veggies and cut down on prep time. It's also very tasty and lower in fat when made with ground turkey breast.

—Cynthia Hudson, Greenville, South Carolina

- 1-1/2 pounds ground beef
- 2 small onions, chopped
- 1/2 cup chopped green pepper
- 1 teaspoon minced garlic
- 2 cans (16 ounces *each*) kidney beans, rinsed and drained
- 2 cans (14-1/2 ounces *each*) stewed tomatoes
- 1 can (28 ounces) crushed tomatoes
- 1 bottle (12 ounces) beer *or* nonalcoholic beer
- 1 can (6 ounces) tomato paste
- 1/4 cup chili powder
- 3/4 teaspoon dried oregano
- 1/2 teaspoon hot pepper sauce
- 1/4 teaspoon sugar
- 1/4 teaspoon salt
- 1/4 teaspoon pepper

In a large saucepan or Dutch oven, cook the beef, onions, green pepper and garlic over medium heat until meat is no longer pink; drain. Add remaining ingredients; bring to a boil. Reduce heat; simmer, uncovered, for 10 minutes. **Yield:** 15 servings.

Speedy Weeknight Chili

Light Chicken Cordon Bleu

Prep: 20 min. | Bake: 25 min.

Since I'm watching my cholesterol, I can't afford to indulge in rich food often. So I trimmed down this recipe that I received in my economics class. —Shannon Strate, Salt Lake City, Utah

    8 boneless skinless chicken breast halves
       (4 ounces *each*)
  1/2 teaspoon pepper
    8 slices lean deli ham (1 ounce *each*)
1-1/2 cups (6 ounces) shredded part-skim mozzarella
       cheese
  2/3 cup fat-free milk
    1 cup crushed cornflakes
    1 teaspoon paprika
  1/2 teaspoon garlic powder
  1/4 teaspoon salt
SAUCE:
    1 can (10-3/4 ounces) reduced-fat reduced-sodium
       condensed cream of chicken soup, undiluted
  1/2 cup fat-free sour cream
    1 teaspoon lemon juice

Flatten the chicken to 1/4-in. thickness. Sprinkle with pepper; place a ham slice and 3 tablespoons of the shredded cheese down the center of each piece. Roll up and tuck in ends; secure with toothpicks. Pour the milk into a shallow bowl. In another bowl, combine the cornflakes, paprika, garlic powder and salt. Dip the rolled-up chicken in milk, then roll in cornflake crumbs.

Place in a 13-in. x 9-in. baking dish coated with cooking spray. Bake, uncovered, at 350° for 25-30 minutes or until chicken is no longer pink. Meanwhile, for the sauce, in a small saucepan, whisk the soup, sour cream and lemon juice until blended; heat through. Discard toothpicks from chicken; serve with sauce. **Yield: 8 servings.**

Smothered Pork Chops

Prep/Total Time: 30 min.

These chops can be prepared in a flash using convenient stuffing mix. It's a dish my Mom used to make when I was still living at home. The sweetness of the apple mixture is a nice complement to the savory stuffing. —Simone Greene, Winchester, Virginia

    1 package (6 ounces) chicken stuffing mix
    4 boneless pork loin chops (6 ounces *each*)
    1 tablespoon butter
    4 medium apples, peeled and cut into wedges
  1/2 cup packed brown sugar
  1/4 cup water
  1/4 teaspoon salt
  1/4 teaspoon ground cinnamon

Prepare stuffing mix according to package directions. Meanwhile, in a large skillet, cook pork chops in butter over medium heat for 2-3 minutes on each side or until lightly browned. Stir in the apples, brown sugar, water and salt. Bring to a boil. Reduce heat; cover and simmer for 8-10 minutes or until apples are tender.

Top with stuffing; sprinkle with cinnamon. Cook, uncovered, over medium heat for 10-12 minutes or until a meat thermometer reads 160°. **Yield: 4 servings.**

Light Chicken Cordon Bleu

Kitchen-Sink Soft Tacos

Kitchen-Sink Soft Tacos
Prep/Total Time: 15 min.

My kids invented this recipe by throwing some taco spice on leftover sloppy joes. I have to admit, they are delicious.
—Darlene King, Estevan, Saskatchewan

- 1/2 cup uncooked instant rice
- 1 can (15 ounces) chili with beans
- 1 teaspoon taco seasoning
- 12 flour tortillas (6 inches), warmed
- 1 cup (4 ounces) shredded cheddar cheese

Cook rice according to package directions. In a microwave-safe bowl, combine chili and taco seasoning. Cover and microwave on high for 2-3 minutes or until heated through.

Spoon rice and chili onto tortillas; sprinkle with cheese. Fold sides of tortilla over filling. **Yield: 6 servings.**

Editor's Note: This recipe was tested in a 1,100-watt microwave.

🍎 Shrimp Cantonese
Prep/Total Time: 30 min.

This recipe proves you don't have to sacrifice good taste when you need something fast. The nutritious stir-fry features tender shrimp, fresh spinach and a package of convenient frozen vegetables. —Bobby Taylor, Michigan City, Indiana

- 2 tablespoons cornstarch
- 1-1/4 cups chicken broth
- 1/4 cup soy sauce
- 1/4 teaspoon pepper
- 2 cups sliced onions
- 2 cups sliced celery
- 2 tablespoons butter
- 3/4 pound uncooked medium shrimp, peeled and deveined
- 8 ounces fresh spinach, torn
- 1 package (16 ounces) frozen stir-fry vegetable blend, thawed

Hot cooked rice

Combine cornstarch and broth until smooth. Add soy sauce and pepper; set aside.

In a large skillet or wok, stir-fry onions and celery in butter for 2-3 minutes or until tender. Add shrimp; cook and stir until shrimp turn pink. Add spinach and mixed vegetables; stir-fry 4-6 minutes longer or until spinach is tender.

Stir broth mixture and add to the shrimp mixture. Bring to a boil; cook and stir for 2 minutes or until thickened. Serve with rice. **Yield: 6 servings.**

Nutrition Facts: 1 cup (made with reduced-sodium broth, reduced-sodium soy sauce and reduced-fat butter; calculated without rice) equals 131 calories, 3 g fat (2 g saturated fat), 91 mg cholesterol, 732 mg sodium, 13 g carbohydrate, 4 g fiber, 13 g protein. Diabetic Exchanges: 2 very lean meat, 2 vegetable, 1/2 fat.

Shrimp Cantonese

fast, delicious & nutritious

If you want fast-to-fix fare that fits today's healthier lifestyle, then you've turned to the right chapter. The light dishes featured here are ideal for those counting calories or trying to reduce calories, fat, sugar or salt in their diet. Best of all, these recipes prove that eating doesn't require hours of work in the kitchen.

Anyone on a special diet, and even those who aren't, will enjoy these delicious and nutritious dishes. Each one includes Nutrition Facts and Diabetic Exchanges.

Chicken Supreme
(recipe on p. 224)

All recipes in this chapter use less fat, sugar or salt and include Nutrition Facts and Diabetic Exchanges.

Fantastic Fish Tacos

Fantastic Fish Tacos

Prep/Total Time: 25 min.

While searching for a lighter substitute to traditional fried fish tacos, I came up with this entree. It's been a hit with friends and family. The orange roughy fillets are so mild that even non-fish eaters are pleasantly surprised by these tasty tacos.

—Jennifer Palmer, Rancho Cucamonga, California

- 1/2 cup fat-free mayonnaise
- 1 tablespoon lime juice
- 2 teaspoons fat-free milk
- 1/3 cup dry bread crumbs
- 2 tablespoons salt-free lemon-pepper seasoning
- 1 egg, lightly beaten
- 1 teaspoon water
- 1 pound orange roughy fillets, cut into 1-inch strips
- 4 corn tortillas (6 inches), warmed
- 1 cup coleslaw mix
- 2 medium tomatoes, diced
- 1 cup (4 ounces) shredded reduced-fat Mexican cheese blend
- 1 tablespoon minced fresh cilantro

In a small bowl, combine the mayonnaise, lime juice and milk; cover and refrigerate until serving.

In a shallow bowl, combine the bread crumbs and lemon-pepper seasoning. In another shallow bowl, combine the egg and water. Dip the fish in the egg mixture, then roll in the bread crumbs.

In a large nonstick skillet coated with cooking spray, cook the fish over medium-high heat for 3-4 minutes on each side or until it flakes easily with a fork. Spoon onto the tortillas; top with the coleslaw mix, diced tomatoes, Mexican cheese and minced cilantro. Drizzle with the mayonnaise mixture. **Yield: 4 servings.**

Nutrition Facts: 1 taco equals 314 calories, 10 g fat (4 g saturated fat), 99 mg cholesterol, 659 mg sodium, 32 g carbohydrate, 3 g fiber, 30 g protein. Diabetic Exchanges: 3 lean meat, 2 starch.

Blueberry Crisp

Prep: 15 min. | Bake: 25 min.

I take advantage of easy-to-use frozen blueberries to make this fruity crisp with a sweet golden topping. Adding a dollop of vanilla yogurt to each serving adds to its homemade taste.

—Betty Geiger, Marion, Michigan

- 2 packages (12 ounces *each*) frozen unsweetened blueberries, thawed
- 2 tablespoons plus 1/2 cup all-purpose flour, *divided*
- 2 tablespoons brown sugar
- 1/4 teaspoon ground cinnamon
- 3 tablespoons cold margarine

TOPPING:
- 1 cup (8 ounces) fat-free plain yogurt
- 1/2 teaspoon vanilla extract

Sugar substitute equivalent to 2 teaspoons sugar

Place the blueberries in an 8-in. square baking dish coated with cooking spray. Sprinkle with 2 tablespoons flour. In a bowl, combine brown sugar, cinnamon and remaining flour; cut in margarine until crumbly. Sprinkle over berries. Bake at 350° for 25-30 minutes or until bubbly and golden brown.

For topping, combine yogurt, vanilla and sweetener; serve with the crisp. **Yield: 6 servings.**

Nutrition Facts: 1 serving equals 198 calories, 7 g fat (0 saturated fat), 1 mg cholesterol, 99 mg sodium, 31 g carbohydrate, 3 g fiber, 5 g protein. Diabetic Exchanges: 1-1/2 fat, 1 starch, 1 fruit.

Freezing Fresh Blueberries

Place fresh berries on a cookie sheet and put them in the freezer until frozen (about 1-1/2 hours). Then place in freezer bags. The berries won't stick together, so you can pour out any portion you desire.

Beef and Bean Macaroni

Prep: 20 min. | Bake: 30 min.

This hearty casserole with ground beef, kidney beans, macaroni, and more is a full meal in itself. Using reduced-fat ingredients makes it lighter, too. —Sally Norcutt, Chatham, Virginia

- 1 pound lean ground beef
- 1 package (7 ounces) elbow macaroni, cooked and drained
- 2 cups (8 ounces) shredded reduced-fat cheddar cheese, *divided*
- 1 can (16 ounces) kidney beans, rinsed and drained
- 1 can (14-1/2 ounces) stewed tomatoes
- 1 medium green pepper, diced
- 1 medium onion, finely chopped
- 1/4 teaspoon garlic powder
Crushed red pepper flakes and pepper to taste
- 2 tablespoons grated Parmesan cheese

In a large skillet, cook the ground beef over medium heat until no longer pink; drain. In a large bowl, combine the macaroni, 1-1/2 cups cheddar cheese, kidney beans, tomatoes, green pepper and onion. Stir in the cooked beef, garlic powder, pepper flakes and pepper.

Spoon into a 13-in. x 9-in. baking dish coated with cooking spray. Sprinkle with Parmesan and remaining cheddar cheese. Cover and bake at 375° for 30 minutes or until heated through. **Yield:** 10 servings.

Nutrition Facts: 1 cup equals 289 calories, 6 g fat (3 g saturated fat), 22 mg cholesterol, 289 mg sodium, 33 g carbohydrate, 6 g fiber, 24 g protein **Diabetic Exchanges:** *2 starch, 2 meat, 1 vegetable.*

Cream Cheese Swirl Brownies

Prep: 20 min. | Bake: 25 min.

I'm a chocolate lover, and this treat has satisfied my cravings many times. No one guesses the brownies are light because their chewy texture and rich chocolate taste can't be beat. —Heidi Johnson, Worland, Wyoming

- 3 eggs
- 6 tablespoons butter, softened
- 1 cup sugar, *divided*
- 3 teaspoons vanilla extract
- 1/2 cup all-purpose flour
- 1/4 cup baking cocoa
- 1 package (8 ounces) reduced-fat cream cheese

Separate two eggs, putting each white in a separate bowl (discard yolks or save for another use); set aside. In a small bowl, beat butter and 3/4 cup sugar until crumbly. Beat in the whole egg, one egg white and vanilla until well combined. Combine flour and cocoa; gradually add to egg mixture until blended. Pour into a 9-in. square baking pan coated with cooking spray; set aside.

In a small bowl, beat cream cheese and remaining sugar until smooth. Beat in the second egg white. Drop by rounded tablespoonfuls over the batter; cut through batter with a knife to swirl.

Bake at 350° for 25-30 minutes or until set and the edges pull away from the sides of the pan. Cool on a wire rack. **Yield:** 1 dozen.

Nutrition Facts: 1 brownie equals 167 calories, 7 g fat (3 g saturated fat), 28 mg cholesterol, 108 mg sodium, 23 g carbohydrate, trace fiber, 4 g protein **Diabetic Exchanges:** *1-1/2 starch, 1 fat.*

Cream Cheese Swirl Brownies

Harvest Soup

Prep: 10 min. | Cook: 25 min.

Loaded with ground beef, squash, tomatoes and two kinds of potatoes, this hearty soup makes a great family meal on a busy night. Go ahead and substitute any of the vegetables with those that better suit your family's tastes.

—Janice Mitchell, Aurora, Colorado

1	pound lean ground beef
3/4	cup chopped onion
2	garlic cloves, minced
3-1/2	cups water
2-1/4	cups chopped peeled sweet potatoes
1	cup chopped red potatoes
1	cup chopped peeled acorn squash
2	teaspoons beef bouillon granules
2	bay leaves
1/2	teaspoon chili powder
1/2	teaspoon pepper
1/8	teaspoon ground allspice
1/8	teaspoon ground cloves
1	can (14-1/2 ounces) diced tomatoes, undrained

In a large saucepan, cook the beef, onion and garlic over medium heat until meat is no longer pink; drain well. Add the water, potatoes, squash, bouillon, bay leaves, chili powder, pepper, allspice and cloves. Bring to a boil. Reduce heat; cover and simmer for 15-20 minutes or until vegetables are tender.

Add the tomatoes. Cook and stir until heated through. Discard bay leaves. **Yield: 6 servings.**

Nutrition Facts: 1-1/2 cups equals 241 calories, 7 g fat (3 g saturated fat), 28 mg cholesterol, 493 mg sodium, 26 g carbohydrate, 4 g fiber, 18 g protein. ***Diabetic Exchanges:*** *2 lean meat, 2 vegetable, 1 starch.*

Chicken Supreme

Harvest Soup

Chicken Supreme

Prep: 15 min. | Bake: 30 min.

I received this wonderful recipe from a friend at church. A light breading seals in the juices of tender chicken breasts, making them special enough to serve company. Sliced almonds top off the eye-catching entree. —Candace Black, Durham, North Carolina

1/2	cup dry bread crumbs
1/2	cup grated Parmesan cheese
2	tablespoons minced fresh parsley
1	garlic clove, minced
1/4	teaspoon pepper
3	egg whites
6	boneless skinless chicken breast halves (4 ounces *each*)
1/4	cup sliced almonds

Refrigerated butter-flavored spray

In a shallow bowl, combine the first five ingredients. In another shallow bowl, beat the egg whites. Dip chicken in egg whites, then coat with crumb mixture. Place in a 13-in. x 9-in. baking dish coated with cooking spray.

Sprinkle almonds over chicken. Spritz with butter-flavored spray. Bake, uncovered, at 350° for 30 minutes or until a meat thermometer reads 170°. **Yield: 6 servings.**

Nutrition Facts: 1 serving equals 224 calories, 6 g fat (2 g saturated fat), 71 mg cholesterol, 304 mg sodium, 8 g carbohydrate, 1 g fiber, 33 g protein. ***Diabetic Exchanges:*** *3-1/2 lean meat, 1/2 starch.*

Garden Frittata

Prep: 25 min. | Bake: 45 min. + standing

I created this dish one day to use up some fresh yellow squash, zucchini and tomato. It's so easy to make because you don't have to fuss with a crust. Give it a different twist by trying it with whatever veggies you have on hand.

—Catherine Michel, St. Peters, Missouri

1	small yellow summer squash, thinly sliced
1	small zucchini, thinly sliced
1	small onion, chopped
1	cup (4 ounces) shredded part-skim mozzarella cheese
1	medium tomato, sliced
1/4	cup crumbled feta cheese
4	eggs
1	cup fat-free milk
2	tablespoons minced fresh basil
1	garlic clove, minced
1/2	teaspoon salt
1/4	teaspoon pepper
1/4	cup shredded Parmesan cheese

In a microwave-safe bowl, combine the squash, zucchini and onion. Cover and microwave on high for 7-9 minutes or until the vegetables are tender; drain well.

Transfer to a 9-in. pie plate coated with cooking spray. Top with the mozzarella, tomato and feta cheese.

In a large bowl, whisk the eggs, milk, basil, garlic, salt and pepper; pour over the cheese and tomato layer. Sprinkle with Parmesan cheese.

Bake, uncovered, at 375° for 45-50 minutes or until a knife inserted near the center comes out clean. Let stand for 10 minutes before serving. **Yield: 8 servings.**

Nutrition Facts: 1 serving equals 126 calories, 7 g fat (4 g saturated fat), 121 mg cholesterol, 316 mg sodium, 6 g carbohydrate, 1 g fiber, 11 g protein. Diabetic Exchanges: 1 lean meat, 1 vegetable, 1 fat.

Garden Frittata

Strawberry Cheesecake Ice Cream

Strawberry Cheesecake Ice Cream

Prep: 10 min. | Freeze: 30 min.

I found the recipe for this creamy and refreshing dessert in an old cookbook. Made in an ice cream freezer, it's wonderful for family gatherings. We love how it tastes like a berry-topped cheesecake.

—Karen Maubach, Fairbury, Illinois

3	cups sliced fresh strawberries
6	ounces reduced-fat cream cheese
2	cans (12 ounces *each*) fat-free evaporated milk
1	can (14 ounces) fat-free sweetened condensed milk
1	teaspoon vanilla extract
1	cup reduced-fat whipped topping

Place strawberries in a blender; cover and process until smooth. In a large bowl, beat cream cheese until smooth. Beat in the evaporated milk, condensed milk, vanilla and pureed strawberries. Fold in whipped topping.

Fill cylinder of ice cream freezer two-thirds full; freeze according to manufacturer's directions. Refrigerate remaining mixture; allow to ripen in ice cream freezer or firm up in freezer for 2-4 hours before serving. **Yield: 2 quarts.**

Nutrition Facts: 3/4 cup equals 234 calories, 4 g fat (3 g saturated fat), 15 mg cholesterol, 171 mg sodium, 38 g carbohydrate, 1 g fiber, 11 g protein. Diabetic Exchanges: 1-1/2 fruit, 1 fat-free milk, 1 fat.

Flavorful Beef Stir-Fry

Flavorful Beef Stir-Fry

Prep/Total Time: 30 min.

I'm a working mom, so I appreciate meals like this one that I can whip up in no time using whatever vegetables I have on hand. What's really great is that even my pickiest eater likes it.
—Tere Abel, Muskegon, Michigan

- 2 tablespoons cornstarch
- 2 teaspoons sugar
- 6 tablespoons soy sauce
- 1/4 cup white wine, apple juice *or* water
- 1 pound boneless round steak, cut into thin strips
- 3 cups fresh broccoli florets
- 2 medium carrots, thinly sliced
- 1 package (6 ounces) frozen pea pods, thawed
- 2 tablespoons chopped onion
- 2 tablespoons canola oil, *divided*
- 1 can (8 ounces) sliced water chestnuts, undrained

Hot cooked rice

In a large resealable plastic bag, combine the cornstarch, sugar, soy sauce and wine, apple juice or water until smooth; add beef. Seal bag and turn to coat; set aside.

In a large skillet, stir-fry the broccoli, carrots, pea pods and onion in 1 tablespoon oil for 1 minute. Stir in water chestnuts. Cover and simmer for 4 minutes; remove and keep warm.

In the same skillet, stir-fry beef in remaining oil until meat reaches desired doneness. Return vegetables to pan; toss. Serve with rice. **Yield: 4 servings.**

Nutrition Facts: 1 serving (prepared with light soy sauce and water; calculated without rice) equals 313 calories, 466 mg sodium, 70 mg cholesterol, 21 gm carbohydrate, 31 gm protein, 12 gm fat, 7 gm fiber. Diabetic Exchanges: 4 lean meat, 1 starch, 1 vegetable.

Tasty Tuna Steaks

Prep/Total Time: 30 min.

Low-carb fans will love these easy-to-fix tuna steaks that are marinated in red wine, soy sauce, ginger and garlic.
—Taste of Home Test Kitchen, Greendale, Wisconsin

- 1/3 cup dry red wine *or* reduced-sodium beef broth
- 1/3 cup reduced-sodium soy sauce
- 2 teaspoons minced fresh gingerroot
- 1 teaspoon minced garlic
- 4 tuna steaks (6 ounces *each*)
- 1 bay leaf
- 1 tablespoon olive oil

Combine the wine or broth, soy sauce, ginger and garlic. Pour into a large resealable plastic bag; add the tuna steaks and bay leaf. Seal bag and turn to coat; let stand for 15 minutes. Drain and discard marinade and bay leaf.

In a large skillet, cook tuna in oil over medium-high heat for 6-8 minutes on each side or until cooked to desired doneness. **Yield: 4 servings.**

Nutrition Facts: 1 serving equals 224 calories, 5 g fat (1 g saturated fat), 77 mg cholesterol, 366 mg sodium, 1 g carbohydrate, trace fiber, 40 g protein. Diabetic Exchanges: 5 very lean meat, 1 fat.

Chicken-Fried Steak

Prep/Total Time: 30 min.

We raise cattle, so beef is a mainstay at our house. I adapted this traditional dish to leave a lot of the fat behind. This lighter version of this American classic dish is now a family favorite.
—Carol Dale, Greenville, Texas

- 3/4   cup all-purpose flour
- 1/4   teaspoon pepper
- 1   pound boneless beef round steak, cut into serving-size pieces
- 1/2   cup fat-free milk
- 2   tablespoons canola oil

GRAVY:
- 2   tablespoons water
- 4-1/2   teaspoons all-purpose flour
- 3/4   cup fat-free milk
- 1/8   teaspoon pepper

In a shallow bowl, combine flour and pepper. Add beef; turn to coat. Remove meat and pound with a mallet to tenderize. Pour milk into another shallow bowl. Heat oil in a skillet. Dip meat in milk, then coat again in flour mixture; add to skillet. Cover and cook over low heat for 10 minutes on each side or until meat is no longer pink. Remove and keep warm.

For gravy, add water to skillet; stir to loosen browned bits from pan. In a small bowl, combine the flour, milk and pepper until smooth. Gradually stir into skillet. Bring to a boil; cook and stir for 1-2 minutes or until thickened. Serve with steak. **Yield:** 4 servings.

Nutrition Facts: 1 serving (calculated without gravy) equals 307 calories, 11 g fat (0 saturated fat), 71 mg cholesterol, 67 mg sodium, 19 g carbohydrate, 1 g fiber, 30 g protein. Diabetic Exchanges: 4 meat, 1-1/2 starch.

Baked Basil Fries

Prep: 10 min. | Bake: 30 min.

A Parmesan cheese and basil coating provides these homemade and baked fries with a pleasant taste. Seasoned with garlic powder and baked in the oven, they're a zippy alternative to deep-fried potatoes.   *—Tammy Neubauer, Ida Grove, Iowa*

- 1/4   cup grated Parmesan cheese
- 1   tablespoon olive oil
- 1   tablespoon dried basil
- 1/4   teaspoon garlic powder
- 4   medium red potatoes

In a large resealable plastic bag, combine the Parmesan cheese, oil, basil and garlic powder. Cut potatoes into 1/4-in. sticks. Add to bag, a few pieces at a time, and shake to coat.

Place in a 15-in. x 10-in. baking pan coated with cooking

spray. Bake at 425° for 15-20 minutes on each side or until crisp and tender. **Yield:** 4 servings.

Nutrition Facts: 1 serving equals 162 calories, 5 g fat (0 saturated fat), 5 mg cholesterol, 117 mg sodium, 27 g carbohydrate, 3 g fiber, 7 g protein. Diabetic Exchanges: 1-1/2 starch, 1 fat.

Kielbasa Apple Kabobs

Prep/Total Time: 25 min.

I rely on sausage to make these colorful kabobs different from most. The meaty chunks are skewered with tart apples and colorful peppers.   *—Edna Hoffman, Hebron, Indiana*

- 1/4   cup sugar
- 1   tablespoon cornstarch
- 3/4   cup cranberry juice
- 2   tablespoons cider vinegar
- 2   teaspoons soy sauce
- 1   pound smoked kielbasa *or* 1 pound smoked Polish sausage, cut into 1-1/2-inch pieces
- 2   medium tart apples, cut into wedges
- 1   medium sweet red pepper, cut into 1-inch pieces
- 1   medium green pepper, cut into 1-inch pieces

In a large saucepan, combine sugar and cornstarch. Stir in cranberry juice, vinegar and soy sauce. Bring to a boil; cook and stir for 1-2 minutes or until thickened.

On metal or soaked wooden skewers, alternately thread sausage, apples and peppers. Grill, uncovered, over indirect heat for 8 minutes or until heated through, turning and brushing with glaze occasionally. **Yield:** 8 servings.

Nutrition Facts: 1 serving (prepared with reduced-fat turkey sausage) equals 168 calories, 6 g fat (2 g saturated fat), 47 mg cholesterol, 455 mg sodium, 19 g carbohydrate, 2 g fiber, 10 g protein. Diabetic Exchanges: 1 meat, 1 vegetable, 1 fruit.

Kielbasa Apple Kabobs

Penne from Heaven

Prep/Total Time: 25 min.

This fast, fresh-tasting side dish comes very close to a delicious treatment for pasta I enjoyed while in Italy. You can also serve it with a green salad and toasted garlic bread for a light meal.

—Dorothy Roche, Menomonee Falls, Wisconsin

6	ounces uncooked penne pasta
1/2	pound fresh mushrooms, sliced
1	tablespoon olive oil
1	can (14-1/2 ounces) diced tomatoes, undrained
1	tablespoon minced fresh basil *or* 1 teaspoon dried basil
1/4	teaspoon salt
1/3	cup crumbled feta cheese

Cook pasta according to package directions. Meanwhile, in a large skillet, saute mushrooms in oil for 5 minutes. Add the tomatoes, basil and salt; cook and stir for 5 minutes. Drain pasta and add to the skillet. Stir in cheese; heat through. **Yield:** 5 servings.

*Nutrition Facts: 1 serving equals 188 calories, 5 g fat (2 g saturated fat), 9 mg cholesterol, 335 mg sodium, 28 g carbohydrate, 3 g fiber, 7 g protein. **Diabetic Exchanges:** 2 starch, 1/2 fat.*

Grilled Asian Flank Steak

Penne from Heaven

Grilled Asian Flank Steak

Prep: 15 min. + marinating | Grill: 15 min.

Chinese five-spice powder and hoisin sauce add a distinctive Asian flair to this tasty grilled flank steak.

—Shawn Solley, Morgantown, West Virginia

1/4	cup Worcestershire sauce
1/4	cup reduced-sodium soy sauce
3	tablespoons honey
1	tablespoon sesame oil
1	teaspoon Chinese five-spice powder
1	teaspoon minced garlic
1/2	teaspoon minced fresh gingerroot
1	beef flank steak (1-1/2 pounds)
2	tablespoons hoisin sauce, warmed
3	green onions, thinly sliced
1	tablespoon sesame seeds, toasted, optional

In a large resealable plastic bag, combine the first seven ingredients; add the steak. Seal bag and turn to coat; refrigerate overnight.

Drain and discard marinade. Grill steak, covered, over medium heat for 6-7 minutes on each side or until meat reaches desired doneness (for medium-rare, a meat thermometer should read 145°; medium, 160°; well-done, 170°). Let stand for 5 minutes.

Thinly slice steak across the grain. Drizzle with hoisin sauce; garnish with onions. Sprinkle with sesame seeds if desired. **Yield:** 6 servings.

*Nutrition Facts: 3 ounces cooked beef (calculated without sesame seeds) equals 193 calories, 9 g fat (4 g saturated fat), 54 mg cholesterol, 241 mg sodium, 5 g carbohydrate, trace fiber, 22 g protein. **Diabetic Exchange:** 3 lean meat.*

Chicken Caesar Salad Pizza

Prep/Total Time: 30 min.

This delectable, cold Caesar salad pizza proves that you can eat well even when you're eating healthy.

—Amber Zurbrugg, Alliance, Ohio

1	tube (13.8 ounces) refrigerated pizza crust
3/4	pound boneless skinless chicken breasts, cut into strips
2	teaspoons canola oil
1/2	cup fat-free creamy Caesar salad dressing
1/2	cup shredded Parmesan cheese, *divided*
1	teaspoon salt-free lemon pepper seasoning
1	garlic clove, minced
1	package (8 ounces) fat-free cream cheese, cubed
4	cups thinly sliced romaine
1/2	cup diced sweet red pepper
1	can (2-1/4 ounces) sliced ripe olives, drained

Unroll pizza crust onto a 12-in. pizza pan coated with cooking spray; flatten dough and build up edges slightly. Prick with a fork. Bake at 400° for 11 minutes or until lightly browned. Cool on a wire rack.

In a nonstick skillet, cook chicken in oil over medium until no longer pink; cool. Meanwhile, combine the dressing, 1/4 cup Parmesan, lemon-pepper and garlic. Combine cream cheese and half of the dressing mixture until well blended.

Combine romaine, red pepper and olives. Add remaining dressing mixture; toss. Spread cream cheese mixture over crust. Top with romaine mixture, chicken and remaining Parmesan. **Yield: 6 servings.**

*Nutrition Facts: 1 serving equals 280 calories, 6 g fat (1 g saturated fat), 43 mg cholesterol, 952 mg sodium, 28 g carbohydrate, 2 g fiber, 25 g protein. **Diabetic Exchanges:** 2 lean meat, 1-1/2 starch, 1 vegetable, 1/2 fat.*

Lemonade Slush

Prep/Total Time: 10 min.

There's nothing quite as refreshing as a cool, lemony drink on a hot summer's day. However, this easy-to-make drink is so delicious that I make it throughout the year!

—Tracy Brousseau, Orem, Utah

2/3	cup lemonade concentrate, partially thawed
1	cup milk
2/3	cup water
1	teaspoon vanilla extract
	Yellow food coloring, optional
12	ice cubes, crushed

In a blender, combine lemonade concentrate, milk, water, vanilla and food coloring if desired; cover and process until blended. While processing, slowly add crushed ice. Process until slushy. Serve immediately. **Yield: 8 servings.**

*Nutrition Facts: 3/4 cup slush (prepared with fat-free milk) equals 56 calories, trace fat (trace saturated fat), 1 mg cholesterol, 17 mg sodium, 13 g carbohydrate, trace fiber, 1 g protein. **Diabetic Exchange:** 1 fruit.*

Chicken Caesar Salad Pizza

Fudgy Brownie Dessert

Pour batter into a 13-in. x 9-in. baking pan coated with cooking spray. Bake at 350° for 20 minutes or until a toothpick comes out clean. Cool on wire rack.

In a large bowl, beat the chilled chocolate mixture until light. Fold in whipped topping; carefully spread over crust. Refrigerate for 2 hours. **Yield: 15 servings.**

*Nutrition Facts: 1 piece equals 220 calories, 8 g fat (0 saturated fat), 1 mg cholesterol, 106 mg sodium, 33 g carbohydrate, 0 fiber, 7 g protein. **Diabetic Exchanges:** 2 starch, 1-1/2 fat.*

Fudgy Brownie Dessert

Prep: 20 min. + chilling | Bake: 20 min. + cooling

I came up with this recipe when searching for a low-fat dessert for my chocolate-loving family. My husband's and son's eyes light up whenever I serve these fudgy brownies.
—Karen Yoder, Bremerton, Washington

1/2	cup sugar
1/4	cup cornstarch
1/4	cup baking cocoa
1	can (12 ounces) fat-free evaporated milk
1/2	cup egg substitute

BROWNIE CRUST:

1	cup unsweetened applesauce
1	cup egg substitute
1/4	cup canola oil
2	teaspoons vanilla extract
1-1/4	cups baking cocoa
1	cup sugar
3/4	cup all-purpose flour
1	teaspoon baking powder
1	carton (8 ounces) frozen reduced-fat whipped topping, thawed

In a large saucepan, combine the sugar, cornstarch and cocoa. Stir in milk until smooth. Cook and stir over medium-high heat until thickened and bubbly. Reduce heat; cook and stir 2 minutes longer. Remove from the heat. Stir a small amount of hot filling into egg substitute; return all to pan, stirring constantly. Bring to a gentle boil; cook and stir 2 minutes longer. Cover and refrigerate.

Meanwhile, for the crust, in a large bowl, combine the applesauce, egg substitute, oil and vanilla. In another large bowl, combine the cocoa, sugar, flour and baking powder. Gradually add to applesauce mixture just until blended.

Grilled Salmon Steaks

Prep/Total Time: 25 min.

Salmon is a popular fish that's rich in nutrients. Seasoned with herbs and lemon juice, these flame-broiled steaks are excellent.
—Robert Bishop, Lexington, Kentucky

3	tablespoons dried rosemary, crushed, *divided*
1	tablespoon rubbed sage
1/4	teaspoon white pepper
1	tablespoon lemon juice
1	tablespoon olive oil
6	salmon steaks (6 ounces *each*)

In a bowl, combine 4-1/2 teaspoons crushed rosemary, rubbed sage, pepper, lemon juice and oil. Drizzle over both sides of salmon steaks. Coat grill rack with cooking spray before starting the grill. Sprinkle the remaining rosemary over hot coals for added flavor.

Place salmon on grill rack. Grill, covered, over medium heat for 6-8 minutes on each side or until fish flakes easily with a fork. **Yield: 6 servings.**

*Nutrition Facts: 1 serving equals 334 calories, 20 g fat (5 g saturated fat), 112 mg cholesterol, 81 mg sodium, 2 g carbohydrate, 1 g fiber, 34 g protein. **Diabetic Exchanges:** 5 lean meat, 1 fat.*

Grilled Salmon Steaks

Spicy Turkey Burgers

Spicy Turkey Burgers

Prep/Total Time: 25 min.

The hot pepper sauce comes through nicely to spark the flavor of these moist turkey burgers. This is a good low-fat burger without the boring taste of typical low-fat foods.
—*Mavis Diment, Marcus, Iowa*

1/2	cup chopped onion
2	tablespoons reduced-fat plain yogurt
1	tablespoon snipped fresh dill *or* 1 teaspoon dill weed
1-1/2	teaspoons hot pepper sauce
1/2	teaspoon salt
1	garlic clove, minced
1	pound lean ground turkey
4	Kaiser rolls, split
4	lettuce leaves
4	tomato slices

In a large bowl, combine the onion, yogurt, dill, hot pepper sauce, salt and garlic. Crumble turkey over mixture; mix well. Shape into four patties, each about 3/4 in. thick.

Grill, uncovered, over medium-high heat for 6-8 minutes on each side or until a meat thermometer reads 165° and the juices run clear. Serve on rolls with lettuce and tomato.
Yield: 4 servings.

Nutrition Facts: 1 serving equals 357 calories, 12 g fat (3 g saturated fat), 90 mg cholesterol, 766 mg sodium, 34 g carbohydrate, 2 g fiber, and 27 g protein. **Diabetic Exchanges:** *3 lean meat, 2 starch, 1 fat.*

Chopping an Onion

To quickly chop an onion, peel, then cut in half through the root. With root attached, place flat side down and cut vertical slits, leaving the root uncut. Then slice across the onion half. Discard the root end.

Bow Tie Chicken Supper

Prep/Total Time: 30 min.

My sister-in-law gave me a recipe for a healthy side dish, and I added chicken to it to make this colorful main course. It's wonderful with a salad and crusty bread.
—*Nancy Daugherty, Cortland, Ohio*

1	pound boneless skinless chicken breasts, cut into 1/4-inch strips
1	tablespoon olive oil
1	small sweet red pepper, julienned
1	small zucchini, cut into 1/4-inch slices
1	small onion, chopped
2	garlic cloves, minced
1/2	cup frozen peas, thawed
1	teaspoon Italian seasoning
1/4	teaspoon salt-free seasoning blend
1	cup bow tie pasta, cooked and drained
2	medium tomatoes, seeded and chopped
1/4	cup shredded Parmesan cheese

In a large nonstick skillet, saute chicken in oil for 3-5 minutes or until no longer pink. Remove and keep warm. In the same skillet, stir-fry red pepper, zucchini, onion and garlic for 3-4 minutes or until vegetables are crisp-tender.

Add the peas and seasonings; stir-fry for 2 minutes. Add the pasta and tomatoes; cook for 1 minute. Remove from the heat. Gently stir in the chicken. Sprinkle with the cheese.
Yield: 4 servings.

Nutrition Facts: 1-1/2 cups equals 256 calories, 7 g fat (2 g saturated fat), 71 mg cholesterol, 219 mg sodium, 15 g carbohydrate, 3 g fiber, and 32 g protein. **Diabetic Exchanges:** *3 lean meat, 1 starch.*

Bow Tie Chicken Supper

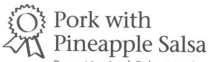
Pork with Pineapple Salsa

Prep: 10 min. | Bake: 30 min.

Nutrition Facts: 4 ounces cooked pork with 1/4 cup salsa equals 259 calories, 6 g fat (2 g saturated fat), 84 mg cholesterol, 255 mg sodium, 19 g carbohydrate, 1 g fiber, 31 g protein. Diabetic Exchanges: 4 lean meat, 1 fruit.

Not only does this easy entree taste awesome, but it's good for you, too. Brown sugar, ground ginger and Dijon mustard give the moist tenderloin its incredible flavor, and the tangy salsa can be made in no time.
— *Nicole Pickett, Oro Valley, Arizona*

1	can (20 ounces) unsweetened pineapple tidbits
1	pork tenderloin (1-1/4 pounds)
3	tablespoons brown sugar, *divided*
2	tablespoons Dijon mustard
1	teaspoon paprika
1/2	teaspoon ground ginger
1/3	cup finely chopped sweet red *or* green pepper
1/4	cup chopped green onions
1/8	teaspoon crushed red pepper flakes, optional

Drain pineapple, reserving 1/4 cup juice. Set aside 1 cup of pineapple (save remaining pineapple for another use). Place the pork on a rack in a shallow roasting pan. Combine 2 tablespoons brown sugar, mustard, paprika and ginger. Spread half over the pork.

Bake, uncovered at 450° for 15 minutes. Spread with remaining brown sugar mixture. Bake 15-20 minutes longer or until a meat thermometer reads 160°.

Meanwhile, for the salsa, combine the red pepper, onions, pepper flakes if desired, remaining brown sugar, reserved pineapple and juice. Let pork stand for 5 minutes before slicing. Serve with salsa. **Yield: 4 servings.**

Raspberry Spinach Salad

Prep/Total Time: 25 min.

My family is always thrilled to see this delicious and refreshing salad. Its sweet raspberry dressing makes an ideal topper for the fresh spinach.
— *Valerie Mitchell, Olathe, Kansas*

3	tablespoons canola oil
2	tablespoons raspberry vinegar
2	tablespoons raspberry jam
1/8	teaspoon pepper
8	cups torn fresh spinach
2	cups fresh raspberries, *divided*
4	tablespoons slivered almonds, toasted, *divided*
1/2	cup thinly sliced onion
3	kiwifruit, peeled and sliced
1	cup seasoned salad croutons

In a jar with a tight-fitting lid, combine the oil, vinegar, jam and pepper; shake well. In a large salad bowl, gently combine spinach, 1 cup of raspberries, 2 tablespoons almonds and onion. Top with kiwi, croutons and remaining berries and almonds. Drizzle with dressing. **Yield: 7 servings.**

Nutrition Facts: 1 cup equals 164 calories, 9 g fat (1 g saturated fat), trace cholesterol, 101 mg sodium, 20 g carbohydrate, 5 g fiber, 4 g protein. Diabetic Exchanges: 2 fat, 1 vegetable, 1 fruit.

Pork with Pineapple Salsa

Grecian Gold Medal Wraps

Prep/Total Time: 20 min.

For a healthy dish, I created these wraps with fat-free yogurt and whole wheat tortillas. Just a small quantity of the Greek olives is needed to give the sandwiches loads of flavor.

—Margee Berry, Trout Lake, Washington

1/2	cup canned white kidney *or* cannellini beans, rinsed and drained
1/3	cup crumbled feta cheese
1/3	cup fat-free plain yogurt
1/4	cup chopped red onion
2	teaspoons lemon juice
2	small tomatoes, chopped
4	whole wheat tortillas (8 inches), room temperature
1	package (6 ounces) ready-to-use grilled chicken breast strips
2/3	cup torn romaine
2	tablespoons chopped pitted Greek olives

In a small bowl, mash beans with a fork. Stir in the feta cheese, yogurt, onion and lemon juice. Fold in tomatoes. Spread 1/4 cup onto each tortilla. Top with chicken, romaine and olives; roll up. **Yield: 4 servings.**

Nutrition Facts: 1 wrap equals 279 calories, 7 g fat (2 g saturated fat), 33 mg cholesterol, 774 mg sodium, 33 g carbohydrate, 5 g fiber, 18 g protein. Diabetic Exchanges: 2 starch, 2 very lean meat, 1 fat

Lemon Feta Chicken

Prep/Total Time: 25 min.

You only need five ingredients to make this moist and flavorful chicken entree. My husband and I prepare this dish often, and it's a hit every time. *—Ann Cain, Morrill, Nebraska*

4	boneless skinless chicken breast halves (4 ounces *each*)
2	to 3 tablespoons lemon juice
1/4	cup crumbled feta cheese
1	teaspoon dried oregano
1/4	to 1/2 teaspoon pepper

Place chicken in a 13-in. x 9-in. baking dish coated with cooking spray. Pour lemon juice over chicken; sprinkle with feta cheese, oregano and pepper.

Bake, uncovered, at 400° for 20-25 minutes or until a meat thermometer reads 170°. **Yield: 4 servings.**

Nutrition Facts: 1 chicken breast half equals 143 calories, 4 g fat (1 g saturated fat), 66 mg cholesterol, 122 mg sodium, 1 g carbohydrate, trace fiber, 24 g protein. Diabetic Exchanges: 3-1/2 very lean meat, 1/2 fat.

Special Summer Berry Medley

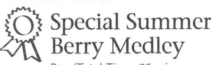

Special Summer Berry Medley

Prep/Total Time: 25 min.

No matter how big the meal, folks always find room for this delightful dessert. With its hint of citrus and mint, it makes a pretty side dish at cookouts or potlucks. Best of all, it's as fast and easy to make as it is to clean up!

—Nancy Whitford, Edwards, New York

1	cup sparkling wine *or* white grape juice
1/2	cup sugar
1	tablespoon lemon juice
1-1/2	teaspoons grated lemon peel
1/2	teaspoon vanilla extract
1/8	teaspoon salt
3	cups sliced fresh strawberries
2	cups fresh blueberries
1	cup fresh raspberries
1	cup fresh blackberries
1	tablespoon minced fresh mint

In a small heavy saucepan, bring wine or grape juice and sugar to a boil. Cook, uncovered, for about 15 minutes or until reduced to 1/2 cup, stirring occasionally. Cool slightly. Stir in the lemon juice and peel, vanilla and salt.

In a large bowl, combine the berries and mint. Add syrup and toss gently to coat. Cover and refrigerate until serving. **Yield: 12 servings.**

Nutrition Facts: 1/2 cup equals 85 calories, trace fat (trace saturated fat), 0 cholesterol, 26 mg sodium, 18 g carbohydrate, 3 g fiber, 1 g protein. Diabetic Exchanges: 1 fruit, 1/2 starch.

breakfast & brunch favorites

Rise and shine for a tasty home-cooked breakfast! This important meal easily gets bypassed during the early-morning rush while heading to work, trying to get the kids to school or other activities. But this chapter is full of quick-to-fix daybreak dishes.

Every recipe is fast to prepare, and most can come together in 30 minutes or less, or assembled the night before. Whether you need a wholesome breakfast or a tasty brunch dish, your whole family will eagerly sit down to these sunrise sensations that start off the day in an energizing way.

 Zucchini Crescent Pie
(recipe on p. 240)

Cheesy Egg Puffs

Cheesy Egg Puffs

Prep: 15 min. | Bake: 35 min.

My father loves to entertain, and these buttery egg delights are one of his favorite items to serve at brunch. The leftovers are perfect to reheat in the microwave on busy mornings, so Dad always stashes a few aside for me to take home once the party is over.

—Amy Soto, Winfield, Kansas

1/2	pound fresh mushrooms, sliced
4	green onions, chopped
1	tablespoon butter plus 1/2 cup butter, cubed, *divided*
1/2	cup all-purpose flour
1	teaspoon baking powder
1/2	teaspoon salt
10	eggs, lightly beaten
4	cups (16 ounces) shredded Monterey Jack cheese
2	cups (16 ounces) 4% cottage cheese

In a skillet, saute the mushrooms and onions in 1 tablespoon butter until tender. In a large bowl, combine the flour, baking powder and salt.

In another bowl, combine eggs and cheeses. Melt remaining butter; add to egg mixture. Stir into dry ingredients along with mushroom mixture.

Fill greased muffin cups three-fourths full. Bake at 350° for 35-40 minutes or until a knife inserted near the center comes out clean. Carefully run the knife around edge of muffin cups before removing. **Yield: 2-1/2 dozen.**

Broccoli Ham Quiche

Prep/Total Time: 30 min.

This is a great way for overnight guests to start the day. Chock-full of cheese, ham and broccoli, this quiche features an easy crust made of frozen hash browns. And because it cooks in the microwave oven, it doesn't heat up the kitchen.

—Sue Armstrong, Norman, Oklahoma

2	cups frozen shredded hash brown potatoes
1	cup (4 ounces) shredded cheddar cheese
1	cup diced fully cooked ham
1/2	cup chopped fresh broccoli
4	eggs
1/2	cup milk
1	teaspoon dried minced onion
1/2	teaspoon garlic powder
1/2	teaspoon salt
1/2	teaspoon pepper

Place hash browns in a greased 9-in. microwave-safe pie plate. Microwave, uncovered, on high for 3 minutes or until thawed. Press onto the bottom and halfway up the sides of plate. Microwave, uncovered, on high for 3 minutes. Sprinkle with cheese, ham and broccoli.

In a large bowl, whisk the eggs, milk and seasonings; pour over the ham mixture. Cover and microwave at 70% power for 5-7 minutes or until a knife inserted in the center comes out clean. Let stand for 5 minutes before cutting. **Yield: 4-6 servings.**

Editor's Note: This recipe was tested in a 1,100-watt microwave.

Frozen Banana Pineapple Cups

Prep: 15 min. + freezing

You can stir together this sweet tangy fruit mixture with just five ingredients, then pop it in the freezer overnight. The frosty results are a refreshing addition to a brunch. In summer, our kids prefer this snack to store-bought frozen treats.

—Alice Miller, Middlebury, Indiana

3	cups water
2-2/3	cups mashed ripe bananas (5 to 6 medium)
1-1/2	cups sugar
1	can (20 ounces) crushed pineapple, undrained
1	can (6 ounces) frozen orange juice concentrate, thawed

In a 2-qt. freezer container, combine all the ingredients together. Cover and freeze for at least 5 hours or overnight. Remove from the freezer 15 minutes before serving. **Yield: 9-12 servings.**

Blueberry Brunch Bake

Prep: 15 min. + chilling | Bake: 50 min.

This recipe is especially nice for overnight company. It's simple to make the day before and then pop in the oven in the morning. Just sit back, enjoy your guests and have a great breakfast.
—Carol Forcum, Marion, Illinois

        1 loaf (1 pound) day-old French bread, cut into
           1/2-inch cubes
    1-1/2 cups fresh *or* frozen unsweetened blueberries
       12 ounces cream cheese, softened
        8 eggs
      1/2 cup plain yogurt
      1/3 cup sour cream
        1 teaspoon vanilla extract
      1/2 teaspoon ground cinnamon
      1/2 cup milk
      1/3 cup maple syrup
    Additional blueberries, optional
    Additional maple syrup

Place half of the bread cubes in a greased shallow 3-qt. baking dish. Sprinkle with blueberries.

In a large bowl, beat cream cheese until smooth. Beat in the eggs, yogurt, sour cream, vanilla and cinnamon. Gradually add milk and 1/3 cup syrup until blended. Pour half over the bread. Top with the remaining bread and cream cheese mixture. Cover and refrigerate overnight.

Remove from the refrigerator 30 minutes before baking. Cover and bake at 350° for 30 minutes. Uncover; bake 20-25 minutes longer or until a knife inserted near the center comes out clean. Sprinkle with additional blueberries if desired. Let stand for 5 minutes. Serve with syrup. **Yield: 6-8 servings.**

Editor's Note: If using frozen blueberries, do not thaw before adding to batter.

Spicy Maple Sausages

Prep/Total Time: 15 min.

Wake up your taste buds with this easy treatment for breakfast sausages from our home economists. Only five items are needed for the sweet and spicy glaze.
—Taste of Home Test Kitchen, Greendale, Wisconsin

        2 packages (7 ounces *each*) brown-and-serve
           sausage links
      1/4 cup maple syrup
      1/4 cup honey
        2 teaspoons Dijon mustard
      1/2 teaspoon ground cinnamon
      1/2 teaspoon cayenne pepper

In a large skillet, cook sausage links until browned; drain. Combine the remaining ingredients; stir into skillet. Bring to a boil; cook and stir for 2-3 minutes or until sausages are glazed. **Yield: 6-8 servings.**

Blueberry Brunch Bake

Carrot Pancakes

Prep/Total Time: 30 min.

When I fix this quick breakfast for overnight guests, they always ask for the recipe. Everyone enjoys the sweet carrot cake flavor and rich cream cheese topping. The pancakes are a snap to make, but you can save even more time by grating the carrots in a food processor. —Denise Rushing, Greenwood, Arkansas

1-1/4	cups all-purpose flour
2	tablespoons finely chopped pecans
2	teaspoons baking powder
1	teaspoon ground cinnamon
1/4	teaspoon salt
1/4	teaspoon ground ginger
1	egg, lightly beaten
1/3	cup packed brown sugar
1	cup milk
1	cup grated carrots
1	teaspoon vanilla extract

CREAM CHEESE SPREAD:

2	tablespoons milk
1/2	teaspoon vanilla extract
4	ounces cream cheese, softened
1/4	cup confectioners' sugar

Dash ground cinnamon

In a large bowl, combine the first six ingredients. In a small bowl, combine the egg, brown sugar, milk, carrots and vanilla. Stir into the dry ingredients just until moistened.

Pour batter by 1/4 cupfuls onto a greased hot griddle. Turn when bubbles form on top of pancake; cook until second side is golden brown.

Meanwhile, in a blender, combine the milk, vanilla, cream cheese and confectioners' sugar; cover and process until blended. Transfer to a small bowl; sprinkle with cinnamon. Serve with pancakes. **Yield:** 4 servings.

Carrot Pancakes

Southwest Sausage Bake

Southwest Sausage Bake

Prep: 15 min. + chilling | Bake: 1 hour + standing

This layered tortilla dish is not only delicious, but it's a real time-saver because it's put together the night before. The tomato slices provide a nice touch of color. I like to serve this eye-opening casserole with sour cream and salsa.

—Barbara Waddel, Lincoln, Nebraska

6	flour tortillas (10 inches), cut into 1/2-inch strips
4	cans (4 ounces *each*) chopped green chilies, drained
1	pound bulk pork sausage, cooked and drained
2	cups (8 ounces) shredded Monterey Jack cheese
10	eggs
1/2	cup milk
1/2	teaspoon *each* salt, garlic salt, onion salt, pepper and ground cumin

Paprika

2	medium tomatoes, sliced

Sour cream and salsa

In a greased 13-in. x 9-in. baking dish, layer half of the tortilla strips, chilies, sausage and cheese. Repeat layers. In a bowl, beat the eggs, milk and seasonings; pour over cheese. Sprinkle with paprika. Cover and refrigerate overnight.

Remove from the refrigerator 30 minutes before baking. Bake, uncovered, at 350° for 50 minutes. Arrange tomato slices over the top. Bake 10-15 minutes longer or until a knife inserted near the center comes out clean. Let stand for 10 minutes before cutting. Serve with sour cream and salsa. **Yield:** 12 servings.

Cheesy O'Brien Egg Scramble

Prep: 20 min. | Bake: 20 min.

This breakfast bake is a snap to prepare. It's perfect for a brunch buffet or when out-of-town guests stay the night. Full of bacon, cheese, hash browns and eggs, the all-in-one dish is a hearty crowd-pleaser. —Margaret Edmondson, Red Oak, Iowa

- 1   package (28 ounces) frozen O'Brien potatoes
- 1/2 teaspoon garlic salt
- 1/4 teaspoon pepper
- 1   can (10-3/4 ounces) condensed cheddar cheese soup, undiluted
- 1   pound sliced bacon, cooked and crumbled
- 12 eggs, lightly beaten
- 2   tablespoons butter
- 2   cups (8 ounces) shredded cheddar cheese

In a large skillet, prepare hash browns according to package directions. Sprinkle with garlic salt and pepper. Transfer to a greased 2-1/2-qt. baking dish. Top with soup. Set aside 1/2 cup of bacon; sprinkle remaining bacon over soup.

In a bowl, whisk the eggs. In another large skillet, heat butter until hot. Add eggs; cook and stir over medium heat until eggs are nearly set. Spoon over bacon. Sprinkle with cheese and reserved bacon. Bake, uncovered, at 350° for 20-25 minutes or until cheese is melted. **Yield: 12 servings.**

Pumpkin Waffles with Orange Walnut Butter

Prep/Total Time: 30 min.

These waffles with yummy butter make a delicious breakfast on a crisp autumn morning. It's easy to delight taste buds with this unique and flavorful recipe. —Brandi Davis, Pullman, Washington

- 1   cup plus 2 tablespoons all-purpose flour
- 2   tablespoons brown sugar
- 1   teaspoon ground cinnamon
- 1/2 teaspoon salt
- 1/2 teaspoon baking powder
- 1/4 teaspoon baking soda
- 2   eggs
- 1   cup milk
- 1/2 cup canned pumpkin
- 2   tablespoons butter, melted
ORANGE WALNUT BUTTER:
- 1/2 cup butter, softened
- 1/4 cup chopped walnuts
- 1   tablespoon grated orange peel
Maple syrup

In a large bowl, combine the first six ingredients. In another bowl, combine the eggs, milk, pumpkin and butter; stir into dry ingredients just until combined.

Bake in a preheated waffle iron according to manufacturer's directions until golden brown.

Meanwhile, for the orange walnut butter, in a small bowl, combine the butter, walnuts and orange peel until blended. Serve the waffles with butter mixture and maple syrup. **Yield: 4 servings.**

Nutmeg Syrup

Prep/Total Time: 15 min.

I'm a music teacher, and I made this for a teachers' breakfast. It was heartily received! The nutmeg adds a rich, homey flavor. —Rochelle Felsburg, Fredericksburg, Virginia

- 1   cup sugar
- 2   tablespoons all-purpose flour
- 1   teaspoon ground cinnamon
- 1/2 teaspoon ground nutmeg
- 2   cups cold water
- 2   tablespoons butter
- 1   teaspoon vanilla extract
- 1/4 teaspoon rum extract, optional

In a large saucepan, combine the sugar, flour, cinnamon, nutmeg and water until smooth. Bring to a boil; cook and stir for 2 minutes or until thickened. Remove from the heat; stir in the butter, vanilla and extract if desired. **Yield: 2-1/3 cups.**

Pumpkin Waffles with Orange Walnut Butter & Nutmeg Syrup

Zucchini Crescent Pie

Zucchini Crescent Pie
Prep: 25 min. | Bake: 20 min.

One of my mother's many recipes designed to take advantage of bountiful zucchini, this easy-to-make pie is inexpensive, nutritious and filling. Refrigerated crescent rolls and cooked ham cut prep time but not taste. My family loves it!
—Susan Davis, Ann Arbor, Michigan

- 1   package (8 ounces) refrigerated crescent rolls
- 2   medium zucchini, sliced lengthwise and quartered
- 1/2 cup chopped onion
- 1/4 cup butter, cubed
- 2   teaspoons minced fresh parsley
- 1/2 teaspoon salt
- 1/2 teaspoon garlic powder
- 1/2 teaspoon pepper
- 1/4 teaspoon dried basil
- 1/4 teaspoon dried oregano
- 2   eggs, lightly beaten
- 2   cups (8 ounces) shredded part-skim mozzarella cheese
- 3/4 cup cubed fully cooked ham
- 1   medium Roma tomato, thinly sliced

Separate the crescent dough into eight triangles; place in a greased 9-in. pie plate with the points facing toward the center. Press onto the bottom and up the side to form a crust; seal seams and perforations. Bake at 375° for 5-8 minutes or until lightly browned.

Meanwhile, in a large skillet, saute zucchini and onion in butter until tender; stir in seasonings. Spoon into crust. Combine the eggs, cheese and ham; pour over zucchini mixture. Top with tomato slices.

Bake at 375° for 20-25 minutes or until a knife inserted near the center comes out clean. Let stand for 5 minutes before cutting. **Yield: 6 servings.**

Bacon Swiss Squares
Prep/Total Time: 30 min.

Not only does this scrumptious breakfast pizza come together easily, it's a cinch to double the ingredients when cooking for an extra-large crowd. Biscuit mix makes it convenient, and the combination of eggs, bacon and Swiss cheese keeps guests coming back for more! —Agarita Vaughan, Fairbury, Illinois

- 2   cups biscuit/baking mix
- 1/2 cup cold water
- 8   ounces sliced Swiss cheese
- 1   pound sliced bacon, cooked and crumbled
- 4   eggs, lightly beaten
- 1/4 cup milk
- 1/2 teaspoon onion powder

In a large bowl, combine the biscuit mix and water; stir 20 strokes. Turn onto a floured surface; knead 10 times. Roll into a 14-in. x 10-in. rectangle.

Place on the bottom and 1/2 in. up the sides of a greased 13-in. x 9-in. baking dish. Arrange cheese over dough. Sprinkle with bacon. In a large bowl, whisk eggs, milk and onion powder; pour over bacon.

Bake at 425° for 15-18 minutes or until a knife inserted near the center comes out clean. Cut into squares; serve immediately. **Yield: 12 servings.**

Sausage Spinach Bake

Prep: 20 min. | Bake: 35 min.

Some years back a friend gave me this delicious recipe that calls for a packaged stuffing mix. A salad and bread of your choice is all you'll need for a filling lunch or dinner. It's so versatile, you can even serve it at brunch.

—Kathleen Grant, Swan Lake, Montana

1	package (6 ounces) savory herb-flavored stuffing mix
1/2	pound bulk pork sausage
1/4	cup chopped green onions
1/2	teaspoon minced garlic
1	package (10 ounces) frozen chopped spinach, thawed and squeezed dry
1-1/2	cups (6 ounces) shredded Monterey Jack cheese
1-1/2	cups half-and-half cream
3	eggs
2	tablespoons grated Parmesan cheese

Prepare stuffing according to package directions. Meanwhile, crumble sausage into a large skillet; add onions and garlic. Cook over medium heat until meat is no longer pink; drain.

In a large bowl, combine the stuffing, sausage mixture and spinach. Transfer to a greased 13-in. x 9-in. baking dish; sprinkle with Monterey Jack cheese. In a small bowl, combine cream and eggs; pour over sausage mixture.

Bake at 400° for 30 minutes. Sprinkle with Parmesan cheese; bake 5 minutes longer or until a thermometer reads 160°. **Yield:** 12 servings.

Sausage Spinach Bake

Breakfast Bake

Prep: 15 min. | Bake: 45 min.

This light, fluffy egg casserole, sprinkled with tasty bacon, retains its fresh flavor after freezing. While it's great for breakfast, it's an easy-to-reheat meal for lunch or dinner, too. The recipe makes two casseroles, so you can serve one right away and freeze the second one for later.

—Kim Weaver, Olathe, Kansas

4-1/2	cups seasoned croutons
2	cups (8 ounces) shredded cheddar cheese
1	medium onion, chopped
1/4	cup chopped sweet red pepper
1/4	cup chopped green pepper
1	jar (4-1/2 ounces) sliced mushrooms, drained
8	eggs
4	cups milk
1	teaspoon salt
1	teaspoon ground mustard
1/8	teaspoon pepper
8	bacon strips, cooked and crumbled

Sprinkle the croutons, cheddar cheese, chopped onion, peppers and mushrooms into two greased 8-in. square baking dishes. In a bowl, combine the eggs, milk, salt, mustard and pepper. Slowly pour over the vegetables. Sprinkle with the crumbled bacon.

Cover one casserole with plastic wrap and aluminum foil and freeze for up to 3 months. Bake the second casserole, uncovered, at 350° for 45-50 minutes or until a knife inserted near the center comes out clean.

To use frozen casserole: Completely thaw in the refrigerator for 24-36 hours. Remove from the refrigerator 30 minutes before baking. Bake, uncovered, at 350° for 50-60 minutes or until a knife inserted near the center comes out clean. **Yield:** 2 casseroles (6-8 servings each).

Broccoli-Ham Puff Pancake

Prep: 20 min. | Bake: 25 min.

You won't have to pay a pretty penny to prepare this special-looking Sunday supper. The golden-brown puff pancake makes a tasty main dish for brunch, lunch or dinner when filled with a creamy ham and broccoli mixture.

—Edna Hoffman, Hebron, Indiana

1/4	cup butter, cubed
1	cup all-purpose flour
4	eggs
1	cup milk

FILLING:

3	tablespoons butter
3	tablespoons all-purpose flour
1	cup plus 2 tablespoons milk
1	package (16 ounces) frozen chopped broccoli, thawed
1-1/2	cups cubed fully cooked ham
1/3	cup sour cream
1-1/2	teaspoons lemon juice
1/8	teaspoon hot pepper sauce

Place the butter in a 10-in. ovenproof skillet; melt in a 425° oven for 3-4 minutes or until melted. In a small bowl, beat the flour, eggs and milk until smooth. Pour into the prepared skillet. Bake at 425° for 22-25 minutes or until puffed and golden brown.

Meanwhile, for the filling, in a large saucepan, melt butter. Stir in flour until smooth; gradually add milk. Bring to a boil; cook and stir for 2 minutes or until thickened. Reduce heat; add the remaining filling ingredients. Cook for 10 minutes or until heated through.

Spoon into center of puff pancake. Cut into wedges; serve immediately. **Yield: 6 servings.**

Broccoli-Ham Puff Pancake

Strawberry Banana Crepes

Strawberry Banana Crepes

Prep: 20 min. + chilling | Cook: 10 min.

My family often has company over for breakfast or brunch, and these light fruit-topped crepes are our favorite dish. The sweet sensations are as fast to make as they are fabulous. You can cook the crepes the night before, refrigerate them with waxed paper in between, then fill and top them in the morning.

—Shelly Soule, Las Vegas, Nevada

1	cup all-purpose flour
1	tablespoon sugar
1/2	teaspoon ground cinnamon
1-1/2	cups milk
2	eggs
1	to 2 tablespoons butter

FILLING:

1	package (8 ounces) cream cheese, softened
1	carton (8 ounces) frozen whipped topping, thawed
1/2	cup confectioners' sugar

TOPPING:

2	cups sliced fresh strawberries
2	medium firm bananas, sliced
1/4	cup sugar, optional

In a large bowl, combine the flour, sugar, cinnamon, milk and eggs. Cover and refrigerate for 1 hour.

In an 8-in. nonstick skillet, melt 1 teaspoon butter. Stir the batter; pour about 2 tablespoons into the center of skillet. Lift and tilt the pan to evenly coat the bottom. Cook until top appears dry; turn and cook 15-20 seconds longer. Remove to a wire rack.

Repeat with the remaining batter, adding butter to the skillet as needed. When cool, stack crepes (on paper towels) with waxed paper in between.

In a large bowl, beat the filling ingredients until smooth. Spread 2 rounded tablespoonfuls on each crepe; roll up. In a large bowl, combine topping ingredients; spoon with crepes. **Yield: 18 crepes.**

Blintz Pancakes

Prep/Total Time: 30 min.

Blending sour cream and cottage cheese, ingredients traditionally associated with blintzes into the batter of these pancakes provides them with their old-fashioned flavor. Top them with berry syrup to add a touch of sweetness.
—Dianna Digoy, San Diego, California

- 1 cup all-purpose flour
- 1 tablespoon sugar
- 1/2 teaspoon salt
- 1 cup (8 ounces) sour cream
- 1 cup (8 ounces) 4% cottage cheese
- 4 eggs, lightly beaten
- Strawberry *or* blueberry syrup
- Sliced fresh strawberries, optional

In a large bowl, combine the flour, sugar and salt. Stir in the sour cream, cottage cheese and eggs until blended.

Pour batter by 1/4 cupful onto a greased hot griddle in batches; turn when bubbles form on top. Cook until the second side is golden brown. Serve with syrup and strawberries if desired. **Yield: 12 pancakes.**

Nutrition Facts: Two pancakes (prepared with reduced-fat sour cream, fat-free cottage cheese and 1 cup egg substitute; calculated without syrup or strawberries) equals 184 calories, 4 g fat (3 g saturated fat), 17 mg cholesterol, 429 mg sodium, 23 g carbohydrate, 1 gm fiber, 14 g protein. Diabetic Exchanges: 1-1/2 starch, 1 lean meat.

Hawaiian Fruit Salad

Prep/Total Time: 30 min.

A simple dressing made with flavored yogurt coats this refreshing combination of fresh and canned fruit. It looks spectacular when presented in a pineapple boat and sprinkled with coconut.
—Taste of Home Test Kitchen, Greendale, Wisconsin

- 1 whole fresh pineapple
- 1 can (15 ounces) mandarin oranges, drained
- 1-1/2 cups sliced fresh strawberries
- 1-1/2 cups green grapes, halved
- 1-1/4 cups pina colada-flavored *or* vanilla yogurt
- 1/2 cup flaked coconut, toasted, *divided*
- 1/4 to 1/2 teaspoon coconut *or* vanilla extract

Stand the pineapple upright and vertically cut a third from one side, leaving the leaves attached. Set cut piece aside. Using a paring or grapefruit knife, remove strips of pineapple from large section, leaving a 1/2-in. shell; discard core. Cut strips into bite-size chunks. Invert shell onto paper towels to drain.

Remove fruit from small pineapple piece and cut into chunks; discard peel. Place shell in a serving basket or bowl.

In another bowl, mix pineapple chunks, oranges, strawberries and grapes. Combine yogurt, 1/4 cup coconut and extract; spoon over fruit and stir gently. Spoon into pineapple shell. Sprinkle with remaining coconut. **Yield: 6 servings.**

Hash Brown Egg Dish

Prep: 25 min. | Cook: 15 min.

I prepare the bacon and vegetables for this casserole the night before, so it's easy to finish in the morning. My family also thinks it's good for dinner. *—Diann Sivley, Signal Mountain, Iowa*

- 3/4 to 1 pound sliced bacon
- 6 cups frozen shredded hash brown potatoes
- 1 small onion, chopped
- 1 medium green pepper, chopped
- 1 jar (4-1/2 ounces) sliced mushrooms, drained
- 3 tablespoons butter
- 6 eggs
- 1/4 cup milk
- 3/4 teaspoon salt
- 1/4 teaspoon dried basil
- 1/8 teaspoon pepper
- 2 cups (8 ounces) shredded cheddar cheese

Place bacon on a microwave-safe plate lined with paper towels. Cover with another paper towel; microwave on high for 5-7 minutes or until crisp. Cool; crumble and set aside.

In a 2-1/2-qt. microwave-safe dish, combine potatoes, onion, green pepper, mushrooms and butter. Cover; microwave on high 5-7 minutes or until vegetables are tender, stirring once.

Whisk the eggs, milk, salt, basil and pepper; stir into vegetable mixture. Cover and cook at 70% power for 4-6 seconds or until eggs are almost set, stirring every 2 minutes.

Sprinkle with cheese and bacon. Cook, uncovered, on high for 30-60 seconds or until cheese is melted. Let stand for 5 minutes before serving. **Yield: 6-8 servings.**

Editor's Note: This recipe was tested in a 1,100-watt microwave.

Hash Brown Egg Dish

Country Brunch Skillet

Country Brunch Skillet

Prep: 10 min. | Cook: 25 min.

Frozen hash browns and packaged shredded cheese shave minutes off preparation of this skillet breakfast. It's an appealing meal-in-one you can do in about 30 minutes.

—Elvira Brunnquell, Port Washington, Wisconsin

- 6 bacon strips
- 6 cups frozen cubed hash brown potatoes
- 3/4 cup chopped green pepper
- 1/2 cup chopped onion
- 1 teaspoon salt
- 1/4 teaspoon pepper
- 6 eggs
- 1/2 cup shredded cheddar cheese

In a large skillet over medium heat, cook bacon until crisp. Remove bacon; crumble and set aside. Drain, reserving 2 tablespoons of drippings. Add the potatoes, green pepper, onion, salt and pepper to drippings; cook and stir for 2 minutes. Cover and cook for about 15 minutes or until potatoes are browned and tender, stirring occasionally.

Make six wells in the potato mixture; break one egg into each well. Cover and cook on low heat for 8-10 minutes or until eggs are completely set. Sprinkle with cheese and bacon. **Yield: 6 servings.**

Speedy Huevos Rancheros

Prep/Total Time: 30 min.

Canned chilies, Mexican-style tomatoes, onion and bacon add plenty of zippy flavor to this delightful poached egg dish. I often make it when we go camping because one skilletful provides a hearty breakfast for the whole family.

—Therese Langolf, Piru, California

- 8 bacon strips, diced
- 3 cans (14-1/2 ounces *each*) Mexican diced tomatoes
- 1 medium onion, chopped
- 1 can (4 ounces) chopped green chilies, drained
- 10 eggs
- 1/2 cup shredded Colby cheese

Flour *or* corn tortillas, warmed, optional

In a large skillet, cook the bacon until crisp; drain. Stir in the tomatoes, onion and green chilies. Simmer, uncovered, until the onion is tender.

With a spoon, make 10 wells in the tomato mixture; break an egg into each. Cover and cook over low heat for 15-20 minutes or until eggs are set. Sprinkle with cheese; cover and cook 1 minute longer or until cheese is melted, about 1 minute. Serve with tortillas if desired. **Yield: 5 servings.**

Open-Faced Omelet

Prep/Total Time: 30 min.

This tasty breakfast dish is a snap to make with convenient frozen hash browns. It gets its colorful look and fresh flavor from broccoli, red pepper and green onions.

—Cynthia Hinkle, Front Royal, Virginia

- 1 cup fresh broccoli florets
- 1/2 cup chopped sweet red pepper
- 1/4 cup thinly sliced green onions
- 1-1/2 cups cubed reduced-sodium fully cooked ham
- 1 cup frozen shredded hash brown potatoes, thawed
- 2-1/2 cups egg substitute
- 1/4 teaspoon pepper
- 1/2 cup shredded reduced-fat cheddar cheese

In a 9-in. or 10-in. skillet coated with cooking spray, saute the broccoli, red pepper and the green onions until crisp-tender. Add the ham and hash browns. Cook for 2 minutes, stirring frequently.

In a bowl, whisk the eggs, water, salt and pepper. Pour over vegetable mixture (mixture should set immediately at edges).

As eggs set, push cooked edges toward the center, letting uncooked portion flow underneath. When the eggs are set; reduce heat. Cover and cook for 10-12 minutes or until set.

Remove from the heat. Sprinkle with cheese; cover and let stand for 5 minutes or until cheese is melted. Cut into wedges. **Yield: 6 servings.**

Nutrition Facts: 1 serving equals 172 calories, 5 g fat (0 saturated fat), 15 mg cholesterol, 490 mg sodium, 10 g carbohydrate, 1 g fiber, 21 g protein. Diabetic Exchanges: 2-1/2 lean meat, 1/2 starch.

Baked Brunch Sandwiches

Prep: 10 min. + chilling | Bake: 30 min.

Serving brunch to your bunch is a breeze when you prepare these scrumptious sandwiches the night before. They combine the popular flavor of grilled ham and cheese (plus a little zip from Dijon mustard) with the puffy, delicate texture of French toast. It's a match made in heaven! —Carolyn Herfkens, Crysler, Ontario

- 3 tablespoons Dijon mustard
- 12 slices bread
- 6 slices fully cooked ham
- 12 slices cheddar *or* Swiss cheese
- 1 medium tomato, thinly sliced
- 3 tablespoons butter, softened
- 4 eggs
- 1/4 cup milk
- 1/4 teaspoon pepper

Spread mustard on one side of six slices of bread. Layer the ham, cheese and tomato over mustard; top with remaining bread. Butter the outsides of the sandwiches; cut in half. Arrange in a greased 13-in. x 9-in. baking dish.

In a small bowl, whisk the eggs, milk and pepper; pour over sandwiches. Cover and refrigerate overnight.

Remove the baking dish from the refrigerator 30 minutes before baking. Bake, uncovered, at 375° for 30 minutes or until the blade of a paring knife inserted in the center comes out clean. **Yield: 6 servings.**

Peach French Toast

Prep: 20 min. + chilling | Bake: 45 min.

Let the aroma of baked peaches, brown sugar and cinnamon wake up your clan when you prepare this homespun dish. Drizzle the golden syrup that bakes at the bottom of this casserole over the tender slices of French toast.
—Geraldine Casey, Anderson, Indiana

- 1 cup packed brown sugar
- 1/2 cup butter, cubed
- 2 tablespoons water
- 1 can (29 ounces) sliced peaches, drained
- 12 slices day-old French bread (3/4 inch thick)
- 5 eggs
- 1-1/2 cups milk
- 1 tablespoon vanilla extract

Ground cinnamon

In a small saucepan, bring the brown sugar, butter and water to a boil. Reduce heat; simmer for 10 minutes, stirring frequently. Pour into a greased 13-in. x 9-in. baking dish; top with peaches. Arrange bread over peaches.

In a large bowl, whisk together the eggs, milk and vanilla extract; slowly pour over the bread. Cover and refrigerate for 8 hours or overnight.

Remove from the refrigerator 30 minutes before baking. Sprinkle with cinnamon. Cover and bake at 350° for 20 minutes. Uncover; bake 25-30 minutes longer or until a knife inserted near the center of French toast comes out clean. Serve with a spoon. **Yield: 6-8 servings.**

Peach French Toast

Hot Fruit Compote

Hot Fruit Compote

Prep: 15 min. | Bake: 40 min.

This sweet and colorful fruit compote is perfect with an egg casserole at a holiday brunch. It can bake right alongside the eggs, so everything is conveniently done at the same time.

—Joyce Moynihan, Lakeville, Minnesota

- 2 cans (15-1/4 ounces *each*) sliced pears, drained
- 1 can (29 ounces) sliced peaches, drained
- 1 can (20 ounces) unsweetened pineapple chunks, drained
- 1 package (20 ounces) pitted dried plums
- 1 jar (16 ounces) unsweetened applesauce
- 1 can (21 ounces) cherry pie filling
- 1/4 cup packed brown sugar

In a large bowl, combine the first five ingredients. Pour into a 13-in. x 9-in. baking dish coated with cooking spray. Spread pie filling over fruit mixture; sprinkle with brown sugar.

Cover and bake at 350° for 40-45 minutes or until bubbly. Serve warm. **Yield: 20 servings.**

Cinnamon Sticky Buns

Prep: 25 min. | Bake: 25 min.

For a generous batch of gooey sticky buns in a hurry, it doesn't get much easier than this recipe. I enjoy giving these sweet treats to friends for a "just because" gift. They reheat in the microwave very well. —Jean Edwards, Indianapolis, Indiana

- 1 cup packed brown sugar
- 1/2 cup corn syrup
- 1/2 cup butter, cubed

- 1 cup coarsely chopped pecans
- 1/2 cup sugar
- 2 tablespoons ground cinnamon
- 2 tubes (17.3 ounces *each*) large refrigerated biscuits

In a saucepan, combine the brown sugar, corn syrup and butter; cook and stir until sugar is dissolved. Add the pecans. Spoon into a greased 13-in. x 9-in. baking pan.

In a shallow bowl, combine sugar and cinnamon. Cut each biscuit in half; dip in cinnamon-sugar. Place, cut side down, over brown sugar mixture.

Bake at 375° for 25-30 minutes or until golden brown. Invert onto a serving plate; serve warm. **Yield: 12-16 servings.**

Sunny-Side-Up Pizza

Prep/Total Time: 30 min.

Preparing this recipe is the best way I know to make sure my family takes time for breakfast. I just call out "pizza's ready!" and everyone dashes to the table. —Rose Koren, Brookfield, Illinois

- 1 prebaked thin Italian bread shell crust (10 ounces)
- 6 eggs
- 1-1/2 cups shredded part-skim mozzarella cheese
- 8 bacon strips, cooked and crumbled
- 1/2 cup chopped sweet red pepper
- 1/2 cup chopped green pepper
- 1 small onion, chopped

Place crust on a greased pizza pan. Using a 2-1/2-in. biscuit cutter, cut out six circles from crust, evenly spaced and about 1 in. from edge. (Remove circles and save for another use.)

Break an egg into each hole. Sprinkle with the cheese, bacon, peppers and onion. Bake at 450° for 8-10 minutes or until the eggs are completely set. **Yield: 6 servings.**

Sunny-Side-Up Pizza

Tex-Mex Cheese Strata

Tex-Mex Cheese Strata

Prep: 15 min. + chilling | Bake: 40 min. + standing

Tortilla chips add a little fun to this south-of-the-border brunch. For spicier tastes, substitute pepper Jack for the Monterey Jack.
—Vickie Lowrey, Fallon, Nevada

- 4   cups coarsely crushed nacho tortilla chips
- 2   cups (8 ounces) shredded Monterey Jack cheese
- 1   small onion, finely chopped
- 1   tablespoon butter
- 6   eggs
- 2-1/2   cups milk
- 1   can (4 ounces) chopped green chilies, undrained
- 3   tablespoons ketchup
- 1/4   teaspoon hot pepper sauce

Arrange tortilla chips in a greased 13-in. x 9-in. baking dish; sprinkle with cheese and set aside. In a skillet, saute onion in butter until tender. In a bowl, whisk the eggs, milk, onion, chilies, ketchup and hot pepper sauce; pour over cheese. Cover and refrigerate overnight.

Remove the strata from the refrigerator 30 minutes before baking. Bake, uncovered, at 350° for 40-45 minutes or until a thermometer reads 160° and a knife inserted near the center comes out clean. Let stand for 5 minutes before cutting. **Yield:** 6-8 servings.

Cheese Biscuits

Prep/Total Time: 25 min.

These savory biscuits couldn't be simpler to make! With from-scratch flavor and a golden-brown cheese topping, they're sure to be a hit.   *—Lynn Tice, Osage City, Kansas*

- 1   tube (12 ounces) refrigerated buttermilk biscuits
- 1/4   cup prepared Italian salad dressing

- 1/3   cup grated Parmesan cheese
- 1/2   cup shredded part-skim mozzarella cheese

Separate biscuits; dip the top of each in salad dressing, then in Parmesan cheese. Place cheese side up on an ungreased baking sheet; sprinkle with mozzarella cheese.

Bake at 400° for 9-11 minutes or until golden brown. Serve warm. **Yield:** 10 biscuits.

Reuben Brunch Bake

Prep: 15 min. + chilling | Bake: 40 min. + standing

I created this when I wanted something different for a graduation brunch for two of our sons. When I realized I had most of the ingredients on hand for the Reuben dip I usually make, I decided to use them in a brunch casserole instead! Everyone asked for the recipe at the meal.   *—Janelle Reed, Merriam, Kansas*

- 8   eggs, lightly beaten
- 1   can (14-1/2 ounces) sauerkraut, rinsed and well drained
- 2   cups (8 ounces) shredded Swiss cheese
- 1   package (2-1/2 ounces) deli corned beef, cut into 1-inch pieces
- 1/2   cup chopped green onions
- 1/2   cup milk
- 1   tablespoon Dijon mustard
- 1/4   teaspoon salt
- 1/4   teaspoon pepper
- 3   slices rye bread, toasted and coarsely chopped
- 1/4   cup butter, melted

In a large bowl, combine the first nine ingredients. Pour into a greased 11-in. x 7-in. baking dish. Cover and refrigerate overnight.

Remove from the refrigerator 30 minutes before baking. Toss bread crumbs and butter; sprinkle over casserole. Bake, uncovered, at 350° for 40-45 minutes or until a knife inserted near the center comes out clean. Let stand for 10 minutes before serving. **Yield:** 8-12 servings.

Freezing Eggs

According to the American Egg Board, to freeze whole eggs, beat them until blended, pour into freezer containers, seal tightly, label with the number of eggs and the date, and then freeze.

Freeze eggs for up to one year. When you're ready to use, thaw overnight in the refrigerator or under running cold water. Use thawed frozen eggs only in dishes that are thoroughly cooked. Substitute 3 tablespoons for 1 large fresh egg.

Pumpkin Pancakes

Prep/Total Time: 20 min.

With four small children, I am always looking for simple, quick and tasty recipes that they'll enjoy. They love pancakes, and these are great with breakfast sausage. I usually double or triple the recipe, depending on how hungry they are.

—Megan Schwartz, Burbank, Ohio

1	cup complete buttermilk pancake mix
1/2	teaspoon ground cinnamon
1/8	teaspoon ground ginger
2/3	cup cold water
1/3	cup canned pumpkin
1	cup maple syrup, warmed
1/4	cup chopped pecans, toasted

In a bowl, combine the pancake mix, cinnamon and ginger. In a small bowl, whisk water and pumpkin until blended; stir into dry ingredients just until moistened.

Pour batter by 1/4 cupfuls onto a hot griddle coated with cooking spray. Flatten with back of spoon. When underside is browned, turn pancakes and cook until second side is browned. Top with syrup and pecans. **Yield: 6 pancakes.**

Bacon & Egg Sandwiches

Prep/Total Time: 15 min.

I came across this yummy grilled combo when I was digging in my mom's recipe box. The crisp bacon, hard-cooked eggs and crunchy green onions make these special sandwiches look impressive when company drops by for lunch. Best of all, they're a snap to assemble. *—Ann Fuemmeler, Glasgow, Missouri*

Bacon & Egg Sandwiches

Pineapple Orange Drink

1/2	cup sour cream
8	slices bread
4	green onions, chopped
4	slices process American cheese
2	hard-cooked eggs, cut into 1/4-inch slices
8	bacon strips, cooked and drained
1/4	cup butter, softened

Spread sour cream on one side of each of four slices of bread. Top with the onions, cheese, eggs and bacon. Top with the remaining bread. Butter outsides of sandwiches. Toast sandwiches for 2-3 minutes on each side or until golden brown. **Yield: 4 servings.**

Pineapple Orange Drink

Prep/Total Time: 10 min.

If you're looking for a creative alternative to coffee or tea, try this refreshing fruit drink. A glass of this sunny slush will wake up your taste buds and put some spring in your step.

—LaChelle Olivet, Pace, Florida

6	cups orange juice
2	cans (8 ounces *each*) unsweetened crushed pineapple, undrained
16	ice cubes

Place half of the orange juice, pineapple and ice cubes in a blender; cover and process until smooth. Repeat with remaining ingredients. Pour into chilled glasses. Serve immediately. **Yield: 8 servings.**

Puff Pancake
With Blueberry Sauce

Prep/Total Time: 30 min.

I collect cookbooks and discovered this recipe while I was in Texas on vacation. The light and puffy pancake really does melt in your mouth! It's a definite crowd-pleaser that's as impressive served at dessert as it is at breakfast. My guests always agree!

—Barbara Mohr, Millington, Michigan

2	tablespoons butter
2	eggs
1/2	cup milk
1/2	cup all-purpose flour
2	tablespoons sugar
1/8	teaspoon ground cinnamon

BLUEBERRY SAUCE:

1/4	cup packed brown sugar
1	tablespoon cornstarch
1/4	cup orange juice
1	cup fresh or frozen blueberries
1/4	teaspoon vanilla extract

Place butter in a 9-in. pie plate; place in a 425° oven for 4-5 minutes or until melted. Meanwhile, in a small bowl, whisk eggs and milk. In another small bowl, combine the flour, sugar and cinnamon; whisk in egg mixture until smooth. Pour into prepared pie plate. Bake for 18-22 minutes or until sides are crisp and golden brown.

Meanwhile, for the sauce, in a small saucepan, combine brown sugar and cornstarch. Gradually whisk in orange juice until smooth. Stir in blueberries. Bring to a boil over medium heat, stirring constantly. Cook and stir 1-2 minutes longer or until thickened. Remove from the heat; stir in vanilla. Serve with pancake. **Yield: 4 servings.**

Puff Pancake with Blueberry Sauce

Baked Apple French Toast

Baked Apple French Toast

Prep: 20 min. + chilling | Bake: 35 min.

This is a simply wonderful brunch recipe that tastes great and will have everyone asking for seconds. I serve it with whipped topping, maple syrup and additional nuts. Some people say it's good enough to be dessert!

—Beverly Johnston, Rubicon, Wisconsin

20	slices French bread (1 inch thick)
1	can (21 ounces) apple pie filling
8	eggs
2	cups milk
2	teaspoons vanilla extract
1/2	teaspoon ground cinnamon
1/2	teaspoon ground nutmeg

TOPPING:

1	cup packed brown sugar
1/2	cup cold butter, cubed
1	cup chopped pecans
2	tablespoons corn syrup

Arrange 10 slices of bread in a greased 13-in. x 9-in. baking dish. Spread with pie filling; top with remaining bread. In a large bowl, combine the eggs, milk, vanilla, cinnamon and nutmeg. Pour over bread. Cover and refrigerate overnight.

Remove from the refrigerator 30 minutes before baking. Meanwhile, for the topping, place brown sugar in a small bowl. Cut in butter until mixture resembles coarse crumbs. Stir in pecans and corn syrup. Sprinkle over French toast.

Bake the French toast, uncovered, at 350° for 35-40 minutes or until a knife inserted near the center comes out clean. **Yield: 10 servings.**

holiday
& seasonal
pleasers

Holidays call for festive fare that
marks the celebration as special.
With the seasonal recipes in this
chapter, you can serve eye-catching
dishes without spending hours and
hours in the kitchen.

Surprise loved ones with wonderful
foods like Valentine's and St. Patrick's
Day treats...frightfully fun goodies for
Halloween...fabulous Christmas
entrees, cookies and appetizers...and
many more holiday favorites.

No matter how busy your schedule
is, these delicious and timely recipes
will help you make the most of
memorable get-togethers throughout
the whole year.

Two-Bread Stuffed Turkey
(recipe on p. 268)

Spring has sprung. What better

way to celebrate the season than with scrumptious food? Whether you're celebrating the Easter holiday, St. Patrick's Day or spring crops such as rhubarb and asparagus at the farmer's market, these recipes won't disappoint!

Marmalade Baked Ham

Marmalade Baked Ham

Prep: 15 min. | Bake: 1-1/2 hours

My family loves the flavor that orange marmalade, beer and brown sugar give this ham. Scoring the ham and inserting whole cloves gives it an appealing look with little effort.
—Clo Runco, Punxsutawney, Pennsylvania

1	boneless fully cooked ham (3 to 4 pounds)
12	to 15 whole cloves
1	can (12 ounces) beer or beef broth
1/4	cup packed brown sugar
1/2	cup orange marmalade

Place ham on a rack in a shallow roasting pan. Score the surface of the ham, making diamond shapes 1/2 in. deep; insert a clove in each diamond.

Pour beer or broth over ham. Rub brown sugar over surface of ham. Cover and bake at 325° for 1-1/4 hours.

Spread with the marmalade. Bake, uncovered, for 15-25 minutes longer or until a meat thermometer reads 140°. **Yield: 12-14 servings.**

🍎 Steamed Artichokes with Lemon Sauce

Prep: 10 min. | Cook: 25 min.

My husband created this smooth tangy sauce awhile back in the 1960's. It complements the steamed artichokes, whether they're served warm or cold. *—Lois Gelzer, Oak Bluffs, Massachusetts*

6	medium fresh artichokes
1-1/2	cups mayonnaise
4-1/2	teaspoons lemon juice
3/4	teaspoon seasoned salt *or* salt-free seasoning blend
3	drops hot pepper sauce

Place the artichokes upside down in a steamer basket; place the basket in a saucepan over 1 in. of boiling water. Cover and steam for 25-35 minutes or until tender.

Combine the mayonnaise, lemon juice, salt and hot pepper sauce. Cover and refrigerate. Serve with the artichokes. **Yield: 6 servings.**

Nutrition Facts: 1 serving (prepared with fat-free mayonnaise and salt-free seasoning blend) equals 102 calories, trace fat (0 saturated fat), 0 cholesterol, 534 mg sodium, 22 g carbohydrate, 7 g fiber, 4 g protein. Diabetic Exchanges: 1 starch, 1 vegetable.

Spring Lamb Supper

Prep/Total Time: 20 min.

Whenever I prepare brown rice, I fix a big batch so I have extra to make this quick dish during the week. Tender lamb is tossed with summer squash, tomatoes and mushrooms.
—Michelle Armistead, Marlboro, New Jersey

1	pound boneless lamb, cut into cubes
2	teaspoons olive oil
2	cups thinly sliced yellow summer squash
1/2	pound fresh mushrooms, sliced
2	medium tomatoes, seeded and chopped
1/2	cup sliced green onions
3	cups cooked brown rice
1	teaspoon salt
1/2	teaspoon garlic powder
1/2	teaspoon pepper
1/2	teaspoon dried rosemary, crushed

In a large skillet, saute lamb in oil until no longer pink; remove from the skillet with a slotted spoon. In the same skillet, stir-fry the squash, mushrooms, tomatoes and onions for 2-3 minutes or until tender. Return lamb to the skillet. Stir in the rice and seasonings; cook and stir until heated through. **Yield: 4 servings.**

Peter Rabbit Cake

Peter Rabbit Cake

Prep: 40 min. | Bake: 25 min.

"Nobunny" will be able to resist a slice of this adorable dessert. Baked and decorated ahead of time, the coconut-topped cake makes an eye-catching, fitting finale to any Easter feast.
— Taste of Home Test Kitchen, Greendale, Wisconsin

- 1 package (18-1/4 ounces) white cake mix
- 1 can (16 ounces) vanilla frosting
- 1-3/4 cups flaked coconut, *divided*
- 2 drops red food coloring
- 2 drops green food coloring
- Assorted jelly beans
- 1 stick black licorice, cut lengthwise into 1/8-inch strips

Mix and bake cake according to package directions, using two greased and floured 9-in. pans. Cool for 10 minutes before removing from pans to wire racks to cool completely.

For bunny's head, place one cake on a 20-in. x 14-in. covered board. Cut remaining cake into two ears and one bow tie. Place ears 4-in. apart on top of head. Place bow tie so it fits in curve of head (see photo).

Frost top and sides of head, ears and bow tie. Sprinkle 1-1/4 cups coconut over head and ears. Divide remaining coconut between two resealable plastic bags; add red food coloring to one bag and green to the other. Seal bags and shake to coat. Place pink coconut on ears to within 1/2 in. of the edges. Place green coconut around the cake.

Use jelly beans for eyes, nose and to decorate bow tie. Cut the licorice into seven 2-in. pieces and seven 3/4-in. pieces. Place six 2-in. pieces next to nose for whiskers. Bend the remaining 2-in. piece into a semicircle and place 3/4 in. below nose for mouth. Connect nose to mouth with one 3/4-in. pieces. Place three 3/4-in. pieces above each eye for eyelashes. **Yield: 12 servings.**

Tart Cherry Crisp

Prep: 10 min. | Bake: 30 min.

Our family first made this dessert after an outing to a cherry orchard. We used the fresh fruit we picked to make several of these crisps. —Chaya Grossman, Brooklyn, New York

- 4 cups pitted fresh tart cherries *or* 2 cans (14-1/2 ounces) pitted tart cherries, drained
- 2 tablespoons sugar
- 1/2 cup all-purpose flour
- 1/2 cup packed brown sugar
- 1 teaspoon ground cinnamon
- 1/4 teaspoon salt
- 1/4 cup cold butter, cubed

Place cherries in an ungreased 9-in. pie plate. Sprinkle with sugar. In a small bowl, combine the flour, brown sugar, cinnamon and salt. Cut in butter until mixture resembles coarse crumbs. Sprinkle over cherries.

Bake, uncovered, at 375° for 30-40 minutes or until top is bubbly. Serve warm. **Yield: 6 servings.**

Country Ham

Prep: 10 min. | Bake: 2 hours

Peach preserves give the easy ham entree a mildly fruity flair. This has been a hit ever since my neighbor gave me the recipe.
—Pamela Proctor, Barlow, Ohio

- 1 boneless fully cooked ham (3 pounds)
- 3/4 cup packed brown sugar
- 2 tablespoons prepared mustard
- 1/4 cup peach preserves

Place ham in a small foil-lined roasting pan; pierce several times with a fork. Combine brown sugar and mustard; spread over ham. Spread with peach preserves.

Cover and bake at 350° for 1-1/2 hours, basting occasionally. Uncover; bake 30-45 minutes longer or until a meat thermometer reads 140°. **Yield: 8-12 servings.**

Country Ham

Corned Beef 'n' Cabbage

Corned Beef 'n' Cabbage

Prep: 10 min. | Cook: 45 min.

I've been making this meal for more than 40 years. It is so easy and so delicious. It's especially good served with a salad of peaches and cottage cheese.

—Ruth Warner, Wheat Ridge, Colorado

    4   cups water
    1   corned beef brisket with spice packet (2 pounds)
    1   medium head cabbage, cut into 8 wedges
    2   large red potatoes, cut into 2-inch chunks
    1   can (14-1/2 ounces) chicken broth
    4   large carrots, cut into 2-inch chunks
    1   medium onion, cut into 2-inch pieces

In a 6-qt. pressure cooker, combine water and contents of corned beef seasoning packet; add beef. Close cover securely; place pressure regulator on vent pipe. Bring cooker to full pressure over high heat. Reduce heat to medium-high and cook for 45 minutes. (Pressure regulator should maintain a slow, steady rocking motion; adjust heat if needed.)

Meanwhile, in a large saucepan, combine the cabbage, potatoes and broth. Bring to a boil. Reduce heat; cover and simmer for 10 minutes. Add carrots and onion. Cover and simmer 20-25 minutes longer or until vegetables are tender; drain.

Remove pressure cooker from the heat; allow pressure to drop on its own. Remove beef to a serving platter. Discard cooking liquid. Serve beef with cabbage, potatoes, carrots and onion. **Yield: 4-6 servings.**

Easter Meringue Cups

Prep: 25 min. + standing | Bake: 45 min. + cooling

These crunchy meringue shells with a lemon curd filling will make guests stop to ooh and ahh at your dessert table. Topped with colorful fresh fruit, they're especially pretty when served as part of a spring meal.

—Taste of Home Test Kitchen, Greendale, Wisconsin

    3   egg whites
  1/2   teaspoon vanilla extract
  1/4   teaspoon cream of tartar
  3/4   cup sugar
  1/2   cup lemon curd
    1   cup sliced fresh strawberries
    2   medium kiwifruit, peeled and sliced
  1/2   cup fresh raspberries
  1/3   cup mandarin oranges
  1/3   cup cubed fresh pineapple

Place egg whites in a large bowl; let stand at room temperature for 30 minutes. Beat the egg whites, vanilla and cream of tartar on medium speed until soft peaks form. Gradually beat in sugar, 1 tablespoon at a time, on high until stiff peaks form.

Drop meringue into eight mounds on parchment paper-lined baking sheet. Shape into 3-in. cups with back of a spoon.

Bake at 275° for 45-50 minutes or until set and dry. Turn off the oven and do not open door; leave meringues in oven for 1 hour. Spread cups with lemon curd and fill with fruit. **Yield: 8 servings.**

Spicy Asparagus Spears

Prep/Total Time: 15 min.

This no-fuss dish gets its zippy taste from Cajun seasoning and crushed red pepper flakes. Even those who don't like asparagus will enjoy these buttery spears. —Marlies Kinnell, Barrie, Ontario

  2 tablespoons butter
1/2 teaspoon onion powder
1/2 teaspoon seasoned salt
1/2 teaspoon Cajun seasoning
Crushed red pepper flakes to taste
1-3/4 pounds fresh asparagus, trimmed

In a large skillet, melt the butter. Stir in the onion powder, seasoned salt, Cajun seasoning and red pepper flakes. Add the asparagus spears, stirring gently to coat. Cover and cook 5-7 minutes or until crisp-tender, stirring occasionally. **Yield: 6 servings.**

Nutrition Facts: 1 serving (prepared with reduced-fat butter) equals 26 calories, 2 g fat (1 g saturated fat), 7 mg cholesterol, 210 mg sodium, 2 g carbohydrate, 1 g fiber, 1 g protein. Diabetic Exchange: 1 vegetable.

Rhubarb Lemon Muffins

Prep: 15 min. | Bake: 20 min.

My father has a rhubarb plant and gives me some every spring. Some of it I stew for him, but I always save some for a new recipe. This is one of the tastiest I've tried.
    —Kathleen Smith, Pittsburgh, Pennsylvania

  2 cups all-purpose flour
  1 cup plus 1-1/2 teaspoons sugar, *divided*
  3 teaspoons baking powder
1/2 teaspoon salt
1/2 teaspoon ground ginger
  2 eggs
1/2 cup buttermilk
1/4 cup canola oil
  1 tablespoon grated lemon peel
1-3/4 cups sliced fresh *or* frozen rhubarb

In a large bowl, combine the flour, 1 cup sugar, baking powder, salt and ginger. In a small bowl, combine the eggs, buttermilk, oil and lemon peel. Stir into dry ingredients just until moistened. Fold in rhubarb.

Fill paper-lined muffin cups two-thirds full. Sprinkle with remaining sugar. Bake at 375° for 20-25 minutes or until a toothpick comes out clean. Cool for 5 minutes before removing from pan to a wire rack. **Yield: 1 dozen.**

Editor's Note: If using frozen rhubarb, measure rhubarb while still frozen, then thaw completely. Drain in a colander, but do not press liquid out.

Clover Crispies

Prep: 30 min. + cooling

These sweet snacks are like the pot of gold at the end of your family's feast. With their yummy peppermint and marshmallow flavor, they'll make even those without Irish hearts happy. And they'll have the cook smiling, too, because they're so easy to assemble. —Taste of Home Test Kitchen, Greendale, Wisconsin

  3 tablespoons butter
  4 cups large marshmallows (about 40)
1/4 teaspoon peppermint extract
  6 cups crisp rice cereal
  6 ounces white candy coating, chopped
  4 drops green food coloring, optional
Green sprinkles

In a large saucepan, melt the butter. Add marshmallows; cook and stir over low heat until melted. Remove from the heat; stir in extract and cereal. With buttered hands, press mixture into a greased foil-lined 13-in. x 9-in. pan. Cool completely on a wire rack.

Turn onto a cutting board; remove foil. Cut with a 3-in. shamrock cookie cutter; reshape shamrock stem if needed (save scraps for another use).

In a microwave, melt candy coating at 70% power for 1 minute; stir. Microwave at additional 10- to 20-second intervals, stirring until smooth.

Stir in food coloring if desired. Spoon over cutouts and spread evenly. Decorate with sprinkles. Let stand until set. **Yield: 15 servings.**

Clover Crispies

Easter Bunny Bread

Prep: 20 min. + rising | Bake: 25 min. + cooling

With its toothy grin, lovely golden crust and tummy that's perfect for serving dip, this charming rabbit is sure to bring a smile to guests young and old. It makes an entertaining appetizer for the Easter holiday!

—Taste of Home Test Kitchen, Greendale, Wisconsin

- 2 loaves (1 pound *each*) frozen bread dough, thawed
- 2 raisins
- 2 sliced almonds
- 1 egg, lightly beaten

Lettuce leaves
Dip of your choice

Cut a fourth off of one loaf of the dough; shape into a pear to form a head. For the rabbit's body, flatten the remaining portion into a 7-in. x 6-in. oval; place on a greased baking sheet. Place the head above the body. Make narrow cuts with the tip of a knife, about 3/4 in. deep, on each side of the head for whiskers.

Cut the second loaf into four equal portions. For ears, shape two portions into 16-in. ropes; fold ropes in half. Arrange ears with open ends touching head. Cut a third portion of dough in half; shape each into a 3-1/2-in. oval for back paws.

Easter Bunny Bread

Cut two 1-in. slits on the top edge for toes. Position on each side of the body.

Divide the fourth portion of the dough into three pieces. Shape two pieces into 2-1/2-in. balls to make the front paws; shape the remaining piece into two 1-in. balls for the cheeks and one 1/2-in. ball for the nose. Place the dough for the paws on each side of the body; cut two 1-in. slits for the toes. Place the cheeks and nose on the face. Add raisins for the eyes and almonds for teeth.

Brush the dough with the lightly beaten egg. Cover and let rise in a warm place until doubled, about 30-45 minutes. Bake at 350° for 25-30 minutes or until golden brown. Remove to a wire rack to cool.

Place the bread on a lettuce-lined 16-in. x 13-in. serving tray. Cut out a 5-in. x 4-in. oval in the center of the body. Hollow out bread, leaving a 1/2-in. shell (discard removed bread or save for another use). Line with lettuce and fill with dip. **Yield: 1 loaf.**

Strawberry Apple Pie

Prep: 15 min. | Bake: 45 min.

I was baking an apple pie for dinner at my in-laws, when I ran short of apples at the last minute. I substituted strawberries for the rest of the apples and didn't tell anyone. But that pie was such a hit, I've been making it ever since!

—Dianne Ebke, Plymouth, Nebraska

- 3-1/2 cups thinly sliced peeled Granny Smith apples (about 3 medium)
- 1-1/4 cups sliced fresh strawberries
- 1 tablespoon lemon juice
- 1/2 cup sugar
- 3 to 4 tablespoons all-purpose flour

Pastry for double-crust pie (9 inches)
- 1/2 teaspoon sugar
- 1/8 teaspoon ground cinnamon

Whipped topping, optional

In a large bowl, combine the apples and strawberries; drizzle with lemon juice. Combine sugar and flour; sprinkle over fruit and toss lightly.

Line a 9-in. pie plate with bottom pastry; trim even with edge of plate. Add filling. Roll out remaining pastry to fit top of pie; place over filling. Trim, seal and flute edges. Cut slits in top. Combine sugar and cinnamon; sprinkle over pastry. Cover edges loosely with foil.

Bake at 450° for 10 minutes. Reduce the heat to 350°; remove the foil and bake 35-40 minutes longer or until the crust is golden brown and the filling is bubbly. Cool on a wire rack. Garnish with the whipped topping if desired. **Yield: 6-8 servings.**

Nesting Chicks

Prep/Total Time: 30 min.

The fun little chicks are a great way to celebrate spring or the Easter holiday with the kids. They're easy to make and great for get-togethers or class treats.

—Taste of Home Test Kitchen, Greendale, Wisconsin

1	package (10-1/2 ounces) miniature marshmallows
2	tablespoons butter
1	teaspoon water
4	drops green food coloring
1-1/2	cups flaked coconut
6	cups Corn Pops
1/2	cup jelly beans
16	Peeps

In a large saucepan, combine the marshmallows and butter. Cook and stir over low heat until melted and smooth. Meanwhile, in a small resealable plastic bag, combine the water and food coloring. Add coconut; seal bag and shake to tint. Set aside.

Place the cereal in a large bowl; add marshmallow mixture and stir until combined. Press into greased muffin cups. Let stand until serving. Remove nests from cups; top with tinted coconut, jelly beans and Peeps. **Yield: 16 servings.**

Beef Wellington Bundles

Prep: 30 min. | Bake: 20 min. + standing

I take advantage of refrigerated pie pastry to fix this sensational main course. Guests dining at my home will find a succulent steak topped with pesto and mushrooms in every flaky bundle.

—Penny Walton, Westerville, Ohio

5	tablespoons olive oil, *divided*
1/2	cup loosely packed basil leaves and fresh parsley sprigs
1/4	cup grated Parmesan cheese
1/8	teaspoon salt
6	beef tenderloin steaks (6 ounces *each*)
4	tablespoons butter, *divided*
1/2	pound fresh mushrooms, chopped
6	sheets refrigerated pie pastry
1	egg, lightly beaten
3	tablespoons all-purpose flour
1-1/4	cups beef broth
1/4	cup dry red wine *or* additional beef broth
1/4	cup water
1/2	teaspoon browning sauce, optional

For pesto, in a food processor, combine 3 tablespoons oil, basil, parsley, Parmesan cheese and salt. Cover and process until smooth; set aside.

Beef Wellington Bundles

In a large skillet, brown steaks in 2 tablespoons butter and remaining oil for 5-6 minutes on each side or until meat reaches desired doneness (for medium-rare, a meat thermometer should read 145°; medium, 160°; well-done, 170°). Remove and keep warm. In the same skillet, saute mushrooms until liquid is absorbed.

Cut each pastry sheet into an 8-in. square (discard scraps or save for another use). Place a steak on each square. Spread steak with about 1 tablespoon of pesto; top with mushrooms.

Bring opposite corners of pastry over steak and pinch seams to seal tightly. Place in a greased 15-in. x 10-in. baking pan. Brush egg over pastry.

Bake at 450° for 18-20 minutes or until golden brown. Let stand for 10 minutes before serving.

For the gravy, melt the remaining butter in the same skillet; stir in the flour until smooth. Gradually stir in the remaining ingredients. Bring to a boil; cook and stir the mixture for 2 minutes or until thickened. Serve gravy with the beef bundles. **Yield: 6 servings.**

Prepping Mushrooms

Here are a few quick hints to help you prepare mushrooms for the Beef Wellington Bundles. Gently remove dirt from the mushrooms by rubbing with a mushroom brush or a damp paper towel. Or, quickly rinse under cold water; drain and pat dry with paper towels. Do not peel mushrooms. Trim stems. Mushrooms can be eaten uncooked, marinated, sauteed, stir-fried, baked, broiled or grilled.

Summer

stays for only a short period of time, so take advantage of those sunny, beautiful days while they're here. The mouth-watering recipes in this section are perfect for lazy-day get-togethers and backyard meals made on the grill. You'll also find wonderful cakes that are perfect for celebrating the Fourth of July holiday or summer birthdays.

Pool Party Cake

Pool Party Cake

Prep: 45 min. + chilling | Bake: 25 min. + chilling

This cleverly decorated cake with its "pool" of cool blue gelatin will steal the show at any gathering! We dipped into our imaginations to come up with the whimsical party cake that doubles as an eye-catching centerpiece.
—Taste of Home Test Kitchen, Greendale, Wisconsin

1	package (18-1/4 ounces) white cake mix
1	package (3 ounces) berry blue gelatin
3/4	cup boiling water
1/2	cup cold water
Ice cubes	
1	package (8 ounces) cream cheese, softened
1/4	cup butter, softened
1	teaspoon vanilla extract
1/8	teaspoon salt
4	cups confectioners' sugar
1	piece red shoestring licorice
14	Swedish Fish candies
5	Peachie-O's candies
5	Necco wafer candies, *divided*
2	Air Head candies
8	Runts candies
1	lollipop stick
2	Now and Later candies
1	stick spearmint chewing gum
1	Life Savers Gummy
98	Smarties candies
1	Sour Brite Octopus candy

Grease two 9-in. round baking pans and line with waxed paper; grease and flour the paper. Prepare cake batter according to package directions. Pour into prepared pans. Bake at 350° for 21-26 minutes or until a toothpick comes out clean. Cool for 10 minutes; remove from pans to wire racks to cool completely.

In a small bowl, dissolve gelatin in boiling water. Pour cold water into a 2-cup measuring cup; add enough ice cubes to measure 1-1/4 cups. Add to gelatin; stir until slightly thickened. Discard any remaining ice. Refrigerate for 30 minutes or until soft-set.

For frosting, in a large bowl, beat cream cheese and butter until smooth. Add vanilla and salt. Beat in confectioners' sugar until smooth and fluffy. Set aside 2 tablespoons frosting for decorating. Place one cake on a glass or plastic board. Frost top of cake with 2/3 cup frosting.

For pool, cut a 5-in. circle (1 in. deep) in the center of second cake (save removed cake for another use). Place over frosted cake. Slowly pour gelatin into circle. Frost top and sides of cake.

For ladder, cut licorice into two 4-in. pieces; gently press 1-1/4 in. apart into frosting, looping top ends for handles. Cut three 1-1/4-in. pieces of licorice for ladder steps; press into frosting. Decorate sides of cake with Swedish Fish and Peachie-O's.

For pool steps, use a small amount of reserved frosting to attach four wafer candies to board. Trim two Air Head candies and bend into chair shapes; with frosting, attach Runts to chairs for legs. For table, attach remaining wafer candy to a lollipop stick; push into cake. Place chairs on cake and board.

For diving board, spread frosting between two Now and Later candies; attach gum to top of candies with frosting. Cut Life Savers Gummy in half; attach to sides of gum. Place on cake.

Arrange Smarties on cake for pool tile. Place a line of Smarties on gelatin to form a buoy rope. Place octopus candy in pool. Refrigerate for 1-2 hours or until gelatin is set. **Yield:** 12-16 servings.

Zesty Grilled Chops

Prep: 5 min. + marinating | Grill: 10 min.

My sister gave me the recipe for this easy five-ingredient marinade. It keeps the meat so moist and tasty that now it's the only way my husband wants his pork chops prepared.
—Bernice Germann, Napoleon, Ohio

- 3/4 cup soy sauce
- 1/4 cup lemon juice
- 1 tablespoon brown sugar
- 1 tablespoon chili sauce
- 1/4 teaspoon garlic powder
- 6 bone-in pork loin chops (8 ounces *each*)

In a large resealable plastic bag, combine the soy sauce, lemon juice, brown sugar, chili sauce and garlic powder. Remove 1/4 cup for basting and refrigerate. Add pork chops to the remaining marinade; turn to coat. Cover and refrigerate for 3 hours or overnight, turning once.

Drain and discard marinade from chops. Grill, covered, over medium-hot heat for 4 minutes. Turn; baste with reserved marinade. Grill 4-7 minutes longer or until juices run clear.
Yield: 6 servings.

Summer Squash Pepper Gratin

Prep: 20 min. | Bake: 30 min.

This satisfying side dish is one of our family's all-time favorites and looks beautiful on a buffet table, too.
—Barbara Nowakowski, North Tonawanda, New York

- 1 large unpeeled potato (12 ounces)
- 3/4 cup thinly sliced green pepper
- 3/4 cup thinly sliced sweet red pepper
- 1 teaspoon olive oil
- 2 small yellow summer squash, thinly sliced
- 2 small zucchini, thinly sliced
- 1 teaspoon dried oregano
- 1/2 teaspoon salt
- 1/8 teaspoon pepper
- 1/2 cup shredded reduced-fat sharp cheddar cheese
- 1 tablespoon butter

Pierce potato with a fork; place on a microwave-safe plate. Microwave, uncovered, on high for 2-3 minutes or until tender but firm. Cool slightly; cut into thin slices.

In a microwave-safe bowl, combine the green and red peppers; drizzle with oil. Cover and microwave on high for 2 to 3-1/2 minutes or until crisp-tender.

In a 1-1/2 qt. baking dish coated with cooking spray, layer half of the sliced potato, yellow squash, zucchini, pepper mixture, oregano, salt, pepper and cheddar cheese. Repeat layers. Dot with butter.

Cover and bake at 375° for 20-25 minutes or until squash is crisp-tender. Uncover; bake 10 minutes longer or until heated through. **Yield: 6 servings.**

Nutrition Facts: 1 cup equals 121 calories, 5 g fat (0 saturated fat), 0 cholesterol, 0 sodium, 0 carbohydrate, 0 fiber, 0 protein.
Diabetic Exchange: 1 vegetable, 1 fat.

Editor's Note: This recipe was tested in a 1,100-watt microwave.

Summer Squash Pepper Gratin

Tomatoes with Horseradish Sauce

Prep/Total Time: 15 min.

This warm dish of lightly sauteed tomatoes and a tangy sauce is very tasty and quick to make. I occasionally use both red and green tomatoes to add even more color.
—Phyllis Shaughnessy, Livonia, New York

Refrigerated butter-flavored spray
  4 large tomatoes, sliced
  3 tablespoons mayonnaise
  2 tablespoons half-and-half cream
  1 tablespoon prepared horseradish
Minced fresh parsley

Coat a large skillet with refrigerated butter-flavored spray. Heat skillet over medium heat. Add tomato slices; cook for 2-3 minutes on each side or until edges begin to brown. In a small bowl, whisk the mayonnaise, cream and horseradish. Spoon over the tomatoes. Sprinkle with parsley. **Yield: 4 servings.**

Nutrition Facts: 1 serving (prepared with fat-free mayonnaise and half-and-half) equals 53 calories, 1 g fat (trace saturated fat), 1 mg cholesterol, 124 mg sodium, 11 g carbohydrate, 2 g fiber, 2 g protein. **Diabetic Exchange:** *2 vegetable.*

Tomatoes with Horseradish Sauce

Watermelon Cake

Watermelon Cake

Prep: 20 min. | Bake: 30 min.

No one will guess how simple this make-ahead melon dessert is to assemble. A package of watermelon gelatin added to the cake batter gives it refreshing flavor while chocolate chips form the seeds. After one bite, kids of all ages will be lining up for seconds.
—Taste of Home Test Kitchen, Greendale, Wisconsin

  1 package (18-1/4 ounces) white cake mix
  1 package (3 ounces) watermelon gelatin
1-1/4 cups water
  2 eggs
  1/4 cup canola oil
2-1/2 cups prepared vanilla *or* cream cheese frosting, *divided*
Red and green gel food coloring
Chocolate chips

In a large bowl, combine the cake mix, gelatin, water, eggs and oil; beat on low speed for 30 seconds. Beat on medium for 2 minutes.

Pour into two greased and floured 9-in. round baking pans. Bake at 350° for 30-35 minutes or until a toothpick inserted near the center comes out clean. Cool for 10 minutes before removing from pans to wire racks to cool completely.

Set aside 2 tablespoons of frosting for decorating. Place 1-1/4 cups frosting in a bowl; tint red. Tint the remaining frosting green.

Place one cake layer on a serving plate; spread with 1/2 cup red frosting to within 1/4 in. of edges. Top with second cake. Frost top with remaining red frosting to within 3/4 in. of edges. Frost sides and top edge of cake with green frosting.

Cut a 1/4-in. hole in the corner of a pastry or plastic bag. Fill the bag with reserved white frosting. Pipe around the top edge of cake where green and pink frostings meet. For seeds, insert chocolate chips upside down into the cake top. **Yield: 12 servings.**

Sirloin Squash Shish Kabobs

Prep: 10 min. + marinating | Grill: 10 min.

When our grill comes out in the spring, this is the first recipe my family asks me to make. You can also use this marinade on six pork chops or a large round steak cut into serving-size pieces.
—*Ronda Karbo, Russell, Minnesota*

- 1 cup packed brown sugar
- 1 cup soy sauce
- 1 teaspoon *each* garlic powder, ground mustard and ground ginger
- 1 pound boneless beef sirloin steak, cut into 1-inch pieces
- 1 medium zucchini, cut into 1/4-inch slices
- 1 medium yellow summer squash, cut into 1/4-inch slices
- 1 medium sweet red pepper, cut into 1-inch pieces
- 1 medium red onion, cut into eight wedges, optional

In a small bowl, combine the brown sugar, soy sauce, garlic powder, mustard and ginger. Place beef in a large resealable plastic bag; add 1 cup marinade. Seal bag and toss to coat. Place zucchini, yellow squash, red pepper and onion if desired in another resealable plastic bag; add remaining marinade and toss to coat. Refrigerate beef and vegetables for at least 4 hours, turning occasionally.

Drain and discard marinade. On eight metal or soaked wooden skewers, alternately thread beef and vegetables. Grill, covered, over medium-hot heat or broil 4-6 in. from the heat for 10 minutes or until meat reaches desired doneness, turning occasionally. **Yield: 4 servings.**

Sirloin Squash Shish Kabobs

Grilled Vegetable Medley

Grilled Vegetable Medley

Prep: 15 min. | Grill: 20 min.

This side dish is our favorite way to fix summer vegetables. Cleanup is a breeze, because it cooks in foil. It makes a great accompaniment to grilled steak or chicken.
—*Lori Daniels, Beverly, West Virginia*

- 1/4 cup olive oil
- 1 teaspoon salt
- 1 teaspoon dried parsley flakes
- 1 teaspoon dried basil
- 3 large ears fresh corn on the cob, cut into 3-inch pieces
- 2 medium zucchini, cut into 1/4-inch slices
- 1 medium yellow summer squash, cut into 1/4-inch slices
- 1 medium sweet onion, sliced
- 1 large green pepper, diced
- 10 cherry tomatoes
- 1 jar (4-1/2 ounces) whole mushrooms, drained
- 1/4 cup butter, cubed

In a large bowl, combine the oil, salt, parsley and basil. Add vegetables and toss to coat. Place on a double thickness of heavy-duty foil (about 28 in. x 18 in.). Dot with butter. Fold foil around vegetables and seal tightly.

Grill, covered, over medium heat for 10-13 minutes on each side or until corn is tender. **Yield: 8 servings.**

Old Glory Dessert

Old Glory Dessert

Prep: 30 min. | Bake: 10 min. + cooling

We took advantage of convenient refrigerated cookie dough to create the crust for this fresh fruit pizza. Easily arranged berries give it an appealing patriotic appearance.
—Taste of Home Test Kitchen, Greendale, Wisconsin

1	tube (18 ounces) refrigerated sugar cookie dough
2	packages (one 8 ounces, one 3 ounces) cream cheese, softened
3/4	cup confectioners' sugar
4-1/2	teaspoons lemon juice
1/2	cup fresh blueberries
2	cups quartered fresh strawberries

Press cookie dough into a greased 15-in. x 10-in. x 1-in. baking pan. Bake at 350° for 10-12 minutes or until golden brown. Cool on a wire rack.

In a large bowl, beat the cream cheese, sugar and lemon juice until smooth. Set aside 1/4 cup. Spread remaining cream cheese mixture over crust. Decorate with blueberries and strawberries to resemble a flag.

Cut a small hole in a corner of a pastry or plastic bag. Insert star tip #16. Fill with reserved cream cheese mixture. Beginning in one corner, pipe stars in the spaces between the blueberries. **Yield: 12-15 servings.**

Editor's Note: 2 cups of any sugar cookie dough can be substituted for the refrigerated dough.

Frozen Lemon-Berry Margaritas

Prep/Total Time: 15 min.

Cool down those summer months with this absolutely fantastic margarita. It's slightly icy, thick and perfect on those warm afternoons. The non-alcoholic version will be a real hit with kids.
—Julie Hieggelke, Grayslake, Illinois

6	lime wedges
3	tablespoons coarse sugar
2/3	cup lemonade concentrate
1	cup frozen unsweetened raspberries
2	cups ice cubes
1	package (16 ounces) frozen sweetened sliced strawberries, partially thawed
1/2	cup frozen blueberries
1	tablespoon sugar
1/2	cup tequila, optional

Using lime wedges, moisten the rims of six glasses. Set limes aside for garnish. Sprinkle coarse sugar on a plate; hold each glass upside down and dip rim into sugar. Set aside. Discard remaining sugar on plate.

In a blender, combine the lemonade concentrate and raspberries; cover and process until blended. Press mixture through a fine meshed sieve; discard seeds. Return raspberry mixture to blender; add ice, strawberries, blueberries, sugar and tequila if desired. Cover and process until smooth.

Pour into prepared glasses. Garnish with reserved limes. **Yield: 6 servings.**

Cucumber Soup

Prep: 25 min. + chilling

I dress up this creamy soup with a colorful selection of savory garnishes. A topping of crunchy almonds contrasts nicely with the smooth texture of the soup.
—Beverly Sprague, Catonsville, Maryland

- 3 medium cucumbers
- 3 cups chicken broth
- 3 cups (24 ounces) sour cream
- 3 tablespoons cider vinegar
- 2 teaspoons salt, optional
- 1 garlic clove, minced

TOPPINGS:
- 2 medium tomatoes, chopped
- 3/4 cup sliced almonds, toasted
- 1/2 cup chopped green onions
- 1/2 cup minced fresh parsley

Peel cucumbers; halve lengthwise and remove seeds. Cut into chunks. In a blender, cover and puree cucumbers and broth in small batches.

Transfer to a large bowl; stir in the sour cream, vinegar, salt if desired and garlic until well blended. Cover and refrigerate for at least 4 hours. Stir before serving. Garnish with tomatoes, almonds, onions and parsley. **Yield: 12 servings.**

Nutrition Facts: 3/4 cup serving (prepared with reduced-sodium broth and fat-free sour cream and without salt) equals 95 calories, 3 g fat (trace saturated fat), 0 cholesterol, 239 mg sodium, 11 g carbohydrate, 1 g fiber, 5 g protein. **Diabetic Exchange:** *1 reduced-fat milk.*

Summer Melon Salsa

Prep/Total Time: 15 min.

I've been experimenting with lots of different fruit salsa recipes, and this one is so good. The refreshing blend of melons is complemented by a slight jalapeno kick. We like it with lime-flavored tortilla chips, but it's also delicious over grilled chicken.
—Sue Gronholz, Beaver Dam, Wisconsin

- 1/2 cup *each* cubed cantaloupe, honeydew and seedless watermelon
- 1/4 cup chopped red onion
- 1 jalapeno pepper, seeded and chopped
- 2 tablespoons minced fresh cilantro
- 1 tablespoon lime juice
- 1/4 teaspoon pepper
- 1/8 teaspoon salt

Tortilla chips

In a small bowl, combine the melon, onion, jalapeno, cilantro, lime juice, pepper and salt. Serve with chips. Refrigerate leftovers. **Yield: 1-3/4 cups.**

Nutrition Facts: 1/4 cup equals 15 calories, trace fat (trace saturated fat), 0 cholesterol, 45 mg sodium, 4 g carbohydrate, trace fiber, trace protein. **Diabetic Exchange:** *Free food.*

Editor's Note: When cutting hot peppers, disposable gloves are recommended. Avoid touching your face.

Grilled Rib Eye Steaks

Prep: 10 min. + marinating | Grill: 10 min.

In summer, I love to marinate these steaks overnight, then grill them for family and friends. —Tim Hanchon, Muncie, Indiana

- 1/2 cup soy sauce
- 1/2 cup sliced green onions
- 1/4 cup packed brown sugar
- 2 garlic cloves, minced
- 1/4 teaspoon ground ginger
- 1/4 teaspoon pepper
- 2-1/2 pounds beef rib eye steaks

In a large resealable plastic bag, combine the soy sauce, onions, brown sugar, garlic, ginger and pepper. Add the steaks. Seal the bag and turn to coat; refrigerate for 8 hours or overnight.

Drain and discard marinade. Grill steaks, uncovered, over medium-hot heat for 8-10 minutes or until the meat reaches desired doneness (for medium-rare, a meat thermometer should read 145°; medium, 160°; well-done, 170°). **Yield: 2-4 servings and about 1-1/4 pounds leftover steak.**

Grilled Rib Eye Steaks

Fall

Fall brings with it, along with brilliantly colored leaves and brisk winds, delicious food. From Halloween treats to Thanksgiving favorites, good taste abounds in these recipes that make cooking a joy!

Butter Pecan Pumpkin Pie

Butter Pecan Pumpkin Pie

Prep: 20 min. + freezing

This pie was always a family favorite at holidays. Everyone thought I'd worked all day to make it, but it's actually so easy to assemble. It's handy to have in the freezer when unexpected company stops in for coffee and dessert.

—*Arletta Slocum, Venice, Florida*

- 1 quart butter pecan ice cream, softened
- 1 pastry shell (9 inches), baked
- 1 cup canned pumpkin
- 1/2 cup sugar
- 1/4 teaspoon *each* ground cinnamon, ginger and nutmeg
- 1 cup heavy whipping cream, whipped
- 1/2 cup caramel ice cream topping
- 1/2 cup chocolate ice cream topping, optional

Additional whipped cream

Spread ice cream into the crust; freeze for 2 hours or until firm. Combine the pumpkin, sugar, cinnamon, ginger and nutmeg; fold in the whipped cream. Spread over ice cream. Cover and freeze for 2 hours or until firm. May be frozen for up to 2 months.

Remove from the freezer 15 minutes before slicing. Drizzle with caramel ice cream topping. Drizzle with chocolate ice cream topping if desired. Dollop with whipped cream. **Yield: 6-8 servings.**

Cran-Apple Salsa

Prep/Total Time: 15 min.

Here's a festive twist on traditional holiday cranberry relish. This salsa packs a tart-sweet blend of fresh flavors, goes together in simply minutes and the colors are beautiful! We think it makes the perfect party dip to celebrate the season.

—*Jody Bauer, Balaton, Minnesota*

- 1 package (12 ounces) fresh *or* frozen cranberries, thawed
- 3 medium apples, cut into wedges
- 1 medium sweet red pepper, cut into pieces
- 1 small red onion, chopped
- 1/2 cup sugar
- 1/3 cup unsweetened apple juice
- 3 tablespoons minced fresh cilantro
- 2 tablespoons chopped jalapeno pepper
- 1 teaspoon grated lime peel

Tortilla chips

In a food processor, process the cranberries, apples, red pepper and onion in batches until coarsely pureed. Transfer to a serving bowl. Stir in the sugar, apple juice, cilantro, jalapeno and lime peel. Refrigerate until serving. Serve with tortilla chips. **Yield: 5 cups.**

Nutrition Facts: 1/4 cup (calculated without chips) equals 45 calories, trace fat (trace saturated fat), 0 cholesterol, 1 mg sodium, 12 g carbohydrate, 1 g fiber, trace protein. **Diabetic Exchange:** *1 fruit.*

Editor's Note: When cutting hot peppers, disposable gloves are recommended. Avoid touching your face.

Cran-Apple Salsa

Marshmallow Witches

Prep/Total Time: 30 min.

Get ready for an assembly line because these no-bake marshmallow witches are easy to prepare, and kids will love helping. They're perfect for gatherings because a dozen can be put together in just 30 minutes.
— *Taste of Home Test Kitchen, Greendale, Wisconsin*

- 1/2   cup vanilla frosting, *divided*
- 36   miniature semisweet chocolate chips
- 12   large marshmallows
- 1   drop *each* green, red and yellow food coloring, optional
- 1/4   cup flaked coconut
- 12   chocolate wafers
- 12   miniature peanut butter cups
- 12   milk chocolate kisses

For the face of each witch, place a dab of frosting on the bottom of three chocolate chips; press two for eyes and one for nose onto each marshmallow.

For hair, combine green food coloring and a drop of water in a small resealable plastic bag; add coconut and shake well. Spread a small amount of frosting on sides of marshmallows; press coconut hair into frosting. Place 3 tablespoons of frosting in a small heavy-duty resealable plastic bag; tint orange with red and yellow food coloring. Set aside.

For hats, spread some of the remaining frosting in the center of chocolate wafers; press peanut butter cups upside down into frosting. Lightly spread bottoms of chocolate kisses with frosting; place on peanut butter cups. Cut a small hole in the corner of pastry or plastic bag; insert a small star tip. Fill the bag with frosting and pipe stars around the base of each peanut butter cup. Secure a hat to each witch with a dab of frosting. **Yield:** 1 dozen.

Apple-Glazed Cornish Hens

Prep: 20 min. | Bake: 1 hour

These golden brown game hens are treated to a cinnamon-apple glaze that's simple but special enough for a standout entree.
— *Donna Mussina, White Oak, Pennsylvania*

- 6   Cornish game hens (22 ounces *each*)
- 1   tablespoon cornstarch
- 1   cup apple juice concentrate
- 3   lemon slices
- 1/2   teaspoon ground cinnamon

Tie legs of each hen together; tuck wings under hens. Place on a greased rack in a roasting pan. In a small saucepan, combine cornstarch and apple juice concentrate until smooth. Stir in the lemon slices and cinnamon. Bring to a boil; cook and stir for 1 minute or until thickened.

Spoon half of the glaze over the hens. Bake, uncovered, at 375° for 1 to 1-1/4 hours or until a meat thermometer reads 180°, basting occasionally with remaining glaze. **Yield: 6 servings.**

Herbed Dinner Rolls

Prep: 20 min. + rising | Bake: 15 min.

After I had my sixth child, a friend dropped off dinner, including these rolls, which start in a bread machine. They were so delicious that I quickly bought my own machine to bake them myself.

—Dana Lowry, Hickory, North Carolina

1	cup water (70°-80°)
2	tablespoons butter, softened
1	egg
1/4	cup sugar
1	teaspoon salt
1/2	teaspoon *each* dried basil, oregano, thyme and rosemary, crushed
3-1/4	cups bread flour
2-1/4	teaspoons active dry yeast

Additional butter, melted
Coarse salt, optional

In a bread machine pan, place the water, butter, egg, sugar, salt, seasonings, flour and yeast in order suggested by manufacturer. Select dough setting (check dough after 5 minutes of mixing; add 1 to 2 tablespoons of water or flour if needed).

When cycle is completed, turn dough onto a lightly floured surface. Divide dough into 16 portions; shape each into a ball. Place 2 in. apart on greased baking sheets. Cover and let rise in a warm place until doubled, about 30 minutes.

Bake at 375° for 12-15 minutes or until golden brown. If desired, brush with butter and sprinkle with coarse salt. Remove from pans to wire racks. **Yield:** 16 rolls.

Editor's Note: We recommend you do not use a bread machine's time-delay feature for this recipe.

Herbed Dinner Rolls

Coconut Sweet Potatoes

Coconut Sweet Potatoes

Prep: 50 min. | Bake: 30 min.

I mash sweet potatoes with pineapples, orange juice and seasonings. With a streusel-like topping of coconut and pecans, its sweet taste and pretty look will garner praise. To switch it up, substitute peanuts for the pecans.

—Hasel King, Nacogdoches, Texas

1-1/2	pounds sweet potatoes (about 6 medium)
1/3	cup crushed pineapple
2	tablespoons butter, melted
1	tablespoon orange juice
1	egg, lightly beaten
1	teaspoon salt
1/4	teaspoon ground mace
1/8	teaspoon ground ginger
1/3	cup flaked coconut
1/3	cup finely chopped pecans
2	tablespoons brown sugar

Place sweet potatoes in a Dutch oven; cover with water. Bring to a boil. Reduce heat; cover and cook for 30-35 minutes or until tender. Drain; cool slightly.

Peel the potatoes and place in a large bowl; mash. Add the pineapple, butter, orange juice, egg, salt, mace and ginger; mix well.

Transfer to a greased 11-in. x 7-in. baking dish. Bake, uncovered, at 400° for 20-30 minutes or until heated through.

Combine the coconut, pecans and brown sugar; sprinkle over the top. Bake 8-10 minutes longer or until topping is lightly browned. **Yield:** 6-8 servings.

Autumn Pork Tenderloin

Prep: 5 min. + marinating | Bake: 40 min.

Sized right for two, this rustic and comforting entree is treated to a combination of apples, raisins and nuts. The fruited sauce adds great flavor. I serve this often, and when I double it for guests, it's greeted with plenty of cheers.

—Tiffany Anderson-Taylor, Gulfport, Florida

1/2	teaspoon salt
1/4	teaspoon pepper
1	pork tenderloin (3/4 pound)
1/2	cup apple juice
1	cup apple pie filling
1/4	cup raisins
1/4	cup chopped pecans
1/4	teaspoon ground cinnamon

Rub salt and pepper over pork. Place in a large resealable plastic bag; add apple juice. Seal bag and turn to coat. Refrigerate for 30 minutes.

Drain and discard the apple juice. Place pork on a rack in a roasting pan. Combine the pie filling, raisins, pecans and cinnamon; spoon over pork. Bake, uncovered, at 400° for 40-45 minutes or until a meat thermometer reads 160°. Let stand for 5 minutes before slicing. **Yield:** 2 servings.

Autumn Pork Tenderloin

Pork Tenderloin Tip

Although a recipe may call for only one pork tenderloin, you can cook up to three in the same time frame. Just place the tenderloins side by side in the roasting pan, making sure there is some space between them. Use the roasting time of only one. Save the remaining pork for another meal.

Yummy Mummy with Veggie Dip

 # Yummy Mummy with Veggie Dip

Prep: 25 min. | Bake: 20 min. + cooling

I came up with this idea for dressing up a veggie tray for our annual Halloween party, and everyone got really "wrapped up" in it. Frozen bread dough and dip mix make this a simple and easy appetizer that's as much fun to display as to eat!

—Heather Snow, Salt Lake City, Utah

1	loaf (1 pound) frozen bread dough, thawed
3	pieces string cheese
2	cups (16 ounces) sour cream
1	envelope fiesta ranch dip mix
1	pitted ripe olive

Assorted crackers and fresh vegetables

Let dough rise according to package directions. Place dough on a greased baking sheet. For mummy, roll out dough into a 12-in. oval that is narrower at the bottom. For the head, make an indentation about 1 in. from the top. Let rise in a warm place for 20 minutes.

Bake at 350° for 20-25 minutes or until golden brown. Arrange strips of string cheese over bread; bake 1-2 minutes longer or until cheese is melted. Remove from pan to a wire rack to cool.

Meanwhile, in a small bowl, combine sour cream and dip mix. Chill until serving.

Cut mummy in half horizontally. Hollow out bottom half, leaving a 3/4-in. shell. Cut removed bread into cubes; set aside. Place bread bottom on a serving plate. Spoon dip into shell. Replace top. For eyes, cut olive and position on head. Serve with crackers, vegetables and reserved bread. **Yield:** 16 servings (2 cups dip).

Two-Bread Stuffed Turkey

Two-Bread Stuffed Turkey

Prep: 30 min. | Bake: 3-3/4 hours

I reach for bacon and canned corn to make this subtly sweet stuffing that combines corn bread and white bread. The moist mixture is terrific with turkey but just as good served solo.
—Fancheon Resler, Bluffton, Indiana

- 6 bacon strips, diced
- 2 cups chopped celery
- 1 cup sliced green onions
- 6 cups cubed corn bread
- 6 cups cubed white bread
- 1 can (15-1/4 ounces) whole kernel corn, undrained
- 1-1/4 cups chicken broth
- 3/4 cup egg substitute
- 1/4 cup butter, melted
- 2 teaspoons rubbed sage
- 1 teaspoon dried thyme
- 1/2 teaspoon salt
- 1/4 teaspoon pepper
- 1 turkey (10 to 12 pounds)
- 2 tablespoons canola oil

In a large skillet, cook bacon over medium heat until crisp. Remove bacon to paper towels to drain. In the drippings, saute celery and onions until tender.

Transfer to a large bowl. Stir in the corn bread, bread, corn, broth, egg substitute, butter, seasonings and bacon. Just before baking, loosely stuff turkey. Skewer openings; tie drumsticks together.

Place on a rack in a roasting pan. Brush with the oil. Bake at 325° for 3-3/4 to 4 hours or until a meat thermometer reads 180° for the turkey and 165° for the stuffing, basting occasionally with the pan drippings. (Cover loosely with aluminum foil if the turkey browns too quickly.) **Yield: 8-10 servings (10 cups stuffing).**

Apple Cranberry Cider

Prep/Total Time: 30 min.

Spiced with cinnamon sticks and cloves, this warm-you-up sipper is sure to chase away winter's chill. Serve brimming mugs of the hot beverage with your family's favorite cookies, muffin or bread.
—Taste of Home Test Kitchen, Greendale, Wisconsin

- 1 quart apple cider *or* juice
- 2 cups cranberry juice
- 1/3 cup packed brown sugar
- 4 whole cloves
- 2 cinnamon sticks (3 inches)

In a large saucepan, combine the apple cider, cranberry juice and brown sugar. Place the whole cloves and cinnamon sticks on a double thickness of cheesecloth; bring up the corners of the cloth and tie with kitchen string to form a bag. Add to the pan.

Bring cider to a boil over medium heat. Reduce the heat; simmer, uncovered, for 15-20 minutes. Discard the spice bag. **Yield: 6 servings.**

Honey-Mustard Turkey Breast

Prep: 10 min. | Bake: 1-3/4 hours

Honey mustard adds subtle flavor to this moist roasted turkey breast. Don't have honey mustard? Use 1/4 cup each honey and brown mustard.

—Taste of Home Test Kitchen, Greendale, Wisconsin

- 1   bone-in turkey breast (6 to 7 pounds)
- 1/2   cup honey mustard
- 3/4   teaspoon dried rosemary, crushed
- 1/2   teaspoon onion powder
- 1/4   teaspoon salt
- 1/8   teaspoon garlic powder
- 1/8   teaspoon pepper

Place the turkey breast, skin side up, on a rack in a foil-lined shallow roasting pan. In a small bowl, combine the remaining ingredients. Spoon over turkey.

Bake, uncovered, at 325° for 1-3/4 to 2-1/2 hours or until a meat thermometer reads 170°, basting every 30 minutes. **Yield: 10-12 servings.**

Jack-o'-Lantern Pops

Jack-o'-Lantern Pops

Prep/Total Time: 30 min.

The faces of your little ghouls and goblins will light up when you surprise them with these sweet, smiling pumpkins. The crispy pops are ideal for school parties.

—Clara Coulston, Washington Court House, Ohio

- 1   package (10-1/2 ounces) miniature marshmallows
- 3   tablespoons butter
- 1/8   teaspoon salt

Red and yellow gel food coloring

- 6   cups crisp rice cereal
- 6   Popsicle sticks
- 3   miniature Tootsie Rolls, cut in half widthwise
- 3   miniature green apple Air Head candies, cut lengthwise into thin strips

Black decorating gel

In a large saucepan, combine the marshmallows, butter and salt. Cook and stir over medium-low heat until melted.

Remove from the heat; tint orange with red and yellow food coloring. Stir in cereal.

With buttered hands, shape mixture into six balls. Insert a Popsicle stick into each ball. Press half of a Tootsie Roll into the top of each for stem. Roll Air Head strips between hands to form vines; press into each pumpkin near stem. Make jack-o'-lantern faces with decorating gel. **Yield: 6 servings.**

Sausage-Stuffed Acorn Squash

Prep/Total Time: 25 min.

Acorn squash gets a sweet-and-savory treatment when stuffed with sausage, onion, spinach and cranberries to make this pretty autumn entree. Cooking the squash in the microwave makes this quick enough for a busy weeknight.

—Taste of Home Test Kitchen, Greendale, Wisconsin

- 2   medium acorn squash
- 1   pound bulk spicy pork sausage
- 1/2   cup chopped onion
- 1   egg
- 2   tablespoons milk
- 1   cup fresh baby spinach, finely chopped
- 1-1/2   cups soft bread crumbs
- 1/2   cup dried cranberries

Cut squash in half; remove and discard seeds. Place squash cut side down in a microwave-safe dish. Cover and microwave on high for 10-12 minutes or until tender.

Meanwhile, crumble sausage into a large skillet; add onion. Cook over medium heat until meat is no longer pink; drain. In a large bowl, beat egg and milk; stir in the spinach, bread crumbs, cranberries and sausage mixture.

Turn squash cut side up. Stuff with sausage mixture. Cover and microwave on high for 2-3 minutes or until a thermometer reads 160°. **Yield: 4 servings.**

Editor's Note: This recipe was tested in a 1,100-watt microwave.

Sausage-Stuffed Acorn Squash

Winter *is the perfect time to*

celebrate with hearty and wholesome fare! The recipes in this section will surely impress your Christmas and New Year's guests—there are plenty of desserts, cookies and appetizers that would add sparkle to any holiday table. No one will believe that many of these recipes require only 20 minutes or less of preparation time.

Burgundy Pears

Burgundy Pears

Prep: 10 min. | Cook: 3 hours

These warm spiced pears elevate slow cooking to a new level of elegance, yet they're incredibly easy to make. Your friends won't believe this fancy-looking dessert came from a slow cooker.
—Elizabeth Hanes, Peralta, New Mexico

6	medium ripe pears
1/3	cup sugar
1/3	cup Burgundy wine *or* grape juice
3	tablespoons orange marmalade
1	tablespoon lemon juice
1/4	teaspoon ground cinnamon
1/4	teaspoon ground nutmeg

Dash salt

Whipped cream cheese

Peel pears, leaving stems intact. Core from the bottom. Stand pears upright in a 5-qt. slow cooker. Combine the sugar, wine or grape juice, marmalade, lemon juice, cinnamon, nutmeg and salt. Carefully pour over pears.

Cover and cook on low for 3-4 hours or until tender. To serve, drizzle pears with sauce and garnish with whipped cream cheese. **Yield: 6 servings.**

Citrus Turkey Roast

Prep: 15 min. | Cook: 5-1/4 hours

I was skeptical at first about fixing turkey in a slow cooker. But once I tasted this dish, I was hooked. With a little cornstarch to thicken the juices, the gravy is easily made.
—Kathy Kittell, Lenexa, Kansas

1	frozen boneless turkey roast, thawed (3 pounds)
1	tablespoon garlic powder
1	tablespoon paprika
1	tablespoon olive oil
2	teaspoons Worcestershire sauce
1/2	teaspoon salt
1/2	teaspoon pepper
8	garlic cloves, peeled
1	cup chicken broth, *divided*
1/4	cup water
1/4	cup white wine *or* additional chicken broth
1/4	cup orange juice
1	tablespoon lemon juice
2	tablespoons cornstarch

Cut roast in half. Combine the garlic powder, paprika, olive oil, Worcestershire sauce, salt and pepper; rub over the turkey. Place in a 5-qt. slow cooker. Add the garlic, 1/2 cup broth, water, wine or additional broth, orange juice and lemon juice. Cover and cook on low for 5-6 hours or until a meat thermometer reads 170°.

Remove turkey and keep warm. Discard garlic cloves. For the gravy, combine cornstarch and remaining broth until smooth; stir into cooking juices. Cover and cook on high for 15 minutes or until thickened. Slice turkey; serve with gravy. **Yield: 12 servings.**

Citrus Turkey Roast

Appetizer Wreath

Easy Gingerbread Cutouts
Prep: 20 min. + chilling | Bake: 10 min./batch

I rely on this tried-and-true recipe during the holidays. The cream cheese frosting complements the cookies' gingery flavor and sets up nicely for easy packaging and stacking.

—Sandra McKenzie, Braham, Minnesota

> 1 package (18-1/4 ounces) spice cake mix
> 3/4 cup all-purpose flour
> 2 eggs
> 1/3 cup canola oil
> 1/3 cup molasses
> 2 teaspoons ground ginger
> 3/4 cup canned cream cheese frosting, slightly warmed

Red-hot candies

In a bowl, combine the cake mix, flour, eggs, oil, molasses and ginger until well blended. Refrigerate for 30 minutes or until easy to handle.

On a floured surface, roll out dough to 1/8-in. thickness. Cut with lightly floured 5-in. cookie cutters. Place 3 in. apart on ungreased baking sheets.

Bake at 375° for 7-10 minutes or until edges are firm and bottom is lightly browned. Remove to wire racks to cool. Decorate with cream cheese frosting as desired. Use red-hots for eyes, nose and buttons. **Yield: 2-1/2 dozen.**

Appetizer Wreath
Prep: 20 min. | Bake: 15 min. + cooling

I have lots of fun with this festive wreath. I often place a bowl of stuffed olives in the center.

—Shirley Privratsky, Dickinson, North Dakota

> 2 tubes (8 ounces *each*) refrigerated crescent rolls
> 1 package (8 ounces) cream cheese, softened
> 1/2 cup sour cream
> 1 teaspoon dill weed
> 1/8 teaspoon garlic powder
> 1-1/2 cups chopped fresh broccoli florets
> 1 cup finely chopped celery
> 1/2 cup finely chopped sweet red pepper

Celery leaves

Remove crescent dough from packaging (do not unroll). Cut each tube into eight slices. Arrange in an 11-in. circle on an ungreased 14-in. pizza pan.

Bake at 375° for 15-20 minutes or until golden brown. Cool 5 minutes; carefully remove to a platter. Cool completely.

In a small bowl, beat the cream cheese, sour cream, dill and garlic powder until smooth. Spread over wreath; top with broccoli, celery and red pepper. Form a bow garnish with celery leaves. **Yield: 16 servings.**

Easier Cookie Cutouts

For easier handling, chill the dough for 1 to 2 hours before rolling it out. Lightly flour the surface and rolling pin. Roll out the dough as evenly as possible. After dipping the cutter in flour, press it into the dough. Lift each cookie with a small metal spatula to support the cookie as it is moved to the baking sheet.

Easy Gingerbread Cutouts

Holiday Sugar Cookies

Prep: 25 min. + chilling | Bake: 10 min.

I add a hint of lemon to these delightful sugar cookies. For make-ahead convenience, freeze the dough up to three months, then thaw in the fridge before baking and decorating them.

—Katie Koziolek, Hartland, Minnesota

- 2　cups butter, softened
- 2　cups sugar
- 3　eggs
- 1　tablespoon grated lemon peel
- 2　teaspoons vanilla extract
- 6　cups all-purpose flour
- 1　teaspoon baking soda

FROSTING:
- 3　cups confectioners' sugar
- 3　tablespoons butter, melted
- 1/4　cup milk

Green food coloring

Red-hot candies

In a large bowl, cream butter and sugar until light and fluffy. Add eggs, one at a time, beating well after each addition. Beat in lemon peel and vanilla. Combine flour and baking soda; gradually add to creamed mixture and mix well. Shape into three 10-in. rolls; wrap each in plastic wrap. Refrigerate for 4 hours or until firm.

Unwrap and cut into 1/4-in. slices. Place 2 in. apart on ungreased baking sheets. Bake at 350° for 10-15 minutes or until edges are lightly browned. Remove to wire racks.

For the frosting, in a large bowl, combine the confectioners' sugar, butter, milk and food coloring until smooth; transfer to a resealable plastic bag. Drizzle over cookies in the shape of a Christmas tree. Place one red-hot at the top of each tree. **Yield: about 9-1/2 dozen.**

Berry Pretty Pork Roast

Holiday Sugar Cookies

Berry Pretty Pork Roast

Prep: 20 min. | Bake: 1-1/4 hours + standing

Berries add such wonderful flavor to recipes. This moist roast is perfect for special dinners. Slices are particularly tasty when served with the cooking juices.

—Paula Marchesi, Lenhartsville, Pennsylvania

- 1　boneless whole pork loin roast (about 2-1/2 pounds)
- 1/2　cup chopped dried plums
- 1/3　cup *each* fresh *or* frozen blueberries, raspberries and sliced strawberries
- 2　garlic cloves, cut into slivers
- 1/4　cup butter, melted
- 1/2　teaspoon dried oregano
- 1/4　teaspoon salt
- 1/4　teaspoon pepper
- 1/2　cup red wine *or* chicken broth
- 1　tablespoon brown sugar
- 1　tablespoon seedless raspberry jam

Make a lengthwise slit down the center of the roast to within 1/2 in. of bottom. Open roast so it lies flat; cover with plastic wrap. Flatten to 3/4-in. thickness. Remove plastic. Combine the fruit; place on one side of roast. Close roast; tie several times with kitchen string and secure ends with toothpicks.

Cut slits in roast; insert garlic slivers. Place in an ungreased shallow baking pan. Drizzle with butter; sprinkle with oregano, salt and pepper.

Combine the wine or broth, brown sugar and jam. Drizzle over roast. Bake, uncovered, at 350° for 75-80 minutes or until a meat thermometer reaches 160°. Let stand for 10 minutes before slicing. **Yield: 8-10 servings.**

Mushroom-Stuffed Tenderloin

Prep: 15 min. | Bake: 1-1/4 hours + standing

These tender beef slices are filled with a delicious mixture of mushrooms, bacon and bread crumbs.
—Marie Steeber, Mishicot, Wisconsin

- 3   bacon strips
- 1   cup chopped fresh mushrooms
- 2   tablespoons chopped onion
- 1   garlic clove, minced
- 3/4 cup dry bread crumbs, *divided*
- 2   tablespoons minced fresh parsley
- 1   beef tenderloin (about 2 pounds), trimmed
- 1   tablespoon butter, melted
- 1   tablespoon grated Parmesan cheese

In a skillet, cook bacon until crisp. Remove bacon; crumble and set aside. Drain, reserving 1 tablespoon drippings. In the drippings, saute the mushrooms, onion and garlic until tender. Remove from the heat; stir in 1/2 cup of bread crumbs, parsley and bacon.

Cut a slit lengthwise three-quarters of the way through the tenderloin. Lightly place stuffing in the pocket; close with toothpicks. Combine butter and Parmesan cheese; spread over top and sides of meat. Press the remaining bread crumbs onto butter mixture.

Place meat on rack in a shallow roasting pan. Bake, uncovered, at 350° for 15 minutes. Cover and bake for 1 hour or until meat reaches desired doneness (for medium-rare, a meat thermometer should read 145°; medium, 160°; well-done, 170°). Let stand for 10 minutes and remove toothpicks before slicing. **Yield: 6-8 servings.**

Cream Wafers

Prep: 25 min. + chilling | Bake: 10 min./batch + cooling

My sons and I used to make these cookies, and now my granddaughter helps. When the smaller grandchildren, they lend a hand, too. *—Linda Clinkenbeard, Vincenr*

- 1/2 cup butter, softened
- 1   cup all-purpose flour
- 3   tablespoons heavy whipping cream

Sugar

FILLING:
- 1/4 cup butter, softened
- 3/4 cup confectioners' sugar
- 1/2 teaspoon vanilla extract
- 1-1/2 to 2 teaspoons heavy whipping cream
- 1   drop *each* red and green food coloring

In a small bowl, beat the butter, flour and cream. Cover and refrigerate for 1 hour or until easy to handle.

On a lightly floured surface, roll out dough to 1/8-in. thickness. Cut with a floured 1-1/4-in. round cookie cutter. Place 1 in. apart on ungreased baking sheets. Sprinkle with sugar. Prick each cookie 3-4 times with a fork.

Bake at 375° for 7-9 minutes or until set. Remove to wire racks to cool.

Combine the butter, confectioners' sugar, vanilla and enough cream to achieve desired consistency. Remove half to another bowl; tint one portion of filling with red food coloring and the other half with green. Carefully spread filling on bottom of half of the cookies; top with remaining cookies. **Yield: 2 dozen sandwich cookies.**

Mushroom-Stuffed Tenderloin

Frosty Peppermint Dessert

Frosty Peppermint Dessert

Prep: 20 min. + freezing

This creamy treat with candy and chocolate crust delivers make-ahead convenience. I often whip up two at the same time so I can freeze one for another time.

—Carolyn Satterfield, Emporia, Kansas

1-1/2	cups chocolate wafers
1/4	cup sugar
1/4	cup butter, melted
1	package (8 ounces) cream cheese, softened
1	can (14 ounces) sweetened condensed milk
1	cup crushed peppermint candies
3	drops red food coloring, optional
2	cups heavy whipping cream, whipped
10	to 14 peppermint candies

Combine the wafer crumbs, sugar and butter. Press onto the bottom and 2 in. up the sides of a greased 8-in. springform pan. Refrigerate the crust.

In a large bowl, beat cream cheese until smooth. Gradually add milk, beating until smooth. Beat in crushed candies and food coloring if desired. Fold in whipped cream. Spoon into crust. Cover and freeze for 8 hours or overnight.

Remove from the freezer 10 minutes before servings. Garnish with whole candies. **Yield: 10-14 servings.**

Christmas Cocoa

Prep/Total Time: 15 min.

A sprinkling of crushed candy canes lends a minty and festive touch to this creamy hot cocoa. You can also place a chocolate mint candy cane in each mug as a stirrer. Serve this heartwarming beverage with Christmas cookies to welcome friends in from the cold after skating, sledding or caroling.

—Lori Daniels, Beverly, West Virginia

4	cups milk
2/3	cup instant chocolate drink mix
5	chocolate mint candy canes, crushed
1-1/2	cups heavy whipping cream
1/4	cup confectioners' sugar
1/2	teaspoon vanilla extract

In a large saucepan, combine the milk with the instant chocolate drink mix. Cook and stir over medium heat until heated through. Remove from the heat. Set aside 1 tablespoon crushed candy canes for garnish. Stir the remaining crushed candy canes into the cocoa; keep warm.

In a small bowl, beat the heavy cream until it begins to thicken. Add confectioners' sugar and vanilla extract; beat until stiff peaks form. Ladle cocoa into mugs. Top with whipped cream; sprinkle with reserved crushed candy canes. **Yield: 4 servings.**

Candied Walnuts

Prep/Total Time: 20 min.

Turn ordinary walnuts into a taste sensation with this simple recipe that's prepared on the stovetop. With plenty of brown sugar and a hint of pepper, the crunchy candied nuts are a nice complement to a fruit and cheese tray. But they can stand on their own, as well, because they're so munchable!
—Taste of Home Test Kitchen, Greendale, Wisconsin

- 2 tablespoons canola oil
- 2 tablespoons balsamic vinegar
- 1/8 teaspoon pepper
- 2 cups walnut halves
- 1/2 cup packed brown sugar

In a large heavy skillet, combine the oil, balsamic vinegar and pepper. Cook and stir over medium heat until blended. Add walnuts and cook over medium heat until nuts are toasted, about 4 minutes.

Sprinkle with brown sugar. Cook and stir for 2-4 minutes or until sugar is melted. Spread on foil to cool. Store in an airtight container. **Yield: 2 cups.**

Nutty Fruit 'n' Cheese Tray

Prep/Total Time: 30 min.

Starting with packaged cheese cubes hurries along this lovely display. Trim your grocery bill by buying blocks of cheese and cutting them yourself, and trim time by using plain walnut or pecan halves instead of making the Candied Walnuts.
—Taste of Home Test Kitchen, Greendale, Wisconsin

- 1 fresh pineapple
- 3 cups (12 ounces) cubed Colby-Monterey Jack cheese
- 3 cups (12 ounces) cubed cheddar cheese
- 3 cups (12 ounces) cubed Swiss cheese
- 3 cups (12 ounces) cubed pepper Jack cheese
- 1 pound green grapes
- 1 pound seedless red grapes
- 1 medium honeydew, peeled, seeded and cubed
- 1 medium cantaloupe, peeled, seeded and cubed
- 1 pound fresh strawberries

Candied Walnuts (see recipe above)

Slice the fresh pineapple in half horizontally. Cut the top half of the pineapple into 1-in. wedges, leaving the leaves intact. Transfer to a serving platter. Peel and cube the remaining pineapple. Arrange cheeses, fruits and walnuts on platter. **Yield: 24 servings.**

Nutty Fruit 'n' Cheese Tray & Candied Walnuts

Christmas Mice Cookies
Prep: 30 min. + chilling

These whimsical cute cookies look like little mice have been a family tradition for 15 years. We enjoy them every year and they always get rave reviews. [faded text]

- cup semisweet chocolate chips
- cups chocolate wafer crumbs (about 40 wafers), divided
- cup sour cream
- 36 red nonpareils
- cup sliced almonds
- 18 pieces black shoestring licorice (2 inches each)

In a microwave, melt chocolate chips; stir until smooth. Stir in 1 cup crumbs and sour cream. Cover and refrigerate for 1 hour or until easy to handle.

For each mouse, roll about 1 tablespoon chocolate mixture into a ball, tapering one end to resemble a mouse. Roll in remaining chocolate crumbs to coat. Position nonpareils for eyes, almond slices for ears and licorice pieces for tails. **Yield: 1-1/2 dozen.**

*Nutrition Facts: 1 cookie equals 135 calories, 5 g fat (2 g saturated fat), 3 mg cholesterol, 89 mg sodium, 22 g carbohydrate, 1 g fiber, 2 g protein. **Diabetic Exchanges:** 1-1/2 starch, 1/2 fat.*

Beef Sirloin Tip Roast

Christmas Mice Cookies

Beef Sirloin Tip Roast
Prep: 10 min. | Bake: 2-1/2 hours

This meaty main course, served with a mouth-watering mushroom gravy, is a snap to assemble and pop in the oven. It's my husband's favorite.
—Mrs. Burgess Marshbanks, Buies Creek, North Carolina

- 1   boneless beef sirloin tip roast
       (about 3 pounds)
- 1-1/4 cups water, *divided*
- 1   can (8 ounces) mushroom stems
       and pieces, drained
- 1   envelope onion soup mix
- 3   tablespoons cornstarch

Place a large piece of heavy-duty foil (21-in. x 17-in.) in a shallow roasting pan. Place roast on foil. Pour 1 cup water and mushrooms over roast. Sprinkle with soup mix. Wrap foil around roast; seal tightly. Bake at 350° for 2-1/2 to 3 hours or until meat reaches desired doneness (for medium-rare, a meat thermometer should read 145°; medium, 160°; well-done, 170°).

Remove roast to a serving platter and keep warm. Pour drippings and mushrooms into a saucepan. Combine cornstarch and remaining water until smooth; gradually stir into drippings. Bring to a boil; cook and stir for 2 minutes or until thickened. Serve with sliced beef. **Yield: 10-12 servings.**

Corn-Stuffed Crown Roast

Prep: 20 min. | Bake: 2-1/2 hours + standing

My mother always made this elegant entree for company dinners and special family celebrations.

—Dorothy Swanson, St. Louis, Missouri

   1   pork crown roast (about 7 pounds and 12 ribs)
 1/2   teaspoon pepper, *divided*
   1   cup chopped celery
   1   cup chopped onion
   1   cup butter
   6   cups crushed corn bread stuffing
   2   cups frozen corn, thawed
   2   jars (4-1/2 ounces *each*) sliced mushrooms, undrained
   1   teaspoon salt
   1   teaspoon poultry seasoning

Place roast on a rack in a large roasting pan. Sprinkle with 1/4 teaspoon pepper. Cover rib ends with small pieces of foil. Bake, uncovered, at 350° for 2 hours.

In a Dutch oven, saute celery and onion in butter until tender. Stir in stuffing, corn, mushrooms, salt, poultry seasoning and remaining pepper. Loosely spoon 1 to 3 cups into center of roast. Place remaining stuffing in a greased 2-qt. baking dish.

Bake roast 30-60 minutes or until a meat thermometer reads 160° and juices run clear. Cover and bake extra stuffing for 30-40 minutes. Transfer the roast to a serving platter. Let stand for 10 minutes. Remove foil; cut between ribs to serve. **Yield: 12 servings.**

Santa Claus Cookies

Prep: 50 min. | Cook: 5 min.

All that's needed to create these cute Kris Kringle confections is just six ingredients. Store-bought peanut butter sandwich cookies are transformed into jolly treats with white chocolate, colored sugar, mini chocolate chips and red-hot candies.

—Mary Kaufenberg, Shakopee, Minnesota

   2   packages (6 ounces *each*) white baking chocolate, chopped
   1   package (1 pound) Nutter Butter sandwich cookies
Red colored sugar
  32   vanilla *or* white chips
  64   miniature semisweet chocolate chips
  32   red-hot candies

In a microwave, melt white chocolate at 70% power for 1 minute; stir. Microwave at additional 10- to 20-second intervals, stirring until smooth.

Dip one end of each peanut butter cookie into the melted white chocolate, allowing the excess to drip off. Place on wire racks. To create Santa's hat, sprinkle the red colored sugar over the top part of the chocolate, leaving the lower part bare for the brim of the hat. Press one vanilla chip off-center on hat for pom-pom; let stand until set.

Dip other end of each cookie into melted chocolate for beard, leaving center of cookie uncovered. Place on wire racks. With a dab of melted chocolate, attach semisweet chips for eyes and a red-hot for nose. Place on waxed paper until set. **Yield: 32 cookies.**

Santa Claus Cookies

New Year's Surf 'n' Turf

Prep: 25 min. | Cook: 10 min.

A mild mushroom sauce pulls together this pleasing pairing of tender steaks and firm shrimp.

—*Taste of Home Test Kitchen, Greendale, Wisconsin*

- 2 cups sliced fresh mushrooms
- 2 tablespoons finely chopped green onion
- 1-1/2 teaspoons minced garlic, *divided*
- 5 tablespoons olive oil, *divided*
- 5 tablespoons butter, *divided*
- 1/2 cup dry red wine *or* beef broth
- 2 tablespoons minced fresh parsley
- 2 tablespoons minced fresh basil
- 1/2 teaspoon browning sauce, optional
- 8 beef tenderloin steaks (1 to 1-1/2 inches thick and 8 ounces *each*)
- 24 uncooked medium shrimp, peeled and deveined

In a large skillet, saute the mushrooms, onion and 1 teaspoon garlic in 2 tablespoons oil and 2 tablespoons butter until tender. Add wine or broth; cook and stir for 1 minute. Stir in the parsley, basil and browning sauce if desired. Remove from the skillet; keep warm.

In the same skillet, cook steaks in 2 tablespoons oil and 2 tablespoons butter over medium heat for 5-8 minutes on each side or until meat reaches desired doneness (for medium-rare, a meat thermometer should read 145°; medium, 160°; well-done, 170°). Return mushroom mixture to the pan; heat through.

Meanwhile, in another skillet, combine the remaining butter and oil. Add the shrimp and remaining garlic; cook and stir until shrimp turn pink. Serve with the steaks. **Yield: 8 servings.**

Mousse Tarts

Prep/Total Time: 10 min.

Rich white chocolate and whipped cream combine in these berry-topped treats. Although the tarts originally called for dark chocolate, I prepare them with white chocolate. I double the recipe when I'm asked to bring a dessert to special events. They're always a hit. —*Angela Lively, Cookeville, Tennessee*

- 3 squares (1 ounce *each*) white baking chocolate
- 1 cup heavy whipping cream
- 1/2 cup sweetened condensed milk
- 1/4 teaspoon vanilla extract
- 6 individual graham cracker tart shells
- 18 fresh raspberries
- 6 mint sprigs

In a microwave, melt white chocolate at 30% power for 2-4 minutes, stirring every 30 seconds. Cool for 1 minute, stirring several times. Meanwhile, in a small bowl, beat cream until stiff peaks form; set aside.

In another small bowl, combine the milk, vanilla and melted chocolate. Add half of the whipped cream; beat on low speed just until combined. Fold in remaining whipped cream. Spoon into tart shells. Garnish with raspberries and mint. **Yield: 6 servings.**

Crab Mornay

Prep/Total Time: 30 min.

I sometimes have unexpected dinner guests, so I keep the ingredients for this easy microwave entree on hand. Prepared pastry shells overflow with a creamy combination of canned crab and mushrooms. I serve this with a packaged salad and receive lots of compliments on the meal.

—Beverly Callison, Memphis, Tennessee

1	package (10 ounces) frozen puff pastry shells
1/2	cup butter, cubed
1	jar (6 ounces) sliced mushrooms, drained
6	green onions, sliced
1	jar (4 ounces) diced pimientos, drained
2	tablespoons all-purpose flour
1	can (12 ounces) evaporated milk
2	cups (8 ounces) shredded Swiss cheese
3	cans (6 ounces *each*) crabmeat, drained, flaked and cartilage removed
1	teaspoon salt
1/8	teaspoon cayenne pepper
1/3	cup minced fresh parsley

Bake pastry shells according to package directions. Meanwhile, place butter in a 2-qt. microwave-safe dish. Cover and microwave on high for 20-30 seconds or until melted. Add the mushrooms, onions and pimientos. Cover and cook on high for 2-3 minutes or until vegetables are crisp-tender.

Combine the flour and milk until smooth; gradually stir into the vegetable mixture. Microwave, uncovered, on high for 2-3 minutes or until thickened, stirring often. Add the cheese, crab, salt and cayenne. Cook, covered, on high for 30-60 seconds or until the cheese is melted. Spoon into the pastry shells; sprinkle with parsley. **Yield:** 6 servings.

Editor's Note: This recipe was tested in a 1,100-watt microwave.

Strawberry Valentine Cookies

Prep: 50 min. | Bake: 10 min./batch + cooling

Start a new Valentine's Day tradition with these pretty cookies. Strawberry is a perfect complement to the chocolate glaze.

—Marna Heitz, Farley, Iowa

2/3	cup butter, softened
2/3	cup sugar
1	egg
1	tablespoon lemon juice
2	cups all-purpose flour
1/3	cup strawberry drink mix
2	teaspoons baking powder
1/2	teaspoon salt

GLAZE:

1	cup (6 ounces) semisweet chocolate chips
1	teaspoon shortening

FROSTING:

1/3	cup butter, softened
2	tablespoons strawberry drink mix
1/8	teaspoon salt
3	cups confectioners' sugar
3	to 5 tablespoons milk

In a small bowl, cream butter and sugar until light and fluffy. Beat in egg and lemon juice. Combine the flour, drink mix, baking powder and salt; gradually add to creamed mixture and mix well.

On a lightly floured surface, roll out dough to 1/4-in. thickness. Cut with a floured 2-1/2- to 3-in. heart-shaped cookie cutter. Place 2 in. apart on ungreased baking sheets. Bake at 350° for 8-10 minutes or until set and edges begin to brown. Cool for 2 minutes before removing to wire racks to cool completely.

For the glaze, in a microwave, melt chocolate chips and shortening; stir until smooth. Spread over cookies; let stand until set.

For the frosting, beat the butter, drink mix and salt until blended. Gradually beat in confectioners' sugar. Add enough milk to achieve desired consistency. Decorate cookies. **Yield: about 2 dozen.**

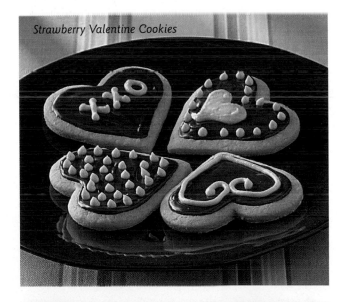

Strawberry Valentine Cookies

Cookie Decorating

To decorate the cookies above, insert a small round tip into a pastry bag, fill with frosting and hold at a 45° angle. Touch cookie's surface with the tip and squeeze frosting out as you go. To stop, release pressure on the bag and touch the cookie with the tip.

delectable
desserts

Almost everyone loves to top off a
tasty supper or lunch with a sweet
finale, but finding the time to create
a dessert can be difficult. Not with
the tantalizing, quick-to-fix recipes in
this chapter! Everyone will think you
fussed when you present these
impressive cakes, cookies and pies.

Whether you want to surprise your
family with a special addition to a
weeknight menu or you need a
dazzling treat for a holiday dinner,
you'll refer to this chapter time and
again for festive desserts that
everyone—including time-crunched
cooks like you—will love!

Makeover Chocolate Truffle Dessert
(recipe on p. 288)

Very Berry Pie

S'more Sandwich Cookies

Prep: 25 min. | Bake: 10 min. + cooling

Capture the taste of campfire s'mores in your kitchen. Graham cracker crumbs added to chocolate chip cookie dough bring out the flavor of the fireside favorite. Melting the marshmallow centers in the microwave makes them simple to assemble.

—*Abby Metzger, Larchwood, Iowa*

3/4	cup butter, softened
1/2	cup sugar
1/2	cup packed brown sugar
1	egg
2	tablespoons milk
1	teaspoon vanilla extract
1-1/4	cups all-purpose flour
1-1/4	cups graham cracker crumbs (about 20 squares)
1/2	teaspoon baking soda
1/4	teaspoon salt
1/8	teaspoon ground cinnamon
2	cups (12 ounces) semisweet chocolate chips
24	to 28 large marshmallows

In a large bowl, cream butter and sugars until light and fluffy. Beat in the egg, milk and vanilla. Combine the flour, graham cracker crumbs, baking soda, salt and cinnamon; gradually add to creamed mixture and mix well. Stir in chocolate chips.

Drop by tablespoonfuls 2 in. apart onto ungreased baking sheets. Bake at 375° for 8-10 minutes or until golden brown. Remove to wire racks to cool.

Place four cookies bottom side up on a microwave-safe plate; top each with a marshmallow. Microwave, uncovered, on high for 10-15 seconds or until marshmallows begin to puff (do not overcook). Top each with another cookie. Repeat. **Yield: about 2 dozen.**

Editor's Note: This recipe was tested in a 1,100-watt microwave.

Very Berry Pie

Prep: 15 min. + chilling

I came up with this quick pie when I needed a dessert for a get-together. My husband raves about the tangy fresh berries and smooth, white chocolate filling.

—*Becky Thompson, Maryville, Tennessee*

1-3/4	cups reduced-fat whipped topping, *divided*
1	reduced-fat graham cracker crust (8 inches)
1	cup fresh raspberries
1	cup fresh blueberries

Sugar substitute equivalent to 1 tablespoon sugar

1	cup cold fat-free milk
1	package (1 ounce) sugar-free instant white chocolate pudding mix

Spread 1/4 cup whipped topping into the crust. Combine berries and sugar substitute; spoon 1 cup over topping.

In a bowl, whisk the milk and pudding mix for 2 minutes; let stand for 2 minutes or until soft-set. Spoon over the berries. Spread with the remaining whipped topping. Top with the remaining berries. Refrigerate for 45 minutes or until set. **Yield: 8 servings.**

Nutrition Facts: 1 piece equals 214 calories, 5 g fat (3 g saturated fat), 1 mg cholesterol, 259 mg sodium, 39 g carbohydrate, 2 g fiber, 2 g protein. Diabetic Exchanges: 1-1/2 fruit, 1 starch, 1 fat.

Editor's Note: This recipe was tested with Splenda no-calorie sweetener.

S'more Sandwich Cookies

Ice Cream Pretzel Cake

Ice Cream Pretzel Cake

Prep: 30 min. + freezing

Our family loved a dessert we had at a local restaurant, so I invented my own version for a birthday party. It's simple to make ahead and pull out of the freezer when you need it.

—Monica Rush, Reading, Pennsylvania

1-1/4	cups crushed pretzels
6	tablespoons cold butter
3/4	cup hot fudge ice cream topping, warmed
2	packages (7-1/2 ounces *each*) chocolate-covered miniature pretzels
1/2	gallon vanilla ice cream, softened
1/4	cup caramel ice cream topping

Place crushed pretzels in a small bowl; cut in butter until crumbly. Press onto the bottom of a greased 9-in. springform pan. Cover and freeze for at least 30 minutes. Spread fudge topping over crust; cover and freeze.

Set aside 16 chocolate-covered pretzels for garnish. Place remaining pretzels in a food processor; cover and process until crumbly. Transfer to a large bowl; stir in ice cream. Spread over fudge topping. Drizzle with caramel topping. Garnish with reserved pretzels. Cover and freeze for at least 8 hours or overnight. **Yield: 16 servings.**

Editor's Note: If you are unable to find chocolate-coated pretzels, use 1 package (11-1/2 ounces) milk chocolate chips, 4 teaspoons shortening and about 110 miniature pretzel twists. In a microwave, melt chips and shortening; stir until blended. With a fork, dip pretzels into chocolate mixture to evenly coat, reheating chocolate if needed. Let stand on waxed paper until set.

Watermelon Ice

Prep: 15 min. + freezing

This sweet frosty snack is so refreshing on hot summer days. It's a snap to scoop and serve in snow cone cups.

—Darlene Brenden, Salem, Oregon

1/2	cup sugar
1/4	cup watermelon *or* mixed fruit gelatin powder
3/4	cup boiling water
5	cups seeded cubed watermelon

In a bowl, dissolve sugar and gelatin in boiling water; set aside. Place watermelon in a blender; cover and puree. Stir into gelatin mixture.

Pour into an ungreased pan. Cover and freeze overnight. Remove from the freezer 1 hour before serving. Spoon into paper cones or serving dishes. **Yield: 4-6 servings.**

Lemon Cheesecake

Prep: 15 min. | Bake: 45 min. + chilling

A homemade chocolate crust complements the light lemon flavor of this delectable little dessert. One of my friends gave me the recipe, which is perfect for birthday dinners, anniversaries...just about any occasion. —Cathy Chan, Calgary, Alberta

- 1/2 cup crushed chocolate wafers
- 2 tablespoons butter, melted
- 1 package (8 ounces) cream cheese, softened
- 1/2 cup sugar
- 1/2 cup sour cream
- 2 tablespoons lemon juice
- 1 tablespoon all-purpose flour
- 1 teaspoon grated lemon peel
- 1/2 teaspoon vanilla extract
- 1 egg, lightly beaten

In a small bowl, combine the wafer crumbs and butter. Press onto the bottom of a greased 6-in. springform pan. Place pan on a baking sheet. Bake at 350° for 7-8 minutes or until set. Cool on a wire rack.

In a large bowl, beat cream cheese and sugar until smooth. Beat in the sour cream, lemon juice, flour, lemon peel and vanilla. Add egg; beat on low speed just until combined. Pour over crust.

Place pan on a baking sheet. Bake for 35-40 minutes or until the center is almost set. Cool on a wire rack for 10 minutes. Carefully run a knife around the edge of pan to loosen; cool 1 hour longer.

Chill for 8 hours or overnight. Remove sides of pan. Refrigerate leftovers. **Yield: 2-4 servings.**

Lemon Cheesecake

Peach Almond Bars

Peach Almond Bars

Prep: 25 min. | Bake: 20 min. + cooling

These delicious, crisp and nutty treats have been a favorite with our family for years—and they're so pretty! When my dad retired, he took over all the baking in our home. He'd make these and say, "Put on a pot of coffee; let's invite company!" What an effortless way to spend time with family and friends. —Justine Furman-Olshan, Willow Street, Pennsylvania

- 1 tube (16-1/2 ounces) refrigerated sugar cookie dough
- 1 jar (18 ounces) peach preserves
- 1-1/2 cups slivered almonds, *divided*
- 4 egg whites
- 1/2 cup sugar

Let dough stand at room temperature for 5-10 minutes to soften. Press into an ungreased 13-in. x 9-in. baking pan. Bake at 350° for 12-15 minutes or until golden brown.

Spread the preserves over crust. Sprinkle with 3/4 cup almonds. In a large bowl, beat the egg whites on medium speed until soft peaks form. Gradually beat in the sugar, 1 tablespoon at a time, on high until stiff glossy peaks form and the sugar is dissolved.

Spread meringue evenly over almonds. Sprinkle with the remaining almonds. Bake for 20-25 minutes or until lightly browned. Cool on a wire rack. Store in the refrigerator. **Yield: 2 dozen.**

Easy Tiramisu

Prep/Total Time: 20 min.

No one can resist this classic, creamy dessert with the winning combination of chocolate and strong-brewed coffee. It's quick to prepare but can be made ahead for added mealtime convenience.
—Nancy Brown, Dahinda, Illinois

1	package (10-3/4 ounces) frozen pound cake, thawed
3/4	cup strong brewed coffee
1	package (8 ounces) cream cheese, softened
1	cup sugar
1/2	cup chocolate syrup
1	cup heavy whipping cream, whipped
2	Heath candy bars (1.4 ounces *each*), crushed

Cut cake into nine slices. Arrange in an ungreased 11-in. x 7-in. dish, cutting to fit if needed. Drizzle with coffee.

In a small bowl, beat cream cheese and sugar until smooth. Add chocolate syrup. Fold in whipped cream. Spread over cake. Sprinkle with crushed candy bars. Refrigerate until serving. **Yield: 8 servings.**

Raspberry Truffle Brownies

Prep: 30 min. | Bake: 25 min. + chilling

This is such a sophisticated dessert! Each rich, fudge-like brownie is bursting with fresh, plump red raspberries and topped with a dreamy, bittersweet ganache. It's true perfection for chocolate lovers of all ages!
—Agnes Ward, Stratford, Ontario

6	squares (1 ounce *each*) bittersweet chocolate, chopped
1/2	cup butter, cubed
2	eggs
1	cup sugar
1	teaspoon vanilla extract
1	cup all-purpose flour
1/4	teaspoon baking soda
1/4	teaspoon salt
1	cup fresh raspberries

FROSTING:

6	squares (1 ounce *each*) bittersweet chocolate, chopped
3/4	cup heavy whipping cream
2	tablespoons seedless raspberry jam
1	teaspoon vanilla extract
12	fresh raspberries

In a microwave-safe bowl, melt chocolate and butter; stir until smooth. In a large bowl, beat the eggs, sugar and vanilla. Stir in chocolate mixture. Combine the flour, baking soda and salt; gradually add to chocolate mixture until combined. Gently fold in raspberries.

Spread into a greased 9-in. square baking pan. Bake at 350° for 25-30 minutes or until a toothpick inserted near the center comes out clean (do not overbake). Cool on a wire rack.

For frosting, in a microwave-safe bowl, combine the chocolate, cream and jam. Microwave at 50% power for 2-3 minutes or until smooth, stirring twice. Transfer to a small bowl; stir in vanilla. Place in a bowl of ice water; stir for 3-5 minutes. Beat on medium speed until soft peaks form.

Cut a small hole in a corner of a heavy-duty resealable plastic bag; insert #825 star tip. Fill with 1/2 cup frosting. Spread remaining frosting over brownies. Cut into 12 bars. Pipe a chocolate rosette in the center of each brownie; top with a raspberry. Cover and refrigerate for 30 minutes or until frosting is set. Refrigerate leftovers. **Yield: 1 dozen.**

Editor's Note: This recipe was tested in a 1,100-watt microwave.

Raspberry Truffle Brownies

Lime Cooler Bars

Lime Cooler Bars

Prep: 15 min. | Bake: 40 min. + cooling

This is a family favorite that's guaranteed to get thumbs-up approval from your gang. Lime juice puts a tangy twist on these tantalizing bars, offering a burst of citrus flavor in every mouth-watering bite. —Dorothy Anderson, Ottawa, Kansas

2-1/2	cups all-purpose flour, *divided*
1/2	cup confectioners' sugar
3/4	cup cold butter, cubed
4	eggs
2	cups sugar
1/3	cup lime juice
1/2	teaspoon grated lime peel
1/2	teaspoon baking powder

Additional confectioners' sugar

In a large bowl, combine 2 cups flour and confectioners' sugar; cut in butter until mixture resembles coarse crumbs. Pat into a greased 13-in. x 9-in. baking pan. Bake at 350° for 20 minutes or until lightly browned.

In a large bowl, whisk together the eggs, sugar, lime juice and grated lime peel until frothy. Combine the baking powder and remaining flour; whisk in the egg mixture. Pour over the hot crust.

Bake for 20-25 minutes or until light golden brown. Cool on a wire rack. Dust with confectioners' sugar. Cut into squares. **Yield: 3 dozen.**

Toffee Oat Cookies

Prep: 15 min. | Bake: 10 min./batch

A friend shared this delicious recipe with me. The crisp yet chewy cookies are bound to satisfy big and little kids alike. They're a hit wherever I take them. —Jean Dandrea, Burkesville, Kentucky

3/4	cup butter, softened
1	cup packed brown sugar
3/4	cup sugar
2	eggs
3	teaspoons vanilla extract
2-1/4	cups all-purpose flour
2-1/4	cups old-fashioned oats
1	teaspoon baking soda
1	teaspoon baking powder
1/2	teaspoon salt
1	package English toffee bits (10 ounces) *or* almond brickle chips (7-1/2 ounces)

In a large bowl, cream butter and sugars until light and fluffy. Add eggs, one at a time, beating well after each addition. Beat in vanilla. Combine the flour, oats, baking soda, baking powder and salt; gradually add to creamed mixture and mix well. Stir in toffee bits.

Drop by rounded tablespoonfuls 2 in. apart onto ungreased baking sheets. Bake at 375° for 10-12 minutes or until golden brown. Cool for 1 minute before removing from pans to wire racks to cool completely. **Yield: about 4 dozen.**

Hawaiian Sunset Cake

Prep: 20 min. + chilling | Bake: 25 min. + cooling

This three-layer orange cake is pretty enough for company, but it's so simple to fix that you'll find yourself making it all the time. A boxed mix keeps it convenient while the pineapple-coconut filling makes it a crowd-pleaser.

—Kara de la Vega, Santa Rosa, California

1	package (18-1/4 ounces) white *or* orange cake mix
1-1/2	cups milk
1	package (3.4 ounces) instant vanilla pudding mix
1	package (3 ounces) orange gelatin
4	eggs
1/2	cup canola oil

FILLING:

1	can (20 ounces) crushed pineapple, drained
2	cups sugar
1	package (10 ounces) flaked coconut
1	cup (8 ounces) sour cream
1	carton (8 ounces) frozen whipped topping, thawed

Toasted coconut, optional

In a large bowl, combine the first six ingredients; beat on low speed for 30 seconds. Beat on medium for 2 minutes.

Pour into three greased and floured 9-in. round baking pans. Bake at 350° for 25-30 minutes or until a toothpick inserted near the center comes out clean. Cool for 10 minutes before removing from pans to wire racks to cool completely.

In a large bowl, combine the pineapple, sugar, coconut and sour cream. Reserve 1 cup; set aside. Place one cake on a serving plate; top with a third of the remaining pineapple mixture. Repeat layers twice.

Fold the whipped topping into the reserved pineapple mixture. Spread over the top and sides of the cake. Sprinkle with toasted coconut if desired. Refrigerate until serving. **Yield: 12-16 servings.**

Helpful Cake Know-How

Stacking cake layers is easier when the layers are level. When the cake is cool, use a long serrated knife to slice the high spot from the bottom layer of the two-layer or the bottom and middle layers of a three-layer cake. You can trim off the crown of the top layer or leave it for a domed effect. Before placing a cake layer on a serving plate to frost it, line the edge with 3-in. strips of waxed paper to keep the plate clean. To keep crumbs from loosening from the cake and mixing into the frosting, first spread a very thin layer of frosting over the top and sides.

Mocha Ice Cream Pie

Prep: 25 min. + freezing

I stir mini marshmallows, mini chocolate chips and crushed sandwich cookies into coffee ice cream to create this irresistible frozen dessert. The fancy look is a snap to achieve by pulling a toothpick through lines of ice cream topping.

—Cherron Nagel, Columbus, Ohio

1-1/2	cups crushed cream-filled chocolate sandwich cookies, *divided*
1/4	cup butter, melted
2	pints coffee ice cream, softened
1	cup miniature marshmallows
1	cup miniature semisweet chocolate chips
2	cups whipped topping
2	tablespoons caramel ice cream topping
2	tablespoons hot fudge ice cream topping, warmed

Additional cream-filled chocolate sandwich cookies, optional

In a small bowl, combine 1-1/4 cups crushed cookies and butter. Press onto the bottom and up the sides of a 9-in. pie plate. In a large bowl, combine the ice cream, marshmallows, chocolate chips and remaining crushed cookies. Spoon into crust. Freeze for 30 minutes.

Spread whipped topping over pie. Alternately pipe thin lines of caramel topping and chocolate topping over pie; gently pull a toothpick or sharp knife through lines in one direction.

Cover and freeze overnight. May be frozen for up to 2 months. Remove from the freezer 10-15 minutes before cutting. Garnish with cookies if desired. **Yield: 6-8 servings.**

Mocha Ice Cream Pie

Makeover Chocolate Truffle Dessert

Prep: 30 min. | Bake: 25 min. + chilling

The original version of this unbelievable, over-the-top truffle dessert took twice as long to make! But after our makeover, it can be made with just 30 minutes of hands-on work, so you can focus on other things before guests arrive.
—Taste of Home Test Kitchen, Greendale, Wisconsin

- 1 package fudge brownie mix (8-inch square pan size)
- 3 cups (18 ounces) semisweet chocolate chips
- 2 cups heavy whipping cream, *divided*
- 6 tablespoons butter, cubed
- 1 tablespoon instant coffee granules
- 3 tablespoons vanilla extract
- 14 to 16 Pirouette cookies, cut into 1-1/2-inch pieces

Prepare brownie batter according to package directions. Spread into a greased 9-in. springform pan; place on baking sheet. Bake at 350° for 25-30 minutes or until toothpick inserted near center comes out clean. Cool on a wire rack.

Place chocolate chips in a food processor; cover and process until finely chopped. In a small microwave-safe bowl, combine 1 cup cream, butter and coffee granules. Microwave, uncovered, on high for 1 to 1-1/2 minutes or until butter is melted; stir until smooth. With food processor running, add cream mixture to chocolate chips in a slow, steady stream. Add vanilla; cover and process until smooth.

Cut a small hole in the corner of a pastry or plastic bag. Fill with 1/4 cup chocolate mixture; set aside for garnish. Transfer remaining chocolate mixture to a large bowl.

Remove the sides of springform pan. Spread half of the chocolate mixture over the brownie layer, spreading evenly over the top and side. In a small bowl, beat the remaining cream until soft peaks form; fold into the remaining chocolate mixture. Spread over chocolate layer. Gently press the cookies into the side of dessert.

Pipe reserved chocolate mixture on top. Cover and refrigerate for at least 4 hours or overnight. Remove from the refrigerator 5 minutes before cutting. **Yield: 12-16 servings.**

Editor's Note: This recipe was tested in a 1,100-watt microwave. The amount of vanilla called for in the recipe is correct.

Cran-Orange Ribbon Dessert

Prep: 30 min. | Bake: 10 min. + freezing

I dress up vanilla ice cream with cream cheese and orange juice concentrate before spreading it over a quick homemade crust. The delicate ribbon of cranberry sauce adds a touch of elegance to each serving. —Deborah Bills, Paducah, Kentucky

- 1-2/3 cups graham cracker crumbs
- 1/4 cup ground pecans
- 3 tablespoons sugar
- 6 tablespoons butter, melted
- 1 package (8 ounces) cream cheese, softened
- 1/2 gallon vanilla ice cream
- 1 can (12 ounces) frozen orange juice concentrate, thawed
- 1 can (16 ounces) whole-berry cranberry sauce
- 1/2 teaspoon almond extract

In a bowl, combine the cracker crumbs, pecans and sugar. Stir in butter until crumbly. Press into a greased 13-in. x 9-in. baking dish. Bake at 350° for 8-10 minutes or until set. Cool on a wire rack.

In a large bowl, beat cream cheese until smooth. Add ice cream. Gradually beat in orange juice concentrate; spread half over crust. Cover and freeze for 1 hour. Refrigerate remaining ice cream mixture.

In a food processor, combine cranberry sauce and almond extract; cover and process until blended. Spread half over ice cream layer. Cover and freeze for at least 30 minutes.

Layer with the remaining ice cream mixture and cranberry mixture. Cover and freeze until firm. May be frozen for up to 2 months. Remove from the freezer about 30 minutes before serving. **Yield: 12-15 servings.**

Makeover Chocolate Truffle Dessert

Frost-on-the-Pumpkin Pie

Prep: 15 min. + chilling | Bake: 10 min.

If you like the aromatic spices in a traditional pumpkin pie, then you'll love this tasty twist. Although this cool and fluffy version of pumpkin pie is special enough for the holidays, I think it's wonderful anytime of year.

—Tammy Covey, Huntington, Arkansas

- 1-1/2 cups graham cracker crumbs (about 24 squares)
- 3 tablespoons sugar
- 1/4 teaspoon ground nutmeg
- 1/8 teaspoon ground cloves
- 1/3 cup butter, melted

FILLING:

- 1 can (16 ounces) vanilla frosting
- 1 can (15 ounces) solid-pack pumpkin
- 1 cup (8 ounces) sour cream
- 1 to 1-1/2 teaspoons ground cinnamon
- 1/2 to 1 teaspoon ground ginger
- 1/4 to 1/2 teaspoon ground cloves
- 1 cup whipped topping

In a small bowl, combine the first five ingredients. Set aside 1 tablespoon for topping. Press remaining crumb mixture onto the bottom and up the sides of an ungreased 9-in. pie plate. Bake at 350° for 7-9 minutes or until crust just begins to brown. Cool on a wire rack.

For the filling, in a large bowl, combine the frosting, pumpkin, sour cream, cinnamon, ginger and cloves. Fold in whipped topping. Spoon into crust. Sprinkle with the reserved crumb mixture. Refrigerate for at least 4 hours before serving. **Yield: 6-8 servings.**

Chocolate Mint Wafers

Prep: 20 min. + standing

I created these melt-in-your-mouth thin mints for a cookie exchange, and everyone raved about them. They're often requested by my family and have become one of my daughter's favorites. To switch up the flavor, try using different extracts instead of peppermint. —Michelle Kester, Cleveland, Ohio

- 4 ounces dark chocolate candy coating
- 1/8 to 1/4 teaspoon peppermint extract
- 18 to 24 vanilla wafers

Place candy coating in a microwave-safe bowl. Microwave, uncovered, on high for 30-60 seconds or until smooth, stirring every 15 seconds. Stir in extract.

Dip vanilla wafers in coating; allow excess to drip off. Place on waxed paper; let stand until set. Store in an airtight container. **Yield: about 1-1/2 dozen.**

Editor's Note: This recipe was tested in a 1,100-watt microwave.

Chocolate-Cherry Ice Cream Pie

Chocolate-Cherry Ice Cream Pie

Prep: 15 min. + freezing

No one would ever dream that the fancy taste and look of this luscious freezer pie comes from only five ingredients! This easy dessert works for an elegant party or a kids' treat.

—Kimberly West, Prairieville, Louisiana

- 1 bottle (7-1/4 ounces) chocolate hard-shell ice cream topping, *divided*
- 1 graham cracker crust (9 inches)
- 1 jar (10 ounces) maraschino cherries, drained
- 1 quart vanilla ice cream, softened
- 2 packages (1-1/2 ounces *each*) peanut butter cups, chopped

Following package directions, drizzle half of the ice cream topping over crust; gently spread to coat bottom and sides. Freeze until firm.

Meanwhile, set aside six cherries for garnish; chop remaining cherries. In a large bowl, combine ice cream and chopped cherries. Spread into prepared crust. Sprinkle with peanut butter cups; drizzle with remaining ice cream topping.

Garnish with reserved cherries. Cover and freeze for 2 hours or until firm. Remove from the freezer 15 minutes before serving. **Yield: 6 servings.**

Dipped Peanut Butter Cookies

Dipped Peanut Butter Cookies

Prep: 30 min. + chilling | Bake: 15 min.

Baking mix makes these soft, moist cookies a snap to stir-up, yet they're pretty enough for parties. I'm often asked to bring them to wedding and baby showers, and they're popular around the holidays, too. I sometimes mix the dough the day before and chill it until it's time to bake the cookies.

—Stephanie DeLoach, Magnolia, Arkansas

1	cup peanut butter
1	can (14 ounces) sweetened condensed milk
1	egg
1	teaspoon vanilla extract
2	cups biscuit/baking mix
3/4	to 1 pound milk chocolate candy coating
1	tablespoon shortening

In a large bowl, combine the peanut butter, milk, egg and vanilla; beat until smooth. Gradually stir in biscuit mix and mix well. Cover and refrigerate for 1 hour.

Shape into 1-in. balls and place 1 in. apart on ungreased baking sheets. Flatten each ball with the bottom of a glass. Bake at 350° for 8-10 minutes or until golden brown. Cool on wire racks.

In a microwave, melt candy coating and shortening; stir until smooth. Dip each cookie halfway into chocolate; shake off excess. Place on waxed paper-lined baking sheets; let stand until set. **Yield: about 5 dozen.**

Secrets to Success

Here are some tips so your cheesecakes turn out great. Grease the bottom and sides of the springform pan to prevent the filling from cracking as the cheesecake cools. For best results, use regular cream cheese, unless a recipe specifically calls for reduced-fat or fat-free products. To avoid lumps, soften cream cheese at room temperature for 30 minutes before mixing. Open the oven door as little as possible while baking the cheesecake. Use a straight-edge knife that has been warmed in hot water to cut a cheesecake.

Candy Bar Cheesecake

Prep: 25 min. | Bake: 1-1/4 hours + cooling

With this recipe, you can easily create a cheesecake that tastes like a fancy, store-bought treat. It's always requested when I'm asked to bring dessert to a function.

—Julie Cervenka, St. Louis, Missouri

1-3/4	cups crushed chocolate wafers (about 28 wafers)
1/4	cup sugar
1/3	cup butter, melted
3	packages (8 ounces *each*) cream cheese, softened
1	can (14 ounces) sweetened condensed milk
1	cup chocolate syrup
2	teaspoons vanilla extract
3	eggs, lightly beaten
6	Snickers candy bars (2.07 ounces *each*), coarsely chopped, *divided*

Additional chocolate syrup

In a small bowl, combine wafer crumbs and sugar; stir in butter. Press onto the bottom and 1-1/2 in. up the sides of a greased 9-in. springform pan. Place pan on a baking sheet. Bake at 325° for 12 minutes. Cool on a wire rack.

In a large bowl, beat the cream cheese, milk, chocolate syrup and vanilla until smooth. Add eggs; beat just until combined. Stir in 2-1/2 cups chopped candy bars. Pour into crust.

Place pan on a double thickness of heavy-duty foil (about 18 in. square); securely wrap foil around pan. Place in a large baking pan. Add 1 in. of hot water to larger pan.

Bake for 75-80 minutes or until center is just set. Cool on a wire rack for 10 minutes. Carefully run a knife around edge of pan to loosen; cool 1 hour longer. Refrigerate overnight.

Remove sides of pan. Top with remaining chopped candy bars; drizzle with additional chocolate syrup. Refrigerate leftovers. **Yield: 12-14 servings.**

Almond Chocolate Torte

Prep: 20 min. + chilling

This no-bake chocolate dessert has a tasty almond crust and smooth, fluffy filling that's almost like a mousse. It's so simple to make ahead of time and so delicious.

—Rhonda Lanterman, Terrace, British Columbia

- 2/3 cup sliced almonds, toasted
- 8 squares (1 ounce *each*) semisweet chocolate
- 2 packages (8 ounces *each*) cream cheese, softened
- 1 cup sugar
- 1 envelope unflavored gelatin
- 1/4 cup cold water
- 2 cups heavy whipping cream, whipped

Set aside 1 tablespoon almonds for garnish. Chop remaining almonds; sprinkle into a greased 9-in. springform pan. In a microwave, melt chocolate; stir until smooth. Cool slightly.

In a large bowl, beat cream cheese and sugar until smooth. Meanwhile, in a small saucepan, sprinkle gelatin over cold water; let stand for 1 minute. Cook and stir over low heat until gelatin is completely dissolved. Beat into cream cheese mixture. Beat in melted chocolate until smooth. Fold in whipped cream.

Pour into the prepared pan. Sprinkle with the reserved almonds. Cover and refrigerate for at least 3 hours. **Yield:** 10-12 servings.

Cookie Fruit Baskets

Prep: 15 min. | Bake: 10 min./batch + cooling

When visiting a friend, I helped organize her recipe collection into scrapbooks. When I found this recipe, I asked to copy it. I served the elegant dessert at my bridge club luncheon to oohs and aahs. Fill these five-ingredient cookie cups with any flavor of ice cream, frozen yogurt or sorbet.

—Theresa Lieber, North Fort Myers, Florida

- 1/4 cup butter
- 1/4 cup packed brown sugar
- 1/4 cup light corn syrup
- 3-1/2 tablespoons all-purpose flour
- 1/2 cup ground pecans
- 1/2 teaspoon vanilla extract

Vanilla ice cream and fresh berries

In a small saucepan, melt the butter over low heat. Stir in the brown sugar and corn syrup; cook and stir until mixture comes to a boil. Remove from the heat. Stir in the flour. Fold in the pecans and vanilla.

Drop by tablespoonfuls 3 in. apart onto parchment paper-lined baking sheets. Bake at 325° for 8-10 minutes or until golden brown.

Cool for 30-60 seconds; peel the cookies off paper. Immediately drape over inverted 6-oz. custard cups; cool completely. Scoop vanilla ice cream into baskets; top with berries. **Yield:** 12 servings.

Cookie Fruit Baskets

 Special Pleasure
Chocolate Cheesecake

Prep: 20 min. | Bake: 40 min. + chilling

When I have time, I enjoy making cheesecakes. In fact, I've come up with a couple of my own recipes, and one of them won second prize at a local bake-off contest. I like this fail-proof dessert because it's so easy to prepare and has just the right mix of ingredients to make it a "special pleasure" for any palate!
—*Benjamin & Sue Ellen Clark, Warsaw, New York*

 1 package (18 ounces) ready-to-bake refrigerated triple-chocolate cookie dough
 1 package (8 ounces) milk chocolate toffee bits
 1 package (9-1/2 ounces) Dove dark chocolate candies
 3 packages (8 ounces *each*) cream cheese, softened
 1 can (14 ounces) sweetened condensed milk
 1 carton (6 ounces) vanilla yogurt
 4 eggs, lightly beaten
 1 teaspoon vanilla extract
Whipped cream

Let dough stand at room temperature for 5-10 minutes to soften. Press nine portions of dough into an ungreased 13-in. x 9-in. baking dish (save remaining dough for another use). Set aside 2 tablespoons toffee bits for garnish; sprinkle remaining toffee bits over dough.

In a small microwave-safe bowl, heat chocolate candies at 70% power for 15 seconds; stir. Microwave in 5-second intervals until melted; stir until smooth.

In a large bowl, beat the cream cheese, milk and yogurt until smooth. Add eggs; beat on low speed just until combined. Fold in vanilla and melted chocolate. Pour over crust.

Bake at 350° for 40-45 minutes or until center is almost set. Cool on a wire rack. Refrigerate for 4 hours or overnight. Garnish with whipped cream and reserved toffee bits. Refrigerate leftovers. **Yield: 24 servings.**

Toffee-Almond Cookie Slices

Prep: 15 min. | Bake: 40 min. + cooling

Make the Christmas season special for family and friends with these crispy coffee-dunkers. Simply bake up a batch, wrap several slices in bright cellophane and add holiday stickers and curly ribbons for last-minute gifts. —Julie Plummer, Sykesville, Maryland

1	package (17-1/2 ounces) sugar cookie mix
1/2	cup all-purpose flour
1/2	cup butter, softened
1	egg
1/3	cup slivered almonds, toasted
1/3	cup miniature semisweet chocolate chips
1/3	cup English toffee bits *or* almond brickle chips

In a large bowl, combine the sugar cookie mix, flour, butter and egg. Stir in the almonds, chocolate chips and toffee bits.

Divide dough in half. On an ungreased baking sheet, shape each portion into a 10-in. x 2-1/2-in. rectangle. Bake at 350° for 25-30 minutes or until lightly browned.

Carefully remove to wire racks; cool for 10 minutes. Transfer to a cutting board. With a serrated knife, cut each rectangle diagonally into 15 slices.

Place cut side down on ungreased baking sheets. Bake for 15-20 minutes or until golden brown. Remove to wire racks to cool. Store in an airtight container. **Yield: 2-1/2 dozen.**

 Coffee Ice Cream Pie

Prep: 30 min. + freezing

While coffee ice cream is great, I sometimes vary the flavor of this family pleaser. It's one dreamy summertime treat that's always highly requested for dessert.
—Velma Brown, Turner Station, Kentucky

2	squares (1 ounce *each*) unsweetened chocolate
1/4	cup butter, cubed
1	can (5 ounces) evaporated milk
1/2	cup sugar
1	pint coffee ice cream, softened
1	chocolate crumb crust (8 inches)
1	carton (8 ounces) frozen whipped topping, thawed
1/4	cup chopped pecans

In a heavy saucepan, melt chocolate and butter over low heat. Stir in milk and sugar. Bring to a boil over medium heat, stirring constantly. Cook and stir for 3-4 minutes or until thickened. Remove from the heat; cool completely.

Spoon ice cream into crust. Stir sauce; spread over ice cream. Top with whipped topping; sprinkle with pecans. Freeze until firm. Remove from the freezer 15 minutes before serving. **Yield: 8 servings.**

Strawberry Banana Pie

Prep: 45 min. + freezing

With its sugar-cone crust and layers of bananas and strawberry ice cream, this pretty pie never seems to last long...especially when our grandchildren visit. It's a favorite year-round, but we really enjoy it in summer, when fresh strawberries are plentiful.
—Bernice Janowski, Stevens Point, Wisconsin

1	packages (5-1/4 ounces) ice cream sugar cones, crushed
1/4	cup ground pecans
1/3	cup butter, melted
2	cups vanilla ice cream, softened
2	medium ripe bananas, mashed
2	large firm bananas, cut into 1/4-inch slices
2	cups strawberry ice cream, softened
1	pint fresh strawberries
1	carton (8 ounces) frozen whipped topping, thawed

In a bowl, combine the crushed ice cream cones, pecans and butter. Press onto the bottom and up the side of a greased 10-in. pie plate. Refrigerate for at least 30 minutes.

In a bowl, combine vanilla ice cream and mashed bananas. Spread over the crust; cover and freeze for 30 minutes. Arrange sliced bananas over ice cream; cover and freeze for 30 minutes. Top with strawberry ice cream; cover and freeze for about 45 minutes.

Hull and halve strawberries; place around edge of pie. Mound or pipe whipped topping in center of pie. Cover and freeze for up to 1 month. Remove from the freezer about 30 minutes before serving. **Yield: 8-10 servings.**

Strawberry Banana Pie

Raspberry Lemon Torte

Prep: 15 min. | Bake: 25 min. + cooling

A box of lemon cake mix, raspberry jam and canned frosting make it a breeze to assemble this lovely layered torte. To split each cake layer evenly, insert toothpicks into the side of the cake layer to mark the halfway point. Wrap a length of dental floss around the cake, resting it on the toothpicks. Cross ends of the dental floss and pull gently to split the cake.
—Taste of Home Test Kitchen, Greendale, Wisconsin

- 1 package (18-1/4 ounces) lemon cake mix
- 1 tablespoon poppy seeds
- 1 tablespoon grated lemon peel
- 1 jar (12 ounces) seedless raspberry jam
- 2-3/4 cups vanilla frosting

Fresh raspberries

Grease two 9-in. round baking pans and line with waxed paper; grease and flour the paper. Prepare cake batter according to package directions; stir in poppy seeds and lemon peel.

Pour into prepared pans. Bake at 350° for 21-26 minutes or until a toothpick inserted near the center comes out clean. Cool for 10 minutes before removing from pans to wire racks to cool completely.

Cut each cake horizontally into two layers. Place bottom layer on a serving plate; top with half of the jam. Top with a second layer; spread with 3/4 cup frosting. Top with a third layer and remaining jam. Top with remaining layer; spread remaining frosting over top and sides of cake. Garnish with fresh raspberries. **Yield: 12 servings.**

Raspberry Lemon Torte

Cookie Lollipops

Prep: 25 min. + freezing

A dip and a drizzle turn crunchy cream-filled cookies into a deliciously different treat! Kids love these lollipops because they taste as good as they look. —Jessie Wiggers, Halstead, Kansas

- 1 package (12 ounces) vanilla chips
- 2 tablespoons shortening, *divided*
- 1 package (16 ounces) double-stuffed Oreo cookies
- 32 wooden Popsicle or craft sticks
- 1 cup (6 ounces) semisweet chocolate chips

In a microwave, melt vanilla chips and 1 tablespoon shortening; stir until smooth. Twist apart sandwich cookies. Dip the end of each Popsicle stick into melted chips; place on a cookie half and top with another half.

Place cookies on waxed paper-lined baking sheets; freeze for 15 minutes. Reheat vanilla chip mixture again if necessary. Dip frozen cookies into mixture until completely covered; allow excess to drip off. Return to baking sheets; freeze 30 minutes longer or until set.

Melt the chocolate chips and remaining shortening; stir until smooth. Drizzle over cookies. Store in an airtight container. **Yield: 32 servings.**

Watermelon Bombe

Prep: 25 min. + freezing

I can't count the times I've made this wonderful dessert. It's a favorite at our summer barbecues. People think you really fussed, but it couldn't be easier—and there are never any leftovers!
—Mary Ann Dell, Phoenixville, Pennsylvania

- 1 pint pistachio ice cream, softened
- 6 drops green food coloring
- 1 pint vanilla ice cream, softened
- 1 pint strawberry ice cream, softened
- 6 drops red food coloring
- 1/2 cup miniature semisweet chocolate chips

Line a 2-qt. freezer-safe bowl with plastic wrap. Place in the freezer for 30 minutes. In a small bowl, combine pistachio ice cream and green food coloring. Quickly spread pistachio ice cream over the bottom and up the sides to within 1/2 in. of the top of bowl. Freeze for 1 hour or until firm. Repeat with vanilla ice cream. Freeze for 2 hours or until firm.

In a small bowl, combine strawberry ice cream and red food coloring; stir in chocolate chips. Spoon into ice cream shell. Cover and freeze overnight.

Remove from the freezer and invert onto a serving plate. Remove the bowl and plastic wrap. Cut into wedges. **Yield: 8 servings.**

Caramel Chocolate Cake

Prep: 25 min. + cooling | Bake: 30 min. + cooling

I love to make this impressive cake for guests or to take to potlucks. Spread with an easy butterscotch frosting and draped with a caramel-nut topping, it looks like it took all day. Yet it's quite simple to make. —Gloria Guadron, Fishers, Indiana

1	package (18-1/4 ounces) German chocolate cake mix
3/4	cup packed brown sugar
6	tablespoons butter, cubed
2	tablespoons heavy whipping cream
1/2	cup finely chopped pecans
1	package (3.4 ounces) instant butterscotch pudding mix
1	cup cold milk
2-1/2	cups whipped topping

Prepare and bake cake according to package directions for two 9-in. round baking pans. Cool for 10 minutes before removing from pans to wire racks to cool completely.

Meanwhile, in a small saucepan, combine the brown sugar, butter and cream. Cook and stir over low heat until sugar is dissolved. Increase heat to medium. Do not stir. Cook for 3-6 minutes or until bubbles form in center of mixture and color is amber brown. Remove from the heat; stir in pecans. Cool at room temperature for 30 minutes, stirring occasionally.

In a small bowl, whisk the pudding mix and milk for 2 minutes. Let stand for 2 minutes or until soft-set. Fold in the whipped topping. Cover and refrigerate until thickened, about 20 minutes.

Place one cake layer on a serving platter; spread with 3/4 cup pudding mixture. Top with remaining cake layer; spread remaining pudding mixture over top and sides of cake.

If necessary, reheat pecan mixture in a microwave for up to 30 seconds to achieve a spreading consistency. Spoon pecan mixture around edge of cake. Store in the refrigerator. Yield: 10-12 servings.

Peanut Butter Chocolate Dessert

Prep: 20 min. + chilling

For me, the ideal dessert combines the flavors of chocolate and peanut butter. So when I came up with this rich treat, it quickly became my all-time favorite. It's a cinch to whip together because it doesn't require any baking. —Debbie Price, LaRue, Ohio

20	chocolate cream-filled chocolate sandwich cookies, *divided*
2	tablespoons butter, softened

Peanut Butter Chocolate Dessert

1	package (8 ounces) cream cheese, softened
1/2	cup peanut butter
1-1/2	cups confectioners' sugar, *divided*
1	carton (16 ounces) frozen whipped topping, thawed, *divided*
15	miniature peanut butter cups, chopped
1	cup cold milk
1	package (3.9 ounces) instant chocolate fudge pudding mix

Crush 16 cookies; toss with the butter. Press into an ungreased 9-in. square dish; set aside.

In a large bowl, beat the cream cheese, peanut butter and 1 cup confectioners' sugar until smooth. Fold in half of the whipped topping. Spread over crust. Sprinkle with peanut butter cups.

In another large bowl, beat the milk, pudding mix and remaining confectioners' sugar on low speed for 2 minutes. Let stand for 2 minutes or until soft-set. Fold in remaining whipped topping.

Spread over peanut butter cups. Crush remaining cookies; sprinkle over the top. Cover and chill for at least 3 hours. Yield: 12-16 servings.

Bing Cherry Sherbet

Bing Cherry Sherbet

Prep: 30 min. + freezing

To whip up this pretty pink sherbet studded with dark, sweet cherries, you'll need an ice-cream maker and a total of only four ingredients! Or try with sliced peaches and peach soda.

—Helen Humble, Longview, Texas

- 4 cups fresh *or* frozen pitted dark sweet cherries, quartered
- 1 cup sugar
- 2 liters black cherry soda, chilled
- 1 can (14 ounces) sweetened condensed milk

In a large saucepan, bring cherries and sugar to a boil over medium heat, stirring constantly. Reduce heat; cover and simmer for 10 minutes, stirring occasionally. Cool slightly. Transfer to a large bowl; cover and refrigerate until chilled.

Stir in soda and milk. Fill ice cream freezer cylinder two-thirds full; freeze according to manufacturer's directions. Refrigerate remaining mixture until ready to freeze. Transfer to a freezer container; freeze for 2-4 hours or until firm. Remove from the freezer 10 minutes before serving. **Yield: about 3 quarts.**

 Mocha Truffle Cheesecake

Prep: 20 min. | Bake: 50 min. + chilling

I went through a phase when I couldn't get enough cheesecake or coffee, so I created this rich dessert. Its brownie-like crust and creamy mocha layer really hit the spot. It's excellent for get-togethers because it can be made in advance.

—Shannon Dormady, Great Falls, Montana

- 1 package (18-1/4 ounces) devil's food cake mix
- 6 tablespoons butter, melted
- 1 egg
- 1 to 3 tablespoons instant coffee granules

FILLING/TOPPING:
- 2 packages (8 ounces *each*) cream cheese, softened
- 1 can (14 ounces) sweetened condensed milk
- 2 cups (12 ounces) semisweet chocolate chips, melted and cooled
- 3 to 6 tablespoons instant coffee granules
- 1/4 cup hot water
- 3 eggs, lightly beaten
- 1 cup heavy whipping cream
- 1/4 cup confectioners' sugar
- 1/2 teaspoon almond extract

In a large bowl, combine the cake mix, butter, egg and coffee granules until well blended. Press onto the bottom and 2 in. up the sides of a greased 10-in. springform pan.

In another large bowl, beat cream cheese until smooth. Beat in milk and melted chips. Dissolve coffee granules in water. Add coffee and eggs to cream cheese mixture; beat on low speed just until combined.

Pour into crust. Place pan on a baking sheet. Bake at 325° for 50-55 minutes or until center is almost set. Cool on a wire rack for 10 minutes. Carefully run a knife around edge of pan to loosen; cool 1 hour longer. Chill overnight.

Remove sides of pan. Just before serving, in a large bowl, beat cream until soft peaks form. Beat in sugar and extract until stiff peaks form. Spread over top of cheesecake. Refrigerate leftovers. **Yield: 12-16 servings.**

Mocha Truffle Cheesecake

Chocolate Raspberry Torte

Prep: 15 min. | Bake: 25 min. + cooling

When our daughter requested this fancy layered cake for her birthday, I was afraid it would be difficult to make. But it's so easy! Everyone oohs and aahs at how pretty it is.

—Rosemary Ford Vinson, El Cajon, California

1	package (18-1/4 ounces) chocolate cake mix
1	package (3 ounces) cream cheese, softened
3/4	cup cold milk
1	package (3.4 ounces) instant vanilla pudding mix
1	carton (8 ounces) frozen whipped topping, thawed
2	cups fresh raspberries

Confectioners' sugar
Fresh mint and additional raspberries, optional

Prepare the cake according to package directions. Pour into three greased and floured 9-in. round baking pans. Bake at 350° for 25-30 minutes or until a toothpick inserted near the center comes out clean. Cool for 10 minutes before removing from pans to wire racks to cool completely.

In a large bowl, beat cream cheese until fluffy. Combine milk and pudding mix; beat into cream cheese until smooth. Fold in whipped topping and raspberries.

Place one cake layer on a serving plate. Spread with half of the filling. Repeat layers. Top with remaining cake; dust with confectioners' sugar. Garnish with mint and raspberries if desired. Store in the refrigerator. **Yield: 12 servings.**

Warm Apple Topping

Prep/Total Time: 30 min.

My husband and I love preparing entire meals on the grill, to the surprise and delight of company. We create this unique dessert for my mother, who can't eat most grain products. She was thrilled with the sweet fruit topping spooned over vanilla ice cream.

—Sharon Manton, Harrisburg, Pennsylvania

3	medium tart apples, peeled
1/3	cup raisins
1	tablespoon lemon juice
1/3	cup packed brown sugar
1/4	teaspoon ground cinnamon
1/4	teaspoon ground cloves
1/8	teaspoon salt
1/8	teaspoon ground nutmeg
2	tablespoons cold butter
1/3	cup finely chopped walnuts

Vanilla ice cream

Cut each apple into 16 wedges; place all on an 18-in. square piece of heavy-duty foil. Sprinkle with raisins; drizzle with lemon juice.

In a bowl, combine the brown sugar, cinnamon, cloves, salt and nutmeg; cut in the butter until crumbly. Stir in walnuts. Sprinkle over apples and raisins.

Fold foil around apple mixture and seal tightly. Grill over indirect medium heat for 18-22 minutes or until apples are tender. Serve with ice cream. **Yield: 3 cups.**

Warm Apple Topping

Frozen Banana Split Pie

Frozen Banana Split Pie

Prep: 25 min. + freezing

This dessert is special enough to make hamburgers and fries a meal to remember! It's so tall and pretty and just like eating a frozen banana split. Make it ahead to save time.

—Joy Collins, Birmingham, Alabama

3	tablespoons chocolate hard-shell ice cream topping
1	graham cracker crust (9 inches)
2	medium bananas, sliced
1/2	teaspoon lemon juice
1/2	cup pineapple ice cream topping
1	quart strawberry ice cream, softened
2	cups whipped topping
1/2	cup chopped walnuts, toasted

Chocolate syrup

8 maraschino cherries with stems

Pour chocolate topping into crust; freeze for 5 minutes or until chocolate is firm.

Meanwhile, place bananas in a small bowl; toss with lemon juice. Arrange bananas over chocolate topping. Layer with the pineapple topping, ice cream, whipped topping and walnuts.

Cover and freeze until firm. Remove from the freezer 15 minutes before cutting. Garnish with chocolate syrup and cherries. **Yield: 8 servings.**

Chocolate and Fruit Trifle

Prep: 20 min. + chilling | Bake: 20 min. + cooling

Layered with devil's food cake, a creamy pudding mixture, red berries and green kiwi, this refreshing dessert is perfect for the holidays. I like making it in a clear glass trifle bowl to show off its festive colors. —Angie Dierikx, State Center, Iowa

1	package (18-1/4 ounces) devil's food cake mix
1	can (14 ounces) sweetened condensed milk
1	cup cold water
1	package (3.4 ounces) instant vanilla pudding mix
2	cups heavy whipping cream, whipped
2	tablespoons orange juice
2	cups fresh strawberries, chopped
2	cups fresh raspberries
2	kiwifruit, peeled and chopped

Prepare cake batter according to package directions; pour into a greased 15-in. x 10-in. x 1-in. baking pan. Bake at 350° for 20 minutes or until a toothpick inserted near the center comes out clean. Cool completely on a wire rack. Crumble enough cake to measure 8 cups; set aside. (Save remaining cake for another use.)

In a large bowl, whisk the milk, water and pudding mix for 2 minutes. Let stand for 2 minutes or until soft-set. Fold in the whipped cream.

To assemble, spread 2-1/2 cups pudding mixture in a 4-qt. glass bowl. Top with half of the crumbled cake; sprinkle with 1 tablespoon orange juice. Arrange half of the berries and kiwi over cake.

Repeat pudding and cake layers; sprinkle with remaining orange juice. Top with remaining pudding mixture. Spoon remaining fruit around edge of bowl. Cover and refrigerate until serving. **Yield: 12-16 servings.**

Chocolate and Fruit Trifle

Watermelon Cookies

Watermelon Cookies

Prep: 30 min. + chilling | Bake: 10 min.

These adorable sugar cookies shaped like watermelon will melt in your mouth. Loved by kids and adults alike, they are the perfect treat to bring to a picnic or bake sale.
—Diane Hunt, Camden, Indiana

1	cup butter, softened
1-1/2	cups sugar
2	eggs
1	teaspoon vanilla extract
3	cups all-purpose flour
1	teaspoon baking soda
1/2	teaspoon salt
1	cup (8 ounces) sour cream
1	can (12 ounces) whipped vanilla frosting

Red and green food coloring
Miniature chocolate chips

In a large bowl, cream butter and sugar until light and fluffy. Beat in eggs and vanilla. Combine the flour, baking soda and salt; gradually add to the creamed mixture alternately with the sour cream, beating well after each addition. Cover and refrigerate for 2 hours or overnight.

On a heavily floured surface, roll out half of the dough to 1/8-in. thickness. Cut with a 3-in. round cookie cutter; cut circles in half. Repeat with remaining dough.

Place on ungreased baking sheets. Bake at 375° for 9-10 minutes or until bottoms are lightly browned and cookies are set. Cool on wire racks.

Place two-thirds of the frosting in bowl; add red food coloring. Add green food coloring to the remaining frosting. Spread pink frosting on tops of cookies. Frost the edges with green frosting, using a pastry bag with a small star tip if desired. Place chocolate chips randomly over the pink frosting for seeds. **Yield: about 8-1/2 dozen.**

Macadamia Berry Dessert

Prep: 30 min. + freezing

My family and friends love this dessert. The crunchy nut crust and colorful filling make it a special finale for guests. During the holidays, I substitute a can of whole-berry cranberry sauce for the raspberries.   —Louise Watkins, Sparta, Wisconsin

1	cup crushed vanilla wafers (about 30 wafers)
1/2	cup finely chopped macadamia nuts
1/4	cup butter, melted
1	can (14 ounces) sweetened condensed milk
3	tablespoons orange juice
3	tablespoons lemon juice
1	package (10 ounces) frozen sweetened raspberries, thawed
1	carton (8 ounces) frozen whipped topping, thawed

Fresh raspberries and additional whipped topping, optional

Combine the wafer crumbs, nuts and butter. Press onto the bottom of a greased 9-in. springform pan. Bake at 375° for 8-10 minutes or until golden brown. Cool completely.

In a large bowl, beat the milk, orange juice and lemon juice on low speed until well blended. Stir in raspberries. Fold in whipped topping. Pour over crust. Cover and freeze for 3 hours or until firm. May be frozen for up to 3 months.

Remove from the freezer 15 minutes before serving. Carefully run a knife around edge of pan to loosen. Remove sides of pan. Garnish with raspberries and whipped topping if desired. **Yield: 12 servings.**

Macadamia Berry Dessert

Streusel Strawberry Pizza

Streusel Strawberry Pizza

Prep: 15 min. | Bake: 30 min.

This is the best dessert pizza I've ever tasted. The fruity treat is easy to put together, too, because it uses a boxed cake mix and canned pie filling. It's great for parties where lots of children will be present. —Karen Ann Bland, Gove, Kansas

1	package (18-1/4 ounces) white cake mix
1-1/4	cups quick-cooking oats
1/3	cup butter, softened
1	egg
1	can (21 ounces) strawberry pie filling *or* flavor of your choice
1/2	cup chopped nuts
1/4	cup packed brown sugar
1/8	teaspoon ground cinnamon

In a large bowl, combine the cake mix, oats and butter until crumbly; set aside 3/4 cup for topping. Add egg to the remaining crumb mixture and mix well.

Press into a greased 12-in. pizza pan. Build up edges and flute if desired. Bake at 350° for 12 minutes.

Spread pie filling over crust to within 1 in. of edges. Combine the nuts, brown sugar, cinnamon and reserved crumb mixture; sprinkle over filling.

Bake for 15-20 minutes or until lightly browned. Cool on a wire rack. Refrigerate leftovers. **Yield: 8-10 servings.**

Pineapple Cherry Ice Cream

Prep: 15 min. + freezing

This cool and fruity treat has been an all-time favorite with my family for years. I use an ice cream freezer to create this colorful crowd-pleaser. For variety, I like to serve the ice cream in sundae glasses and top it with whipped cream and toasted, chopped nuts. It's always a surefire success! —Johanna Gimmeson, Powell, Wyoming

2-1/2	cups sugar
1	package (6 ounces) cherry gelatin
2	cups boiling water
4	cups milk
4	cups heavy whipping cream
1	can (20 ounces) crushed pineapple, drained
1/3	cup lemon juice

In a large bowl, dissolve the sugar and the cherry gelatin in boiling water. Refrigerate for at least 1 hour or until the gelatin mixture is completely cool, but not set.

Stir in the milk, cream, pineapple and lemon juice. Fill cylinder of ice cream freezer two-thirds full; freeze according to manufacturer's directions. Refrigerate remaining mixture until ready to freeze.

When the ice cream is frozen, transfer to a tightly covered freezer storage container; freeze for 2-4 hours before serving. **Yield: 3 quarts.**

Mandarin Orange Cream Pie

Prep: 10 min. + chilling

I never heat up my kitchen when this heavenly sensation is on the menu. That's because the pie's delightful layers of orange gelatin, creamy whipped topping and mandarin oranges rely on the refrigerator instead of the oven. —Gusty Crumb, Dover, Ohio

- 1 package (3 ounces) orange *or* sparkling mandarin orange gelatin
- 1/2 cup boiling water
- 1-1/4 cups cold club soda
- 1 graham cracker crust (9 inches)
- 1/2 cup whipped topping
- 1 can (11 ounces) mandarin oranges, well drained

In a bowl, dissolve gelatin in boiling water. Stir in soda. Set aside 1/2 cup at room temperature. Refrigerate remaining gelatin mixture for 20 minutes or until slightly thickened; pour into crust. Refrigerate for 30 minutes or until set.

Whisk whipped topping into reserved gelatin mixture. Slowly pour into crust. Arrange orange segments over the top and press down lightly. Refrigerate for at least 3 hours or until firm. **Yield: 6-8 servings.**

Coffee Shop Fudge

Prep: 15 min. + chilling

This recipe is one that my son, Jackson, and I worked on together. After several efforts, we decided this version was a winner. It is smooth, creamy and has an irresistible crunch from pecans. The coffee and cinnamon blend nicely to provide subtle flavor. —Beth Osborne Skinner, Bristol, Tennessee

- 1 cup chopped pecans
- 3 cups (18 ounces) semisweet chocolate chips
- 1 can (14 ounces) sweetened condensed milk
- 2 tablespoons strong brewed coffee, room temperature
- 1 teaspoon ground cinnamon
- 1/8 teaspoon salt
- 1 teaspoon vanilla extract

Line an 8-in. square pan with foil and butter the foil; set aside. Place the pecans in a microwave-safe pie plate. Microwave, uncovered, on high for 3 minutes, stirring after each minute; set aside.

In a 2-qt. microwave-safe bowl, combine the chocolate chips, milk, coffee, cinnamon and salt. Microwave, uncovered, on high for 1 minute. Stir until smooth. Stir in vanilla and pecans. Immediately spread into the prepared pan.

Cover and refrigerate until firm, about 2 hours. Remove from pan; cut into 1-in. squares. Cover and store at room temperature (70°-80°). **Yield: 2 pounds.**

Editor's Note: This recipe was tested in a 1,100-watt microwave.

Maple-Mocha Brownie Torte

Prep: 30 min. | Bake: 20 min. + cooling

This impressive-looking dessert is at the top of my list of speedy standbys. It's simple to make because it starts with a boxed brownie mix. The nutty brownie layers are topped with a frosting that has a rich creamy texture and irresistible maple taste. —Amy Flory, Cleveland, Georgia

- 1 package brownie mix (13-in. x 9-in. pan size)
- 1/2 cup chopped walnuts
- 2 cups heavy whipping cream
- 2 teaspoons instant coffee granules
- 1/2 cup packed brown sugar
- 1-1/2 teaspoons maple flavoring
- 1 teaspoon vanilla extract

Chocolate curls *or* additional walnuts, optional

Prepare batter for brownie mix according to package directions for cake-like brownies. Stir in walnuts. Pour into two greased 9-in. round baking pans.

Bake at 350° for 20-22 minutes or until a toothpick inserted 2 in. from the edge comes out clean. Cool for 10 minutes before removing from pans to wire racks to cool completely.

In a large bowl, beat cream and coffee granules until stiff peaks form. Gradually beat in brown sugar, maple flavoring and vanilla.

Spread 1-1/2 cups over one brownie layer; top with second layer. Spread remaining cream mixture over top and sides of torte. Garnish with chocolate curls or walnuts if desired. Store in the refrigerator. **Yield: 12 servings.**

Maple-Mocha Brownie Torte

odds & ends

Do you like to try a wide variety of recipes? Want something new for a backyard barbecue or for family night? You'll find foods that fit all of these categories in this chapter.

Enjoy grilled specialties and festive foods perfect for outdoor get-togethers, such as Chili Sauce Chicken, Barbecued Alaskan Salmon, Tummy Dogs (cheese-filled, bacon-wrapped hot dogs) and refreshing Kool-Aid Sherbet.

There are also plenty of fun-filled sweet treats, such as Apple Spice Cupcakes, Heart's Delight Torte and Pecan Toffee Fudge, that are perfect for almost any occasion.

Scrabble Brownies
(recipe on p. 311)

Onion-Beef Muffin Cups

Combine mozzarella cheese and 1/4 cup Parmesan cheese; sprinkle over filling. Fold dough over completely to enclose filling. Sprinkle with remaining Parmesan cheese.

Bake at 375° for 12-15 minutes or until golden brown. Let stand for 2 minutes before removing from pan. Serve warm. **Yield: 4 servings.**

Kool-Aid Sherbet

Prep: 10 min. + freezing

The recipe for this frosty treat is more than 30 years old, and kids love it. You'd never guess that powdered soft drink mix provides the yummy flavor. —Elizabeth Stanton, Mt. Vernon, Washington

  1   cup sugar
  1   envelope unsweetened orange soft drink mix *or* flavor of your choice
  3   cups milk

In a large bowl, combine the sugar, dry soft drink mix and milk until sugar is dissolved. Pour into a shallow freezer container; cover and freeze for 1 hour or until slightly thickened.

Transfer to a large mixing bowl; beat until smooth. Return to freezer container; cover and freeze until firm. Remove from the freezer 20 minutes before serving. **Yield: about 3 cups.**

Guacamole Burgers

Prep/Total Time: 30 min.

Take classic bacon cheeseburgers to a whole new level with zippy green chilies and melted Monterey Jack cheese. A dollop of guacamole adds a delicious twist.

—Patricia Collins, Imbler, Oregon

  8   bacon strips
  1/2 cup chopped onion
  1   can (4 ounces) chopped green chilies
  1   pound ground beef
  4   slices Monterey Jack cheese
  4   sandwich buns, split and toasted
  1/4 cup guacamole

In a large skillet, cook bacon over medium heat until crisp. Remove to paper towels to drain. Meanwhile, in a small bowl, combine onion and green chilies; set aside. Shape beef into eight patties. Top half of the patties with onion mixture. Cover with remaining patties and firmly press edges to seal.

Grill, covered, over medium heat for 5-7 minutes on each side or until a meat thermometer reads 160° and juices run clear. Top each with bacon and cheese. Grill 1 minute longer or until cheese is melted. Serve on buns with guacamole. **Yield: 4 servings.**

Onion-Beef Muffin Cups

Prep: 25 min. | Bake: 15 min.

A tube of refrigerated biscuits makes these delicious bites so quick and easy! They're one of my tried-and-true, great lunch recipes and always bring raves. In fact, I usually double the recipe just to be sure I have leftovers. —Barbara Carlucci, Orange Park, Florida

  3   medium onions, thinly sliced
  1/4 cup butter, cubed
  1   boneless beef top sirloin steak (1-inch thick and 6 ounces), cut into 1/8-inch slices
  1   teaspoon all-purpose flour
  1   teaspoon brown sugar
  1/4 teaspoon salt
  1/2 cup beef broth
  1   tube (16.3 ounces) large refrigerated flaky biscuits
  3/4 cup shredded part-skim mozzarella cheese
  1/3 cup grated Parmesan cheese, *divided*

In a large skillet, cook onions in butter over medium heat for 10-12 minutes or until very tender. Remove and keep warm. In the same skillet, cook steak for 2-3 minutes or until no longer pink.

Return onions to pan. Stir in the flour, brown sugar and salt until blended; gradually add broth. Bring to a boil; cook and stir for 4-6 minutes or until thickened.

Separate biscuits; split each horizontally into three portions. Press onto the bottom and up the sides of eight ungreased muffin cups, overlapping the sides and tops. Fill each with about 2 tablespoons beef mixture.

Honey Barbecue Chicken

Prep/Total Time: 30 min.

I love chicken with pineapple, yet I wanted to try something different. So I came up with this sweet and tangy chicken that doesn't take long to prepare and only uses one pan.
—Carrie Price, Uneeda, West Virginia

1	can (20 ounces) pineapple chunks
4	boneless skinless chicken breast halves (4 ounces *each*)
1	teaspoon curry powder
1	tablespoon canola oil
1/2	cup chopped onion
1/2	cup chopped green pepper
1	bottle (18 ounces) honey barbecue sauce

Hot cooked rice

Drain pineapple, reserving juice; set fruit and juice aside. Sprinkle chicken with curry powder. In a large skillet, brown chicken on both sides over medium-high heat in oil. Remove and keep warm.

In the same skillet, saute the onion, green pepper and pineapple until vegetables are tender and pineapple is golden brown. Stir in barbecue sauce and reserved pineapple juice. Return chicken to the pan. Cover and simmer for 15 minutes or until a meat thermometer reads 170°. Serve with rice.
Yield: 4 servings.

Tummy Dogs

Prep/Total Time: 15 min.

Looking for a fun and flavorful way to jazz up hot dogs? Try these bacon-wrapped versions with zippy Dijon mustard. They don't take long to fix.
—Myra Innes, Auburn, Kansas

8	bacon strips
8	hot dogs
4	ounces Monterey Jack cheese, cut into strips
1/4	cup butter, softened
1/4	cup Dijon mustard
8	hot dog buns
1	small onion, thinly sliced, optional
1	can (4 ounces) diced green chilies, optional

Partially cook bacon; drain on paper towels. Cut a 1/4-in. lengthwise slit in each hot dog; place cheese in each slit. Starting at one end, wrap bacon in a spiral around hot dog; secure with toothpicks.

Split buns just halfway. Combine butter and mustard; spread inside buns. Set aside.

On a covered grill over medium heat, cook hot dogs with cheese side down for 2 minutes. Place buns on grill with cut side down; grill until lightly toasted. Remove toothpicks from the hot dogs; serve in buns with onion and chilies if desired.
Yield: 8 sandwiches.

Tummy Dogs

Pork with Watermelon Salsa

Pork with Watermelon Salsa

Prep: 15 min. | Grill: 25 min.

A colorful combination of watermelon, strawberries, kiwifruit and peaches makes a sweet salsa that's ideal to serve alongside grilled pork basted with peach preserves.

—Taste of Home Test Kitchen, Greendale, Wisconsin

1	cup seeded chopped watermelon
1/2	cup chopped strawberries
1/2	cup chopped kiwifruit
1/4	cup chopped peaches
3	tablespoons lime juice
4	teaspoons honey
1/2	teaspoon grated lime peel
1	to 2 mint leaves, chopped
1/2	cup peach preserves
3	pork tenderloins (3/4 pound *each*)

Coat grill rack with cooking spray before starting. Prepare grill for indirect heat. For salsa, in a small bowl, combine the fruit, lime juice, honey, lime peel and mint; set aside. In a saucepan or microwave, heat the preserves for 1 minute.

Grill pork, covered, over indirect medium-hot heat for 15 minutes. Turn; brush with some of the preserves. Grill 10-15 minutes longer or until juices run clear and a meat thermometer reads 160°, basting occasionally with preserves. Serve with salsa. **Yield:** 6 servings (2 cups salsa).

Saltine Toffee

Prep: 30 min. | Bake: 10 min. + chilling

Easy to prepare using pantry staples, this recipe is always a hit. The unique bites start with saltine crackers and are drizzled with white chocolate for an elegant and easy accent.

—Jo Ann Dalrymple, Claremore, Oklahoma

37	saltines cracker squares
1	cup butter, cubed
3/4	cup sugar
2	cups (12 ounces) semisweet chocolate chips
1	square (1 ounce) white baking chocolate
1	teaspoon shortening

Place crackers in a single layer in a foil-lined 15-in. x 10-in. x 1-in. baking pan. In a large saucepan, bring butter and sugar to a boil. Reduce heat; simmer, uncovered, for 5-6 minutes or until mixture is thickened and sugar is completely dissolved. Spread over crackers.

Bake at 350° for 7-8 minutes or until bubbly. Sprinkle with chips. Bake 3-5 minutes longer or until chips begin to melt; spread chocolate evenly over top.

In a microwave, melt white chocolate and shortening; stir until smooth. Drizzle over toffee. Chill for 15-20 minutes or until set; break into pieces. Store in the refrigerator. **Yield:** about 1-3/4 pounds.

Butterscotch Muffins

Prep: 20 min. | Bake: 15 min.

Butterscotch pudding gives a distinctive flavor to these muffins topped with brown sugar and nuts. My son made them for a 4-H competition and they won first-place ribbons.

—Jill Hazelton, Hamlet, Indiana

- 2 cups all-purpose flour
- 1 cup sugar
- 1 package (3.4 ounces) instant butterscotch pudding mix
- 1 package (3.4 ounces) instant vanilla pudding mix
- 2 teaspoons baking powder
- 1 teaspoon salt
- 1 cup water
- 4 eggs
- 3/4 cup vegetable oil
- 1 teaspoon vanilla extract

TOPPING:
- 2/3 cup packed brown sugar
- 1/2 cup chopped pecans
- 2 teaspoons ground cinnamon

In a large bowl, combine the flour, sugar, instant pudding mixes, baking powder and salt. Combine the water, eggs, vegetable oil and vanilla extract; stir into the dry ingredients just until moistened.

Fill greased or paper-lined muffin cups two-thirds full. Combine the topping ingredients; sprinkle over batter. Bake at 350° for 15-20 minutes or until a toothpick comes out clean. Cool for 5 minutes before removing from pans to wire racks. **Yield: about 1-1/2 dozen.**

Chili Sauce Chicken

Prep: 30 min. + marinating | Grill: 30 min.

Zesty chili sauce with plenty of olive oil, minced garlic, basil and a dash of wine adds huge flavor to these moist and tender chicken thighs. We enjoy this delicious grilled chicken not just in the summertime, but throughout the year.

—Marilyn Waltz, Idyllwild, California

- 1 bottle (12 ounces) chili sauce
- 1/3 cup white wine *or* chicken broth
- 1/4 cup olive oil
- 10 to 12 garlic cloves, minced
- 4-1/2 teaspoons dried basil
- 1/2 teaspoon salt
- 1/8 teaspoon pepper
- 8 bone-in chicken thighs (4 ounces *each*)

In a large resealable plastic bag, combine the first seven ingredients. Remove 1/3 cup for basting; cover and refrigerate. Add chicken to bag; seal and turn to coat. Chill for at least 2 hours.

Drain and discard the marinade from the chicken. Grill, covered, skin side down, over medium heat for 20 minutes. Baste the chicken as it grills with half the reserved marinade. Turn; grill 10 minutes longer or until a meat thermometer reads 180°, basting frequently with the reserved marinade. **Yield: 8 servings.**

Chocolate Coconut Candies

Prep: 30 min. + chilling

These yummy candies disappear just as fast as I put them out. They're a snap to whip up and make a beautiful presentation on any holiday cookie plate. I mound them high, sprinkle with a little coconut and watch them vanish.

—Mary Ann Marino, West Pittsburg, Pennsylvania

- 1-3/4 cups confectioners' sugar
- 1-3/4 cups flaked coconut
- 1 cup chopped almonds
- 1/2 cup sweetened condensed milk
- 2 cups (12 ounces) semisweet chocolate chips
- 2 tablespoons shortening

In a large bowl, combine the confectioners' sugar, coconut, almonds and milk. Shape into 1-in. balls. Refrigerate until firm, about 20 minutes.

In a microwave, melt chocolate chips and shortening; stir until smooth. Dip balls in chocolate; allow excess to drip off. Place on waxed paper; let stand until set. Store in an airtight container. **Yield: 2-1/2 dozen.**

Chocolate Coconut Candies

Octopus and Seaweed

1 egg
1/2 cup cola, *divided*
1/2 cup crushed saltines (about 15)
6 tablespoons French salad dressing, *divided*
2 tablespoons grated Parmesan cheese
1/4 teaspoon salt
1-1/2 pounds ground beef
6 hamburger buns, split

In a large bowl, combine the egg, 1/4 cup cola, crushed cracker crumbs, 2 tablespoons salad dressing, Parmesan cheese and salt. Crumble the ground beef over mixture and mix well. Shape into six 3/4-in. thick patties (the mixture will be moist). In a small bowl, combine the remaining cola and salad dressing; set aside.

Grill patties, uncovered, over medium-hot heat for 3 minutes on each side. Brush with cola mixture. Grill 8-10 minutes longer or until a meat thermometer reads 160°, basting and turning occasionally. Serve on buns. **Yield: 6 servings.**

Editor's Note: Diet cola is not recommended for this recipe.

Octopus and Seaweed
Prep/Total Time: 15 min.

Add a little fun to lunch with easy-to-make ramen noodles and hot dogs. Kids will go crazy for the silly look of this creative dish while enjoying every scrumptious bite.
—*Kerry Tittle, Little Rock, Arkansas*

1 package (3 ounces) beef ramen noodles
4 hot dogs
5 drops liquid green food coloring, optional
Prepared mustard

In a large saucepan, bring 1-1/2 cups water to a boil. Add the noodles and contents of seasoning packet. Boil for 3-4 minutes or until noodles are tender.

Meanwhile, add 4 in. of water to another large saucepan; bring to a boil. Cut each hot dog lengthwise into eight strips to within 2 in. of one end. Drop into boiling water; cook until heated through.

Add food coloring to noodles if desired. Drain if necessary. Place noodles on serving plates; top with hot dogs. Add eyes and mouth with dabs of mustard. **Yield: 4 servings.**

Cola Burgers
Prep/Total Time: 30 min.

The unusual combination of cola and French salad dressing added to the ground beef gives these hamburgers fabulous flavor. The mixture is also used as a basting sauce on the moist burgers, which are a family favorite.
—*Melva Baumer, Millmont, Pennsylvania*

Cool-Kitchen Meat Loaf
Prep: 10 min. | Grill: 30 min.

Juicy slices of this tender meat loaf are wonderful served with a homemade sweet-and-sour sauce. It's an easy way to fix supper.
—*Susan Taul, Birmingham, Alabama*

1 cup soft bread crumbs
1 medium onion, chopped
1/2 cup tomato sauce
1 egg
1-1/2 teaspoons salt
1/4 teaspoon pepper
1-1/2 pounds lean ground beef
SAUCE:
1/2 cup ketchup
3 tablespoons brown sugar
3 tablespoons Worcestershire sauce
2 tablespoons white vinegar
2 tablespoons prepared mustard

In a large bowl, combine the first six ingredients. Crumble the ground beef over mixture and mix well. Shape into two loaves; place each loaf in a disposable 8-in. x 4-in. loaf pan. Cover with foil.

Prepare grill for indirect heat. Grill, covered, over medium heat for 30 minutes or until the meat is no longer pink and a meat thermometer reads 160°.

Meanwhile, for the sauce, in a small saucepan, combine remaining ingredients. Cook and stir over low heat until sugar is dissolved. Spoon over meat loaves before serving. **Yield: 2 loaves (3 servings each).**

Barbecued Alaskan Salmon

Prep/Total Time: 25 min.

*We eat salmon all summer long, and this is our favorite way to
fix it. The mild sauce—brushed on as the fish grills—really
enhances the taste.* —Janis Smoke, King Salmon, Alaska

2	tablespoons butter
2	tablespoons brown sugar
1	to 2 garlic cloves, minced
1	tablespoon lemon juice
2	teaspoons soy sauce
1/2	teaspoon pepper
4	salmon steaks (1-inch thick and 6 ounces *each*)

In a small saucepan, combine the first six ingredients. Cook
and stir until sugar is dissolved.

Meanwhile, grill salmon, covered, over medium-hot heat for
5 minutes. Turn salmon; baste with the butter sauce. Grill
7-9 minutes longer, or until the salmon flakes easily with a
fork, turning and basting occasionally. **Yield: 4 servings.**

Purchasing & Storing Salmon

*When purchasing salmon, be sure you are buying it
from a reputable source. Fillets and steaks should
have a smooth, clean appearance and a fresh smell.
The skin should be firm and glossy.*

*To preserve its freshness, store salmon in the
refrigerator or freezer as soon as possible after you
purchase it. If refrigerated, wrap salmon loosely in
clear plastic and use within two days.*

Apple Spice Cupcakes

Prep: 25 min. | Bake: 20 min. + cooling

*Not only do these adorable cupcakes complement an apple theme
party, but they're super sellers at bake sales, too. A spice cake
mix makes the moist treats a snap to stir up and a fast frosting
helps them stand out from an orchard of goodies.*
—Taste of Home Test Kitchen, Greendale, Wisconsin

1	package (18-1/4 ounces) spice cake mix
1-1/4	cups water
3	eggs
1/3	cup applesauce

FROSTING:

1	package (8 ounces) cream cheese, softened
1/4	cup butter, softened
1	teaspoon vanilla extract
4	cups confectioners' sugar

Red paste *or* liquid food coloring

24	pieces black licorice (3/4 inch)
12	green spice gumdrops

In a large bowl, beat the cake mix, water, eggs and
applesauce on low speed for 30 seconds. Beat on medium
for 2 minutes.

Fill paper-lined muffin cups two-thirds full. Bake at 350°
for 18-22 minutes or until a toothpick inserted near centers
comes out clean. Cool for 10 minutes before removing from
pans to wire racks to cool completely.

In a small bowl, beat the cream cheese, butter and vanilla
until fluffy. Gradually add the sugar, beating until smooth.
Stir in food coloring.

Frost tops of cupcakes. Insert licorice into centers for apple
stems. Cut gumdrops in half; flatten and pinch to form
leaves. Place one leaf next to each stem. **Yield: 2 dozen.**

Apple Spice Cupcakes

Grilled Jerk Chicken Wings

 Grilled Jerk Chicken Wings

Prep/Total Time: 30 min.

I've been making this recipe ever since I can remember. It's so simple to fix, doesn't take a lot of ingredients or time, and is always a favorite with my guests. You can change it up for different crowds by varying the seasonings for a mild to extra-spicy kick. —Caren Adams, Fontana, California

- 1/2 cup Caribbean jerk seasoning
- 18 fresh chicken wingettes (2 to 3 pounds)
- 2 cups honey barbecue sauce
- 1/3 cup packed brown sugar
- 2 teaspoons prepared mustard
- 1 teaspoon ground ginger

Coat grill rack with cooking spray before starting the grill. Place jerk seasoning in a large resealable plastic bag; add chicken wings, a few at a time, and shake to coat. In a small bowl, combine the barbecue sauce, brown sugar, mustard and ginger; set aside.

Grill chicken wings, covered, over medium heat for 12-16 minutes, turning occasionally. Brush with sauce. Grill, uncovered, 8-10 minutes longer or until juices run clear, basting and turning several times. **Yield: 6 servings.**

Editor's Note: Caribbean jerk seasoning may be found in the spice aisle of your grocery store.

Jewel Nut Bars

Prep: 10 min. | Bake: 35 min. + cooling

With the eye-catching appeal of green and red candied cherries and the crunchy goodness of mixed nuts, these colorful bars are certain to become a holiday staple year after year.
—Joyce Fitt, Listowel, Ontario

- 1-1/4 cups all-purpose flour
- 2/3 cup packed brown sugar, *divided*
- 3/4 cup cold butter, cubed
- 1 egg
- 1/2 teaspoon salt
- 1-1/2 cups mixed nuts
- 1-1/2 cups green and red candied cherries, halved
- 1 cup (6 ounces) semisweet chocolate chips

In a bowl, combine the flour and 1/3 cup brown sugar; cut in the butter until the mixture resembles coarse crumbs. Press into a lightly greased 13-in. x 9-in. baking pan. Bake at 350° for 15 minutes.

In a large bowl, beat the egg. Add the salt and the remaining brown sugar. Stir in the mixed nuts, candied cherries and chocolate chips.

Spoon the cherry-nut mixture evenly over the crust. Bake for 20-25 minutes or until set. Cool on a wire rack. Cut into bars. **Yield: 3 dozen.**

Teddy Bear Biscuits

Prep/Total Time: 20 min.

Children can't resist helping to assemble these cute cinnamony bears before baking. Refrigerated biscuit dough makes them easy, convenient and fun! —Catherine Berra Bleem, Walsh, Illinois

1	tube (7-1/2 ounces) refrigerated buttermilk biscuits (10 biscuits)
1	egg, lightly beaten
2	tablespoons sugar
1/4	teaspoon ground cinnamon
9	miniature semisweet chocolate chips

For each bear, shape one biscuit into an oval for the body and place on a greased baking sheet. Cut one biscuit into four pieces; shape each piece into a ball for arms and legs. Place next to body.

Cut one biscuit into two small pieces and one large piece; shape into head and ears and place above body. Brush with egg. Combine sugar and cinnamon; sprinkle over bears.

Bake at 425° for 8-10 minutes (the one remaining biscuit can be baked with the bears) or until golden brown. Place chocolate chips on head for eyes and nose while the biscuits are still warm. **Yield: 3 bears.**

Teddy Bear Biscuits

Scrabble Brownies

Scrabble Brownies

Prep: 20 min. | Bake: 25 min. + cooling

One bite will send snackers scrambling for their dictionaries to describe these unbeatable blond brownies. With a nutty texture and chocolaty frosting, the treats are letter-perfect for dessert. —Taste of Home Test Kitchen, Greendale, Wisconsin

1	cup butter, softened
3	cups packed brown sugar
4	eggs
2	teaspoons vanilla extract
3	cups all purpose flour
1	teaspoon baking powder
1	teaspoon salt
1	cup chopped nuts
1	can (16 ounces) chocolate frosting
1	cup vanilla frosting

In a large bowl, cream the butter and brown sugar until light and fluffy. Add eggs, one at a time, beating well after each addition. Beat in the vanilla. Combine the flour, baking powder and salt; add to the creamed mixture and mix well. Fold in the chopped nuts.

Spread into a greased 15-in. x 10-in. x 1-in. baking pan. Bake at 350° for 25-30 minutes or until a toothpick comes out clean. Cool.

Frost brownies with chocolate frosting. Cut into 1-1/2-in. squares. Place vanilla frosting in a small heavy-duty resealable plastic bag; cut an 1/8-in. hole in one corner. Pipe letters on brownies and arrange on a serving platter to form words. **Yield: 5 dozen.**

Chipotle Chicken Fajitas

Prep: 30 min. + marinating | Grill: 10 min.

I've had this recipe for three years and my husband and I just love it. Be careful with the chipotle peppers as they can be very hot. I changed it up a little to fit our taste. You may want to adjust the amount to your preference.

—Melissa Thomeczek, Hannibal, Missouri

1	bottle (12 ounces) chili sauce
1/4	cup lime juice
4	chipotle peppers in adobo sauce
1	pound boneless skinless chicken breasts, cut into strips
1/2	cup cider vinegar
1/3	cup packed brown sugar
1/3	cup molasses
4	medium green peppers, cut into 1-inch pieces
1	large onion, cut into 1-inch pieces
1	tablespoon olive oil
1/8	teaspoon salt
1/8	teaspoon pepper
10	flour tortillas (8 inches)
1-1/2	cups chopped tomatoes
1	cup (4 ounces) shredded Mexican cheese blend

Place the chili sauce, lime juice and chipotle peppers in a food processor; cover and process until blended. Transfer 1/2 cup to a large resealable plastic bag; add chicken. Seal bag and turn to coat; refrigerate for 1-4 hours.

Pour remaining marinade into a small bowl; add the vinegar, brown sugar and molasses. Cover and refrigerate.

On six metal or soaked wooden skewers, alternately thread the chicken, green peppers and onion. Brush with olive oil; sprinkle with salt and pepper. Grill, covered, over medium heat for 10-16 minutes or until the chicken is no longer pink, turning occasionally.

Chipotle
Chicken Fajitas

Candy Corn Cookies

Unskewer chicken and vegetables into a large bowl; add 1/2 cup chipotle-molasses mixture and toss to coat. Keep warm.

Grill tortillas, uncovered, over medium heat for 45-55 seconds on each side or until warmed. Top with chicken mixture, tomatoes, cheese and remaining chipotle-molasses mixture. **Yield: 5 servings.**

Candy Corn Cookies

Prep: 20 min. + chilling | Bake: 10 min.

Get a head start on these buttery cookies by shaping and chilling the homemade dough ahead of time. When you're ready, just slice and bake the tricolor treats.

—Taste of Home Test Kitchen, Greendale, Wisconsin

1-1/2	cups butter, softened
1-1/2	cups sugar
1/2	teaspoon vanilla extract
3	cups all-purpose flour
1	teaspoon baking soda
1/2	teaspoon salt

Yellow and orange paste food coloring

In a large bowl, cream butter and sugar until light and fluffy. Beat in vanilla. Combine flour, baking soda and salt; gradually add to creamed mixture and mix well.

Divide dough in half. Tint one portion yellow. Divide remaining dough into two-thirds and one-third portions. Color the larger portion orange; leave smaller portion white.

Shape each portion of dough into two 8-in. logs. Flatten top and push sides in at a slight angle. Place orange logs on yellow logs; push the sides in at a slight angle. Top with white logs; form a rounded top. Wrap in plastic wrap. Chill for 4 hours or until firm.

Unwrap the logs and cut into 1/2-in. slices. Place 2 in. apart on ungreased baking sheets. Bake at 350° for 10-12 minutes or until set. Remove to wire racks to cool. **Yield: about 5 dozen.**

Grilled Scallop Salad

Prep: 20 min. + marinating | Grill: 15 min.

I created this green salad with scallops, asparagus, bacon and walnuts. The recipe calls for prepared vinaigrette, but I often make a version with walnut oil and balsamic vinegar.

—Dennis Reed, Henry, Illinois

24	asparagus spears, trimmed
2	tablespoons olive oil
1	teaspoon soy sauce
24	sea scallops
2	cups sliced fresh mushrooms
2	cups torn red leaf lettuce
2	cups torn Bibb lettuce *or* Boston lettuce
1/4	cup crumbled cooked bacon
1	cup chopped walnuts, toasted
2	tablespoons grated Romano cheese
1/2	cup balsamic vinaigrette salad dressing

In a large saucepan, bring 6 cups water to a boil. Add asparagus; cover and boil for 3 minutes. Drain and immediately place asparagus in ice water. Drain and pat dry; set aside. In a large resealable plastic bag, combine oil and soy sauce; add scallops. Seal bag and turn to coat. Let stand for 10 minutes.

Drain and discard marinade. Coat grill rack with cooking spray before starting the grill. Grill scallops, uncovered, over medium heat for 7-8 minutes on each side or until the scallops are firm and opaque.

Arrange mushrooms on a 9-in. square piece of heavy-duty foil coated with cooking spray. Grill mushrooms on foil, uncovered, over medium heat for 10-15 minutes or until tender, stirring often.

Arrange the lettuce on four serving plates. Top with the asparagus, scallops, mushrooms, bacon, walnuts and cheese. Drizzle with dressing. **Yield:** 4 servings.

Tender Flank Steak

Prep: 10 min. + marinating | Grill: 15 min.

This mildly marinated flank steak is my son's favorite. I usually slice it thinly and serve it with twice-baked potatoes and a green salad to round out the meal. Leftovers are great for French dip sandwiches. —Gayle Bucknam, Greenbank, Washington

1/4	cup soy sauce
2	tablespoons water
3	garlic cloves, thinly sliced
1	tablespoon brown sugar
1	tablespoon canola oil
1/2	teaspoon ground ginger
1/2	teaspoon pepper
1	flank steak (1 pound)

In a large resealable plastic bag, combine the first seven ingredients; add steak. Seal bag and turn to coat. Cover and refrigerate for 8 hours or overnight, turning occasionally.

Drain and discard the marinade. Grill, covered, over medium-hot heat for 6-8 minutes on each side or until the meat reaches desired doneness (for medium-rare, a meat thermometer should read 145°; medium, 160°; well-done, 170°). **Yield:** 4 servings.

*Nutrition Facts: 1 serving (prepared with reduced-sodium soy sauce) equals 209 calories, 11 g fat (0 saturated fat), 59 mg cholesterol, 326 mg sodium, 3 g carbohydrate, trace fiber, 24 g protein. **Diabetic Exchange:** 3-1/2 lean meat.*

Grilled Scallop Salad

Microwave Mexican Manicotti

Microwave Mexican Manicotti

Prep: 15 min. | Cook: 30 min.

With this time-saving recipe, you don't need to precook the pasta or beef. Everything goes in the microwave...and the result is a delicious, change-of-pace dish. —Nancy Ensor, Oviedo, Florida

1/2	pound uncooked lean ground beef
1	cup refried beans
1	teaspoon dried oregano
1/2	teaspoon ground cumin
8	uncooked manicotti shells
1-1/4	cups water
1	cup taco *or* picante sauce
1	cup (8 ounces) sour cream
1/4	cup finely chopped green onions
1/4	cup sliced ripe olives
1/2	cup shredded Monterey Jack cheese

In a large bowl, combine the beef, beans, oregano and cumin. Stuff into manicotti shells; place in an ungreased 11-in. x 7-in. microwave-safe dish.

Combine water and taco sauce; pour over shells. Loosely cover dish; microwave on high 3-4 minutes. Turn shells with tongs. Microwave 3-4 minutes; turn shells again. Cover; cook at 50% power for 12-15 minutes or until pasta is tender and meat is no longer pink, turning dish a half turn once.

Spoon sour cream lengthwise down center; sprinkle with onions, olives and cheese. Microwave, uncovered, on high for 1-2 minutes or until cheese is melted. **Yield: 4 servings.**

Editor's Note: This recipe was tested in a 1,100-watt microwave.

Chili Flank Steak

Prep: 10 min. + marinating | Grill: 15 min.

I started making this recipe when we moved from Idaho to Kentucky several years ago. It gets so hot here during the summer months that we use our outdoor grill as often as possible to keep the kitchen cool. My husband loves the flavor of this juicy steak and its tasty sauce. I like that the meat marinates overnight so mealtime the next day is a snap.

—Karma Henry, Glasgow, Kentucky

2/3	cup packed brown sugar
2/3	cup V8 juice
2/3	cup soy sauce
1/2	cup olive oil
4	garlic cloves, chopped
2	tablespoons chili powder
1/4	teaspoon ground cumin
1	beef flank steak (about 1-1/2 pounds)

In a large bowl, combine the first seven ingredients. Pour half of the marinade into a large resealable bag; add the flank steak. Seal the bag and turn to coat; refrigerate for 8 hours or overnight, turning occasionally. Cover and refrigerate the remaining marinade.

Drain and discard the marinade from the steak. Grill the steak, covered, over medium-hot heat for 6-10 minutes on each side or until the meat reaches desired doneness (for medium-rare, a meat thermometer should read 145°; medium, 160°; well-done, 170°).

Serve with the reserved marinade. **Yield: 4-6 servings.**

Heart's Delight Torte

Pecan Toffee Fudge

Prep: 20 min. + chilling

This quick fudge is always popular wherever it shows up and makes great gifts for loved ones and friends. People love the crunchy toffee bits blended into the creamy texture. And it's so easy, even kids can join in the fun of making it.
—Diane Willey, Bozman, Maryland

1	teaspoon butter
1	package (8 ounces) cream cheese, softened
3-3/4	cups confectioners' sugar
6	squares (1 ounce *each*) unsweetened chocolate, melted and cooled
1/4	teaspoon almond extract

Dash salt

1/4	cup coarsely chopped pecans
1/4	cup English toffee bits

Line a 9-in. square pan with foil and grease with butter; set aside. In a large bowl, beat cream cheese until fluffy. Gradually beat in confectioners' sugar. Add melted chocolate, extract and salt; mix well. Stir in pecans and toffee bits.

Spread into prepared pan. Cover and refrigerate overnight or until firm. Using foil, lift fudge out of pan. Gently peel off foil; cut fudge into 1-in. squares. Store in an airtight container in the refrigerator. **Yield:** 2-1/2 pounds.

Nutrition Facts: 1 piece equals 49 calories, 3 g fat (1 g saturated fat), 3 mg cholesterol, 15 mg sodium, 7 g carbohydrate, trace fiber, 1 g protein. **Diabetic Exchanges:** *1/2 starch, 1/2 fat.*

Heart's Delight Torte

Prep: 25 min. | Bake: 30 min.

Cherry pie filling dresses up homemade chocolate cake layers in this impressive dessert. I found the recipe on a newspaper we used for packing material when we moved to our new home. Our family enjoys it so much, it has become the traditional birthday cake at our house. —Nancy Heesch, Sioux Falls, South Dakota

1/3	cup shortening
1	cup sugar
1	egg
3/4	cup buttermilk
1	teaspoon vanilla extract
1	cup plus 2 tablespoons all-purpose flour
1/3	cup baking cocoa
1/2	teaspoon baking soda
1/2	teaspoon salt
2	cans (21 ounces *each*) cherry pie filling
1	cup whipped topping
2	tablespoons semisweet chocolate chips

In a large bowl, cream the shortening and sugar until light and fluffy. Beat in the egg. Stir in buttermilk and vanilla extract. Combine the dry ingredients; gradually add to the creamed mixture and mix well.

Pour into a greased and floured 9-in. heart-shaped or round baking pan. Bake at 350° for 30-35 minutes or until a toothpick inserted near the center comes out clean. Cool for 10 minutes before removing the cake from the pan to a wire rack to cool completely.

Split cake in half; place one layer on a serving plate. Spread with one can of pie filling; top with second cake layer. Pipe whipped topping around edge; garnish with chocolate chips.

Spoon cherries from the second can of pie filling onto the top of the cake (refrigerate any remaining filling for another use). **Yield:** 10-12 servings.

Pecan Toffee Fudge

Melting Chocolate

Chop chocolate and melt in a dry, heavy saucepan over low heat; stir until smooth. To melt in the microwave, place in a microwave-safe bowl and melt at 50% power in 10-second intervals. Stir until chocolate is melted; do not overheat.

General Recipe Index

This handy index lists every recipe by food category, major ingredient and/or cooking method, so you can easily locate recipes to suit your needs.

✓Recipe includes Nutrition Facts and Diabetic Exchanges

✓Recipe includes Nutrition Facts and Diabetic Exchanges

✓Recipe includes Nutrition Facts and Diabetic Exchanges

✓Recipe includes Nutrition Facts and Diabetic Exchanges

✓Recipe includes Nutrition Facts and Diabetic Exchanges

✓Recipe includes Nutrition Facts and Diabetic Exchanges

✓Recipe includes Nutrition Facts and Diabetic Exchanges

✓Recipe includes Nutrition Facts and Diabetic Exchanges

✓Recipe includes Nutrition Facts and Diabetic Exchanges

✓Recipe includes Nutrition Facts and Diabetic Exchanges

✓Recipe includes Nutrition Facts and Diabetic Exchanges

✓Recipe includes Nutrition Facts and Diabetic Exchanges

✓Recipe includes Nutrition Facts and Diabetic Exchanges

✓Recipe includes Nutrition Facts and Diabetic Exchanges

Alphabetical Index

This handy index lists every recipe in alphabetical order, so you can easily find your favorite recipes.

✓Recipe includes Nutrition Facts and Diabetic Exchanges

✓Recipe includes Nutrition Facts and Diabetic Exchanges

✓*Recipe includes Nutrition Facts and Diabetic Exchanges*

✓Recipe includes Nutrition Facts and Diabetic Exchanges

✓Recipe includes Nutrition Facts and Diabetic Exchanges

✓Recipe includes Nutrition Facts and Diabetic Exchanges